FACING THE PHOENIX

ALSO BY ZALIN GRANT

Survivors
Over the Beach

FACING THE PHOENIX

ZALIN GRANT

W. W. NORTON & COMPANY

NEW YORK   LONDON

Library of Congress Cataloging in Publication Data

Grant, Zalin.

Facing the phoenix / Zalin Grant.

p.   cm.

Includes bibliographical references.

1. Vietnamese Conflict, 1961–1975.   2. Vietnam—Politics and

government—1945–1975.   I. Title.

DS557.7.G72   1991

959.704'3–dc20   90–7207

ISBN 0–393–02925–5

W.W. Norton & Company, Inc.

500 Fifth Avenue, New York, N.Y. 10110

W.W. Norton & Company, Ltd.

10 Coptic Street, London WC1A IPU

1 2 3 4 5 6 7 8 9 0

To Claude

"You know you never beat us on the battlefield," I told my North Vietnamese Army counterpart, Colonel Tu, during a meeting in Hanoi a week before the fall of Saigon. "That may be so," he replied, "but it is also irrelevant."

—*AN AMERICAN COLONEL*

And ye shall know the truth, and the truth shall
make you free.

—*INSCRIBED AT THE CENTRAL INTELLIGENCE AGENCY*

Blood is thicker than water.

—*OLD SAYING*

"All the News That's Fit to Print"

—*MOTTO OF THE* NEW YORK TIMES

CONTENTS

FOREWORD

WHAT BEFELL TRAN NGOC CHAU in 1970 is the subject of this book: how a Vietnamese nationalist, brave and incorruptible, one of the most imaginative strategists of the war in the field of political action and pacification, was brought down by the venality of power politics involving his own government and the government of the United States. Chau was pushed into disgrace and jailed on trumped-up charges, despite efforts to save him by a small group of his American friends, who, like him, were unconventional warriors, mavericks in their own bureaucracies. The oldest of Chau's friends, and the symbolic leader of the group, was Edward G. Lansdale, the legendary intelligence operative; and in a larger sense this is an account of the political action programs that were attempted in Vietnam, and a tale of the American failure to comprehend the kind of war that was being fought in that ravaged land.

The questions posed in this book, indirect as they are, revolving around the experiences of Chau and Lansdale and their friends, have nothing to do with whether the United States should or should not have been in Vietnam, whether the war was just or unjust, moral or immoral. Rather, I have accepted Vietnam as a historical fact and have tried to show the way the strategy for fighting the war evolved, how it ultimately came down to a choice between a heavy-handed military approach, which was adopted, and a more subtle application of political and military programs, which was advocated by Chau and his unconventional friends. It is perhaps the least known, and certainly the most misunderstood, aspect of the Vietnam War.

Z.G.

17

I

YE
SHALL
KNOW

1

SAIGON 1970

TRAN NGOC CHAU negotiated the streets of Saigon like a guerrilla at night, hiding from the police. He walked by the American embassy and turned up Tu Do Street, passing the ugly redbrick cathedral in the square renamed to honor the murdered John F. Kennedy. He was headed to that narrow five-block section of Tu Do stretching from the Continental Hotel to the Saigon River, which served as a rowdy combination of Paris's Champs-Elysées and New York's Forty-second Street. There, among the crowds, he would be invisible, perhaps taken for another hustler, dressed as he was in dark slacks and a white shirt and wearing cheap sandals.

Celebrations of the lunar new year, Tet, when all of South Vietnam momentarily forgot the war, were over, and the occidental year of 1970 had been confirmed by the oriental calendar. Chau knew that police agents would be returning to the job after the holidays and that the danger to him was growing. He carried a medal, South Vietnam's highest decoration, which looked out of place pinned to his civilian clothes, but which he treated as a talisman, confident the award would protect him from harm. Now a politician, Chau had won the medal and made his early reputation as an army colonel who specialized in devising the kind of political and economic programs that were classified under the broad heading of "pacification" to distinguish them from purely military operations. He was a key Vietnamese theorist on guerrilla warfare, and yet his formal education, except for his military training, had ended with high school. By sheer ability he had risen to become chief of one of South Vietnam's forty-four provinces, later mayor of Da Nang, the country's second largest city, then head of the pacification training program, and finally secretary-general of the National Assembly, a position roughly equivalent to that of speaker of the U.S. House of Representatives. With each step along the way he had won more supporters among certain American civilians, including those visiting congressmen and senators who agreed with him that the United States had taken a wrong turn in its strategy for fighting the war.

Chau, who was forty-six, loved philosophical debate. Stocky for a Vietnamese, of medium height, he had dark eyes that took on a sparkling intensity as he tried to explain to one of the endless stream of visiting American officials from Washington what he believed a guerrilla war to be all about. First and foremost, he would say in his flawed but urgent English, it was not necessarily about killing guerrillas. Body counts could be irrelevant and even detrimental to winning such a war. That was usually enough to stun most Americans into a befuddled silence. Then Chau went on with his exposition, describing Vietnam as a war that from the beginning had been fought on three different levels. The communists' military strength consisted of (1) regular troops backed by (2) guerrillas who were directed and supported by (3) a politically organized base.

To Chau the key to winning the war lay in defeating the communists' political organization. It was as a province chief—the equivalent of state governor—that he had developed most of his ideas. The communist rebels, who were known as the Viet Cong, had their own governor in Chau's state, as well as a tightly controlled administrative organization that descended straight down to the smallest villages, each with its own clandestine Viet Cong mayor and a number of assistants to carry out various functions, such as collecting taxes and spreading propaganda against Chau's administration. The Viet Cong governor was also recruiting his own version of a national guard to fight the Saigon government troops that were under Chau's command. And the Viet Cong governor could count on the support of regular, well-armed soldiers who were sent from North Vietnam to South Vietnam by Ho Chi Minh and his communist administration in Hanoi.

Chau did not want to kill the Viet Cong guerrillas. He wanted to win them over to the government side. After all, most of them were young men, often teenagers, poorly educated and not really communists but simply the children of poverty-stricken rice farmers who were badly treated—or at best, completely ignored—by the central government in Saigon. Chau realized that, while some of the young men had been forcibly conscripted by the communists' political organization, on the whole, most of them were fighting because they had legitimate grievances.

His first step, then, was to identify and try to remove their complaints against the Saigon government and to demonstrate that he offered them a better path to the future than the communists. He formed what he called "census grievance teams" and sent them to every village to talk to the rice farmers and to register their complaints. Then he tried to act on them. If a village needed a well for drinking water, he made sure it was dug. If the village was without a school, he brought in a teacher.

At the same time, he started an amnesty program. He encouraged anyone who was a Viet Cong to quit and return to the Saigon government side. Chau assured them they would not be punished. Rather, he would help them find work and treat them as deserving citizens. Because Chau was a popular province chief and known for his honesty, many of the Viet Cong took him at his word and turned themselves in.

Chau was convinced that the war could be won by concentrating on political and not military action. But he was also a realist who understood that there were dedicated men in the communists' political/administrative organization who would never give up. He spent long hours tracking the moves of his counterpart on the other side, the Viet Cong province chief. He did not view his opponent with personal rancor. He would have liked to engage him in a debate about democracy versus communism. But Chau did in fact detest the Viet Cong province chief's methods. When Chau brought in a new village schoolteacher, the Viet Cong chief sent his men to assassinate her, as part of his campaign to terrorize the rice farmers to keep them from supporting the Saigon government. Certainly, Chau thought, the Viet Cong province chief would have to be eliminated, either by capturing him, or, if necessary, by killing him.

But how was he to do this? Chau knew that if he sent regular combat troops after the communist province chief they would probably kill innocent people during their search and wind up making more Viet Cong. He could call in airstrikes or artillery on a village where he had information the province chief might be hiding. But what would that accomplish beyond destroying the village and killing more people? No, Chau decided, he had to keep his operation small and focused

on a single target. Using intelligence techniques, he would first identify and locate the members of the Viet Cong's political/administrative
organization in his province and then send three-man teams to capture or kill them. Since the Viet Cong used terror as a weapon to
dominate the rice farmers, Chau called his three-man units "counterterror teams." This was the beginning of what later became known as
the Phoenix program, the most controversial undertaking of the war.

In the early 1960s, when Chau was developing his unorthodox
strategy for fighting the war, he found it difficult to explain his methods to the United States military officers who were being sent to
South Vietnam in increasing numbers to serve as advisers as the Viet
Cong made gains throughout the country. When he talked about the
communists' political organization, he drew blank looks from most of
the American military men. First, they understood little about the
country and the Viet Cong's organizational techniques; and, second,
they had been trained to kill enemy soldiers—not to track down the
Viet Cong's administrative and governing apparatus.

What Chau said made sense to them on one level: the Viet Cong
province chief, who could recruit hundreds of guerrilla fighters, was
obviously more valuable to the other side than one soldier who carried a rifle and did what he was told. But how could they find and
identify the Viet Cong province chief? In America a state governor
lived in a mansion, rode in a big car, and appeared on television. In
South Vietnam the Viet Cong governor lived a clandestine life, was
always on the move, wore the same simple black pajama-type clothes
of the ordinary rice farmer or the guerrilla, and used a number of
aliases. It was all very confusing.

Besides, Chau did not always make a good impression on American
officers when he talked to them about political action. It wasn't so
much that he tended to be impatient and arrogant at times, anxious to
get on with the job of winning of the war. The Americans had grown
accustomed to Vietnamese officers who, seemingly to overcompen-
sate for their position as the dirt-poor oriental ally, acted arrogantly.
They knew that, sooner or later, the arrogant-acting Vietnamese
would humble himself by asking them for something, a gift from the
post exchange, a recommendation for promotion; or he might reveal
by his actions on the battlefield that he lacked courage; or his dealings
with the rice farmers would show him to be a corrupt bribetaker.
Chau was different. He was brave, he was honest (certainly by Saigon
standards), and he asked for nothing. The problem that many Ameri-

can military men had with Chau was that he acted—well, he acted truly equal. That was so rare in Vietnamese-American relationships as to be disconcerting.

Thus, much of what Chau said was discounted or ignored, and the American military men continued to treat one guerrilla the same as the other, province chief or illiterate farmboy. Kill enough of the Viet Cong, no matter who they were, military officers believed, and eventually they would give up.

Nevertheless, Chau had not been discouraged in his efforts to devise programs to beat the communists at their own game, even though the province to which he was assigned—Kien Hoa, to the south of Saigon—was one of the most communist-dominated states in the country. To make matters more difficult, Chau and his wife had been born and raised in Hue, in central Vietnam, and they were looked on at first with suspicion by the southerners of Kien Hoa because of their strange accents and different tastes in food. It was as though someone from New York had been appointed governor of Arkansas without the consent of that state's people.

But Chau and his attractive wife had quickly overcome the suspicion of the people in Kien Hoa. They were relaxed and unpretentious among the rural Vietnamese, and they were well on their way to building a family of six children, which met with the approval of the prolific southerners. Chau knew how to walk into a group of rice farmers and squat on his haunches to talk to them, without showing the superior attitude that might be expected of most Vietnamese who came from upper-class families, as he and his wife did. He was full of energy and in good shape—he didn't smoke, and he drank little—and he popped up unannounced in every part of his state.

When Chau took over as province chief of Kien Hoa, only 80,000 out of a population of 530,000 could be said to be under Saigon government control. Within a year Chau had upped the number to 220,-000. Moreover, his successes came when other provinces in South Vietnam were falling increasingly under communist control.

"Give me a budget that equals the cost of only one American helicopter," Chau would often say, "and I'll give you a pacified province. With that much money I can raise the standard of living of the rice farmers, and government officials in the province can be paid enough so that they won't think it necessary to steal."

While U.S. military officers did not know what to make of Chau, there was a small group of Americans, mostly civilians employed by the government, who understood his strategy and were opposed to the Pentagon's way of fighting the war by concentrating on body counts. The symbolic leader of the group was Edward G. Lansdale, the political operative who glued together the first Saigon government after the 1954 French defeat by Ho Chi Minh's forces. They were alike, Chau and Lansdale, two officers, unrestrained and out- spoken, who were convinced the war could be won only by emphasiz- ing political techniques over bombs and bullets. And the Americans who supported Chau were, in one way or another, Lansdale men— operatives who had served with him, or men who thought like Lans- dale and believed that progress could be made only by approaching the war as an integrated political-military conflict. Significantly, they disagreed on many other issues, and some of them could be called conservatives, others moderates or liberals, but they all found com- mon cause in their support of Chau.

It was largely through their efforts that a number of the programs Chau had developed in his province were started countrywide. His census grievance teams were merged with the people's action teams devised by another Vietnamese officer, and the result became the pacification program's chief hope for winning the rice farmers over to the Saigon government side. His amnesty program, which allowed the Viet Cong to surrender without punishment, was established in every province. And his counterterror teams for tracking down the Viet Cong's political/administrative organization grew into the Phoenix program.

It was of the highest irony that Chau, who believed that the com- munists should be killed only as a last resort, turned out to be the father of something the antiwar movement labeled in later years an "assassination" program. For the Phoenix program came to stand in the minds of some Americans for all that was wrong and immoral about the Vietnam War. In fact Phoenix, which was little understood and enveloped in notorious publicity, became a shorthand to describe the entire pacification program and the failure of American efforts.

Still, Chau's supporters knew the real story, knew that his pro- grams had been taken out of context and that he remained one of the most imaginative thinkers of the war. And they understood too that the unorthodox ideas of both Chau and Lansdale had made them few friends—and many enemies.

In Chau's case, the most important enemy was an old friend. It was

Nguyen Van Thieu, the president of South Vietnam, who sent the police to search for Chau. In the days when they taught at a military academy and shared the same home, Chau had once saved Thieu's wife from an accidental death by asphyxiation from the charcoal cooking fumes in her kitchen. But in the intervening years the beliefs of the two Vietnamese officers about how the war should be fought had diverged. In the first place, Chau believed, the Viet Cong could not be defeated so long as the Saigon government was riddled with corruption. He also thought it time to begin negotiations with the communists and turn the war into a political struggle. Which Thieu detested more, Chau's call for peace negotiations or his charges of governmental corruption, would be hard to say. It was clear though that Chau, from his important position in the National Assembly, had become a political threat to Thieu and his cronies.

Thieu was looking for a way to neutralize Chau, when his police captured a high-ranking communist spy and intelligence officer from North Vietnam by the name of Tran Ngoc Hien. Under interrogation, Hien confessed that he was Chau's blood brother and that after sixteen years of separation they had re-established contact from 1965 to 1968.

It didn't take long for Thieu's men to spread the word that Chau had seen his brother and was doubtless a communist spy himself. This was the beginning of a campaign to strip Chau of parliamentary immunity so that he could be arrested and thrown in jail. At first Chau was unconcerned by the revelation. Yes, he had seen his brother, he said, and he had immediately reported the contact to the American embassy. Then he sat back to wait for the ambassador and the CIA station chief to come to his rescue. But as Thieu marshaled his campaign against him, no word in Chau's favor came from the offices of Ambassador Ellsworth Bunker or CIA chief Theodore Shackley.

Astonished, then angered, the small group of Chau's American friends began to react to what was happening. Chau was being framed, they believed, and the embassy and the CIA appeared ready to abandon him in the interest of supporting Thieu and the goal of political stability. They were ready to fight for Chau, because they believed that in fighting for him they were fighting for America's conscience, although they would have shied away from reducing the matter to—as they would have seen it—such melodramatic terms. Yet however stated, the issue could not be fudged or clouded or weaseled away. Chau had been a loyal friend of the United States, a dedicated Vietnamese nationalist who stood for the democratic ideals that were often given as the reason that so many young Americans were dying and so much treasure was being expended on a war so far from home. To abandon Chau, his supporters believed, would be to betray the principles that had brought them to Vietnam.

And so as Chau moved down Tu Do Street with the crowds, boldly pausing for a moment in front of the National Assembly building, which was guarded by the police, his American friends began preparing an operation to save him from his own government—and theirs.

FROM THE AIR Saigon appeared to shimmer in the sunshine. Light was reflected from the surrounding rivers and canals and from the tin roofs of thousands of shacks. Even the blue haze of pollution that rose from the city and was visible fifty miles away seemed to accentuate rather than dull its brightness. The narrow streets and tree-shaded boulevards were clogged with military trucks, bicycles, cars, pedicabs, and motorbikes, but from a helicopter the noise was unheard and the vehicles looked like small, harmless insects.

It was once you were on the ground that the true character of the city emerged. The temperature was hot and sticky. The traffic jams were accompanied by the roar of engines and the honking of horns. The blue haze was throat-constricting. The sidewalks were crammed with vendors selling vegetables, fruits, watches, cigarettes, lottery tickets, whisky, beer, laundry detergent, military gear, and toothpaste. Beggars, whores, and petty thieves roamed the streets looking for targets of opportunity. Away from the French-style villas and hotels where Americans lived with their air conditioners, alleys were filled with scrawny dogs, barbed wire, chickens, tin cans, and children everywhere. The shacks that glinted so charmingly from the air had walls made of pressed sheets of beer-can tin. One family might live behind a façade of hundreds of Miller High Life emblems, while a next-door neighbor sported the brighter logos of Budweiser or Pabst Blue Ribbon. The shacks had no electricity, no running water, no toilets. Adults and children slept side by side in a single room. And they were the lucky ones—others slept on sidewalks, beneath bridges, or in unused sewer pipes.

By 1970 Saigon had become the most densely packed city in the world. A large part of the rural population, upward of four million people, had been shot and bombed out of their farmlands and had fled to the cities and towns, which now overflowed with nearly half of the country's inhabitants. Many civilians had been killed during this mass uprooting. The pacification program, which Edward Lansdale and his operatives had established years before with the idea of using friendly political and economic measures to win the people over to the Saigon government and away from the communists, had turned into an organization that devoted much of its energy and resources to cleaning up after U.S. military operations. Standardized and computerized, the pacification program offered compensation calibrated to cover every type of destruction in the countryside. The survivors of a Vietnamese civilian accidentally killed in a military operation, for example, received the equivalent of forty dollars if the deceased was fifteen years or older, twenty dollars if he or she was younger. The head of a household got thirty dollars for a house destroyed between 20 and 50 percent and a fifteen-day rice supply. If the home was damaged over 50 percent, the family received seventy-five dollars, ten sheets of tin roofing, and a thirty-day rice supply. By 1970 the U.S. government had paid out $4,732,750 to civilians in compensation for accidental destruction, about a dollar for each Vietnamese farmer who had been driven from his land.

The migration to urban areas, forced as it was, had changed the face of the war. In the rice fields there were fewer recruits for the communists. But even more important to this change was the fact that Chau's strategy of destroying the Viet Cong's political and administrative organization as a prerequisite for winning the war almost had been brought about—though not in a manner envisioned by Chau, but, rather, largely as a result of a miscalculation—by the Viet Cong themselves. That mistake came when the Viet Cong launched a massive attack against the cities during the Tet holidays, in 1968, believing that it would provoke a general uprising among South Vietnam's population, forcing the Americans to leave the country. In perhaps the fiercest irony of the war, the Viet Cong were decimated in the Tet offensive, which stirred no uprising among the populace, but they emerged from defeat, to their surprise, with a great psychological victory. To a war-weary public in the United States, the spectacle of guerrillas attacking the American embassy in Saigon was taken as final proof that the war could not be won, and a withdrawal of American forces was begun the following year.

Nonetheless, the communists knew the price of their psychological victory, even if the American public did not. Some of the Viet Cong, who were made up of southern communists, suspected that their North Vietnamese comrades had encouraged them to launch the Tet offensive fully realizing that they would be decimated and thus removed forever as challengers to the primacy of the northern communists in directing the course of the war. Whatever the case, the Viet Cong's losses at Tet, combined with the first successes of the Phoenix program in tracking down and eliminating their shadow government, which had moved into high gear the year after the offensive, meant the communists were hurting as they never had before.

Just how badly they were hurting was apparent to the CIA station in Saigon, which was located on the top two floors of the six-story embassy. CIA analysts were poring over a freshly captured document, a major policy statement by the communist high command. Though couched in ambiguous terms, the document—called COSVN Resolution Nine—was an admission by the communists that they had been severely wounded by the Tet offensive and would be incapable of any sustained operations, in the CIA's opinion, for at least two years.*

At the same time, a Vietnamese-speaking official of the pacification program was conducting an informal public opinion survey in the countryside. Avoiding the inhibiting presence of Saigon government authorities, the American official drove down dirt roads in a civilian car, and when he saw Vietnamese threshing rice in the fields, he stopped to talk with them, slowly taking his time to get around to the subject that interested him. The farmers usually mistook him for a Frenchman who had lived in Vietnam all his life. He learned that they continued to give the communists a significant degree of support, not out of ideological reasons but because they had suffered personally from the armed conflict. Their homes had been bombed or shelled, and they blamed the Americans and the Saigon government for the destruction.

---

*The CIA assessment was correct. The next offensive came in 1972 at Easter and was carried out by regular North Vietnamese troops, practically unassisted by Viet Cong guerrillas, who were beaten back by U.S. airpower. The guerrillas ceased to be a major factor at the exact moment American public opinion had given up on the war.

Thus, as 1970 opened, the best assessment of the situation could be gained by combining the CIA's analysis of the communist high command's policy statement with the results of the interviews conducted by the pacification official. The communists were hurting badly. But that didn't mean that Thieu and the Saigon government had the support of the population. The first part of the assessment, however, was the more discernible. Roads were safe for travel. Who could remember when that could be said? Though inflation was raging in the artificial war economy, a large segment of the population seemed in spite of the refugee problem to be increasing its standard of living. American officials had been burned too many times by the news media to confess openly to optimism. But progress was clearly being made. As for the less tangible problem of lack of support for the Saigon government, Ambassador Ellsworth Bunker was working on that. So was Theodore Shackley, chief of the CIA station, whose files contained the real story of Chau's meetings with his communist brother.

CHAU HAD WORKED CLOSELY with the CIA on pacification projects, but his relationship with the agency had been strained, sometimes on the verge of open warfare. He got along best with the political operatives who had the Lansdale touch in dealing with the Vietnamese, patient and easygoing Americans with a talent for achieving their goals by indirection. Ted Shackley was not a Lansdale man; in fact, he was just the opposite. Shackley was, though, whatever the criticism to be leveled at him, an intelligence officer with a first-rate mind and a large capacity for work. He spoke tersely, to the point. Facts and figures poured from him. He was so quick that he made other bright people around him seem slow by comparison. Because he was tall and rather pale, had a shock of blond hair, wore horn-rimmed glasses and favored baggy suits, his subordinates nicknamed him "the blond ghost." Shackley, who was forty-two and a graduate of the University of Maryland, began to shake up the station, which at eight hundred men was the largest in the world, as soon as he arrived in 1969.

"Ted Shackley was an object of awe in the station because he had just come from running the secret war in Laos," said Frank Snepp, a CIA analyst. "Before that he had headed the Miami station in the peak anti-Castro days and served in Germany. He was an operative par excellence—so it was thought. He surrounded himself with can-do people who were all very exciting if you were young and a CIA person."

Frank Snepp wasn't the only one in the station who quickly perceived that Ted Shackley was deadly serious about advancing his career. Shackley was rumored to be on track for the top job at the CIA, director of the agency. That was down the road apiece, but Shackley appeared to keep his eye focused on the horizon. Yet he had run into a patch of bad luck shortly after arriving in Saigon. It had come in the form of the assassination of a Vietnamese interpreter for the U.S. Special Forces.

The Special Forces dispatched commando teams across South Vietnam's border into Cambodia, and on one such raid on a North Vietnamese camp in May 1969, they captured a photograph of what appeared to them to be their Vietnamese interpreter from headquarters talking to a North Vietnamese officer in the jungle. A lie-detector test seemed to confirm that the interpreter, Thai Khac Chuyen, was a double agent. The Special Forces men shot Chuyen in the head, weighted his body with chains, and dumped it into the ocean. The act was subsequently discovered and a court-martial investigation begun.

The Special Forces men, trying to justify their action, said that they had sought advice from their CIA liaison officer on what to do about Chuyen and had been told they ought to terminate him with extreme prejudice—a euphemism they took to mean "kill him." A New York lawyer who arrived to defend the Green Berets and who was not overly modest about seeking publicity launched a campaign to lay the blame on the CIA. He quoted the agency liaison officer as saying Ted Shackley "had been responsible for two hundred and fifty political killings in Laos and one more wouldn't make any difference."

At bottom the only confirmable fact was that the Vietnamese interpreter had been murdered. The CIA had once directed the Special Forces and still helped them with logistics, in the area of psychological warfare, and as liaison officers—but the agency no longer had command responsibility. That belonged to the Special Forces and to the army itself. Despite what the CIA liaison officer may have recommended, the Special Forces men were not under his orders and presumably understood the rules of warfare. Nor was it likely that the newly arrived Shackley had anything to do with the affair.

Whatever the truth of the matter, the case had far-reaching consequences for the CIA station because of the reaction of General Creighton Abrams, the military commander in Vietnam. General Abrams was furious that the Special Forces had brought dishonor to his command. Like many officers of the regular army, he disliked the Green Berets on principle for their self-promoted image of eliteness and flamboyance. In Abrams's case, it may have been even more personal since he had served as a tank officer with George Patton's army in Europe during World War Two, and Patton's men were considered an elite of that war, hard-chargers whose actions did their talking—not some guys prancing around in berets claiming to be counterinsurgency experts and singing songs about themselves.

In any event, General Abrams reacted strongly against the Special Forces. The promising career of the unit's commander was destroyed. Abrams then turned with a vengeance on the CIA. He cut the agency off from his military command and tried to isolate the station. The consequences of his action were potentially devastating to Ted Shackley, if for no other reason than that General Abrams was held in such high esteem by Ambassador Ellsworth Bunker. Not long after his arrival in Saigon, Shackley, the up-and-comer with an eye on greater things, found himself on the outside of two powerful men who could be the determining influences on his career.

"The case soured relations beyond belief," Frank Snepp said. "To such an extent that when Abrams briefed Bunker, Shackley would sometimes be cut out. So what happened in nineteen seventy was that Shackley and the station were determined to sort of weasel their way back into Ambassador Bunker's confidence and offset the competition from the military. Half our time was spent giving Shackley information that would pretty up the agency's image. I sat up late with Shackley many nights at his house writing briefs for him or taking dictation and then turning it into something he could use to impress Bunker with."

Ambassador Bunker's major concern was to cement the power of Nguyen Van Thieu as president of South Vietnam. Bringing about the political stability of the Saigon government had been the focus of the embassy for sixteen years, since the arrival of Ngo Dinh Diem from exile in 1954, and had taken on an air of desperation after Diem was overthrown in 1963. With Bunker as ambassador the Saigon government appeared more stable than it had for years.

"Under Shackley the station established two major divisions— COD and POD—the Communist Operations Division and the Political Operations Division," Snepp said. "The second was set up to manipulate South Vietnamese politics and/or propaganda, so as to enhance the seeming legitimacy of the Thieu regime. Of course there were other purposes too."

"Yes, that was certainly a big objective," agreed Bill Kohlmann, another analyst in the station. "I think Bunker very strongly believed that Thieu was pretty much the only hope of having a stable government, so he supported him all the way. And he authorized Shackley to do whatever he could to build him up."

The CIA had kept track of Chau for years. There was plenty of information about him in the files. When Chau got into the fight with Thieu, Shackley ordered the analytical branch to compile a dossier on him for circulation in Washington and Saigon.

"I went through the files," Frank Snepp said, "to come up with information to respond to Shackley's query: 'Do you have any evidence showing that Chau is a communist?' "

"You were not asked, 'Would you weigh the evidence on all sides and present a balanced analysis of the likelihood that this man is a communist,' " Bill Kohlmann said. "You were asked if there was *any* evidence that he was a communist."

"In my own defense, I have to say that I wasn't the only analyst going through the files," Snepp added. "There were three or four of us who did this. If we had been asked what were the countervailing pieces of evidence about Chau, we would have come up with that answer too. But the question wasn't posed. Did we have evidence indicating that Chau was in contact with the communists? It was overwhelming that he had been in contact with his brother Hien. And this is what we came up with."

2

SANTA MONICA 1970

DANIEL ELLSBERG had taken steps to get Chau out of the country. He arranged for the Rand Corporation, a California think tank where he worked, to invite Chau to serve as a consultant for a study on pacification. That would remove him from Thieu's grasp. But the invitation to Chau, which had to be cleared by the Saigon embassy, had hit a snag. Ellsberg, who first met the Vietnamese in 1965 when he went to Saigon as a member of Lansdale's pacification team, was one of Chau's closest American friends. He believed the CIA was setting Chau up for a hanging out of revenge for an earlier fight with the agency over the pacification program.

"Chau wanted to keep his independence, but at the same time he very much respected the CIA," Ellsberg said. "He was happy to take their financial support for his programs. What he wanted was the way the early members of Ed Lansdale's team had dealt with him. 'Well, you have a good idea there, Chau. Here's some money. Go do it.' That was sort of the Lansdale approach, which Chau thought was fine. But the attitude of most Americans of course was, 'Screw that! You take our money, and we want you to do it our way.' Chau didn't fully understand this at first. And that's when the CIA began to get pissed off at him."

The relationship between Chau and Ellsberg was close enough for each to perceive and accept the other's weaknesses. "I loved Chau like an older brother," Ellsberg said. "By the time I left Vietnam he and John Paul Vann were my closest friends in the whole world. Most of what I learned about pacification I learned from Chau or Vann—and

Vann got it from Chau. But even then Chau seemed to me somewhat unrealistically schematic. He was given to elaborate plans with sub-headings and had a rather American style of reading books. He was a very proud guy—egotistical. He wanted *his* programs. And he didn't like to be told by anyone what to do."

Chau realized that in Ellsberg he had a friend who was brilliant but sometimes driven to extremes. Ellsberg, he knew, had turned against the war, opposing it now as passionately as he had once supported it. Chau was not aware, however, that at that very moment Ellsberg was perpetrating the biggest theft of government secrets in American history with the idea of ending U.S. involvement in Vietnam. Ellsberg had used his position as a Rand employee and Pentagon consultant to gain access to a classified study that traced America's links to Vietnam up through the period when the country seemingly had become enmeshed in an unending commitment to the war. Known later as the Pentagon Papers, the study was authorized in 1967 by Secretary of Defense Robert McNamara. He assigned the project to Morton H. Halperin, his assistant for international security affairs, who brought in his own assistant, Leslie Gelb, as editor of the history-writing task force. At first they thought the assignment might be completed with six researchers in six months, but in the end it took thirty-six scholars working eighteen months to assemble the final massive file, which contained three thousand pages of analysis and history and four thousand pages of secret documents. Dan Ellsberg worked for a while with the study group, but he was weak, recovering from a bout of hepatitis contracted in Vietnam, and much of his research was rewritten by someone else. No one other than Leslie Gelb, though, had plowed though the whole thing as Ellsberg had, and he had brought a copy with him from the Pentagon to Rand. As he went through the Pentagon Papers and saw the many discrepancies and contradictions between what government officials were secretly telling each other and what they were telling the public about Vietnam—sometimes outright lies—Ellsberg became convinced that he could end the war by releasing the documents and stirring a general uprising of outrage across America.

By profession Dan Ellsberg was a specialist in what he termed "decision-making under uncertainty," a weighty subject that conjured up a picture of its practitioner as a domed professor of grave demeanor and reflective pauses but that did not describe Ellsberg at all. Born on April 7, 1931, he was about five-eleven, slender, well-built, with dark curly hair, and he sprang from a family of Jewish converts to Christian Science. His Harvard Ph.D. thesis, on subjective probability and statistical inference—entitled Risk, Ambiguity, and Decision— began: "To act reasonably one must judge actions by their consequences. But what if their consequences are uncertain? One must still, no doubt, act reasonably: the problem is to decide what this may mean." Since most of the information to which he applied subjective probability and statistical inference—sometimes called game theory—was, as he conceded in his thesis, "highly ambiguous, scanty, marked by gaps, or obscure and vague, of dubious relevance or contradictory import"—in other words, shades of gray—it would have been useless and futile to go through his methodology to come up with just another shade of gray. He arrived at a specific formulation, at least specific enough to set up cases for "game-playing," to reach a possible solution. As a specialist in defense matters, mostly involving nuclear weapons, he was, then, in effect, a man of opinions, and those opinions were based on his examination of information of the most abstract kind, opinions that, luckily for the world, were not proved or disproved—in a word, a rational dogmatist. He was of course much more than that and could apply his analytical skills to other matters with good results. But any man who chose such an arcane specialty was obviously not lacking in intellectual self-confidence, nor was it likely he would present himself to the world as one more ambivalent academic. A bit of self-righteous certitude, in Ellsberg's case, was indispensable to his professional credibility.

Actually Ellsberg got into his field almost by chance. His mother, who was killed in an automobile accident when he was fifteen, hoped he would grow up to be a concert pianist, and he spent long hours of childhood practicing. His father, a structural engineer who experienced some hard times during the Depression and moved his family from Chicago to Springfield to Detroit, always emphasized to his children that the man with the plan should not stop at drafting blueprints but should make on-site inspections, get his hands dirty, be an activist, ensure that paper logic was translated properly into the reality of concrete and steel. Dan himself, who was under the political influence of an older, left-leaning brother, wanted to be a labor organizer. He won a scholarship to a Michigan prep school, which recommended him for a Pepsi Cola scholarship to Harvard ("a brilliant superior student . . . inclined at times to feel superior, but no recluse"), and his classmates voted him the graduate "most likely to make a contribution to human progress." At Harvard his field was labor economics. A tutor urged him to switch to game theory his senior year so that he could write a better thesis. Ellsberg took the advice and received a summa, class of 1952. (His senior honors thesis wasn't praised unconditionally. A faculty comment: "If there is one principal shortcoming in his work it is an unfortunate tendency to be somewhat erratic in the pursuit of a single line of investigation which leads to a lack of depth and completeness.") Labor unions seemed less compelling, and he abandoned his plan to become an organizer. At the same time, his political orientation began to change. While remaining on the left in domestic matters, he turned strongly anticommunist. This came about primarily as a result of his concern about what was happening in Europe during this period—the Berlin airlift, the Czech trials—but the Alger Hiss case was also a critical factor in shaping his beliefs. Hiss, a former State Department official, was undergoing a second trial for perjury in connection with a communist spy case.

"Everybody I knew was sure that Alger Hiss was innocent," Ellsberg said, "and that Whittaker Chambers was lying. I did a lot of research and read everything available and concluded that Hiss was really guilty. That led to what I considered a credibility gap on the left, not just so far as my left-wing brother was concerned, but my liberal friends at Harvard I felt had been much too quick to assume Hiss was not guilty. It was about that time I began to think of myself as very liberal at home—pro-union, pro-civil rights—but tough abroad, very critical of the Soviets."

Daniel Ellsberg had become a classic liberal hawk, and a nascent member of the academic clique that shuttled between government and university. But unlike many other governmental academics, Ellsberg had more than just a theoretical knowledge to draw from about military matters. He joined the Marine Corps after attending graduate school.

"Virtually all of my friends went to law school," Ellsberg said, "and why I thought I had the responsibility to join, when I had no bent toward the military, is an interesting question that I've spent some time considering. I can look into my childhood and see perhaps some reasons. But it was strictly based on a feeling of responsibility. There was also this feeling, if you are going into the military, at least get some new experience out of it. I joined the marines for the same reason the posters recruit most people: 'Are you man enough to be in the marines?' To test myself."

There was an additional factor. During his junior year at Harvard, Ellsberg married Carol Cummings, a Radcliffe sophomore. Carol's father, Gayle Cummings, a widower then studying law at nearby Boston University, was a career marine officer who had been promoted to general upon retirement. Ellsberg's friends recalled that he was worried about the possible contrast between himself, the disheveled student, and his father-in-law, who would be wearing the full-dress uniform of a marine general. They settled on an informal ceremony at an Episcopal church, attended mostly by college friends.

"The thing was," Ellsberg said, "my wife had grown up on marine reservations. She loved the marines and would have liked to be a marine herself. This was something I could do that would make her feel good. And it did make her feel good. She was astounded when I told her I was going to enlist. It never occurred to her that I would do such a thing."

He almost washed out of Quantico the first month, but to his own surprise turned out to be an outstanding officer, among ten out of eleven hundred men to be offered a regular commission at the end of the training period. He took a reserve commission instead, meaning that he would have to stay in for only two years, and commanded one of the best companies in his division, a company well disciplined and organized, with the highest rifle scores and lowest absentee rate. He extended for a short time, hoping to get into the fight being predicted for the Middle East, but when a warlike situation failed to develop he left the marines and took a fellowship at Harvard, joining the elite Society of Fellows in early 1957.

He took his first permanent job in June 1959, as a consultant for the Rand Corporation, which had its headquarters in an old warehouse in Santa Monica. Established originally to conduct studies for the air force, Rand was one of the first of the think tanks that would proliferate in the following years with the help of government contracts. Ellsberg would spend one year, 1964–65, as a third-level bureaucrat in the defense department—an assistant to Robert McNamara's deputy—and, beginning in 1965, a couple of years as a member of Lansdale's pacification team in Vietnam, but Rand was where he would pass most of his career. And it was at Rand that he thought he could help Chau by inviting him to make a pacification study.

Unknown to Ellsberg, however, the American embassy in Saigon was quietly shooting down his attempt to get Chau out of Vietnam. A cable had gone out from the embassy over Ellsworth Bunker's name to the State Department, declaring the embassy's intention to prevent Chau from leaving the country.

"We were informed . . . that Chau had received a letter from Ellsberg of Rand telling him that the invitation was to be extended and that only remaining formality was embassy clearance which still in process of being obtained," said the secret cable, in part. "We suggest Department may wish to advise Rand of the delicacy of Tran Ngoc Chau's position here which makes it desirable that invitation be shelved for the time being. Department may also wish to make point that since Rand officer prematurely informed Chau that they had approved the project, which we think should not have been done in the absence of USG clearance, they should now cooperate with us in taking responsibility for shelving the project in a discreet manner so as not to embarrass the USG."

Even had he known of the cable it was unlikely that Dan Ellsberg would have been concerned, for he was convinced that Chau's problems would be washed away with the tidal wave he was creating by stealing the Pentagon Papers. Ellsberg's career had centered on decision-making in government, and Vietnam was his obsession. To him, the Pentagon Papers combined the richness of the *Iliad* with the shock of the Dead Sea scrolls. They told of America's first secret moves in Vietnam, which went back to World War Two, and described the Tonkin Gulf incidents in 1964, which resulted in a wider U.S. commitment—accounts that conflicted with what the government had told the people of the United States. Like others attracted to power, Ellsberg was intrigued by the idea of secrecy and liked to describe the security clearances he had held beyond Top Secret, exotic clearances few people had ever heard of. And here were the most intimate secrets of all, revealing the deceptions and lies surrounding America's involvement in Vietnam, gathered by men of similar academic backgrounds as himself, written in a style to which he was accustomed.

To practically everyone else, though, the Pentagon Papers that Ellsberg believed might end the war had a big flaw: devoid of human life, written in a bureaucratic language, and thousands of pages long, they were almost impossible to get through. Stories like Chau's were missing, and so were other crucial elements in telling how the war developed. How about the journalists who reported from Saigon? And the men who shaped the political side of the war—what were they like? These questions, the human element, the Pentagon Papers ignored, and that was perhaps the most important part of the story of Vietnam. To understand what happened to Chau, in fact, one had to go back to the day a pretty young girl was looking out the window of her home in Hanoi.

3

HANOI 1945

"ELYETTE BRUCHOT, get away from that window! Tu m'ecoutes?"

I pretended not to hear my mother. I continued to look through the louvers. There was a big meeting going on in Hanoi's Place de la Théâtre. I could see everything. The communists led the meeting. Since the Japanese had ordered us five months before, in March 1945, to pack up and leave our home, a big villa, that window had been my link to the outside world. We left everything, just took our clothes, and moved to this apartment, which belonged to a childhood friend of my mother's. When the Japanese made us leave our villa, they arrested my stepfather and all the other Frenchmen in Hanoi and put them in jail. Everything began to fall apart. The Japanese didn't know anything about running Vietnam. That had been done for them until now during World War Two by the French like my stepfather. Nothing worked anymore. The dikes in the countryside started to crumble; the fields were flooded and the rice destroyed. All the Vietnamese farmers came to town, but there was nothing for them there. A famine broke out. Thousands died. Tractors pulled trailers piled with bodies past our apartment. We ran and closed the window because of the smell. The only thing we could do was sip cognac to keep the microbes away. I was fifteen and strong, and we had enough food for the moment, though I wasn't sure it would last. But on this day, August 22, 1945, as I looked out the window, something happened that changed everything. Suddenly, in the sky, across the river above the airport, I saw a parachute. Then two planes. The word spread fast. The Americans had come. It was the Patti mission. Most of the American OSS officers were in one plane, Jean Sainteny

43

and the Free French officials in the second. The OSS man who parachuted and touched ground first was Captain Lucien Conein—my future husband.

LOU CONEIN volunteered to parachute in before the American planes landed, to determine how they would be received by the Japanese, who controlled the Hanoi airport with armed soldiers and who had not yet surrendered their forces in Indochina. Atomic bombs had been dropped on Hiroshima and Nagasaki, two weeks earlier, on August 6 and 9, and it was assumed that the war was over, but no one could predict how the Japanese might react to the coming of the Americans. The Japanese soldiers greeted Conein without hostility, however, if with no great enthusiasm, and he signaled the two airplanes that had arrived from Kunming, in South China, that the way was clear to land.

Unlike Archimedes Patti, the major who headed the Vietnam mission of the Office of Strategic Services—the forerunner of the CIA—Lou Conein got on well with the Frenchmen, who were anxious to reestablish a French presence in their longtime colony as World War Two came to a close. Archimedes Patti and Jean Sainteny, chief of the French delegation, despised each other, for both professional and personal reasons. Conein, a naturalized American, was born in Paris and spoke French; and he had a profane, hard-drinking manner, combined with a witty, easygoing personality that could charm practically anyone. When Sainteny later pinned him with France's Legion of Honor, it was the highest compliment to Conein's ability to get along with both sides.

Archimedes Patti and Jean Sainteny were operating largely on personal assumptions rather than on specific instructions from their respective governments—and that was the problem. This tense situation, full of petty animosity, had developed through little fault of their own beyond their natural prejudices as an American and as a Frenchman: one of them, a first-generation American of Italian descent and a fervent anticolonialist, felt superior because of his country's victory in the war; the other, perhaps of larger intelligence and very proud, was sensitive to his country's humiliations and weaknesses. But at fault, really, were the ambivalence and lack of clear policy on Indochina of both their countries in the chaotic, concluding days of World War Two; and the confusion of policy was greatest on the American side.

Personally, Franklin D. Roosevelt never had a doubt about what he wanted to do with Vietnam, Laos, and Cambodia, all of which made up Indochina. When his secretary of state asked about Indochina, in light of past American commitments to help restore the French colonial empire after the war, Roosevelt, on January 24, 1944, said: "Each case must, of course, stand on its own feet, but the case of Indochina is perfectly clear. France has milked it for one hundred years. The people of Indochina are entitled to something better than that." But turning his personal inclination into political reality was another matter. The big powers—America, Britain, Russia—were busy redrawing the boundaries of the world as their victory came into sight, and Roosevelt wanted to take Indochina away from the French and place it in a "trusteeship," presumably with America, Britain, and Russia as its guardians, and France and China as lesser partners, until a process, some sort of elections as a means of self-determination, could be worked out to let the Vietnamese take over their country for themselves. Roosevelt's gut feeling corresponded to the anticolonial sentiments of most Americans.

On this point, however, Franklin Roosevelt found himself in vigorous disagreement with his ally and friend, Britain's Winston Churchill. Roosevelt and Churchill were in accord on most matters concerning France. Neither of them particularly liked Charles de Gaulle, the brigadier general who had shown up in London after the fall of France and announced that he represented the Free French. Nobody had elected or appointed de Gaulle but himself, and his air of superiority, extraordinary even for a Frenchman, grated on Roosevelt and Churchill. Besides, they did not see why, as the elected leaders of the world's two greatest democracies, they should help foist de Gaulle on postwar France simply by dint of his own brand of self-determination. Still de Gaulle, to them, was much better than the French who had turned tail at the first instance of the German invasion and fled Paris to set up a government near the center of France, at Vichy, to cooperate with the Nazis, in order to "help" their country—patriots all, as they saw themselves—through a difficult period of history. The Vichy French had cooperated with the Japanese in Indochina, Elyette Bruchot's stepfather among them, until the final days, when they made a play to overturn the Japanese but were crushed and thrown into prison before the plot got off the ground. The Vichy collaboration in Indochina was another reason, in Roosevelt's opinion, for taking the colony away from France.

Nevertheless, Winston Churchill opposed Roosevelt's plan—not out of love for France, but because it threatened the continuing rule of Britain's own colonies. What about Burma, Singapore, Malaya, and India, holdings of Churchill's United Kingdom? Should they be granted the right to self-determination too? Churchill told Roosevelt, "I have not become the King's first minister in order to preside over the liquidation of the British Empire." The two leaders had made a number of tradeoffs during the war, and, in hard truth, Indochina was not a large concern in the overall context of problems to be resolved. Roosevelt floated his idea of a trusteeship for Indochina at meetings with Churchill and Stalin in Cairo and Tehran, then later at Yalta. When the proposal could not get past the Englishman, he didn't push it. Instead, he settled on an in-between policy. A year after he told his secretary of state that the people of Indochina were entitled to something better than French rule, Roosevelt, exhausted and near death, now equivocated, saying, "I still don't want to get mixed up in any Indochina decision." To hell with it. He certainly wasn't going to help the French colonialists retake Indochina, but neither would he help the Vietnamese kick the French out.

It was under these circumstances that Archimedes Patti and Lou Conein and other members of the Office of Strategic Services were dispatched to Kunming, in southern China, the closest post to Indochina. Patti had been recalled from Europe to Washington in mid-1944 by General William Donovan, head of the OSS. Donovan took Patti to lunch and told him he wanted Patti to set up an intelligence organization in Indochina. Patti spoke French, which seemed to be his major qualification for the job. Indochina was somewhere in Asia, Patti knew, but he had to ask Donovan exactly where. When he got it located, Donovan told him about the phone call he had received from President Roosevelt, to discuss what their policy should be in Indochina. It sounded nebulous to Patti. Apparently there was no written policy, just a series of statements that had been made by Roosevelt, his secretary of state, and the joint chiefs of staff.

"The policy was—and as given to me by General Donovan—that in my mission to the Far East I was not to support the French objective of retaking their former colony, nor necessarily to assist the Vietnamese in achieving their independence," Patti later told a reporter. With that order from General Donovan, Patti went to an office assigned him at OSS headquarters on Constitution Avenue and began going through the skimpy files on Indochina. There he would remain for the next six months.

As Archimedes Patti was reading up on Indochina, Lou Conein was preparing to parachute into the south of France as the leader of a three-man OSS team. Conein was six feet tall (actually five-eleven-and-a-half but like most men he rounded it off to his advantage), and he had dark brown hair; the hooded blue eyes, along with the full lips and the cowlick, gave him the look of a drowsy lion. Lou Conein was born on the rue de Vaugirard in Paris on November 29, 1919. His father, who had served with the French army, died shortly afterward, and his mother sent him, at age five, to live with her sister, who had married an American and settled in Kansas. Lou grew up as an American and forgot whatever French he had learned as a child. He was not good in school. "I was a mediocre student," Conein said. "Low mediocre, I should say." But he was far from stupid. *Canny* and *shrewd* were words that people who knew him later would use to describe Conein. "I had no feeling growing up of being French, but in nineteen thirty-nine I decided to join the French army, basically because there was nothing to do in Kansas, and I wanted a little adventure, so I took a cattleboat that was carrying Missouri mules to Bordeaux." Probably there was more to it than that. He sought out his real mother in Paris, and she eventually was to live with him and Elyette for the last nineteen years of her life. He was assigned to a regular French army division as a basic soldier and was posted near the Belgium border just in time to face the German Blitzkreig. Like everybody else, Conein ran and didn't stop till he got to the southwest of France, in Basque country, above the Pyrenees. Along with a friend, he survived by stealing from nearby farms, and waited, not doing much of anything, until the country was organized into German-occupied and Vichy France, and then made his way to North Africa, from there to Martinique and on to New York, where he joined the United States Army in late 1941 and wound up in Hawaii as a corporal of the field artillery. "I got down on my knees and thanked God for the army," Conein said. "Otherwise, I would have still been in Kansas shoveling horseshit." One did not easily imagine Lou Conein in the posture of prayer, but his point was taken. In 1943 he was picked to be trained as an officer. "They needed cannon fodder, and anybody who could read and write was sent to Officer Candidate School. Three OSS recruiters came down to Fort Benning and asked to see anybody who spoke a foreign language. They gave me a bunch of forms and I sent them in and soon received orders to go directly to OSS from Officer Candidate School, where I graduated as a second lieutenant. They sent me to the Congressional Country Club outside Washington, and I stayed there for a while. Then one day they called us in and said they needed volunteers to be trained by the British and parachuted into Europe to help resistance groups against the Germans."

It was as a British-trained OSS commando that Lou Conein found his métier. Naturally strong, in excellent shape, and recklessly brave, he liked blowing up things and was good at it. What's more, he got along well with different nationalities. He parachuted into southwestern France on August 15, 1944, the day of the invasion of southern France in Operation Anvil.

"A British officer and his female radio operator had been there for two years, so we didn't have the kind of problems like some who had to go in and organize from scratch," Conein said. "Our resistance group had about two thousand members. One of our biggest problems was with the communist arm of the resistance. At that point, I wasn't intellectually developed enough to even understand what communism was. A fault of the OSS program was the lack of political indoctrination. We didn't realize there were conflicts between generals Charles de Gaulle and Henri Giraud and between Roosevelt and de Gaulle. We didn't understand the struggle between the Free French and the Colonial French. And then one day I found myself being shot at by French communists. We had a pitched battle with them in the center of Toulouse. People were killed on both sides. It was crazy."

Conein remained in France until December 1944, when he was brought back to the United States and told to prepare for China. The war in Europe was coming to a close. OSS operatives were being sent to Kunming to get ready for the anticipated invasion of Japan. He was assigned to train Nationalist Chinese commandos. In April 1945, his commanding officer sent for him.

"I hear you speak French," the colonel said.

"Yessir," Conein replied.

"Well, you're going to Indochina."

"Where's that, sir?"

"Some place where the Japs just knocked over the French, and they've asked our help. We're going to send in some training teams."

Kunming was the headquarters of four military missions—American, British, French, and Chinese. When the Japanese arrested Vietnam's Vichy administration in March 1945, an element of the eighty-five-hundred-man colonial garrison escaped across the border onto the China mainland. Conein, by now a captain, gathered a team of five men, drew some weapons and supplies, and arranged for an airplane to drop them over a French group's location. The French element contained a hundred and fifty men, including a few native Vietnamese, among them Nguyen Van Vy, a future Saigon general, and several others Conein would work with years later as a CIA man. After arming and training them, Conein led them on a march over the mountains into Indochina, to attack a Japanese divisional headquarters. The attack was successful, and the group retreated back into China. A few days later, Conein received a message ordering him to return to Kunming. "You are going to Hanoi," he was told.

Archimedes Patti, meanwhile, was making a five-day tour near the Vietnam border, to survey OSS operations. He ran into an OSS agent who was going to Vietnam to set up an escape and evasion network for American pilots shot down while flying missions against the Japanese. With the agent was a Vietnamese called Ho Chi Minh, who was going along to introduce him to Vietnamese resistance fighters who could staff the network. Patti would be acquainted with Ho Chi Minh for the following six months and see him with some frequency for about five weeks, from August 26, 1945, when Ho entered Hanoi, until October 1, when the Patti mission was disbanded.

At the time of their first meeting, Ho Chi Minh was fifty-five and had been a Moscow-trained political agitator for the past twenty-five years, nearly as long as Patti had lived. Multilingual, a world traveler, he had spent thirty of his last thirty-five years living in exile outside Vietnam under several names. He was a founding member of both the French and the Indochinese communist parties. He had returned to South China five years earlier and helped organize the League for the Independence of Vietnam—shortened in the original language to *Viet Minh*—which was formed at a 1941 meeting of the Indochinese Communist Party. The Viet Minh included noncommunist elements and was open to any individual or group who wanted to join the struggle for "national liberation"—although its main emphasis, at the time, was on anti-Japanese resistance. Ho Chi Minh and his associates spent the next two years building the Viet Minh's political organization. Its first guerrilla units were established at the end of 1943, but it took them some time to become operational. In fact, the OSS buildup in South China and the Viet Minh's ability to mount operations against the Japanese in Vietnam developed almost simultaneously. Archimedes Patti was later asked what impression Ho Chi Minh first made on him.

"Really he didn't impress me very much, to be honest about it," Patti said. "To me, he was just another old Vietnamese. Except for one thing, that in parting he had said: 'Now if you need any help, contact the following people,' and he gave me a list of names, which at the time meant nothing to me, in Kunming. Well sure enough, those people started to come into Kunming headquarters at our compound and brought us some interesting order of battle information on the Japanese in Indochina. We were beginning to get information which was free—no charge connected to it, which was unusual. It was reasonably accurate. At first we paid no credence to it at all. But it contradicted the French intelligence. And we were more or less compelled after a while to really read the information that was coming from the Vietnamese, and it was good. . . . I was telling my headquarters in Chungking, with respect to Ho Chi Minh he was definitely a communist, no question in my mind about it. But he was not a Moscow communist. He was more a nationalist who was using the communist techniques and methods to achieve his ends."

After the Vietnam War became unpopular, Patti and several of his lieutenants were among those who promoted the theory of the "missed opportunity," the idea that Ho Chi Minh was a likely pro-American, or at least a potential Tito, who had been driven to the Soviet side by Washington's stupidity—*a nationalist first and a communist second.* But what did that mean? Was Lenin a communist first and a Russian second? Was Mao Tse-tung a communist first and a Chinese second? Was bronze made of copper and tin, or tin and copper? In fact, the only significant modern revolutionary who might be considered a communist first and a nationalist second was Che Guevara, whose efforts later came to naught in Bolivia largely for that reason. Being a communist and being a nationalist, in any successful modern revolutionary terms, were inseparable. What this meant ultimately was that Ho Chi Minh, not necessarily a Russian or a Chinese puppet, was a nationalist dedicated to bringing a communist dictatorship to his country, while there were other Vietnamese nationalists, not necessarily French or American puppets, who supported democratic principles. The difference between the two groups was that Ho Chi Minh and his communists were better organized and disciplined and more adept—some observers thought—at manipulating the

Americans, particularly Archimedes Patti, to help them walk into the political vacuum at the end of World War Two and take over Hanoi.

Ho Chi Minh was short, fragile-boned, poorly dressed, almost emaciated, spoke politely and self-effacingly, avoided eye contact, had few possessions, and was not even very successful at growing a beard— "just another old Vietnamese." To Patti he seemed sincere but insubstantial. He simply did not measure up in American terms. But it was his country, and Patti felt a sympathy for him. Patti's grandfather had fought with Garibaldi's Red Shirts during the Italian revolution, and Patti detested French colonialism.

Yet, in truth, it was no more Ho Chi Minh's country than it was the country of any of a dozen other noncommunist revolutionary leaders who were fighting to free Vietnam from foreigners at the same moment.

"Was it obvious to you that the Americans were vital to Ho Chi Minh in helping him establish his authority as a leader?" Patti was later asked. "After all, the man was completely unknown inside Indochina—do you agree with that?"

"Yes, that is true," Patti said. "He did use us, and I know it. I knew he was using us, and I didn't mind frankly because the use he made of us was more one of image rather than substance. Really what he was trying to do was to say: 'Well, look, even the Americans believe in my cause'—when speaking to the Vietnamese. But at the same time he did use us, yes."

As Patti observed, Ho Chi Minh and his followers adapted Leninist organizational techniques (as modified by the Chinese communists and then themselves) to their Asian situation, but they did not seem to espouse communist goals. Partly this was because they did not want to scare off potential noncommunist supporters; many who served in the Viet Minh had no idea that it was controlled by the communists. But it also had something to do with their brand of communism. For the fact was that they had few revolutionary goals beyond driving out a foreigner and imposing a vaguely stated Marxism; and driving out a foreigner was a traditional dynamic of Vietnamese history, not limited to the communists.

The lack of revolutionary goals could be traced to their backgrounds. The Chinese communists were their major organizational influence, but almost every important Indochinese communist leader had spent his ideologically formative years in Paris. Many others had been trained in French schools in Indochina. Theirs was a Marxism as seen by Vietnamese eyes through the lens of French cultural influences. Both the French and the Vietnamese communist parties shared certain resemblances.

The French Communist Party was a reflection of the French personality. It was characterized by propaganda and organization, but had few specific revolutionary goals beyond the Marxist orthodoxy of calling for a classless society brought about by the dictatorship of the proletariat and the abolition of private property. The French communists, who parroted the Moscow line, placed little emphasis on such concrete measures as, for example, eradicating illiteracy and improving health care. This may have been because any of a dozen reformist democratic elements in France supported such measures and to the French there was nothing revolutionary about them.

While short on goals, the French communists were long on talk, which took the form of ideological hair-splitting and a kind of Left Bank utopianism based on the theory that the destruction of the capitalist system and a change to communism, without being specific about it, would bring about a more perfect society. There were, on the other hand, definite goals attached to Cuba's later revolution, and Fidel Castro's country was more like Ho Chi Minh's in terms of underdevelopment than France was like Vietnam. Ten years after the Cuban revolution, Fidel Castro could run on endlessly about what had been accomplished, the number of schools and clinics built, the pigpens made. Ten years after the Vietnamese communists drove the last Americans out of Saigon, a *Washington Post* reporter asked a high official from Hanoi what the revolution had accomplished. Well, the official replied without a trace of irony, the whole country was desperately poor, but at least it was now a classless society—everybody shared the same poverty. Nguyen Van Linh, who took over as head of Vietnam's communist party in 1987, said frankly that his predecessors had left the country without an economic and social strategy. The clearest postwar indication of the lack of ideas could be found in the Cambodia led by Pol Pot and his chief associates, all of whom had been formed ideologically in Paris. They abolished money and tried to turn the country into a pastoral commune, ridding it of Western influences by killing all intellectuals, defined as anyone who wore eyeglasses. That was not communism but simply perverted Left Bank utopianism carried to a genocidal extreme.

Still, it would be overstating the case to say that Ho Chi Minh was completely unknown in Indochina. But neither did he ride into Hanoi on a wave of public support. Compared to Lenin, Mao, or Castro at the same stage of their revolutionary careers, he was indeed virtually unknown. Perhaps he might have had more public support if the political situation under the French had been different. He had a persona the Vietnamese masses found attractive, even opponents of communism. Ascetic and soft-spoken, he projected the air of a kindly uncle, although this did not quite square with his documented ruthlessness. At any rate, the French did not permit political parties to exist in Vietnam, not until the Popular Front took over France in 1936. They hounded and jailed and sometimes shot anyone they considered to be a political agitator. So Vietnamese politics, whether nationalist or communist, or both, developed in an atmosphere of conspiracy and intrigue. The situation was so confused that Ho Chi Minh, known earlier as Nguyen Ai Quoc and Nguyen That Thanh, had assumed his final name only several years before, and many people were not sure that the three names represented the same person. Ho Chi Minh was aware of the shakiness of his position. Moreover, he undoubtedly knew that he could expect little assistance from the Soviet Union, which had been devastated by the war and was interested first in securing its European backyard for communism. Nor could he expect much help from the Chinese communists, who were involved in their own revolution. Certainly it wasn't lost on him that the United States would emerge from the war as the dominant factor in world affairs and that he would have to try to deal with that fact to his advantage.

In mid-August 1945, Ho Chi Minh's forces entered Hanoi and took over the government administration. Their timing seemed perfect. It came in the middle of the political vacuum that would exist in Vietnam for approximately one month, between the moment atomic bombs were dropped on Japan and the time allied occupying forces would arrive.

Jean Sainteny, the Free French representative, had been trying to get from Kunming to Hanoi for two weeks, ever since it became obvious the war was over. Charles de Gaulle had designated him as the commissioner for Indochina. As Sainteny later admitted, his instructions from Paris were scarcely more specific than Patti's. "The only telegram I received at the time of the Japanese capitulation," Sainteny said, "was 'well, we've been overtaken by events. We are counting on you . . . to manage on your own.' " Sainteny took that to mean he should reestablish the French presence. But he had no transport of his own, and Patti refused for days to give him a flight. Patti said he didn't want to help Sainteny because he had been ordered not to aid the French. During the same period, however, Patti sent one of his OSS officers to accompany Ho Chi Minh's military commander, Vo Nguyen Giap, and his Viet Minh troops on a march from southern China to Hanoi. Patti said it was an operation to mop up Japanese resistance, but the Viet Minh also burned their way through places in the countryside to establish their control over Vietnamese villagers, and the net result was to allow Ho Chi Minh and his forces to enter Hanoi before the French.

Patti and his OSS men had free run of Hanoi, but Sainteny and the French encountered a different reception from the Japanese upon their arrival. They were placed under guard, and Sainteny thought Patti had something to do with it. "I was permanently guarded by Japanese sentries with fixed bayonets," Sainteny said, "and Patti used to come regularly to make sure we were really properly guarded by the Japanese—our common enemy—who had capitulated two weeks earlier."

Meanwhile, Patti and his OSS men were photographed at the side of Ho Chi Minh and General Giap. Ho Chi Minh called Patti one afternoon and asked if he knew the wording of America's Declaration of Independence. Ho said he wanted to use it in the speech he planned to make on September 2, 1945, announcing the establishment of the Democratic Republic of Vietnam. Patti couldn't remember the exact wording but tried to help him.

Ho Chi Minh gave his speech from the balcony of the opera house, across the square from Elyette Bruchot's apartment, where she watched from her window. It began: "All men are created equal. They are endowed by the Creator with certain unalienable rights; among these are Life, Liberty, and the Pursuit of Happiness. . . . Nevertheless, for more than eighty years, the French imperialists, abusing the standard of Liberty, Equality, and Fraternity, have violated our Fatherland and oppressed our fellow citizens. Their acts are the opposite of the ideals of humanity and justice. . . ."

Ho's ceremony was getting underway when a flight of American planes appeared overhead in an impressive formation. The pilots dipped their wings. Patti said that the flight was merely a coincidence. The American planes, he said, happened to be passing by and probably dipped their wings from curiosity about the crowd gathered below. Whatever the case, the crowd took the dip of wings as a salute and as further proof, if any were needed, that the Americans firmly supported Ho Chi Minh and his communists.

Archimedes Patti, left to his devices because of a lack of clear-cut Washington policy on Indochina, had helped bring Ho Chi Minh to power. For in truth, Harry Truman, who assumed office after Roosevelt died on April 12, 1945, had adopted the same policy of ambivalence as his predecessor. Truman said that he would leave the matter of Indochina up to his military commanders. In July 1945, at the Potsdam Conference, the combined chiefs of staff decided that the southern part of Vietnam would fall under the command of Admiral Lord Mountbatten, supreme commander of the Southeast Asia theater. This led to the decision to send the Nationalist Chinese troops of Generalissimo Chiang Kai-shek into North Vietnam to accept the surrender of the Japanese in Hanoi and a small British force to Saigon in the South to accept the surrender there. The Nationalist Chinese were ready to acknowledge Ho Chi Minh's government in the North, but in the South the British deferred to the French, who began maneuvering to retake that part of the country from the Viet Minh. On September 12, 1945, the British landed a Gurkha battalion and a company of Free French soldiers in Saigon. Eleven days later, with British help, the French overthrew Ho Chi Minh's representatives in Saigon. With the southern part of Vietnam back under French control, the scene shifted to the North, where Ho Chi Minh was having second thoughts.

Ho soon realized that his problems were such that he would have to negotiate with the French. The country was in the grip of a famine, brought about by a poor rice harvest and a breakdown of farming after the Japanese took over from the Vichy French. In one of his first acts he had abolished taxes, and his treasury was empty. He sought recognition and aid abroad, but his letters, including several to President Truman, went unanswered, and not even the Soviet Union appeared interested in helping. He was left with a Nationalist Chinese occupying force in North Vietnam numbering fifty thousand, and the Chinese were acting more and more like warlords who had no intention of leaving.

When Ho began to negotiate with the French, he was attacked by some elements within the Viet Minh. He told them to remember their history. The last time the Chinese came, he said, they stayed for a thousand years. The French, on the other hand, were weak and colonialism was dying out. "As for me," Ho said, "I prefer to smell French shit for five years, rather than Chinese shit for the rest of my life." Negotiations brought the Vietnamese, Chinese, and French together. The Chinese reluctantly agreed to leave. Jean Sainteny signed an accord with Ho Chi Minh on March 6, 1946, which recognized Tonkin (the traditional name for North Vietnam) as a free state within the French Union. Under its terms, fifteen thousand French troops would be stationed in the North, to be relieved progressively by the Viet Minh troops the French agreed to train and equip over the following five years.

Ho was called to France to work out the final terms of the agreement, and he departed on a French warship. The day before, the French high commissioner in Saigon, apparently acting on his own, declared South Vietnam to be a free state under the same terms that Ho's government in Hanoi had been recognized—a move that, in effect, firmed up French control of the South, known by its traditional name of Cochinchina. The negotiations in France did not go well. At the last moment Ho signed an agreement that confirmed the accord made with Jean Sainteny, with further negotiations supposed to take place in early 1947. But events were moving out of control.

In retrospect, it seemed inevitable that the French and the Vietnamese would go to war. Ho Chi Minh's declaration of independence had proved popular with the people and made them touchy and resentful when French troops returned under the terms of the accords. The French government, led by the socialists under Premier Leon Blum, appeared conciliatory toward Ho Chi Minh but was too far away to exert the kind of control needed to prevent the outbreak of local disputes between French soldiers and the Viet Minh, who were rubbing against each other with increasing friction, which produced shooting incidents, leaving dead on both sides. In November 1946, a fight erupted in Haiphong and a French ship opened fire from offshore. In the panic six thousand Vietnamese civilians were killed by gunfire or trampled to death. The tension continued to build, and on December 19, 1946, Vietnamese troops cut off Hanoi's water and electricity and then attacked French posts with small arms, mortars, and artillery. The French responded and recaptured the parts of Hanoi that had been taken by the Viet Minh. Ho Chi Minh and his lieutenants fled to the jungle, where they began to direct guerrilla attacks against the French throughout the whole of Vietnam. The war was on.

By then Lou Conein was in Germany. After World War Two ended, Conein had examined his résumé. He was good at espionage and sabotage; he knew how to kill with his hands, could field-strip a weapon in seconds, and was an experienced parachutist. But that did not seem to qualify him for a position in the private sector. There was only one civilian job he knew and was trained in to some proficiency: shoveling horseshit in Kansas. Conein decided to stay in the army. The OSS was abolished, but a special intelligence unit was soon set up, an interim organization that would last until the CIA was established in 1947, and Conein signed on, not realizing that it was only a matter of time before he returned to Vietnam as a member of Lansdale's team.

4

SAIGON 1970

JOHN PAUL VANN had known Chau for eight years, and he was determined to help him, even if it meant going against the American embassy and his superiors in the pacification program. Chau was not only his best Vietnamese friend but also the most important influence in shaping Vann's approach to the war. Short, blond, balding, with a voice that at its gentlest had the quality of sandpaper, Vann had become the most controversial American official in Vietnam by his outspoken advocacy of a war strategy that paralleled Chau's belief in using political-military methods. Like Chau, Vann detested the massive military operations run by the United States, and his criticisms had made him many enemies among American officers.

"John Vann had a rough exterior and a country-boy accent," Dan Ellsberg said. "But he also had a very high intelligence and a fantastic capacity for facts. He was not much for strategy or theory, and that's where Chau came in. Chau gave him concepts for pacification."

Vann, who was born on July 2, 1924, enlisted in the army during World War Two with the hopes of becoming a pilot. He wound up as a navigator instead and after the war switched to the infantry. He distinguished himself in Korea, added to his education by taking a degree at Rutgers, and arrived in Vietnam in 1962 as a lieutenant colonel, assigned to advise a South Vietnamese division in the Mekong Delta. Vann quickly reached the conclusion that the Vietnamese troops were badly led. Their officers, he believed, consistently avoided combat with the enemy. He challenged the assessment of Washington and the military command that the war was going well and became a major source of pessimism for newspaper reporters.

"Ironically, while a handful of reporters were privately being criticized by the Pentagon for our pessimistic tone and for being left wing, one of our key sources was the conservative Vann," wrote David Halberstam of the *New York Times.*

After Vann met Chau he began to formulate his ideas for fighting the war. Like Chau he came to believe that Vietnam was essentially a political war that could be won if it was not fought in a wrongheaded way. The best weapon for such a war was a knife and the next best a rifle, he said. "The worst is an airplane, and after that the worst is artillery. You have to know who you're killing." To a military establishment whose strategy for fighting the war was evolving into one of high-intensity technological destruction, Vann's comments seemed heretical, and his outspokenness brought him a reprimand from the military command. Disgusted and apparently at the end of his possibilities for promotion because of an earlier indiscretion stemming from his unreined-in sex drive, Vann resigned from the army and applied for a civilian job as an official in the pacification program. As a civilian he was assigned once again to the delta, the most populous area of South Vietnam, and as a civilian he was no more hesitant about voicing his strong opinions than he had been as an army officer, which continued to get him in trouble with his superiors.

As Vann worked his way up the ladder of the pacification bureaucracy, he and Chau developed an even closer professional and personal relationship. And it was Vann to whom Chau turned when his communist brother Hien got in touch with him in 1965. The timing of the contact was more than coincidental, Vann thought, and could lead to a possible breakthrough in the war. Hien wanted Chau to help him set up a channel of communications between Hanoi and Washington. He asked Chau to arrange through Vann for him to see Ambassador Henry Cabot Lodge for a private meeting. Vann carried Hien's request to the embassy, but was turned down by the ambassador. Vann also knew that Chau had told the CIA about his contacts with Hien, though without identifying him as his brother.

So when Vann realized that neither the embassy nor the CIA was ready to help Chau refute Thieu's claims that he was a communist agent, Vann decided to move himself. At first he did what he often did: he tried to drum up press support for Chau. Probably no American official served as a greater source of information for journalists in

Vietnam (though he was usually identified as just that—"an American official"), and Vann, cynical about such things and brusque by nature, made little effort to disguise the fact that he was using the press to fight whatever cause he was interested in. In this case, he was able to stimulate several reporters to write about Chau, who, having learned from Vann the value of publicity, was ready to make himself available.

But the stories had not deterred Thieu from his campaign to destroy Chau, and Vann realized that he would have to think of something else if Chau were to be saved. Vann got in touch with Evert Bumgardner, who like Vann was a Virginian and a kindred spirit in his opposition to the Pentagon's strategy for fighting the war. Bumgardner, a psychological warfare specialist in the pacification program, was also a friend of Chau's. They devised a plan to get Chau out of the country. They had to work secretly because they knew they could wind up getting fired from their jobs and kicked out of the country. Vann was already in trouble with Ambassador Ellsworth Bunker, who, when reading a critical news story, could spot the source identified as an "American official" as easily as anyone in Saigon. Bunker had talked seriously about firing Vann on two occasions.

John Vann and Ev Bumgardner decided to hide Chau in Can Tho, the largest town in the delta, and then smuggle him by boat to Cambodia. They would leave some of his possessions to be washed up on shore, to try to create the impression that he had drowned while fleeing the country. Time was needed to work out the details on the Cambodian end. They had to arrange for a boat and someone to meet him; money would have to be transferred for living expenses. Vann and Bumgardner decided, though, to go ahead with the first step of the plan by getting him out of Saigon.

Ev Bumgardner drove to the house of a journalist, a friend of Bumgardner's, where Chau was staying under cover, then took him on a long jeep ride through the city. They were tailed by Thieu's agents. Bumgardner and Vann had prepared for the possibility of surveillance. Following their plan, Bumgardner drove to an area that had an entrance but no exit. The police agents realized there was no way for Bumgardner's jeep to leave without being spotted, and their attention wandered while they awaited further orders from headquarters.

"They hadn't counted on Vann's helicopter to come swooping in and take Chau away," Bumgardner said. "We got him to Can Tho and hid him out."

5

HANOI 1946

AFTER WORLD WAR TWO French troops returned and tried to drive out the communists. The fright was with us all the time. We were aware of everything around us. The New French, as we called them, did not understand the Viet Minh. They were not always on their guard as we were, and on the evening of December 19, 1946, the communists struck. Our home was near Hanoi's Citadel, so we were safe. But my Aunt Marguerite lived on the other side of town. She was giving a dinner party that night for two French pilots when the communists burst in. They killed the pilots and took her captive. There was devastation everywhere. The communists tore up money and threw it to the wind. Houses were burned to the ground. It was as if they were euphoric with craziness, absolutely wild. Then after days of fighting Hanoi was retaken and the communists fled to the jungle. It was the start of the war. They kept their prisoners moving, always changing places. Aunt Marguerite was tiny, about four-nine, but strong. A lot of wealthy Frenchmen were in her group. They couldn't use their money any longer. She buried twenty men. We got a package to her through the Red Cross. The package included a deck of playing cards. The Viet Minh were superstitious. They would give Aunt Marguerite a bowl of rice or an aspirin to tell their fortunes. She was able to survive five years by reading the cards for the Viet Minh, until they released her.

ELYETTE BRUCHOT'S GRANDFATHER arrived in Vietnam in the late 1880s. He was among the first colonialists. From Burgundy and

63

trained as a lawyer, he was, as Elyette described him, an adventurer who came to make his fortune. He established a thousand-acre coffee plantation near Vinh, toward the Laos border, an area of no particular distinction. Elyette's grandmother was Vietnamese. She did not marry and, as native mistresses often did, left when Elyette's mother was born in 1904. Elyette's mother was educated in a French convent. After Elyette's grandfather died in a hunting accident, her mother, at age sixteen, took over the plantation and ran it with the help of a friend of Elyette's grandfather and a Japanese foreman, who later returned during World War Two as a colonel in Japan's army. Elyette's mother met another adventurer from France, an engineer named Bruchot, who was searching the mountains of Indochina for mineral wealth, hoping to strike it big. They were married, and Elyette was born in 1929. The engineer's womanizing led to a divorce. Elyette's mother then chose a Frenchman of a more settled nature, Charles Dufour, from Lille, a graduate of the Hautes Etudes Commerciales, one of France's best schools. Dufour was the quintessential colonialist, president of Hanoi's Chamber of Commerce as well as the Cercle Sportif, the most exclusive social club in Indochina.

Like other countries to be colonized, Vietnam was initially penetrated by sailors and missionaries. Though who got there first remained cloudy, Alexandre de Rhodes, a thirty-five-year-old French priest who came to promote Catholicism in the mid 1600s, was the most important. Alexandre de Rhodes assembled the Vietnamese language, which was then written in brush strokes of Chinese characters, and converted it into a Latin alphabet. Since it was a tonal language, with the meaning of a word changing depending on how it was pronounced, he devised a series of diacritical marks—a period under a letter to indicate a glottal stop, a question mark above to indicate a mid-low tone, and so on—which satisfied the tongue's imperatives, while leaving it the only Oriental language to have a French- and American-style alphabet. Grammatically, Vietnamese was simple, with no conjugations and only present, past, and future tenses, although the six tones made it difficult for a Westerner to master. But the alphabet made it easier for a Vietnamese to learn French than for a Chinese, say, to go from Chinese to French. Thus the door was opened wider to Western influences.

Alexandre de Rhodes's work was symbolic of the rationale that evolved for colonizing Indochina. No colonial power looked upon itself as an exploiter. Britain's justification for its empire was to bring

64

administration and law to people who were thought to have no sense of self-government, to shoulder the white man's burden. The French rationale turned on the assumption that France should act as a civilizing influence on the underdeveloped world. Jules Ferry, France's architect of colonialism, was a forward thinker at home, commemorated today as the father of compulsory free education, a policy he advocated more than a hundred years ago as France's minister of education; his name appears on high schools and streets across the country. Ferry also had an obsessional drive to colonize Indochina when he later served as foreign minister. He explained himself in a debate in the Chamber of Deputies in 1885. "The superior races have rights in relation to the inferior races," Ferry said. "Rights because they have obligations—the obligation to civilize all inferior races." His doctrine of a "civilizing mission," which found resonance among other politicians and intellectuals, was to remain the justification for France's colonial policy.

The French took it seriously. The British may have built better roads in Asia, but the French established impressive high schools in Hanoi and Saigon. And it had to be said that the French were not racists in the Anglo-Saxon sense, which was quick to disqualify a person simply on the basis of skin color. Though the French as colonialists were far from egalitarian and capable of reprehensible acts, a native could aspire to become a born-again Frenchman in a way that was seldom open under the British, who maintained separate schools, clubs, and churches and who kept their subjugated at arm's length. Elyette Bruchot, for example, who was one quarter Vietnamese, would have been considered an Anglo-Indian under the British raj and treated accordingly, whereas under the French she was accepted as being completely French, though a word existed—*mélisse*—to describe a person of mixed blood. She attended an integrated school with French and Vietnamese students. Intermarriages were frequent between the two races, more so than among the British in their colonies. A soldier who fathered a child out of wedlock could, under French law, recognize the child without an obligation to marry the mother. Instead of producing a lot of illegitimate children of mixed blood with no place to turn, as the Americans later did, the French produced a lot of Vietnamese who held French passports and were free to emigrate to France if they could find the money.

This attitude of racial acceptance was the most generous aspect of French colonialism, even if tied to the arrogant conviction that anyone should thank his or her lucky stars to hold French nationality. Yet it was to have a major negative impact on American efforts in Vietnam. For the natives who aspired to become born-again Frenchmen were not of course the poor rice farmers but Vietnamese of family background and wealth who were smart enough to excel in French-style schools—that is, the country's natural leadership elements. American political operatives discovered when they arrived that there were few "pure" noncommunist Vietnamese, except for the illiterate rice farmer who seldom had traveled five miles from his birthplace and who was susceptible to the most primitive sort of communist propaganda. The nature of French colonialism ensured, moreover, that the educated Vietnamese would be exposed to some of the worst aspects of the French national character, which in its least sensitive moments was inclined to an exasperating pettiness, an idolatry for bureaucratic form, and a class-inspired need to show superiority. Unlike Britain's colonial service, which produced a future writer like George Orwell as a policeman in Burma, the French colonial service often attracted applicants from the poorer and less educated areas of southern France and the island of Corsica, where a position as a colonial functionary was considered a big step up the social and economic ladder. The functionaries were joined in Indochina by business opportunists, quite often from poverty-stricken Corsica, who could be described unkindly but accurately in Faulknerian terms as poor white trash. There were well-educated and cultivated Frenchmen like Elyette Bruchot's stepfather Charles Dufour, who ran Hanoi's public transportation system of tramways. But even this small group of lawyers and engineers and planters had an exaggerated sense of their eliteness.

Colonial society in Hanoi and Saigon revolved around the Cercle Sportif, which was similar to an exclusive American country club but without the golf, the two main activities being swimming and tennis. Hanoi's Cercle Sportif had a big ballroom opening onto a terrace overlooking the swimming pool, and swimming became the prime social activity in Hanoi (Elyette was a champion diver), with tennis playing secondary. At Saigon's Cercle Sportif, where the terrace overlooked the tennis courts, the relative social importance of tennis and swimming was the reverse of what it was in Hanoi. Food and wine were excellent at both clubs, thanks to daily flights from Paris. Formal balls were held on France's national holidays. Elyette's stepfather was devoted to bridge, and card parties were frequent. As president of the Hanoi club, he made sure that only selected members of the professional and commercial classes entered its gates. Of the military, French officers could apply for membership; and a few Vietnamese were allowed to join. "But you had to be of a certain class," Elyette said. And be able to afford the stiff membership fee. "Not even all the French were accepted. It was very difficult to get in. My stepfather was very tough, very bourgeois, very snob. It was just terrible. But, you know, they were all snobs. He was in his milieu. Nevertheless, he was a good man."

The colonialists developed into a hybrid nationality that, beyond the romantic ideal, felt little connection to metropolitan France. "In nineteen forty-seven, we went to Paris for six months," Elyette Bruchot said. "People asked us if tigers walked the streets of Vietnam. They wanted to know what we ate. They thought we were all millionaires. Why else would we be in Indochina? We had to be careful when we brought gifts to friends in Paris, for if the gifts were not sufficiently expensive, they would get upset with us. France was a beautiful country, but I realized that my life was in Vietnam."

A number of writers, mostly French and including Bernard Fall, argued that the widely held American view of French colonialism as being nothing more than exploitation on a massive scale was false. Bernard Fall pointed out that, in the early years, trade with Indochina accounted for only 10 percent of France's total foreign trade, which in turn accounted for 3 percent of the country's gross national product. As Fall suggested, the question was probably more complex than perhaps most Americans were ready to concede. Indochina was of minor importance to the lives of the majority in France. If the average Frenchman vaguely supported military efforts to retain control there, it was because he believed a great power should not give up its empire (and lose in the process "credibility," as Americans of a later era might have phrased it), not because he feared economic loss. The French sensitivity was acute because of their defeat in World War Two. There were those who feared economic loss, however, companies such as the one that employed Elyette Bruchot's stepfather, and they made up a small but vociferous lobby in Paris that joined with the military establishment to back the fight in Indochina.

And so the war went on. Elyette knew the terminology associated with French military strategy—*tache d'huile, ratissage, pacification.* But the fighting was confined to the countryside, and life in the towns remained gay and exciting. She took a job as the first ground hostess for Air France in Hanoi. The forty-eight passengers who left on the daily flight to Saigon en route to Paris on a trip that took four days were allowed to choose individual menus, and Elyette had to get up at five every morning to make sure that each box contained the proper food, and then, dressed in the neat uniform that emphasized her lithe figure, she would hop on the bus and travel around the city collecting the passengers to take them to Gia Lam airport. Receptions were held in the evening at the Cercle Sportif for high-ranking generals and government officials passing through on inspection tours, and Elyette was expected to be in attendance to display her coquetry and charms. After her mother died of cancer, she became the *maitresse de maison,* and her father allowed her to entertain her own special group of friends once a week for dinner and dancing. There were reminders of what was happening: a girlfriend was engaged twice and twice lost her future husband to combat; the pilot who loved to dance to Glenn Miller records failed to show up one evening.

"You saw friends and then you didn't see them anymore," Elyette said. "But we never spoke about the war. It was just there."

THE EDUCATION THE FRENCH GAVE THEM created a paradox for himself and his friends, Tran Ngoc Chau said. The more they learned, the more they admired French culture, and the more they loved French history and philosophy, the more they hated the French colonialists. They saw, he said, that liberty, equality, and fraternity did not apply to Vietnamese and that the French colonialists who addressed them by the familiar *tu* had no relation to the Montesquieu they revered. Besides, they were fiercely proud of their own history, which was devoted almost entirely to fighting to maintain their independence from foreign invaders—a two-thousand-year cycle of invasion, seige, occupation, and rebellion. And so Tran Ngoc Chau was among the first to answer the call of the Viet Minh.

Unlike many others of his class, Chau was always to remain close to his roots, which went back to the imperial capital of Hue in central Vietnam and to the religion of Buddhism. His forebears had served the Nguyen dynasty of Vietnamese emperors for generations. His grandfather was a member of the royal cabinet, his father a judge. It was a family of small wealth and large pride. Later, when Ngo Dinh Diem, head of the Saigon government, who was also from Hue, asked to meet Chau's father, Chau had a hard time persuading the old man to go through with it. Chau's father considered Diem's status to be inferior to his own. After all, he said, their family had been more loyal to the country than Diem's, which had converted to Catholicism—the French religion—and adopted Western customs.

It was in this atmosphere of strong national pride that Chau and his four brothers and two sisters grew up on the Perfume River in Hue. The pride was reinforced by a feeling of regional differentness. Historically, Vietnam was divided into three separate areas—north (Tonkin), center (Annam), south (Cochin)—each with its own dialect, customs, food—each suspicious of the other. The French used these sectional differences as a basis for their strategy of divide and rule. According to the theory of climate and fertility, the northerner lived a harder life than the southerner and was therefore more mentally alert and aggressive. But no one could explain adequately why most of Vietnam's national leaders were born or educated in the center, including Ngo Dinh Diem, Ho Chi Minh, Pham Van Dong, and Vo Nguyen Giap, although there was a theory that since the center was the poorest region of the country, it was fertile ground for the growth of revolutionaries.

At any rate, Chau, who was a Boy Scout in 1942—actually a *Routier,* the French equivalent of Explorer Scout—was recruited into the Viet Minh by a professor who was a prominent member of the international scout movement. Although Chau did not realize it, the professor was organizing clandestine units for Ho's Viet Minh. The Boy Scouts, along with the Youth and Culture Clubs founded by the Vichy French and modeled on the lines of the Hitler Youth, provided much of the leadership for the Viet Minh, since no other military training was open to a Vietnamese not directly serving the French.

After World War Two was over and the French returned, Chau and his brothers and sisters, all but the youngest boy, joined the Viet Minh in the jungle for the war against the colonialists. It was a time of confusion. They were given thirty days of training, twenty devoted to political indoctrination, ten to military tactics. Chau's squad had only six weapons, a couple of old French muskets, the rest a mix of Japanese and German rifles. One youth killed himself by firing the wrong kind of ammunition in his weapon. There was such a lack of military knowledge among them that a Boy Scout leader from Hue was given five months training and then made commander of the Viet Minh Fifth Interzone, which stretched from above Da Nang southward to Phan Thiet, an area of such vastness that it made up three separate military regions during the American war. Chau's brother Hien, who was older by a year, had been a boyhood friend of the scout, and Hien was appointed the chief of intelligence for the Fifth Interzone. So many Vietnamese volunteered for the Viet Minh that there was not enough rice to feed them. They were called to a meeting, and the leader asked those who did not feel healthy enough to thrive in the jungle with little food to return home and wait until more supplies and weapons were available. The speaker made it sound as though anybody who chose to leave at that moment was a patriot, and only years later did Chau realize it had been a communist technique to weed out the weak and less dedicated. Among those who left were two young men who later became prominent Saigon generals. Chau stayed because he felt healthy and did not want to abandon the cause.

Chau was soon promoted to company commander. The Viet Minh developed a cycle whereby an officer was rotated from the field to a base camp to a training course and back to the field. This narrowed the exposure to combat, but casualties were still high, and Chau was wounded three times. He was prepared to give his life for his country. He had heard talk about the communists but knew little about them and was not interested in politics. He was ready to follow anyone who could lead the Viet Minh to victory over the French.

His political awakening came in a roundabout manner. Each large unit of the Viet Minh had a political commissioner as well as a military commander. The military officer was responsible for tactics and leading the fighting. The political man was responsible for indoctrination and motivating the troops. Although much depended on the personalities and competence of the two men, it often seemed that the political commissioner was more important than the military man. You could be a good military leader without necessarily being politically aware, and politics was the lifeblood of the Viet Minh organization, flowing straight up the chain of command to Ho Chi Minh.

Chau was a friend of his battalion political officer. One day, after the Viet Minh burned a Catholic church, the political man was arrested and brought to trial, accused of ordering the burning. Chau knew that he had done no such thing, yet the political officer was forced to get up in front of everyone and confess that, yes, he had given the order to destroy the church. Chau saw that he was being made a scapegoat by communists behind the scenes who wanted to get rid of him for political reasons. He was sentenced to death. On top of that, Chau was made the new battalion political officer to replace his friend.

Not long afterward another old friend showed up. He was also from Hue. Chau estimated there to be only three or four communists in the whole regiment at the time, and his friend was one of them. He was chief of staff for political affairs and worked for the regimental political commissioner, Chau's boss. The fact that his friend was a communist did not bother Chau. Chau admired him very much. He had been imprisoned by the French, and his life as a revolutionary was exemplary. To Chau, his friend outshone the regimental military commander. Nevertheless, Chau was taken aback when his friend began to try to recruit him for the communist party. Chau knew little about communism, but he assumed he would be considered a poor risk for recruitment as he came from what the communists called a "reactionary" family, one of relative wealth and property. Also, he wondered if his friend had forgotten that he was religious. Or maybe his friend didn't believe he was a serious Buddhist, which was an error on his part. As a high-school student, Chau had won a countrywide essay contest on what it meant to be a Buddhist.

Buddhism was the predominant religion of Vietnam, although to call Vietnam a Buddhist country was as misleading as to call Spain a Catholic country, as many were only nominal Buddhists and serious adherents probably numbered no more than 20 or 25 percent of those who claimed the religion. Confucianism, which was not really a religion but more a social philosophy, was a second influence, followed by the superstition-filled Taoism and a variety of sects, such as the Hoa Hao and Cao Dai. Catholics, though small in number, rivaled, and often exceeded, the Buddhists in influence, mainly because of their militarylike organization and because a Vietnamese interested in advancing under the French might do well to adopt the religion of his master. Chau would remain, however, a strong Buddhist his entire life, even when faced by communists who dismissed all religions, or by ambitious colleagues like Nguyen Van Thieu who converted to Catholicism. He believed in the Four Noble Truths formulated by Buddha, that (1) man was born to suffer, and he suffers from one life to the next; (2) craving is the cause for suffering: craving for pleasure, possessions, and cessation of pain; (3) the cure for craving is nonattachment to all things including self; (4) to achieve nonattachment one must take the eightfold path of right conduct, right effort, right intentions, right livelihood, right medications, right mindedness, right speech, and right views.

Chau tried to hide his surprise when his friend tried to recruit him. He did not turn him down flatly. Chau told him he did not have time to study the theory behind communism and would only join the party when he was convinced he knew what it was all about. Chau added that he didn't enjoy politics and was interested only in fighting the French. To be truthful, he said, he did not think he could stand as a role model like his friend and the other communists he had seen. His friend seemed to accept his explanation and returned to headquarters.

Abruptly, Chau was removed from his position as battalion political officer. He had liked his work and pursued his job in a conscientious manner. There was no question in his mind but that he was being fired for refusing to join the communist party. The point was hammered home when the friend who tried to recruit him now assigned him to a training course devoted to political indoctrination. The course was run by the head of the Department of Cadres, a communist who later became defense minister of the National Liberation Front during the American war.

A cadre was a unique creation of the communist system, a political functionary who, at his most effective, combined the inspirational enthusiasm of a Rotary Club president with the responsibility and dedication of a fireman, backed by the hard eyes and enforcement of a policeman. The cadre was the singlemost important cog in the communists' political-military machine, the one who performed chores ranging from recruiting guerrilla fighters to collecting taxes and making sure that propaganda was kept at maximum pitch. Though armed and sometimes caught up in the fighting, the cadre was not a soldier but someone more valuable, in fact indispensable, to the communist success. Nearly twenty years later, under Chau's direction, the Americans would create their own revolutionary cadres, while trying to eliminate communist cadres with the Phoenix program.

The techniques of communist organization he learned would prove helpful to Chau years later in fighting them, but at the moment he was dissatisfied, depressed, and even embarrassed to be assigned to the Department of Cadres with no specific job. Life in the jungle had been hard. He and his fellow guerrilla fighters had eaten little, made their shoes by cutting old rubber tires into Ho Chi Minh sandals, suffered malaria, and slept in hammocks in the rain and cold. But they were a family. Chau missed them. He felt like a shirker. He approached the head of cadres and told him he wanted a job, told him he could not endure headquarters any longer. The chief advised him to be patient. But he received no assignment and Chau kept prodding. Finally, the chief of cadres told him he could be the special observer of the Da Nang region. He would travel around the area and make reports that would be used for training purposes. It was a made-up title and a make-work job, but Chau jumped at it and set out to turn it into a position that would help the cause.

For the first time in years, Chau could move about and talk to people on the outside, read newspapers, listen to the radio. What he saw and heard was a shock. Britain was granting India independence. All signs indicated that colonialism was on its last legs. The French appeared to be making concessions too. Bao Dai, the exiled emperor, was brought back by the French and ostensibly put in charge of Vietnam. Chau's family had served the emperor, and he took this as a good sign—too politically immature to realize that Bao Dai's restoration was but a French ruse to maintain their control through a puppet. Chau felt exhausted. He had fought in the jungle for four years and, with the poor diet, had never properly recovered from his wounds. The French seemed overwhelmingly strong, unbeatable. It looked to him as though the bloodletting would go on for years, leading to the slaughter of the best of Vietnamese youth.

Chau decided to leave the Viet Minh. Looking back, he could not put his finger on any single reason for his decision. It was a combination of many factors, including his own weakness. He suffered, he said, a sudden lack of confidence in the Viet Minh leadership and in how the war was being conducted. He held a grudge against the communists for the way he had been treated, not that he was necessarily against communism as a political program. He still knew little about it. Chau was never comfortable talking about his decision, and his attitude contrasted with that of many Saigon officers who served with the Americans, who would flatly assert that they had deserted the Viet Minh because they knew that communists and communism were bad.

It was a painful moment for Chau. A sister and two of his brothers, including Hien, were serving nearby, but he decided not to tell them. If they could continue to believe in the Viet Minh, he would not attempt to change their minds. Anyway, he did not feel strong enough in his own convictions to try to persuade them. So one morning in late

1949 Chau got up and put on the uniform of a regular Viet Minh officer and walked to the headquarters of the province chief outside Da Nang. The guards were astonished to see a Viet Minh officer come strolling up. To calm them, Chau said that he was a relative of the province chief—not true—and asked to see him. The province chief knew Chau's father and received him cordially. The French were informed of his defection. "The special observer of the Da Nang region," they said, delighted. The title made Chau sound like one of the highest-ranking Viet Minh ever to defect. The French treated him accordingly. They flew him to Nha Trang, farther down the coast, and lodged him in a hotel. He was assigned a car and escort. French intelligence believed he knew everything about Viet Minh strategy and organization. The interrogations began. For ten days, French intelligence flew him around the country and asked him to point out Viet Minh locations. He showed them places he was certain the Viet Minh had abandoned. During the interrogations he tried not to lie; he simply did not tell everything he knew. At the end, the French captain in charge said, "I think you are sincere. I was in the resistance during the war. If we fought for our independence, we have no reason to fight against what you tried to do. Unfortunately, it takes time. It is not people like us who make the policy. We are in the line. I hope you will not look at the French as your enemy anymore."

The French official in Hue knew Chau's father, who was living as a retired judge, and Chau was sent home with instructions to report to the police every week. Chau felt like a displaced person. He looked for some way to rebuild his life. Hoping to promote reconciliation between Vietnamese on both sides, he founded a magazine called *Fatherland*. He advocated independence for Vietnam under a step-by-step program. The magazine lasted four months. The Vietnamese governor called Chau in and told him he would have to cease publication. It was too controversial.

Chau began to talk to other Vietnamese who had left the Viet Minh. He studied communist theory. He discovered that his experiences with the communists had not been an isolated incident but typical of what had happened to many others. Anyone who opposed the communists was removed and sometimes killed. By 1950, they had taken over almost every important position in the Viet Minh. Vietnam had never known democracy, but Chau realized he was seeing something worse than the usual Asian authoritarianism. What he saw was a meticulously organized totalitarianism that allowed for no dissent or deviation from the party line. It was now that he became an anticommunist. This did not mean he believed the friends he had fought beside in the jungle were monsters. He thought they were good people, dedicated, most of them, but victims of a specious indoctrination. Likewise, he could respect what Ho Chi Minh was trying to do in ridding the country of the French. Ho's idea was patriotic. But Chau believed that Ho and the communists were putting the country on a track that would lead to a horrible future.

It was not Chau's nature to remain inactive or to play the role of a French-tainted intellectual content to criticize all sides from the safety of a café in Saigon or Hanoi. Having decided that he was anticommunist, it followed by his logic that he had to join with French forces and fight against the Viet Minh, at the same time supporting independence for Vietnam. The French had recently established a military academy in the mountain resort of Dalat, and Chau was selected as a member of the first Vietnamese class. After completing the yearlong course, he was picked as one of two from the class to stay on as instructors. Shortly afterward, eight more Vietnamese instructors arrived at the academy, among them Nguyen Van Thieu. Thieu had gone to a regional military school and had been sent to France for additional training. He and Chau were second lieutenants. Both were newly married. They began to talk and discovered that Chau's father-in-law and Thieu's older brother had been classmates in school. That kind of family connection was important. Thieu and his wife had no place to stay. Chau lived in a three-bedroom villa. He offered to share his home with Thieu.

Chau and Thieu lived together for a year. The two couples became good friends. Chau was impressed by Thieu's intelligence. Thieu was one of the brightest officers Chau had met, definitely on the top level. Not only that, Thieu was pleasant-natured and seemed to be a man of standards. One day Chau finished teaching early and returned home. His wife was taking a siesta in their upstairs bedroom. He smelled a sharp odor. He went to the ground-floor kitchen and looked in. Because it was a cold day, Thieu's wife and her cook had sealed the kitchen windows tightly, and they had been overcome by fumes from the charcoal cooking stove. Chau broke down the door and carried their unconscious bodies to fresh air. He phoned Thieu, who was at the school, and told him his wife was dying. The two men often joked together, and Thieu replied, "Good. I'll get another." No, it was not a joke, Chau said, but it took a long time to persuade Thieu that Chau wasn't trying to put something over on him, Thieu being innately skeptical and cautious. The school doctor arrived, then Thieu, and his wife and the cook regained consciousness. Another hour, the doctor said, and she would have been gone. The two couples did not talk about the incident, except to laugh about it.

Their shared life ended after Chau got into an argument with a French captain at the academy. Beauvisage was his name, commander of the service company, and Chau acidly pointed out that Captain Pretty Face had come all the way from France just to manage housekeeping duties. The head of the academy asked Chau to apologize, but he refused. Chau told the colonel that he was an instructor at the school against his will and requested a transfer to a combat unit. An assignment to an airborne battalion came through in a few days, sending Chau to fight the Viet Minh.

6

WASHINGTON 1949

AT THE MOMENT CHAU was deciding to leave the Viet Minh, the American government was also moving toward a crucial decision on Vietnam. Chau and the United States shared the same dilemma. Neither liked French colonialism, but both were opposed to the communists. In its way, Washington's decision was as tortured bureaucratically as Chau's was personally. The difference was that many of the communists were Chau's friends, including his brothers and sisters, and however misguided he considered their ideology, he knew them as patriots—not as faceless members of a Moscow-directed conspiracy, as Washington saw them. Acting in their own interests, the French played on America's growing nervousness about international communism by couching their requests for aid in terms that suggested they were the last bulwark in Asia against the spreading red menace. The idea could not be dismissed out of hand as Ho Chi Minh had obviously gone to Moscow to learn communist organizational techniques.

Taken in the context of the times it is not difficult to trace why President Harry Truman and his administration moved from a policy of ambivalence on Indochina to one of active support for the French. The warnings about Russian expansionist tendencies had begun before World War Two was concluded, and Soviet actions in taking over Eastern Europe justified the worries of reasonable men. Then in early 1947 the British informed Washington that they were withdrawing from the area of Greece and Turkey, which were both under communist pressure. The United States was left with a choice of staying out of this strategic area and taking what appeared at the time a sizable risk that the communists would move in or developing a strategy of intervention that would counter the threat. The decision, announced in Harry Truman's speech to Congress on March 12, 1947, requesting an aid program for Greece and Turkey, became known as the Truman Doctrine.

Prior to the Truman speech the United States had no policy to stand as a basis for intervention around the world, and the role that George Kennan of the State Department played in helping formulate it became legend-encrusted over the ensuing years—the Long Telegram from Moscow, the anonymous *Foreign Affairs* article of July 1947, signed "X," in which he developed the thesis that United States policy toward the Soviet Union should be "long-term, patient but firm" and asserted that "Soviet pressure can be contained by the adroit and vigilant application of counterforce at a series of shifting geographical and political points...." But according to Kennan, President Truman gave the policy of containment a more sweeping interpretation than its author had intended. Truman described the conflict between democracy and communism in Manichaean terms, as a struggle between good and evil to be decided on a worldwide scale. "I believe," Truman said in his speech to Congress, "that it must be the policy of the United States to support free peoples who are resisting attempted subjugation by armed minorities or by outside pressure." Kennan objected to the phrase "to support free peoples" as being too general and not limited to clearly defined American interests vis-à-vis Russian expansionism. Fourteen years later John F. Kennedy restated the Truman Doctrine in his inaugural address and, seeking elegant phrasing with the kind of rhetoric the plain-speaking Truman never used, actually broadened its implications: "Let every nation know, whether it wishes us well or ill, that we shall pay any price, bear any burden, meet any hardship, support any friend, oppose any foe to assure the survival and success of liberty." The doctrine had moved from supporting "free peoples" to supporting "any friend."

The Truman Doctrine, and the question of whether the United States should act as the policeman of the world, as the policy of containment suggested to its critics, was usually argued in political and philosophical terms, with the concrete method of its application often little considered. Yet containment was applied in two distinctly separate ways, one based on historical precedent concerning the use of military force, which succeeded, the second on an unproved assumption widely thought to be flawed from the beginning, which indeed failed. The method of containment generally agreed to be successful involved the setting up of the North Atlantic Treaty Organization in Europe. (An equivalent organization, SEATO, was attempted in Asia but remained toothless and eventually faded away.) Reduced to its most primal, NATO was nothing more than a banding together of different tribes in an uneasy alliance in order to concentrate their brute force the better to deter or defeat a perceived threat from another band of tribes. The strategy for NATO—the massing of troops in an alliance, the development of new and ever more powerful weapons—had evolved in an unbroken line over centuries and had demonstrated its value in countless struggles throughout history.

One was hard put, however, to find any historical evidence that the other military application of the containment policy, the sending of small groups of advisers to the armies of foreign countries, had worked to a significant degree to win wars or deter threats. It didn't take a brilliant strategist to realize that such a piecemeal introduction of forces could lead to immense trouble, and for this very reason the Congress of the United States had turned down military requests to send advisers around the world. Congress had made an exception in 1926 for an advisory effort to Latin America, considered the backyard of the United States under the Monroe Doctrine and therefore open to forceful intervention if the advisers got into trouble, and in 1946 to the Philippines, which had been granted its independence after serving as a U.S. colony for half a century.

But Congress's attitude could be seen in the way it treated the matter of a military mission to help Chiang Kai-shek's Nationalist Chinese against Mao Tse-tung's communists. In late 1945, when it appeared the communists would occupy parts of north China being vacated by the defeated Japanese, Washington sent fifty thousand marines to hold the territory until Chiang Kai-shek's troops could get there. This brought the Americans into hostile contact with the communists, and the U.S. commander in China recommended that the marines be strengthened or withdrawn. The troops were withdrawn, but Truman established a military mission on February 25, 1946, by claiming that the war powers authority giving the president leeway in such cases was still in effect. The Senate didn't think so, however, and refused to approve the military mission the following year, although army and air force units were continued under presidential order without authorization by statute. When a bill authorizing a naval advisory unit in China did get through both the House and the Senate, Congress added this restriction: "United States naval or Marine Corps personnel shall not accompany Chinese troops, aircraft, or ships on other than training maneuvers or cruises."

So when President Truman asked for advisers to be sent to Greece and Turkey under his new policy of containment, the reaction of Congress was not unexpected. Seeking to head off opposition, the administration included in its draft of the bill the self-imposed restriction that these military personnel, "limited in number," would serve "in an advisory capacity only." Still, there was widespread skepticism and reluctance on the part of Congress to grant Truman's request. Opposition to sending military advisers was particularly strong in the House of Representatives. Many members wanted a strict limitation to the number of advisers so they could be withdrawn quickly. Representative Jacob Javits of New York suggested that instead of a numerical limitation, the vague phrase "in an advisory capacity only" be replaced by "in the instruction and training of military personnel, and in the procurement of military equipment and supplies only." "We are worried," said Javits, "that one day an American captain will be found in the mountains advising a Greek officer how to fire on a guerrilla." There was considerable worry among other members that after the United States put its prestige and credibility on the line by sending a few advisers, withdrawal might become difficult or impossible and the country could be sucked into an unwanted war.

All these considerations were deeply debated, but the Truman administration made a persuasive case that the wolf was at the door, and the Greek-Turkey aid bill was passed by Congress, committing American military advisers to a foreign country for the first time as an arm of the policy of communist containment. The unclear and foggy atmosphere surrounding the way this came about—with ambivalence and skepticism on the part of many members of Congress and a lack of a specific definition of the advisory role by the White House—was to carry over to the introduction of military advisers in Vietnam, leaving the United States' policy of containment there in a similar but more dangerous mist of indeterminacy.

The first step into Indochina came with the Mutual Defense Assistance Act of 1949, which was passed at the time Mao Tse-tung and his communists were taking over China and the Russians were exploding their first atomic bomb. The purpose of the bill was to provide military assistance to countries in Europe, with only Korea and the Philippines covered in Asia, but an amendment was added to help the "general area" of China, and when asked what this meant, a State Department official replied, "It might be used in other areas of the Far East which are affected by the developments in China. That would include such areas of Burma, the northern part of Indochina, if it became desirable to suppress communism in that country." The act authorized the president to send military personnel to any "agency or nation" as noncombatant advisers, which became the legal basis for the advisory mission Truman sent to Vietnam in 1950 and the authority by which Kennedy increased their number to about twenty thousand in 1963.

The battle over the sending of advisers to foreign countries had been fought during the debate on the Greek-Turkey aid bill. Congress passed the assistance act that would be used to justify intervention in Indochina with little reservation or discussion. When Secretary of State Dean Acheson announced in May 1950 that the United States would begin giving direct aid to Vietnam, Cambodia, and Laos, as well as continue aid to the French, which had begun earlier, the *New York Times,* echoing public sentiment, applauded the move with an editorial agreeing that the fall of Indochina would have a domino effect on the rest of Southeast Asia.

7

MANILA 1950

THE PASSING OF the Mutual Defense Assistance Act of 1949, which occurred as Chau was leaving the Viet Minh, triggered the chain of events that brought him and other anticommunists in contact with an exuberant personality by the name of Edward Geary Lansdale. For Lansdale the road to Saigon led through Manila, and how he happened to get sent to the Philippines was so typical of the man that it is best told in his own words:

> Mindful of the part played by Americans in the recent Greek struggle against communist guerrillas, I talked to U.S. leaders about giving similar help to the Philippines. This was the spring of 1950. Few U.S. officials wanted even to think about going through another experience such as Greece, although they admitted that the Philippine situation seemed to be worsening. It was suggested that I draw up a modest plan for simple measures that could be added to the U.S. military and economic assistance already being given to the Philippines. I went to work on a plan for an input of less conventional actions against the political-military tactics of the [communist guerrilla] Huks.

Many years later, when asked what he considered the oddest aspect of Lansdale, William Colby, a former director of the CIA, thought for a moment and said, "That he became an air force general." Indeed, Ed Lansdale was one of the most unusual professional officers that *any* military service had ever seen. This anomaly could not be detected in his appearance, for he was conventionally handsome, nearly five-eleven, slim, with brown hair and eyes. His uniform was neatly pressed and his shoes shined. Perhaps a hint came with the Clark Gable mustache and the way he settled into a civilian sprawl when he sat down, shifting about with nervous energy, lighting one cigarette after another. But it was when he began to talk, in his informal and easy manner, the ideas spilling out, that one really had trouble believing he was a military man.

Born in Detroit on February 6, 1908, Ed Lansdale was number two of four brothers whose father worked in the automotive industry, sometimes as a vice president, usually in sales. His mother was from California, and when his father changed jobs, as he frequently did, his mother returned home, taking Ed with her. Except for a time when they lived outside New York, in New Jersey, Lansdale grew up in Michigan and California, where he graduated from high school and entered UCLA. He hoped to major in journalism, but the college did not have a school of journalism, so he concentrated on English and devoted his outside time to editing the campus humor magazine. He was scheduled to graduate with the class of 1931, but lacking three or four credits and short of money, he left without taking a degree and headed to New York.

Editors at two newspapers had offered him jobs, but when he arrived in the city, with less than a dollar left, he discovered that one of the papers had folded and that the other, the *World-Telegram,* was laying off journalists because of the Depression. He had a choice between washing dishes in a restaurant or working as a file clerk for a railroad. Several months later he met Helen Batcheller, a petite and pretty young woman who worked as a secretary for a hardware business. It was a case of opposites attracting, for Helen was quiet and reserved, while Ed was outgoing and warm—a difference that was to grow like a hedge between them over time and leave their friends with the impression that Lansdale was happiest when traveling around the world in a state of quasi-bachelorhood. After their marriage, they moved to Greenwich Village and settled down to work but Lansdale soon grew bored, and when his brother, Phil, who was the advertising director for a men's clothing chain in Los Angeles, offered him a job as his assistant, he quit New York and moved to California. The job was low-paying and the brothers found they didn't get on well working together, so Ed scouted San Francisco with letters of introduction and took a job with an advertising agency there.

Lansdale did well in advertising, and was promoted to chief copy-writer. "I liked it because I could be very independent," Lansdale said. "I hated people who told lies about products, and I refused to do it." Instead, he made field trips to talk to executives whose products he was promoting. With his inquisitive mind and upbeat nature, he was usually able to find something good to say about anything.

After the attack on Pearl Harbor, Lansdale announced that he intended to join the army. The head of his advertising agency told him he was crazy, that at thirty-three, married, with two kids, he should leave the heroics to others. When Lansdale insisted that he intended to do his duty, his boss fired him on the spot. Another agency heard he was free and offered him a job with a pay increase, providing Lansdale agreed they could check with his former employer for a reference. His old boss said, hell yes, Ed Lansdale was the best copy-writer he'd ever seen, but like all good copywriters he was a little crazy and the idiot wanted to join the army. Lansdale turned down the job. His commission as a first lieutenant in the army's Military Intelligence Service came through, and he was attached to the OSS office in San Francisco.

Ed Lansdale's interest in intelligence work was shaped by his earlier interests in journalism and advertising. He looked at it as a chance to be creative. He was the opposite of paramilitary operatives like Lou Conein and many OSS officers who would later staff the CIA. He had little interest in the craft of espionage and sabotage, of jumping out of airplanes and blowing up things. Most of his war service was spent on the West Coast writing reports on esoteric subjects. If that sounded dull to other intelligence officers, Lansdale approached the work with great enthusiasm. It was the kind of stuff he loved, in a sense a continuation of his product research as an advertising man.

"I was fascinated by intelligence," Lansdale said. "We were fighting around the world, and we needed to know about different peoples and cultures and geography. I found all kinds of amazing experts. One was an ichthyologist at Stanford whom I interviewed about poisonous fishes in the Pacific—what to look for, how to handle them. The report I did went out to American troops and got tremendous circulation."

Lansdale saw no overseas service during the war, but on August 21, 1945, the day before Lou Conein and other OSS officers were moving into Hanoi, he received orders to report to the Philippines as the chief of analysis in the intelligence division at army headquarters. With the war over, most Americans were eager to get home, but the newly arrived Lansdale was intrigued by the possibility of playing a role in the postwar development of the Philippines, which was set to receive its independence from the United States on July 4, 1946. He volunteered to stay on and was promoted to deputy chief of intelligence for the army command. His boss, Colonel George A. Chester, described Lansdale "as one of the most able men I have ever met, combining idealism, ability and aggressiveness."

When friction developed between the Filipinos, who had been given their independence, and some Americans who tended to ignore that fact, Lansdale was appointed as the command's public information officer. The assignment brought him into contact with various elements of Philippine society, and it was then that he first displayed the talent that would be the subject of debate in future years. Lansdale could form an immediate bond with another nationality. He had an indefinable quality that inspired trust and confidence among non-Americans. Not only was he learning the dynamics of another culture, he was also gaining experience through his intelligence work in combating the communist-led guerrilla insurgency that had flared up in the Philippines during World War Two. When his tour ended, a hundred Filipino friends escorted him and his family to the gangplank of the ship, showering them with flowers.

While in the Philippines, Lansdale applied to join the newly formed United States Air Force. He decided to make the military a career and reasoned that in a new service he would have a better chance for promotions and interesting jobs. Lansdale almost immediately regretted the decision, for he discovered that pilots had the inside track for promotions and good jobs, and he was no pilot. He was furious when he received orders to report to air force intelligence school in Denver on February 24, 1949, as an instructor. It seemed to him that he had jumped to a new service straight into an unwanted career as a teacher. Restless and upset, he got in touch with his old boss from the Philippines, Colonel Chester, who had been assigned to the Pentagon, and Chester told him he would recommend him to a new intelligence organization that was being formed.

William Donovan, the chief of the OSS, urged an unreceptive President Truman to establish a peacetime intelligence organization as World War Two came to a close, presumably with Donovan as its head. Instead, viewing Donovan as a possible political rival, and under pressure from the FBI and the Pentagon, who feared their turf might be threatened by such an organization, Truman abolished the OSS on September 20, 1945. It became clear, however, that some form of centralization was necessary to give coherence to intelligence collection, and four months later Truman took a step in that direction by establishing the National Intelligence Authority, consisting of the secretaries of war, navy, and state, with Admiral William D. Leahy serving as his personal representative. The NIA had a staff called the Central Intelligence Group, made up of eighty volunteers from the three departments involved. When this organization proved not up to the task, Truman signed into law the National Security Act on September 15, 1947, which, among other things, established the Central Intelligence Agency. The CIA was given the authority to hire and train its own employees and to act as an arm of the executive branch in intelligence matters. Still, the CIA as originally set up did not have the kind of covert political action capability that some officials thought necessary to carry out the cold war policy of containment. George Kennan, from his post as director of the State Department's policy planning staff, recommended that Truman establish an organization designed solely to carry out covert activities such as paramilitary operations and support of anticommunist guerrilla movements. The organization would be run by a director selected by the secretary of state and approved by the secretary of defense. Thus was the innocuous-sounding Office of Policy Coordination formed in May 1948, as a direct descendant of the Office of Strategic Services and staffed mostly by former OSS officers who had been marking time since the end of the war, waiting for such an opportunity to get back into action.

The Office of Policy Coordination eventually merged into the CIA's covert action branch, but the merger was not completed until 1952, under the insistent hand of CIA director Walter Bedell Smith, and in the beginning OPC was a separate organization with its own head, Frank Wisner, a former OSS officer, and it relied on the CIA mainly for administrative and logistics support—room and board. When Lansdale joined OPC in November 1949, heaving a sigh of relief at having escaped the teaching job that lasted nine months, the organization had a staff of 302, including secretaries and other nonoperatives.

The initial difference between CIA and OPC, which after the merger looked to the outsider to be only a bureaucratic blip (CIA did not admit to the existence of OPC and the true history of its covert action branch until 1982), was extremely important to the development and attitude of Lansdale as an intelligence operative. He was, in effect, a military officer who received his pay and promotion from the air force while detached to a highly secret intelligence organization that itself was attached to the CIA. One could hardly imagine a greater blurring of the lines of bureaucratic control over an operative who was already inclined to go his own way. Moreover, Lansdale's brilliant and driven boss at OPC, Frank Wisner, who later committed suicide after falling into depression and mental instability, was as flamboyant and freewheeling as Lansdale and shared his contempt for bureaucracy. From the Philippines to Vietnam, Lansdale felt he was attached to the CIA but not really a part of it, and he coveted his independence to the point of not hesitating to fight with the agency. The end result was that Lansdale, more so than any covert operative, became the instrument of his own policy.

That policy was concentrated on the country he knew best, and by the sheer force of his energy and personality he soon became Washington's expert on the Philippines. Colonel Chester, his old boss from the Philippines who recruited Lansdale for OPC, sounded more like an awed booster than an objective superior when he wrote his efficiency report during this period. "He has the highest potential value of any air force officer I have known," Chester recorded, "with a steel-trap mind and a driving purpose in a relaxed body."

Lansdale persuaded the Philippines' military attaché at its Washington embassy to allow him to give any Filipino officers who were in the United States as students a postgraduate course in psychological warfare, which he set up in a vacant office at the Pentagon. Then he began drafting his own plans on how to fight the communist insurgency and, more to the point, began lobbying his superiors to send him to Manila to carry them out.

It was at this time, in the spring of 1950, that a friend introduced Lansdale to Ramón Magsaysay, a Philippine congressman who was on a trip to the United States. At forty-three, Magsaysay was about Lansdale's height, which was tall for a Filipino, a little heavier, and six months older. He had fought the Japanese as a guerrilla in an American-led unit during the war and had become a popular politician afterward, known for his quick smile and warm personality. Lansdale was immediately taken with Magsaysay. He spent much of the first night

after dinner talking to him and planning a campaign against the communist Huk guerrillas, apparently deciding on the spot that he was
going to engineer Magsaysay's appointment as the Philippines' defense secretary. Lansdale's superiors were also impressed with Magsaysay but not as anxious as Lansdale to intervene in Philippine affairs
in such a heavy-handed way. After Lansdale persisted, Frank Wisner,
the head of OPC, agreed to send Colonel Chester and Livingston
Merchant, who was the State Department's liaison with OPC, to Manila to pressure President Quirino to put Magsaysay in charge of
defense. Quirino realized he had no choice but to acquiesce if he
wanted continued American aid, and in September 1950 Magsaysay
became secretary of defense. The only step left in Lansdale's plan,
which had been bubbling in his head since he landed in Washington,
was to get himself assigned to the Philippines so that he could work
with Magsaysay against the communists. His superiors cooled to the
idea, particularly when Lansdale announced that he intended to take
with him Charles Bohannan, who was an officer and friend from his
first tour, and a communications specialist as members of his "team."
Lansdale's persistence won yet again, though, and pressure was applied once more on President Quirino, this time to invite Lansdale to
Manila as his adviser on intelligence matters. His work was considered so secret that not even John Richardson, the CIA's regular station chief in Manila, was informed about what was going on. With his
propensity for grabbing the bull by the horns *and* the tail, Lansdale
turned his ninety-day temporary assignment in September 1950 into a
tour that lasted nearly four years and propelled him onward to Vietnam.

On the surface the communist rebellion in the Philippines resembled the Viet Minh insurgency in Vietnam. Both developed during
World War Two at about the same time, both were ostensibly aimed
at defeating the Japanese, and both received organizational help from
Chinese communist veterans. Therefore Lansdale gained an earlier
understanding of communist guerrilla warfare than most Americans
of the period. He had a flexible and curious mind that looked at the
problem beyond the usual shallow level of anticommunist sloganeer-
ing. Using the same talents for market research that he had cultivated
as an advertising man, he got out in the field and talked to ordinary
people about their lives and aspirations, about what worked with the
government and what didn't. His response to the problem also drew

from his background. Lansdale did not want to kill the communists. He wanted to win them over to the government side. Almost every technique he developed was based on psychological and political warfare, the military equivalent of promotion and advertising. Lansdale was selling a product he believed superior: democracy. He was the personification of the United States that emerged from World War Two. If the British had imposed law and administration on foreign peoples and France had been determined to civilize the under-developed world, then Americans would assert themselves as the new leaders by promoting democracy and economic improvement while not incidentally trying to contain communism. What separated Lansdale from many cold warriors who joined the fight was that he actually believed in what he was selling. The idea of democracy and free elections, to him, was not just a cover of soap suds in an all-out fight to counter communism, as it often appeared to be where others were concerned. One could imagine Lansdale, in another context, trying to persuade Franco of Spain to accept democratic reforms, something not easily imagined of many intelligence officers.

Yet below the surface the situation in the Philippines was greatly different from that in Vietnam. The Philippine communists were led not by an accomplished revolutionary like Ho Chi Minh but by a twenty-seven-year-old former tailor of little talent. During World War Two the Chinese communists who were training the Filipinos threw up their hands at their amateurishness and formed their own separate unit against the Japanese. By late 1950 the security of the Filipino communists was so lax that Lansdale was able to mount an operation that captured almost the entire Politburo leadership, which immensely enhanced his prestige.

Another crucial difference was found in the government official through whom Lansdale was able to do his wheeling and dealing. It was impossible to tell who influenced whom the most—Lansdale or Magsaysay. Each night the two of them sat up late discussing the political and military situation. Lansdale tried to channel, as subtly as possible, Magsaysay's gush of ideas into effective action. Magsaysay was ambitious, and Lansdale involved himself in plotting domestic moves for his friend, as well as devising tactics to use against the communist guerrillas, two things he saw as related since he considered the Quirino government to be hopelessly conventional and not up to the fight against the communists. Lansdale aroused the anger of other politicians by pushing Magsaysay to the fore, and there was talk of kicking him out of the country. But he stayed on, and eventually Magsaysay rose to head the government, only to be killed in a plane crash a few years later. Magsaysay was a rare democratic leader, and his likes were not to be found in any other Southeast Asia country, especially Vietnam; and much of Lansdale's success in the Philippines could be attributed to him.

But the biggest difference between the Philippines and Vietnam was in their recent histories. The Philippines were for nearly fifty years a colony of the United States, which intended to bestow independence, and before that were ruled by Spain. Under American tutelage, the Filipinos were encouraged to adopt democratic attitudes, and over the years an acceptance of democratic forms grew. Politics, while rough and tumble, were out in the open. When Lansdale talked to Magsaysay about moves in their fight against the communists, they were speaking the same language, literally and figuratively. It wasn't like Vietnam, where political parties had operated for eighty years in an underground atmosphere of conspiracy and distrust.

Nevertheless, Lansdale's Philippine experience was to become the greatest influence on the American political approach to Vietnam. Undeniably, he had done a good job and proved himself to be an effective operative. The word of his accomplishments spread. China might have been "lost," went the thought, and Korea bogged down into a stalemate, but look at what an infusion of aid and advisers had done in Greece, and then Lansdale had succeeded in the Philippines.

A second major influence was Britain's success in countering communist guerrillas in Malaya during the period of the Philippines insurgency. As in the case of the Philippines, the situation in Malaya was different from Vietnam. Among other things, the communists there were mostly of Chinese extraction and could be identified and isolated from the general population, not like Vietnam, where communist guerrillas looked like ordinary farmers. To some Americans, however, it appeared that the British had a winning formula. Robert Thompson and veterans of the Malaya campaign soon established themselves as experts on counterguerrilla warfare and as advisers to their American cousins, whom they considered, with few exceptions, hopeless neophytes.

Oddly enough, the least important influence on the American approach to Vietnam was the French experience in Indochina. The French had nearly a century's worth of knowledge of the country. The Viet Minh they fought evolved into the Viet Cong the Americans fought—same leaders, same tactics, same battlefields.* Chau's brother Hien did not change, except to become better at his job. Yet the American military, from private to general, considered the French experience not only ancient but prehistoric. Some graybeards could speak about the period of 1954 to 1963. But for most Americans Vietnam emerged from the murk around the time of the Diem coup; for the combat soldier, history went no farther back than 1965. Even civilian officials such as Dan Ellsberg and his friends regarded the French with unnuanced disdain, calling them the "bad" colonialists, as opposed to the British, who were the "good" colonialists. Books written about their experiences went unread and were not translated into English until the United States was already in up to its knees. Only then was there a certain stirring of interest.

---

*The term *Viet Minh,* which was shortened from the Vietnamese name for the front group the communists set up to fight the French—League for the Independence of Vietnam—was acceptable to all sides. The name given the guerrillas during the American war, *Viet Cong,* for "Vietnamese communist", was considered pejorative by those it was applied to and never used by them. The farmers in the countryside, aware of the nuance involved, called the guerrillas Viet Cong when they were speaking to Americans, but cautiously addressed the communists by such names as *Ong Giai-Phong*—"Mr. Liberation," as in National Liberation Front—when speaking to them.

8

HANOI-SAIGON 1954

I GAVE A BIRTHDAY PARTY in the spring of 1954, and everybody had a good time. One of the men who came owned an airplane, and he said, "Elyette, I've got a surprise for you." Because of a military shortage, civilians were hired to airdrop supplies for the French base at Dien Bien Phu, which was under seige by the Viet Minh, and my pilot friend was scheduled to make a run later that afternoon. He invited us to fly with him. My parents were strict. I had to tell them before I went anywhere, and I couldn't reach them by telephone, so I didn't go. Three of my girlfriends went on the drop. The plane was shot down. They were killed. The war was coming closer. Many French returned home. Besides the military, only civilians connected with the government, schoolteachers, and a few doctors were left in Hanoi. Censorship was imposed, so we knew only what the government wanted us to know. Then an official from the British consulate dropped by my home at eleven o'clock on May 7, 1954, and said, "Did you hear the news about Dien Bien Phu?" I said, "Yes, I understand everything is going better." He said, "No, the French have capitulated. You'll have to leave soon." I just couldn't believe it. We had the best fighters, you know. We just didn't have what the Americans had—the best equipment. And in Paris there was a strong feeling they didn't want to fight anymore. Too many dead.

WHEN DIEN BIEN PHU FELL in 1954, Chau was in Hanoi a short distance from Elyette's house, taking a course at the French war college. He had been identified as one of the most outstanding officers

93

in the army, on his way up, sure to succeed under the French. But Dien Bien Phu changed everything, and from then on his fate would be decided in another faraway city, not on the Seine but on the Potomac.

During the year preceding the fall of Dien Bien Phu, Washington had been concerned about what could be done to prevent Indochina from going to the communists. As President Dwight Eisenhower saw it at a National Security Council meeting on May 6, 1953, unless the French made it clear to the Indochinese that they were serious about granting them independence and at the same time appointed an effective military commander for the fight against the Viet Minh, nothing could possibly save the situation and "continued United States assistance would amount," said Eisenhower, "to pouring money down a rathole." Vice President Richard Nixon agreed. A CIA estimate predicted that the political and military situation would continue to deteriorate the following year. There was a brief moment of optimism after the French, in May 1953, appointed General Henri-Eugène Navarre as their new military commander in Indochina. Washington sent the army commander in the Pacific, Lieutenant General John (Iron Mike) O'Daniel to confer with Navarre. O'Daniel was accompanied by a dozen assistants, including Ed Lansdale, who took time out from his work in the Philippines. The O'Daniel mission had been told to prod the French into more aggressive action and encourage them to put greater emphasis on guerrilla warfare and the use of officers like Chau in more native Vietnamese units. General Navarre knew in advance what the Americans would be pushing, and he beat them to it by presenting a written statement that became known as the Navarre plan, which incorporated just those things. In his report to Washington, O'Daniel was ambivalent about French prospects for success but tried to put the best face on it. Ed Lansdale was frankly pessimistic. "I didn't see how Navarre was going to win," he said, "unless he made radical changes to get the Vietnamese nationalists much more deeply involved."

By the time of a key national security meeting on January 8, 1954, Dien Bien Phu was beseiged, and Washington, after avoiding the subject as much as possible during the last ten years, was compelled to make a decision. Dwight Eisenhower was against sending ground troops to help the French. According to notes taken at the meeting, Eisenhower said, "There was just no sense in even talking about United States forces replacing the French in Indochina. If we did so,

94

the Vietnamese could be expected to transfer their hatred of the French to us. I cannot tell you, said the President with vehemence, how bitterly opposed I am to such a course of action. This war in Indochina would absorb our troops by divisions!"

Eisenhower had a couple of hard-liners among his advisers who advocated strong action, including Secretary of State John Foster Dulles and joint chiefs of staff chairman Admiral Arthur Radford. Contingency planning for a possible intervention continued until a few weeks before Dien Bien Phu was overrun. Admiral Radford, in particular, seemed to be discombobulated on the question, swinging from moods of optimism and assuring Congress that everything was going just dandy to having visions of the apocalypse and calling for the use of tactical atomic bombs to wipe out Viet Minh positions around Dien Bien Phu. Eisenhower was often portrayed as being a captive in foreign affairs to his secretary of state, but there was no evidence that he followed either Dulles or Radford on this issue.

As the situation worsened, Eisenhower shifted around, called for "united action" by allied forces, and considered launching a covert air strike to help the French, but he did not change his mind about the unilateral use of American troops. He was strongly supported in this by Army Chief of Staff James Ridgway, who had developed second thoughts about waging warfare in Asia after his experiences in Korea. The administration's plan for aiding the French turned to supplying them with pilots and aircraft mechanics and planes under CIA cover, a low-risk tactic suggested by Eisenhower himself.

At the same time, Washington began to look beyond the French. Dien Bien Phu was a symbol for the French defeat, but there was a deeper underlying cause and that was war-weariness in France. The French had begun to talk about negotiating their way out of the morass long before Dien Bien Phu fell, to the agitation of American officials, who hoped they would hold on. It was France, over Washington's objections, that insisted on putting Indochina on the agenda at the five-power conference in Geneva beginning in April 1954, which would first deal with Korea. A special committee on Indochina set up by Eisenhower around this time began considering alternatives. As early as February 16, 1954, three months before Dien Bien Phu fell, Under Secretary of State Walter Bedell Smith told the Senate Foreign Relations Committee what the administration had on its mind. Bedell Smith said that if the French were forced to withdraw, "the first possible alternative line of action" would be "a kind of walling off an area and supporting native elements who are willing to be supported in the other part of the area." Months later, Vietnam was divided into North and South at the seventeenth parallel.

Washington also began to reach a consensus as to why the French had failed and how America could do better. The failure could be traced, Washington thought, to the fact that the French were colonialists. They had not made use of the nationalist elements among the Vietnamese (people like Chau) who could provide an alternative to communism for their country. The French claimed they favored creating a large national army made up of Vietnamese, but they hadn't done much about it. There were only several thousand officers like Chau in the entire French Union forces, and none held important command positions. Vice President Richard Nixon, at the national security meeting on January 8, 1954, said that the French were "aware that if the Vietnamese become strong enough to hold their country alone, they would proceed to remove themselves from the French Union." Nixon's analysis seemed to be illustrated by France's refusal to let Americans get involved in advising the Vietnamese. It was thought the French were afraid the Americans would encourage an independence movement. The U.S. military advisory group, which was assigned to Saigon in 1950 by President Truman, worked solely through the French and was concerned mainly with procuring military equipment. France wanted supplies and money but no advice. As the situation worsened, and as they turned desperate for aid, the French were forced to become more flexible. In early 1954, General Navarre agreed to let five American liaison officers be attached to his military command. CIA director Allen Dulles recommended that Lansdale of the Philippines be dispatched to Saigon.

ED LANSDALE AND LAWRENCE OF ARABIA shared a number of obvious similarities. Both were freewheeling operatives who were considered mavericks by their governments and tolerated because they were effective in dealing with the natives. The two also shared a more subtle link in terms of their public image. The reputations of Britain's

Lawrence and America's Lansdale were formed in books written by authors of the other's nationality. In the case of Lawrence of Arabia it was a book of nonfiction by American broadcaster Lowell Thomas that first brought attention to his exploits as an adviser to the Arabs who were waging a desert guerrilla war against the Ottoman Empire. Lowell Thomas portrayed T. E. Lawrence as a man of great simplicity and artless sincerity who was imbued with the single idea of fighting for freedom. It was years before Thomas's version was corrected by other writers who showed that Lawrence was considerably more complex and that he had manipulated the Arabs to enhance Britain's influence in the Middle East at the expense of France.

In Lansdale's case, three books were published using him as a model, all of them fiction.* The most influential in fixing his public image was *The Quiet American* by British author Graham Greene. In Greene's novel, as narrated by a cynical English journalist, the theme that good intentions could lead to deadly results was illustrated through an American who arrived in Saigon during the French Indochina War and tried to create a third force for democracy as an alternative to the French colonialists and the Vietnamese communists. The American operative, named Pyle, was, like Lowell Thomas's version of Lawrence of Arabia, a man of great simplicity and artless sincerity. The difference between the two was that Thomas's Lawrence was a force for good, whereas Greene's Lansdale-like character was a well-meaning but inadvertent force for evil—or a symbol, in Greene's mind, for what he considered America's naïve tendency to stick its nose where it had no business and didn't understand what it was doing. As a work of art, Greene's novel was unsurpassed at setting the mood in Saigon. Depending upon one's political views, it could be argued that his theme was not far off the mark. And his fictional character captured an aspect of Lansdale. But Lansdale was not Pyle, though that became his tag with a large segment of the influential reading public, a misapprehension disseminated by journalists who turned against the war. Dan Ellsberg, who continued to regard Lansdale with affection, almost as a father figure, even after he became an opponent of the war, worked with Lansdale as a foreign

---

*The books are *The Quiet American* by Graham Greene (New York: Viking, 1956); *The Ugly American* by William J. Lederer and Eugene Burdick (New York: W. W. Norton, 1958); and *Yellow Fever* by Jean Larteguy, translated by Xan Fielding (New York: E. P. Dutton, 1965).

service officer and observed him closely. To Ellsberg there were three Lansdales:

"The first was the Lansdale who was reputed to have a magical touch with foreigners. Most people assumed he could speak the language. Of course he spoke no language but English. He worked through a translator. What I saw him do with the Vietnamese—and I learned from him—was to listen to them, instead of lecturing or talking down to them, as most Americans did. He treated them respectfully as though they were adults worthy of his attention—not deferentially, just respectfully as equals. That was ninety percent of his rapport. And they would almost cry with gratitude that they were being accepted as deserving human beings. Lansdale was excellent with them, much better than he was with Americans.

"The second Lansdale who dealt with American bureaucrats often came across as a kind of idiot—a guy with crazy wild ideas, naïve and simplistic. He was not at all afraid to appear simpleminded to anyone he did not want to reveal himself to, which was ninety-nine out of a hundred people. To journalists, other than a couple he was close to like Robert Shaplen of *The New Yorker,* he was very guarded and careful about what he told them. To put them off, he spoke in the most basic terms about democracy and Vietnamese traditions.

"Then there was the third Lansdale you saw only if you were on his team or worked with him closely. After giving a journalist his hayseed routine, he would join us and his mood would change immediately. He would present an analysis of a situation that was filled with shrewd and perceptive, even cynical, detail about who was doing what to whom."

Joe Redick, a CIA officer who served with Lansdale on both of his tours, thought he was far from naïve. "Lansdale would deal with the Vietnamese and some of them were real bastards, no question about it," Redick said. "Corrupt as hell. And he would treat them as though they were actually working for the good of their country. Then they sort of felt like they really had to do it."

So the Ed Lansdale who arrived in Saigon on June 1, 1954, was a talented and experienced covert operative. His mission was to undercut the French and work directly with native Vietnamese to establish an alternative to the communists. When Lansdale stepped off the plane, he became in effect the first American to serve in the Second Indochina War.

LANSDALE REALIZED THAT HE NEEDED SOMEONE to operate through in Vietnam. But instead of finding a Ramón Magsaysay he wound up with a Ngo Dinh Diem. Lansdale had nothing to do with Diem's being picked as the new prime minister to replace a succession of puppets who had served under the French. Diem was proposed by the Emperor Bao Dai, who had been reinstalled by the French for appearance's sake, as head of the Vietnam government, from his exile on the Côte d'Azur, and vetted and approved by Washington. The choice of Diem reflected the reality that pickings were slim among non-Viet Minh elements. Most potential leaders, if not aspiring to be born-again Frenchmen, were tarred in some way by their past associations with the colonialists. Officials at the American embassy in Paris who examined Ngo Dinh Diem before he went to Saigon cabled their assessment to Washington. Calling Diem a "Yogi-like mystic," they said they were prepared to accept the "seeming ridiculous prospect" that Diem become prime minister of the Saigon government "only because the standard set by his predecessors is so low." That was a rather tough assessment, but not out of line with what a lot of people thought.

Diem's attraction was that he had opposed both the French and the communists and had a countrywide reputation as a nationalist. The CIA may have had a hidden hand in promoting his appointment by Bao Dai, whose virtue, if not for sale, could be leased. Robert Amory, then deputy director of the agency, related how he had attended an after-theater party at the home of TV journalist Martin Agronsky where he chatted with Supreme Court justice William O. Douglas, who told him, "Do you know who's the guy to fix you up in Vietnam. He's here in this country, and that's Ngo Dinh Diem." Amory recorded the name in his notebook, Z-I-M, and brought it up with agency officials the next morning. Nobody had heard of Diem, said Amory, but he was looked into and it was decided that he was just the ticket.

Amory's story was possibly true, for Justice Douglas, later known as the liberal's liberal on the Supreme Court, had become a one-man lobbying effort on behalf of Ngo Dinh Diem. Douglas, an adventurous sort, made a trip to Vietnam in 1953 and hiked through isolated parts of the country that few Americans had seen. Justice Douglas was disgusted by the Eisenhower administration's support of the French colonialists. As a liberal democrat, he was seeking his own alternative for Vietnam. Most of the Vietnamese he met were fence-sitters who cozened the French for protection from the communists but hated them and dreamed of independence, talking about it quite a bit over tea. One name kept coming up: Ngo Dinh Diem, a government official who had left Vietnam in 1950, when the communists sentenced him to death and the French said they couldn't guarantee his safety. Diem, a bachelor and celibate whose dedication to Catholicism would have shamed many a priest, took refuge with the Maryknoll fathers in New Jersey, after being encouraged by Wesley Fishel, an American academic and friend, to make the United States his temporary home. When Justice Douglas returned from Vietnam, he asked Diem to come to Washington to meet with influential leaders. Douglas arranged a luncheon at the Supreme Court in May 1953, and one of the guests was a young senator named John F. Kennedy. Douglas particularly wanted Kennedy to meet Diem, because the senator had taken an interest in foreign affairs and as a congressman had traveled to Vietnam, where he had angered the French by suggesting that the Vietnamese could not be expected to fight the communists unless they were given their own freedom. At any rate, the name of Ngo Dinh Diem took root among Washington's movers and shakers.

Diem's reputation from the beginning was a little misleading. He had opposed the French and the communists, that much was true. He came from an impressive background and had served in government. His father founded the school in Hue where Ho Chi Minh and Diem himself studied. He was stubborn. He was a nationalist. But being a stubborn nationalist did not a revolutionary leader make. By nature he was sedentary and contemplative. The idea of the fastidious Diem tramping through the jungle singing patriotic songs was unimaginable. When things got too hot for him, he simply withdrew into his cocoon. He was willful, supremely self-confident, yet not given to making the kind of grand gestures that would inspire others. He was convinced of his own rightness of purpose and saw no need to take much trouble to try to persuade anybody else.

Ed Lansdale had not heard of Diem until his appointment as prime minister. Different as they were, Lansdale and Diem shared an important connection: both were outsiders. If either was to succeed, he needed the other. Lansdale had already managed to irritate his fellow officers in the short time he was in Saigon before Diem arrived. Trying to make the point that he was not being taken seriously enough and had not even been assigned a car, he pulled up at a formal military reception in a bicycle-propelled *cyclo-pousse,* the transportation of the poor Vietnamese, and hopped out and saluted smartly, which caused muttering among the starchy American officers present, who thought he was an embarrassment to their side in front of the despised French. Nevertheless the tactic worked and he was assigned a car— sort of. It was an old Citroën *deux chevaux,* with a front seat made of wide rubber bands, and a lopsided suspension. He used it to drive to the airport to watch the arrival of Ngo Dinh Diem.

"In the distance we could hear a wail of sirens and the *pop-popping* of motorcycles," Lansdale recalled. "As the sounds grew louder, the crowds pushed forward, the better to see. Suddenly, motorcycles in a police phalanx came roaring by. Whizzing past the crowd and hugging a position just behind the motorcycles came a big black limousine, Vietnamese flags fluttering from holders on its fenders, windows closed, passengers invisible in its deep interior. *Whoosh!* Limousine and entourage were past. The crowds of people looked at one another in disappointment."

Dismayed by what he'd seen, Lansdale jumped into his car and drove to the embassy, where he described Diem's arrival to Ambassador Donald Heath. "Diem should have ridden into the city slowly in an open car, or even have walked, to provide a focus for the affection that the people so obviously had been waiting to bestow on him," he said. Lansdale, who had spent a total of twenty-five days in Vietnam, thought perhaps Diem had been away from his country too long and could do with some advice on how to act toward his countrymen. He suggested to Ambassador Heath that he prepare a paper for Diem's consideration. Heath gave his okay. Lansdale spent the rest of the day and night drafting a plan of action for Diem. He showed it to the ambassador the next morning. Heath said that it was not something the United States could present a new prime minister officially but that Lansdale could give it to Diem as a personal suggestion.

Lansdale found an American who could speak French to act as his translator and headed for the palace. No guards stopped them. They barged into an office and asked for Diem. A middle-aged Vietnamese looked up from a document he was reading and said, "I am Ngo Dinh

Diem." Diem didn't look very impressive to Lansdale: "A rolypoly figure dressed in a white sharkskin doublebreasted suit, his feet were not quite touching the floor . . . black hair, combed strictly, topped a broad face in which the most prominent feature was high rounds of flesh over the cheekbones, as if they had been pushed up there by constant smiling." Lansdale and his translator introduced themselves and stated their mission. The translator had forgotten his reading glasses. Diem loaned him his own so he could translate the document aloud. Diem listened but asked few questions. Then he thanked Lansdale for his consideration, folded the paper, and put it in his pocket. That was the end of their first meeting.

This initial encounter said a great deal about both men. Lansdale thought that Diem should have arrived in Saigon like an American-style political figure, as he had encouraged Magsaysay to be in the Philippines, waving to the crowd and stopping to press the flesh; and he assumed the people were upset that he had not done so. Yet Vietnam had a system of social values very different from America's. It was a society of such formality that instead of Miss, Mr., Ms., and Mrs., the Vietnamese had nearly ten different ways of referring to each other, depending on one's family or social status. Even Ho Chi Minh, who managed to establish himself as an informal presence but who didn't wade into crowds either, was called "Uncle Ho" as a mark of respect, not the equivalent of Ike or Jack. Had Diem acted like an American politician, as Lansdale would've preferred, the crowd probably would not have known what to make of him. Diem could have pointed this out to Lansdale, but he chose not to, politely thanking him for his advice. He undoubtedly recognized that Lansdale could be a valuable ally and that mixed in with the well-meaning nonsense were nuggets of sound advice.

"I think Diem was impressed by Lansdale's record in the Philippines and sort of liked him as a person," Joe Redick said. "But you wouldn't have called them close friends. I doubt that Diem had any close friends. He wasn't that kind of person. Still, he and Lansdale got along well."

Lansdale began to see Diem almost on a daily basis. He set out to do what he had done in the Philippines, to help consolidate a politician's power while fighting against the communists by using psychological and political warfare. The equation was different in Vietnam, however, not only culturally and historically but also because of the addition of the French factor.

The Geneva negotiations on Indochina, which began the day after Dien Bien Phu fell and three weeks before Lansdale arrived in Saigon, actually turned out better than the Americans and the French thought they would, even though the United States and South Vietnam refused to sign the final agreements. Considering that the communists held a strong psychological advantage and were capable of continuing the war, their demands at Geneva were relatively moderate. They agreed to a cease-fire and settled on occupying only half the country, with the issue of reunification to be decided by a referendum two years hence. John Foster Dulles speculated that either the North Vietnamese were restrained by China and Russia, who feared the outbreak of a general war, or they believed their victory over the whole country was inevitable and they could afford to take it one bite at a time.

In any event, the French got a partial reprieve at Geneva and were only forced to pull back into South Vietnam at the seventeenth parallel, an area that comprised part of central Vietnam plus the entire south, with its Mekong Delta, the richest part of Vietnam, and where most of France's economic interests were concentrated. All in all, it didn't turn out so badly for them, and they intended to try to maintain their hold on South Vietnam.

But the French hadn't counted on an operator like Ed Lansdale. During the months following the end of the First Indochina War, their intelligence services and Lansdale's small band of operatives would wage an unofficial guerrilla war to see who would control the Saigon government. Lansdale was fighting for what he considered the strategic interests of the United States in assuming primacy in Vietnam to stop the spread of communism, at which the French had failed. His mission, never formally stated and at times based on his personal initiative in a chaotic situation, had been discussed by the secretary of state and the director of Central Intelligence, who happened to be brothers, but had not been worked out as official policy by the White House or Congress. Underlying Lansdale's actions, and a reason he was able to operate so freely, was the belief of most American officials going back to Franklin Roosevelt's time that nothing could be accomplished in Vietnam until the colonial French were removed from the picture.

With a three-pronged fight shaping up—against the communists, the French, and Diem's sundry opponents—Lansdale needed help. The Geneva accords had added an unforeseen complication by freezing the number of Americans who could enter Vietnam after a certain deadline. Hastily, the call went out for officers to rush to Saigon to join Lansdale. Because they were already assigned to Asia and could react swiftly, most of the twelve officers were sent from Korea, Japan, and Okinawa. Only two came directly from CIA headquarters in Washington—and the contrast between the two could not have been greater.

Joe Redick was picked mainly because of his language proficiency. He became Lansdale's translator and handyman for paperwork. A brown-haired man of medium height and build who wore no-nonsense glasses, Joe Redick was a Phi Beta Kappa with a Ph.D. in French who'd served as a Japanese linguist in Naval Intelligence during World War Two and who also spoke Spanish. After the war Redick taught school, as his father had, but became bored with the job and low pay and applied to the CIA.

"There weren't many French speakers in the agency, or at least ones who wanted to go to Vietnam," Joe Redick said. "When I told a friend who worked on the Philippine desk I was going out to Indochina, he said, 'Oh my God!' I said, 'What do you mean?' He explained that Lansdale was accepted in the agency as a very effective operator, but was unusual and a little hard to handle."

Redick and Lansdale hit it off immediately, even though they were opposite sides of a coin. Joe Redick had the manner of a schoolmaster, precise and punctilious, which made him a sturdy bridge to the bureaucracy that Lansdale detested but knew he needed. The team member Joe Redick didn't much cotton to was the fellow CIA officer sent from Washington—Lou Conein—and later Redick found Conein's relationship with Elyette Bruchot difficult to comprehend.

"I knew Elyette very well," Redick said. "She was a lovely girl, very nice and very bright. But Lou? Lou was a thug."

Lou Conein had returned to Washington the year before after spending six and a half years in Germany as an intelligence officer. He was in the army but assigned to the agency. "I was still military," Conein said. "But nobody gave me orders. I think they forgot I even existed. It was very unusual. I was in the Western Europe division of the agency, shuffling papers. My personnel form had a little slot that said I'd been in Vietnam before, and nobody knew the hell where the goddamn country was, so I got sent."

Lou Conein had not met Ed Lansdale. He received a briefing about him before he left Washington. When he arrived in Saigon, an officer took him to see his new boss. "Lansdale was a very strange air force colonel, and I was a very strange infantry parachute major," Conein said. "He was a guy with a lot of ideas. He told me about the Philippines and about what he was going to try to do in Vietnam. Then he asked for my ideas. That's one thing about Ed Lansdale. If you had an idea and he went for it, he would back you all the way. I think he disliked the French because he had been badly received by them when he first reached Saigon. The French resented any Americans being around. Also, Lansdale's idea was that all the little brown brothers in Asia should become one big happy family and help one another. So the thing was to get rid of the colonial system and let them fight the communists."

Rufus Phillips, a second lieutenant just turned twenty-five, had no idea that he would be working with Ed Lansdale and Lou Conein. Assigned to Korea, he suddenly received orders to report to the military advisory group in Saigon. Phillips had gone through CIA training but had left the agency and volunteered for the army. Someone thumbing through his personnel file evidently noted his background and the fact that he'd studied French and spent a summer in France. A shambling, handsome man who talked with a soft Virginia drawl and stood six feet tall and weighed over two hundred pounds, Rufe Phillips looked more like a varsity football tackle—which he had been—than like an honors student at Yale on an academic scholarship—which he also had been.

Phillips was given a room at the Majestic Hotel, on the Saigon waterfront, and waited there while the other team members trickled in, not having the slightest idea about what was going on. Saigon was in turmoil, a lot of Vietnamese were preparing to flee to France, and merchants and moneychangers were accosting every American they saw, trying to buy dollars. No one was giving odds over 20 percent that South Vietnam could be held together as a country. Phillips was disappointed by his first meeting with Lansdale, who seemed enigmatic and unable to give him a clear idea of his assignment. When he heard that Lou Conein and several other team members were being sent to Hanoi, Phillips thought it sounded exciting. But he still could not understand what possible use he could be to Lansdale in Saigon. Then one day Lansdale said, "There's a psychological warfare office at Vietnamese army headquarters. Why don't you go out and meet them and see if you can provide some help." When Phillips returned, he told Lansdale, "They really need a training course on what they ought to be doing in psywar, but I don't know anything about it."

Lansdale dug out his copy of Paul Linebarger's influential book, *Psychological Warfare,* and handed it to Phillips, who was on his way to becoming one of the team's experts on psywar.

The Lansdale team moved into houses and apartments around the city. All of them, whether career CIA men or not, were given cover as military officers attached to the United States Military Advisory Group. Joe Redick, for example, reverted to his World War Two rank of navy lieutenant and had the documents to prove it. Lansdale decided to call his group the Saigon Military Mission, which sounded at once suitably innocuous and rather grand. They had their own special uniform of khaki shorts and long socks, a variation of the French uniform, cut by a Saigon tailor. After working at their cover jobs by day, they got together at night to plot their moves. Cognac was plentiful and cheap, and brandy and soda became the team's preferred drink, though Lansdale took it straight. After Lou Conein got to Hanoi, he "liberated" some black Citroën sedans left behind by the French, the kind used in Jean Gabin cops-and-robbers movies, then shipped them to Saigon, and soon everybody was in motion.

"Lansdale kept track of things," Rufe Phillips said. "But he really ran his operation very loosely. First of all, he had too many things to do, so people reported to him on an informal basis. He never pulled rank on anybody, rather his authority flowed from the fact that he knew what he was doing." Another team member was confident he also knew what he was doing. "Lansdale and Conein used to have some terrible arguments," Phillips added. "About what to do in certain circumstances. Lou wasn't, I don't think, very fond of Diem. He just didn't like the guy. So there were arguments and everything. But you could argue your case with Lansdale and he didn't hold it against you."

Ed Lansdale and Lou Conein liked each other personally. Lansdale was amused by Conein, who could curse with more inventiveness than anyone he'd ever heard, switching easily from English to French. In Conein's vocabulary, *espèce de con* and *salaud* were relatively friendly descriptions. And Lansdale respected Lou's abilities as an intelligence officer. But there was, from the start, a difference in operational philosophy between the two based on their past experiences. Lansdale was a believer in achieving his ends by political action. Conein, the former OSS commando, preferred tactics that included a bit of a bang.

"I agreed with Lansdale in principle," Conein said. "But I told him,

'We're going to have to establish certain things outside political action.' You wanted to win the hearts and minds of the people, but other things, I thought, had to be put in place before you could do that. My idea was to nurture a resistance movement among political and military groups."

Lou Conein argued for the need of creating a movement in the North to oppose the communists. After hearing him out, Lansdale approved the operation and dispatched Conein to Hanoi as head of a three-man team. Except for a daylong visit to Hanoi with the general who commanded the military advisory group, Lansdale stayed out of North Vietnam and let Conein handle operations there. Under the Geneva accords, both communist and noncommunist Vietnamese were given a time period during which they could regroup in the North or the South before the border between the two countries became permanent. Conein and his team flew to Hanoi ostensibly to help oversee the movement of refugees from North to South, but their chief mission was to launch a campaign against the new government of North Vietnam. Conein followed the chain of command, clearing what he proposed to do with Lansdale, who in turn asked Washington's approval. But CIA headquarters was far away, communications weren't very good, and Conein's operations fell under the broad guidelines of "stirring up trouble for the communists," which had been discussed and approved in a general way by the Dulles brothers. Owing to the chaotic situation and lack of specific policy directives, along with Lansdale's easygoing leadership style, Conein had a great degree of flexibility in choosing his operations.

He sought out members of political parties with nationalist tendencies who had been purged by the communists and tried to organize them into a resistance movement. This led him, he said, to launch a sabotage campaign against Hanoi's transportation system. "In any resistance organization, you have to have what is called a 'carnival,' " Conein said. "You can't expect people to join if nothing is going on. So I wanted a carnival, which meant there would be a bang here, something happening there, so as to show people there really was a resistance movement, to create something that would make the doubters join."

One might suspect that Conein was also reacting in part to the old commando itch to blow up things. In any case, Conein devised an elaborate plan of sabotage that called for the technical help of the CIA station in Japan. Years later David Halberstam would write in his book

The Best and the Brightest that the Lansdale team had put sugar in the gas tanks of Hanoi's buses, an error picked up and repeated by other journalists, much to Conein's exasperation. Sugar? Lou said. That was a high-school trick, something a goddamn amateur might do, not a professional. Actually, Conein set about to attack the copper bearings of Hanoi's buses and streetcars with acid.

He bought fifty drums of oil of the kind used by the Hanoi system; then he and his team doctored the oil with acid one night, almost fainting from the fumes, and placed the drums among the transportation company's normal oil supplies, so that they would be used unwittingly in the following months. To try to disable North Vietnam's trains, Conein asked the CIA's technical experts to create an explosive that looked like the compressed bricks of coal burned in the steam-powered trains. The CIA shaped the plastique into coallike form and sent it to Saigon, where it was forwarded to Hanoi in several hundred footlockers, which Conein hid in the American consulate until he could secretly mix the exploding bricks among the coal piles used by the North Vietnamese, though he never learned if the tactic was effective.

He then set his sights on a bigger target—the storage tanks at Haiphong owned by Standard Oil and Shell. Two tanks stood side by side, and Conein believed he could blow up both by wiring one with a lot of plastique explosive and relying on a sympathetic detonation to get the other. After setting everything up, he flew to Saigon to tell Lansdale what he was going to do. "Generally, I had a free hand," Conein said, "but this time Ed said, 'President Eisenhower has sent a special envoy here by the name of General J. Lawton Collins, and I think you ought to tell him what you intend to do.' " Collins objected to Conein's sabotage and ordered him to dismantle his device. Conein returned to Haiphong, hired a boat, and dumped the plastique in the sea.

Meanwhile, his assistants in Hanoi were packing noncommunist refugees into airplanes for the trip to the South. Lansdale and the American embassy had persuaded the French government to award the Civil Air Transport a contract to fly the refugees to Saigon. The idea for the airline went back to pre-Pearl Harbor days, when Washington devised a covert scheme to provide Chiang Kai-shek's Chinese, who were already at war with Japan, with American pilots and planes. The covert plan was being put into effect at the time of Japan's attack on Pearl Harbor and was then modified to be carried out openly by General Claire Chennault's Flying Tigers. After the war, Chennault, who had taken part in the original covert scheme, worked with Washington to form the Civil Air Transport, which became the secret airline for the CIA. Two dozen civilian pilots hired by the CIA flew resupply missions for Dien Bien Phu in CAT planes and two of them were shot down and killed. After its cover was blown, the airline metamorphosed into Air America, which continued to fly covert missions for the CIA in Indochina while transporting people and supplies openly for other government agencies. With the deal made to fly the refugees, Lou Conein and his team gained a means of moving around the country.

Washington insisted at Geneva that the Vietnamese be allowed to relocate if they so desired after the cease-fire. The Americans wanted to ensure that as many anticommunists as possible, especially the well-organized northern Catholics, reinforced the weak political base in the South. The United States Information Service launched a publicity campaign and leaflets appeared in Hanoi saying "Christ has gone to the South." Four-fifths of the approximately one million refugees who fled to South Vietnam were Catholics. Lansdale was involved in trying to scare them to leave, which he admitted to frankly but added, probably correctly, that his efforts weren't decisive.

"I pointed out to the people in the North what was going to happen," Lansdale said. "But people don't leave ancestral homes that they care a lot about without a very good reason, particularly in Asia. So it took tremendous personal fear to get them to leave, and when a million of them did, it wasn't just words and propaganda making them do it."

Lou Conein carried out propaganda operations but also believed the Lansdale team was given too much credit—or blame—for persuading the refugees to flee. "You see, we had an additional problem," Conein said. "We were also supposed to retrieve and ship to the South all the equipment in the North that the United States had given the French. And that was a mess. The refugee thing was decided by Washington. I was just told, 'You are going to have so many planes'—they gave the number—'flying into Hanoi each day. Load them up.' So I would go to the political groups and the Catholics and tell them what was coming." The situation was so hectic and confused that one day Conein's team scooped a child and tossed him on an airplane heading south, only to have the boy's parents demand the return of their son, who was at the airport to tell a relative goodbye. They solved the problem by putting the parents on the next plane, turning them into instant refugees. However much the Lansdale team influenced the exodus, the refugee operation from Washington's point of view was judged a success, and in future years it would often seem that the war against the Viet Cong in South Vietnam was being led and fought mainly by former Catholic refugees from the North.

Lou Conein's resistance organization was taking shape. He recruited agents for two groups, code-named the Hao and the Binh, neither of which was aware of the other. A second paramilitary team was set up in Saigon under another major to handle their training. They were taken first to a CIA base outside Vietnam, and then flown to the Philippines for last-minute instructions, after which they were infiltrated into North Vietnam, not difficult given the movement of refugees both ways. With the help of the navy, Conein's team smuggled about eight and a half tons of supplies for the twenty-one agents of the Hao resistance group, including fourteen radios, three hundred carbines, fifty pistols, and three hundred pounds of plastique explosive. Conein hid most of the equipment at points along the banks of the Red River.

"At the time I thought the Hanoi operation was a success," Conein said. "The resistance nets existed about four years, before they finally died out."

Conein also thought the sabotage operations had gone well. On that he had been lucky. He knew nothing about how to attack the transportation system, but he had been provided with expert advice by the one man in Hanoi who did know—Elyette Bruchot's stepfather, Charles Dufour, who was the local head of the French company that ran Hanoi's buses and streetcars.

THE AMERICAN CONSUL SAID, *"Elyette, we've received notification that you are a friend of the United States, so we have space for you on a plane, and it will be leaving Hanoi the last of July nineteen fifty-four." Instead of being grateful, I was secretly offended. How could an American tell me when I had to leave? I'd lived in Hanoi all my life. I thanked him and said, "That's very kind of you. But don't worry. I have a French friend with a plane, and I'll choose my own departure date."*

There was a deadline for everybody, and I left on the last day. In the meantime, the consul invited me to the final cocktail party. I asked my oldest friend Eliane to go with me. I said, "I hear an American officer is going to be there who might be fun to meet. He has been going around Hanoi bragging that there are two things every Frenchman hopes to have before the age of fifty—the Legion of Honor and a case of gonorrhea. And he says he had both before he was twenty-five!" Well, one of the vice consuls introduced me to Lucien that evening, and he invited me to dance. He was witty and spoke French with an American accent, but I didn't think about him after the party. Shortly before I left Hanoi, I was having dinner with friends at the Metropole, and he sent me an apéritif from the bar and then came over and introduced himself. He said, "Madamoiselle, I'd like to get in touch with you in Saigon. Do you know where you'll be staying?" I told him I did not. He said, "This is my Saigon phone number. Please call me." So I went to Saigon and Pan Am hired me right away to work in their office on the rue Catinat, next to the Continental Hotel. The American vice consul in Saigon invited me to dinner one evening at the Continental, and I accepted. I'm very near-sighted, but I never wear my glasses when I go out, because of vanity. So here comes this man and I don't recognize him, and he says to the vice consul, "Please excuse me, but I have to ask your date why she didn't call me." The vice consul was furious. I realized then who he was. I said, "I lost your number." He said, "Will you please call me tomorrow. I'll be waiting." I called the next day and Lou was by his phone. He said, "Can I invite you to dinner?" Silence. "Lunch?" I said, "Fine, lunch." He introduced me to the people he worked with. Ed Lansdale seemed like a very kind man. I didn't know what he was doing. To me he was just a colonel, and I'd met all the generals of the French army. Rufus Phillips—I liked Rufe Phillips very much. He was nice, handsome, a dreamboy, always dating a different girl. Anyway, Lou flew to Hanoi and asked my stepfather for my hand. My stepfather was still there, because he had to teach somebody to run the tramways before he left. And my stepfather, who never thought anyone was good enough for me, was impressed by Lou. He sent me a wire and said he had talked to Lou and would give me his blessing.

WITH LOU CONEIN operating in Hanoi, Ed Lansdale turned his attention to getting things moving in Saigon. Lansdale was not overwhelmed by the team members that had been assigned him. "They had been selected for me by personnel officers in Washington who must have had a Korean-style conflict in mind and disregarded my own written list of requirements," he complained. "They were an ideal crew for guerrilla combat, for blowing up things, for jumps behind enemy lines, and for sensitive intelligence work against communist infiltrators, saboteurs, and terrorists. But none had an inkling of psywar, the one activity in which I already was helping the Vietnamese army, nor did they know anything about military civic action as practiced in the Philippines or the subjects which I had outlined to the new prime minister as worth doing and with which we might be asked to assist."

In addition to settling the refugees from the North, Lansdale was concerned about filling the vacuum in the areas of South Vietnam that had been controlled by the Viet Minh. Under the terms of the Geneva accords, the communists were required to withdraw from South Vietnam over a phased time period, just as the French were required to withdraw from North Vietnam. The Viet Minh had controlled their areas not only militarily but administratively, and the question was, who would replace their governing structure? Lansdale didn't want the French involved, because it would look as though they were maintaining their colonial system in the South, and the Geneva accords called for the complete independence of South Vietnam. Though heavily French-influenced, the Vietnamese national army was the only group in the country well enough organized to take over the former Viet Minh areas.

In late September 1954, when the Viet Minh started evacuating the areas they controlled in the South, Lansdale sent Rufe Phillips to the delta to see what could be done about establishing a Saigon government presence and coaxing the rice farmers to support Diem rather than Ho Chi Minh. After making his survey, Phillips believed that their support might be won by providing them with mosquito nets, blankets, and food, and by improving roads and bridges, almost nonexistent in many areas, so that the farmers could get their crops to market. Phillips and the Vietnamese team formed to make the survey returned to Saigon and wrote a report for Diem, urging him to adopt a strategy of economic improvement for the farmers. Lansdale then arranged for Phillips to escort the team, which was essentially Diem's planning group, to the Philippines, where they were shown by Ramón Magsaysay himself what could be accomplished against a guerrilla insurgency with a sensitive combination of military and civilian programs. The planning group flew home with enthusiasm and got down to work at developing an approach to assuming control over the areas once owned by the Viet Minh.

"We tried to find a name to describe what we were doing, but nothing seemed to work," Rufe Phillips said. "Actually, what we were doing was reoccupying the areas and providing the people who lived there with essential supplies. Since the Vietnamese officials we were dealing with all spoke French but little English, we finally decided on calling it *pacification*— and the term, which had been used during the French war, stuck."

Pacification was a term the Americans were never happy with, and they tried, without much success, to find an alternative, using over the years such descriptions as *rural construction, revolutionary development,* or simply *the other war.* The problem was that there was no exact definition of what made up pacification. It was best defined by what it was not: a soldier shooting at another soldier during a military operation.

In the Philippines, Lansdale had talked Magsaysay into setting up a Civil Affairs Office, which was designed to wage psychological warfare against the enemy and also, more important, to indoctrinate government troops in the correct way to act toward the people—or, as Lansdale put it, "to make the soldiers behave as brothers and protectors of the people in their everyday military operations, replacing the arrogance of the military at highway checkpoints or in village searches with courteous manners and striving to stop the age-old soldier's habit of stealing chickens and pigs from the farmers." To describe this brotherly attitude of the military toward the people, Lansdale coined the term *civic action,* which was soon picked up and used by armies around the world.

The theory behind pacification included civic action and several other elements. The first step was to bring security to an area, to stop the armed violence, which meant ridding it of the communist presence. The first pacification operation was the easiest of all in this respect, since the communists withdrew from their areas voluntarily, under the terms of the Geneva accords. Never again would that happen. Second, the lives of the rice farmers had to be improved materially. That meant trying to break down the inherited French system of centralization that made Saigon—like Paris—a bottleneck for permission to do anything; it also meant fighting the endemic corruption among Vietnamese officials to ensure that supplies reached their intended recipients, the rice farmers, and trying to organize the various squabbling agencies of the American bureaucracy well enough to oversee the effort. Third, Vietnamese soldiers had to be taught how to act toward their fellow citizens and perform good works under civic action. Stopping them from stealing chickens from the farmers was easier ordered than done, as several generations of American military advisers were to discover. All this, according to theory, was supposed to add up to the final and most important element of pacification: winning the allegiance of the people.

But winning their allegiance to what? or whom?

"The question was," Rufe Phillips said, "if you had a country with no leadership, how did the leadership establish itself? What was the political process to be used? Lansdale had very clear notions about this and a strong commitment to democratic ideals. The next question then became, how did one work to achieve those ends? His method was to encourage the Vietnamese to come up with suggestions that he could shape into coherent and practical form, and then persuade them that what he was telling them was their idea in the first place. Ed was a good listener, and he projected something that convinced people he sincerely wanted to help them, and he did. There was a kind of chemistry there. And of course part of it was his ideas."

Yet before Lansdale could put into effect any of his ideas, he was confronted by the basic and immediate need to keep Ngo Dinh Diem from being overthrown by his own military officers. The cycle of coups d'état and rumored coups d'état, which would last as long as the war, began shortly after Diem took over as prime minister. His would-be successor of the first instance was the chief of staff of the armed forces, a born-again Frenchman by the name of Nguyen Van Hinh. He was backed by the head of the psywar office that Rufe Phillips was trying to help organize and equip. This, too, would establish a precedent to be followed many times afterward. While the Americans tried to train the Vietnamese military for the fight against the communists, the Vietnamese often used what they learned to better fight among themselves for political power.

The Hinh coup was hatched in confusion, and it was never really clear. Lansdale took it seriously and believed he was able to thwart it by packing off Hinh's key aides on a junket to the Philippines. Then he maneuvered Hinh himself out of the country. He was sent to Paris, where he completed his transformation from tadpole and served out his career as a general in France's air force.

Lansdale and Diem drew a number of lessons from this first coup attempt. Diem had barely settled down at his desk when he found himself threatened by one of his military officers. Since he had no political base and the military establishment was the strongest force in the country, he recognized that he would have to bring it under control. He could neither survive in office nor fight the communists if he was going to be stabbed in the back by a lieutenant. It was simple common sense that he should put officers who were loyal to him in key positions. So Diem established the principle of arranging the army on the basis of, first, preventing a coup d'état, and, second, fighting the communists. But if loyalty to Diem was the primary criterion in selecting military leaders, then qualities such as honesty and competence obviously became secondary considerations. Thus the circle was closed: Diem could not stay in office without loyal support; neither could he accomplish anything if his loyal supporters were incompetent and dishonest opportunists, as many of them were. The Diem principle of coup d'état prevention, which turned out to be less than foolproof, was nevertheless to endure throughout the war, no matter who happened to head the Saigon government.

The coup attempt also pushed Diem into a further reliance on his family. In Vietnam, family was everything, a concrete fact of daily life, while the nation-state was an abstract concept. If a politician or a military officer couldn't help a fourth cousin on his wife's aunt's side, who could he be expected to help? The unmarried Diem sat at the head of the table at family meals, but he was often overshadowed in discussions by his brothers. One of them was sent to London as ambassador; another remained in Hue as the Catholic archbishop and the de facto power in central Vietnam. A younger brother who was considered the family intellectual became Diem's chief aide in Saigon. His name was Nhu. He spoke French better and was thought brighter than his brother by Americans who knew them. He was also more arrogant and harder to deal with. Nhu was married to a pretty woman who didn't mind speaking up either.

"Diem was a man who loved his country and the people," Ed Lansdale said. "He was a rare commodity. But his brother Nhu had a tremendous ego and was self-seeking. I liked Nhu's wife and felt sorry for her. She had been raised by a mother who was a beauty and who trained her daughter to marry someone rich and influential. She would come in while I was talking to Diem and Nhu and say, 'Anybody like some piano music?' and sit down to play. I'd say, 'No, no, we're too busy.' She'd been taught to do that, you know. She got in close to some American wives in Saigon and somehow or other they insulted her. She was good-looking, and I guess they were worried about their husbands. After that, she turned sort of anti-American."

Lansdale believed that Nhu committed errors on his brother's behalf, which grew from his efforts to keep Diem in power. Nhu detested the French and was always seeing plots to overthrow his brother. His paranoia wasn't unfounded. The French were working to get rid of Diem. Nhu became head of his brother's intelligence service to help stamp out the plots and to monitor the endless intrigue that went on in Saigon. To consolidate Diem's power in the countryside, he began developing a semisecret political organization called the Can Lao, with a membership composed largely of Catholics whose loyalty to Diem was unquestioned. Nhu then appointed them to key military and administrative positions, at the expense of the Buddhists and other religious and political groups, a tactic that created dissension and unrest, and one, incidentally, that Lansdale opposed from the beginning for just that reason.

Lansdale, for his part, took several important steps after the attempted coup d'état. When he went to see Diem at the height of the trouble, he discovered that the palace guards had fled, leaving Diem unprotected. Lansdale asked Magsaysay to send one of his battalion commanders to train a unit of bodyguards. Diem and Nhu saw the advantages of having their own personal forces. Later, when the United States sent the Special Forces to Vietnam, Diem and Nhu had them organize and train a unit of Vietnamese Special Forces, which they adopted for their personal protection and to carry out duties independent of the army command.

Lansdale also began to look for outside support for Diem. He thought he found it in an armed sect led by a general named Trinh Minh The, who had opposed the communists and the French for years. Vietnam had a number of armed sects but none so colorful as the Cao Dai, who controlled the territory around their headquarters sixty-two miles from Saigon, in Tay Ninh province, near the Cambodian border. The Cao Dai, whose symbol was an all-seeing eye, had assembled their order in an eccentric but pacific manner, taking bits and pieces from the world's major religions and installing a canon of saints that included Jesus, Buddha, Victor Hugo, Joan of Arc, and others of intriguing diversity.

Lansdale recognized that making contact with Trinh Minh The and his guerrillas would be a controversial move. He talked it over with Diem, who first brought up The's name, and then discussed it with Ambassador Donald Heath and General John (Iron Mike) O'Daniel, on whose team Lansdale had made his initial visit to Vietnam and who now headed the military advisory group. O'Daniel wanted to integrate the various armed sects into Vietnam's national army, and he and Ambassador Heath gave their approval to Lansdale's proposal.

Lansdale and five of his team members put on civilian clothes, hid their weapons, and drove to the guerrilla leader's hideout. "I couldn't get over how young and boyishly merry a person he was to be either the notorious monster of the French or the famed patriot of the Vietnamese," Lansdale recorded. "I found myself liking him instinctively." Joe Redick translated Lansdale's remarks into French, and someone else then translated them into Vietnamese for The. The Lansdale team had no Vietnamese linguist. The conversation moved slowly, but Lansdale found that Trinh Minh The's declarations of freedom from French colonialism "reminded me, deeply and touchingly, of some other people of bygone days, the Americans who had founded my own country." The upshot was that Trinh Minh The and his three thousand guerrillas were integrated into the national army to become supporters of Diem, albeit fickle supporters at best.

Lansdale always emphasized the idealistic aspects of his recruitments for Diem. Trinh Minh The, according to him, was a patriot of the highest order. He minimized the money that changed hands. In Trinh Minh The's case, Lansdale said, financial support was given only to sustain his guerrilla operations. The evidence indicated nevertheless that Lansdale's team did not hesitate to strengthen idealistic tendencies with a sackful of cash. In 1955 the team spent $228,000 on operational matters, which, considering the year and country, was an impressive amount. That did not include the cost of weapons and supplies or their salaries. Nor did some other people see Trinh Minh The in quite the same way as Lansdale. To them, he was a warlord and terrorist who used ideology to justify his activities. The French hated Trinh Minh The and put a price on his head. Their antipathy, Lansdale conceded, was not totally unwarranted. The's men had assassinated a top officer and then planted explosives at the opera house, in the center of Saigon, hoping to wipe out the French command, but the attempt had failed.

The French had been suspicious of Lansdale from the moment he arrived, and they turned wildly against him after they learned he was aiding Trinh Minh The. Some of them began plotting his assassination. The British author Graham Greene was visiting Saigon during this period to write journalism and collect material for a book. "I never met Graham Greene," Ed Lansdale said. "But he used to sit at the sidewalk cafe outside the Majestic Hotel with all the French officers. He was very francophile, and eventually made his home in France. One day I went to the Majestic to pick up a reporter and his wife from the *New York Times,* friends of mine, and Graham Greene was there. The French officers were yelling at me, calling me dirty names. The wife of the *Times* reporter came out and kissed me on the cheek. Then she turned to the crowd and stuck out her tongue and said, 'We love him.' My little dog Pierre ran over to a table and bit a Frenchman on the ankle. That didn't make me too popular, either. The book Greene wrote, which had Trinh Minh The as a character, and later the one called *The Ugly American,* hindered my work quite a bit with other Americans. You have to get normal bureaucrats to work with you to accomplish anything, and they didn't trust me after reading one of those books. They said I was undisciplined, that I tried to get ahead by knocking on everybody around me."

The anti-Lansdale forces were growing. The dispute between the French and the Americans over who would train Vietnam's army and thereby gain the most influence in the country had been resolved by a compromise that integrated the two staffs and distributed the key positions equally, with a French section leader assigned an American deputy and an American section leader a French deputy. Lansdale elbowed his way into command of the most important training division, the one concerned with pacification, although trying to avoid the French term he named it "the office of national security." His French deputy was mild-mannered and likable, but the French loaded their other slots in Lansdale's division with intelligence agents whose job it was to monitor his activities. Finally they complained so vehemently about Lansdale to the American embassy that it was decided to hold a meeting at the CIA station chief's home to examine their charges.

Lansdale was on special assignment for the CIA as head of the Saigon Military Mission. But the agency also had a regular station of intelligence officers who operated out of the embassy. One of the duties of the Saigon station chief, as in other countries, was to stay in friendly liaison with the French intelligence services. This dual arrangement, with Lansdale running operations that were essentially against the French and the regular CIA station chief trying to maintain a degree of cooperation with them as part of his job, was bound to create friction. Apparently CIA director Allen Dulles, who made a secret trip to Saigon and enjoyed being spirited about town, telling Lansdale that it reminded him of his days during World War Two, was content to let the two of them fight it out.

"We didn't get along worth a damn," Lansdale said. "The station chief was supposed to support me with funds and so on, but he wouldn't lift a little finger. He used to keep me waiting outside his office door when I went to see him. Once he began giving me a lecture, telling me that I had to learn something about intelligence, that he'd gone to school and been trained for it, and was real good. Oh, he was terrible."

The station chief took notes to send to Washington as the French intelligence officers registered their complaints. One of their charges was that Lansdale had airdropped weapons to the Hoa Hao, another armed sect that he was trying to recruit to support Diem. But the French had their dates wrong about the alleged airdrop, and Lansdale was able to prove that he hadn't been in the area at the time. He contended that all the charges were manufactured in an effort to neutralize him. The one exception, he said, was the charge that his team in North Vietnam was planning to blow up the Haiphong harbor. Lansdale admitted there had been such talk, but dismissed it as a practical joke by Lou Conein and his men. Their team house in Haiphong was next to the French admiral's house, he said, and they noticed that the admiral spent a long time sitting on his toilet every morning. Conein and the boys discussed throwing a firecracker through the admiral's bathroom window, to stir him into action. But they decided instead to talk loudly about blowing up the harbor, knowing he would overhear and rush to radio the news to Saigon. The practical joke was quite conceivably something Lou Conein might pull. Then again, blowing up the Haiphong harbor was too. Whatever the case, Lansdale's explanation got him off the hook, and the French gave up on trying to get him sacked by the CIA.

But Lansdale's relations with the station chief did not improve. "He was lying about me in his cables to Washington," Lansdale said. "He kept other incoming cables addressed to me and wouldn't give them to me. I finally called him to my house one day when nobody was there, and said, 'You are younger than I am. You are bigger; you've got the reach. But you are a sonofabitch.' He wouldn't fight. I called him a coward. Later on, I told Frank Wisner, an agency official, about him, and got him removed."

Lansdale's bureaucratic war with the CIA station chief was a mere brushfire compared to what broke out when the new American ambassador, General J. Lawton Collins, took over in November 1954. Lansdale considered Ambassador Donald Heath, who was in Saigon during Dien Bien Phu and the Geneva negotiations, a little too pro-French, but they had got on well. Heath was impressed by Lansdale's work in the Philippines and slightly overwhelmed by his personality. On one occasion, when Heath found himself serving as Lansdale's translator during conversations with Diem about the refugee problem, the ambassador chided Lansdale that he was violating protocol by treating Heath as his assistant. Still, it was Lansdale's advice that Diem took. Lansdale was also usually able to get his way with General Iron Mike O'Daniel, chief of the military advisory group, a gruff but genial man. O'Daniel recognized that he was outclassed by the air force colonel when it came to dealing with the Vietnamese.

Even so, events were moving at such a swift pace that President Eisenhower decided to replace Ambassador Heath, a State Department careerist, with a personal friend whom he could trust not to let things get out of control. As he often did in such moments, he turned to a general who had served under him in World War Two. J. Lawton (Lightning Joe) Collins had commanded the army corps that broke out of Normandy. He was not a man easily overwhelmed by anyone, which he was ready to demonstrate at the first meeting of American officials in Saigon. Ambassador Heath had run his meetings with a tolerant informality, and allowed the heads of various agencies to argue out a proposal, which gave the confident and articulate Lansdale an advantage in pushing his ideas. General Collins informed them that his meetings would be run with military precision. Each official would make a concise oral report and then sit down to await Collins's decision.

At the first meeting, Ambassador Collins listed the priorities he wanted them to work toward. They were to try to strengthen the Saigon government but also prepare for cutting the size of Vietnam's army, which Washington thought was beginning to cost too much money. When Collins finished, Lansdale rose and talked about *his* priorities: that they try to establish democratic institutions in the country before the scheduled 1956 vote on reunification with North

Vietnam; and that they integrate the armed sects into the national army before starting to think about cutting its size.

"I am the special representative of the president of the United States," General Collins said, furious. "As such, I am the one who establishes the priorities, not you, and we don't need to discuss them. Understand, Colonel?"

"Yes, sir," Lansdale said. "I understand. I guess there's nobody here as the personal representative of the people of the United States. The American people would want us to discuss these priorities. So, I hereby appoint myself as their representative—and we're walking out on you." Without a further word, Lansdale left and went to a nearby embassy office, where he started making notes on what he had to do before leaving Vietnam, in case Collins ordered him out of the country.

It was a brash move. But Lansdale's seemingly spontaneous gestures usually were made with a shrewd appreciation of the odds, and he probably guessed that Collins, who might begin to maneuver to remove him later, would hardly be prepared to dismiss on the first day someone who was not the personal representative of the people, as he claimed, but who was the personal representative of the CIA director. If so, Lansdale guessed right. After a while, an emissary told Lansdale that the meeting was over and that General Collins wanted to see him in his office. Collins was seated at his desk doing paperwork. He spoke to Lansdale reproachfully but in fatherly tones, telling him he was disappointed by the way he had acted in the meeting. As a military man, Lansdale should understand there could be but one commander who gave the orders, Collins said, and in this case it was the ambassador. But appealing to Lansdale as a professional officer was about as effective as appealing to a gambler as a professional businessman. Lansdale turned on the charm and argued with Collins that he wanted to help make policy. He said he'd heard that Collins's nickname was given him because of his ability to think through a problem quickly and come up with a solution. Perhaps Lightning Joe, he suggested, could do his thinking out loud in private meetings with Lansdale, who would then add his own thoughts to the problem under consideration. Collins smiled and said that wouldn't be possible. He explained that he usually did his heaviest thinking in bed after lunch, when he took a short rest.

"Good," Lansdale said. "I'll come over to your house right after lunch and join you in your room, sitting quietly while you rest. If you want to talk, okay, we'll talk. If you just want to rest, I'll not say a word."

Ambassador Collins thought Lansdale was joking and was distinctly displeased to see him after lunch that day. Lansdale cajoled him cheerfully. "Come on. Let's give it one try anyhow, now that I'm here." Reluctantly, Collins led the way to his room and sprawled out on the bed. Lansdale pulled up a chair beside him. They had a long talk. Lansdale realized that Collins was still suffering from plane lag, and he apologized for insisting on the meeting. "You would've been better off taking a nap," Lansdale said. Collins agreed. Lansdale beat a retreat.

Looking back years later, Ed Lansdale admitted that he had acted outrageously. "If I had been the ambassador, I would have kicked me out of the country immediately," Lansdale said—but with a chuckle.

That was the beginning of their stormy relationship. Collins thought that Lansdale had become too emotionally involved with Vietnam. He was anxious to rein in this upstart colonel who was riding at will over the embassy's turf. Collins was irritated to learn when he arrived that Lansdale was completing a deal to bring in civic action teams from the Philippines. Lansdale claimed the idea had been suggested by an official from the Philippine Chamber of Commerce during a visit to Saigon. Lansdale, however, was one of the early practitioners of suggesting to non-Americans that they officially ask the Americans to do something, permitting a we're-just-responding-to-the-request-of-a-friendly-nation explanation for the particular action. Even Diem had been against importing the Philippine teams, telling Lansdale that the Vietnamese didn't need the help of orators or nightclub musicians, alluding to the fact that the Filipinos were the dance band and entertainment specialists of Asia. But Lansdale prevailed over both the embassy and the Diem government. Philippine teams of doctors and nurses, later mechanics and technicians, spread out not only in Vietnam but in Laos as well, hoping to innoculate the Indochinese against the disease of communism through good works and civic action, carrying out Lansdale's idea—as Lou Conein put it, with his unapologetic cynicism—"that all the little brown brothers in Asia should become one big happy family and help one another."

As Lansdale saw it, Ambassador Collins understood little about Vietnam and, worse still, had fallen under the influence of the French commander in Saigon, General Paul Ely. Ely was a courteous and reasonable man who knew how to get along with Americans and had made a favorable impression when he visited Washington at the time of the Dien Bien Phu crisis. He and Collins were World War Two generals, members of a special fraternity who understood each other. General Ely disliked Diem and thought he should be removed. What part of Ely's attitude was based on his assessment that Diem was a poor leader and what part was based on his realization that with the anti-French Diem in power France eventually would have to pack up and go home was not known. In any case, within a month after his arrival, and after talking to Ely, Collins became convinced that his French colleague was right. This meant that Diem had been in office scarcely five months before the ranking French and American officials in Saigon were trying to oust him.

General Ely had a short-list of candidates to replace Diem—all born-again Frenchmen, naturally. Collins first took another tack and urged Diem to appoint Pham Huy Quat, a medical doctor who was a born-again Frenchman in mind but a Vietnamese at heart, as a deputy prime minister, as a prelude to his taking over. When Diem refused, Collins began his campaign to persuade Washington to get rid of him. It was, Collins allowed, a decision arrived at reluctantly.

Washington, particularly John Foster Dulles, tried to put Collins off. But Collins was Eisenhower's special envoy and friend with sizable clout, and when he insisted, the president and the secretary of state started coming around to his way of thinking. Dulles said after conferring with the president that they were "disposed to back" Collins's final decision. But they wanted to make sure Collins understood their position. What was happening in Vietnam, Dulles said, was the result of "a basic and dangerous misunderstanding" between France and the United States. Getting rid of Diem, Eisenhower and Dulles believed, would not solve the problem, but would simply mean "that from now on we will be merely paying the bill and the French will be calling the tune."

At the same moment, the issue was being forced. Under French rule, an armed sect of cutthroats known as the Binh Xuyen controlled the police in Saigon and all the vice, gambling, and narcotics. The Binh Xuyen paid off French and Vietnamese notables, including, it was rumored, the Emperor Bao Dai. When Diem pushed for measures that would remove the Binh Xuyen, the gang, backed by two other armed sects, the Cao Dai and Hoa Hao, rose up in rebellion to try to crush Diem and his military forces. Diem's men in Saigon were outnumbered and had to depend on the military support of the French.

There was so much double-dealing going on by all parties that it was impossible to say who was behind what, but it was strongly suspected that the French encouraged the revolt of the Binh Xuyen in an attempt to topple Diem. No one necessarily thought the orders came from Paris or even from General Ely. If Lansdale and his team sometimes operated as free agents, as they clearly did, then it was not unreasonable to believe that French intelligence officers, encouraged by the remnants of the colonial establishment that had taken roost at Saigon's Cercle Sportif, were likewise inclined to turn the French policy of getting rid of Diem into the freelance action of stirring up a mini civil war.

The uprising of the sects called for all of Lansdale's ingenuity. He first had to try to split off his earlier recruitments, the Cao Dai and the Hoa Hao, from the Binh Xuyen. He began to persuade Trinh Minh The and the Hoa Hao leader that they were true patriots who were being manipulated by the gangster Binh Xuyen for financial motives. When he had them half convinced, Lansdale set up a meeting of the two sect generals with Ambassador Collins. Collins began by telling them how shocked he was as a military man by the disloyal behavior of the two generals toward their government. Joe Redick was doing the translating. Lansdale stopped Redick before he could tell them what Collins said. Lansdale asked Collins not to chastise the two generals but to congratulate them for remaining loyal to the government. This led to a prolonged argument between Collins and Lansdale, as Trinh Minh The and the Hoa Hao leader looked on, puzzled. Lansdale broke off the meeting. He was able to coax Trinh Minh The back on the government side. Fighting soon broke out. The French military intervened and were not shy about showing their preference for the Binh Xuyen.

Ambassador Collins flew to Washington for consultations. He assured Lansdale before he left that he would support Diem, but in fact he pressed Eisenhower to dump him, which, under the circumstances, also meant dumping Lansdale, probably not a dismaying prospect, as Collins saw it. Using up his line of credit, Collins was able to persuade Eisenhower and then Dulles. On April 27, 1955, a cable was sent to the Saigon embassy proposing a scheme for getting rid of Diem. The overt policy of the United States would be one of continued support for Diem, the cable said, while covertly Collins and Ely were given the green light to act as "catalysts" in finding a replacement whom they could encourage Bao Dai to appoint.

The cable arrived in Saigon as fighting was going on between the Binh Xuyen and Diem's forces. The city was turned into a battlefield. Lansdale realized the psychological importance of what was happening and immediately portrayed the battle as being won by Diem's forces, even though embassy officials were skeptical at that point. Lansdale insisted on sending his own cable to Washington describing the impending victory. John Foster Dulles was at a dinner party when the cable arrived. He excused himself and went to the White House to tell Eisenhower. Meanwhile, led by Senator Mike Mansfield, there had been a strong reaction in Congress against abandoning Diem. Faced with congressional opposition, and with Lansdale's quick cable in hand declaring victory for Diem, the White House reversed itself three days later. Orders went out to burn the April 27 cable withdrawing support. It was to be sink or swim with Ngo Dinh Diem. The first to be sunk was Collins himself. He had made a play that came down to an either/or choice between him and Lansdale. In less than a month Collins was gone, replaced as ambassador by G. Frederick Reinhardt, a professional foreign service officer.

Diem's victory touched off a final spasm of rage by the French in Saigon. Lansdale was shot at as he drove the streets. A Frenchman who had a car similar to his and who resembled him was gunned down by assassins. Stories in the French press described Diem as a butcher controlled by his American adviser.

"The journalistic attack was bearable," Ed Lansdale said. "What happened next wasn't. A group of soreheads among the French in Saigon undertook a spiteful terror campaign against American residents. Grenades were tossed at night into yards of houses where Americans lived. American-owned automobiles were blown up or booby-trapped."

Lansdale collected intelligence to identify who was behind the attacks. It appeared to be the French colonel who was chief of staff of the combined American-French training mission and a few of his subordinates. Lansdale went to see the colonel, told him he knew who was behind the attacks, and said, "Don't forget that you are ten thousand miles from metropolitan France. Whatever happens to you from now on is on your own heads."

The same night grenades exploded outside the quarters of the suspected French terrorists. The French colonel Lansdale had threatened protested to the American embassy, and Lansdale was called on the carpet the next morning. He was unrepentant. He told the new ambassador about the three junior French officers who had been caught redhanded by the Vietnamese police, with explosives in their jeep and a list of American targets in their pocket. Lansdale was ordered to stop his guerrilla actions.

In the war of grenades, Ed Lansdale had the help of Lou Conein and his team, who had earlier left North Vietnam, as required by the Geneva accords. Conein downplayed the importance of his role during this time. "I was just a go-fer for Lansdale, a liaison with people he wanted me to talk to," Conein said, which sounded uncharacteristically modest to those who knew him.

Elyette recalled a startling incident from this period. Lou did not discuss his work with her. She was usually exposed to his French side, the side of Conein that could be discreet and well-mannered, the one that enjoyed good food and wine. Lansdale had a lovely apartment that opened onto a rooftop garden, but Elyette and Lou did not dine with him a single time. Lansdale was indifferent to food, and Elyette and Lou preferred to take advantage of the many excellent French restaurants in Saigon. Sometimes Lou would wear the rosette of the Legion of Honor, and Elyette could sense the other diners eyeing them. She felt proud. It was one night after they'd dined out that the incident occurred.

"It was around nine in the evening," Elyette recalled. "We were driving slowly past the home of the American ambassador. Lou took something—I didn't know what it was, it was hissing—and threw it. *Boom!* He had thrown a grenade in the ambassador's yard. I couldn't believe it. I said, 'But why, Lou? You're crazy!' He said, 'This is the order of Ed Lansdale.' We drove away and luckily nobody came after us. I had seen a lot of things in my life, but I was a very proper person. Lou was very exciting, though, because he was never the same."

In retrospect, Elyette Bruchot believed that Lou Conein had thrown the grenade at the American ambassador's residence to warn him to increase his personal security and, indeed, barricades went up the next day. But at the time French officers were throwing grenades at Americans, and Lansdale had been ordered by his ambassador not to reciprocate. One might surmise that Lansdale, through Conein, was sending the new ambassador a message that was supposed to look as though it bore a French stamp.

The French had had enough. General Ely ordered a stop to the terror. Ambassador Collins had negotiated with the French to take over all the training of the Vietnamese army, and now the French decided to pull out completely. At a meeting in Paris on May 8–11, 1955, the French foreign minister, Edgar Faure, said that Diem was crazy, *un fou,* and warned that Lansdale was playing a game that would lead to disaster. John Foster Dulles disagreed and said that the only choice the United States had was to support Diem or withdraw. In April 1956, after Diem formally requested the move, the French military command was dissolved, and the last French troops left Vietnam.

Lansdale and Diem had stood together and had experienced one crisis after another. After a year of it, they were spoiled for each other. Undoubtedly, Diem had read one newspaper story too many about how he was thought to be the American's puppet. Their relations cooled. Lansdale no longer had the same access. Diplomats who arrived at the palace did not find him frolicking on the floor with Nhu's children, as before. Lansdale did the only thing to be done. He requested reassignment to Washington.

The CIA decided that the technique of giving Diem a personal adviser had worked well, and a search was begun for Lansdale's successor. The job was offered to a young intelligence officer who'd made a name for himself within the agency for his success at manipulating political parties in Italy to outmaneuver the communists there. But William Colby asked to be allowed to finish his tour in the Rome station, and his request was granted. Lansdale had brought a specialist in Asian agriculture to Vietnam by the name of Wolf Ladejinsky, a naturalized American who had been born and raised in Russia. Ladejinsky had the Lansdale touch in dealing with the Vietnamese and a lower profile; he became Diem's personal adviser and practically a member of the palace staff from 1956 to 1961, paid by the CIA. Wesley Fishel, Diem's oldest American friend, also served as an adviser. Fishel helped assemble a team of academics from Michigan State University, and, funded covertly by the CIA, they picked up where Lansdale left off, to try to encourage democratic institutions and help Diem consolidate his power during the late nineteen fifties. The CIA used the Michigan State group as a cover to train Diem's police.

Ed Lansdale was effective in Vietnam, but not as effective as he had been in the Philippines. The leader he left in place was wounded. Partly this was Diem's fault, the result of his own large deficiencies, but it also had to do with the way he was obliged to take over in the face of unceasing French opposition, which set the tone for the way he was received by influential Vietnamese. From the first day he assumed office, the country's intellectual class, those who aspired to be born-again Frenchmen, perched like magpies in Saigon and began a relentless campaign of criticism of his government, which had the effect of pushing the stubborn Diem ever deeper into his cocoon. For better or for worse, South Vietnam was now solely the client of the United States, thanks in significant part to Edward Geary Lansdale, U.S. Air Force/Central Intelligence Agency. But the French, with nearly a hundred years to create their own special ghost, were still there in spirit if not in body.

9

FORT BENNING 1956

WITH LANSDALE OUT OF THE PICTURE, the military advisory group in Saigon began to train the South Vietnamese in tactics that proved disastrously inappropriate to the situation. Instead of preparing the South Vietnamese to face a communist-inspired guerrilla war inside their country at the village level, the Americans trained them to oppose an invasion of conventional forces from North Vietnam. The Saigon army was turned into a pale replica of the United States Army, with tiny Asian footsoldiers clanking through the countryside with their bulky American gear, conducting maneuvers-by-the-book that were devised at the infantry school in the red clay and pine barrens of Fort Benning, Georgia.

A number of officials opposed the Pentagon's decision to turn the South Vietnamese into an American-style army—Lansdale of course, but including, perhaps surprisingly, Secretary of State John Foster Dulles, who wasn't generally noted for his unconventional thinking. In this case Dulles was on the mark in his conviction that the emphasis should be placed on counterguerrilla warfare. Yet, as crucial as the error turned out to be, even Lansdale was ready to admit that it had stemmed less from unconscionable ignorance than from an almost historical inevitability based on the United States' experience in Korea only five years earlier, when the communist North had invaded the American-supported South. The Korean experience was fresh in the mind and worries of Lieutenant General Samuel (Hanging Sam) Williams, who had served there, and who took over as the commanding general of the Saigon military group in late 1955. The intelligence

129

reports Williams received indicating that the North Vietnamese were equipping their army with Soviet weapons and turning it into a conventional force further convinced him that he should do the same with the South Vietnamese. Moreover, Ngo Dinh Diem preferred a conventional army, partly because he too feared an invasion from the North but also because he feared probably as much that villagers who were armed to fight a guerrilla war inside the country might turn on him. With a conventional army, he could at least manipulate its commanders to ensure his continuing power.

For the following decade, the American public, when it read or heard about Vietnam, was exposed to an array of theories about "counterinsurgency" and how to fight "a people's war," theories that seemed confusing and astonishingly exotic. The basic question was quite simple, though. How did a conventional anti-invasion force fight an unconventional internal guerrilla force? The mistake had been made before the United States barely had completed its takeover from the French.

Chau saw it coming. He quickly realized that the Americans understood less about Vietnam than the French and showed little capacity for learning. The French war's end had found him being groomed for higher command. He had done well as the commander of a company that was part of a French strike force called a *groupe mobile.* He was wounded in action several times, and after one particularly harsh battle, his wife visited the morgue for three consecutive days to try to determine if Chau, as most of his battalion, had been killed. When Ngo Dinh Diem arrived in Saigon, Chau was taking command of a battalion outside Da Nang.

Chau was soon drawn into the plotting against Diem by the chief of staff, Nguyen Van Hinh, the born-again Frenchman. One of Hinh's backers flew from Saigon to enlist Chau in the conspiracy. Chau had nothing against Diem, who, after all, had just become head of Vietnam a couple of months before, but many of his friends were supporting the coup, and he agreed to take part. It was arranged that he would be transferred to Hue as commander of a military school and a strike force, making him the conspirators' chief lieutenant in South Vietnam's second largest city. After Ed Lansdale smothered the coup attempt, the leaders of the plot told Chau that they had miscalculated, that nothing could be done without the approval of the Americans, and so they had failed. Now it was necessary, they said, for Chau to apologize to one of Diem's brothers, Ngo Dinh Can, who lived in Hue and who was the de facto power in central Vietnam. Apologize? responded Chau. Never. He was not a leader of the coup but an officer who had been enlisted by his superiors. Well, in that case, they said, he could not remain in Hue. The best that could be done for him was to reassign him as commandant of cadets at the Dalat military academy, where he had once taught.

So Chau wound up in Dalat as a major. He was soon joined there by Nguyen Van Thieu. Thieu was already a lieutenant colonel and was picked to head the school. Chau and Thieu did not share a home as they had before, but they remained good friends and worked well together. They watched as Diem took steps to consolidate his power. The Emperor Bao Dai, encouraged by the French, tried to fire Diem at the time of the uprising of the sects. But Diem refused to give up power and announced that he would hold a referendum to decide whether the country preferred Bao Dai as chief of state or himself as president of a republic. Lansdale advised Diem on the elections and chose the cheerful color of red, associated with good luck, for Diem's ballots, while coloring Bao Dai's ballots an uninspiring green, hoping to give Diem an edge with the rice farmers. But that proved unnecessary.

"I told Diem not to cheat," Lansdale said. "And then he came up with ninety-eight percent of the vote. Jesus!"

Diem also announced that he had no intention of taking part in a referendum to decide the question of reunification of North and South Vietnam, as called for by the 1954 Geneva accords. Diem told Lansdale he didn't trust the communists to play fair in an election. Lansdale did not oppose his decision, and may have encouraged it. He persuaded Diem to hold elections for a constituent assembly to legitimize his government and brought someone from the Philippines to help write the constitution. Elections were held, and the National Assembly that followed became a rubber stamp for Diem's quasi-dictatorship.

But these events seemed distant to Chau from his teaching position in Dalat, whose rolling hills and small lakes gave it the quiet air of a college town. He and the other Vietnamese officers at the military academy were caught up in their own transition: they had learned to speak French and the formality that went with the French way of doing things; now they had to learn to speak English and accustom themselves to the sometimes shocking informality of the Americans. For Chau, the transition was deeply unsettling.

"It was taking me time to recover from a feeling of self-betrayal," he said, "as if I were allying myself with a new group of foreigners, the Americans, just to make a living—after having spent years trying to break away from another group of foreigners, the French."

Still, he was pleased to receive orders to report to Fort Benning, Georgia, to take a ten-month infantry course. He would get to see the United States at first hand and make up his mind about these new foreigners. Of the twenty-five officers in his group heading to Benning, none spoke English well enough to carry on a simple conversation. After they landed in San Francisco, they grew excited by the possibilities of this fabulous new country. But the day before they were scheduled to leave by train for Georgia, their excitement came crashing down when the American captain in charge of the group informed them that they were to take Yellow Cabs to the train station. They had heard much about racism in America. Were they being put in Yellow Cabs because they were yellow people? The group was divided as to what to do. Some counseled that they say nothing, but others wanted to protest the humiliation. Finally, Chau got up his courage and spoke to the American captain. When the captain was able to grasp the question Chau was asking in his broken English, he threw back his head and laughed. No, he said, Yellow Cabs had nothing to do with racism but was simply the name of a cab company.

The Vietnamese officers were relieved and laughed at their mistake, but Chau remained wary. On matters of race, the Americans were not the French. He saw an example when he attended a Nat King Cole concert in Phoenix, Alabama, not far from Fort Benning. A fight suddenly broke out, ending the concert, and Chau was told that it was caused by a black man embracing a white woman on the stage. Only when he took a trip to Washington and stayed with a family named Klein did Chau begin to warm up to Americans. Chau found the Kleins generous and kind, immediately ready to accept a stranger and an Asian like himself as a member of the family. They were wonderful people, he decided, and his stay with them did much to ease the feelings of mistrust he felt about Americans in general.

Like other foreign student officers, he could not help but be overwhelmed by the spectacular displays of modern firepower at Fort Benning—the "mad minute" of concentrated infantry fire, the long-range cannons, the tanks, the jets, the bombers, all there to cover the foot soldier. And dispite his misgivings that this might not be the best way to fight a guerrilla war, he returned to the military academy at

Dalat full of enthusiasm after his graduation from Fort Benning in September 1956.

The changes at the Dalat academy were immediately apparent. The transition was over. The Americans seemed to be everywhere. Some American wives and their children had joined their officer husbands. At a reception Chau was shocked to see an American sergeant sitting on the same couch with a lieutenant colonel's wife and talking to her as if they were equals. Never had he seen anything similar to that with the French, nor could it ever happen among the Vietnamese. This amazing informality would take some getting used to.

Yet the social informality of the Americans was accompanied by a certain professional rigidity. Chau was assigned as the director of instruction at the school and was told to work with his American counterpart, a West Point major, in preparing a four-year program of instruction to train Vietnamese officers. Chau was enthusiastic about the work because he thought the time ripe to break with the old French system and create a new breed of officer, but he believed too that modern military techniques should be balanced by maintaining traditional Vietnamese cultural ideas in the program of instruction. His American counterpart showed little interest in Chau's project, however, and told him that the system used at the U.S. Military Academy and its replica in the Philippines could be transferred intact to Vietnam.

Chau had little time to protest the Americanization of the military academy because he was removed from his job in May 1957. The cause was politics. Nguyen Van Thieu had been removed earlier as the school's commandant through the machinations of Diem's brother's political party, the Can Lao, whose heavily Catholic membership was being given key positions throughout the army and government. Whether this raw power play led Nguyen Van Thieu to a greater spiritual understanding of Catholicism was uncertain, but he soon converted from Buddhism to the religion of political influence. Then Chau, the faithful Buddhist, came under Can Lao pressure, and was transferred from the academy. He was made temporary chief of staff of a division commanded by an old friend. Saigon refused to make his assignment permanent and replaced him with a Can Lao member. Chau was transferred again, this time to a training center.

It looked as though Chau's career had come to a dead end. Because of his participation in the aborted Hinh coup, he was considered to be anti-Diem, though that was not true; and he had refused to join Nhu's

Can Lao party. He had not been promoted a single time since the French war ended. A number of his friends and contemporaries were already generals. Nguyen Van Thieu was a colonel. Chau was not complaining, though. The general commanding the training center had served as the chief of security for the French police during the war, and Chau disliked all Vietnamese who had been associated with the French in jobs other than what he considered the honorable one of a military man fighting against the communists on the battlefield, but to his surprise he and the general got on well, and their wives became friends. The general was sent on an observation mission to Israel, and when he returned, he asked Chau to help him write his report. Chau worked hard to make the general and his report look as impressive as possible.

Not long afterward Chau received a message to come to Saigon for an interview with President Diem. Chau did not know it but the general's report had been well received, and the general had mentioned that Chau helped write it. When Chau entered the president's office, Diem greeted him and asked him to sit down, then began to speak about Chau's family. Diem knew Chau's father, the retired judge, and he said that although they were not on good political terms, he respected him as a man of integrity. "What about you?" Diem asked. Chau replied that he tried to be a good son and follow the precepts of service to his country laid down by generations of his ancestors. On that note the interview ended, and Chau returned to his training center. Chau was accustomed to Vietnamese indirection, to his countrymen's distaste for approaching any subject head on, but he did not know what to make of his interview with Diem. The general at the training center assured him, however, that he wouldn't be around much longer. Diem was taking his measure, he said, and evidently had plans for him.

A week later Chau was assigned to be the inspector of the civil guard. Diem called him to another interview. This time the president was direct. The job he was giving Chau, Diem said, was one he considered extremely important because it was at the civil guard level that the relationship between the military and the people was formed. Diem wanted Chau to spend three months traveling around the country talking to average citizens to see what they thought of the military. This was the first serious attempt by the Diem administration, no doubt prodded by the CIA, to come to grips with the error that had been made in turning the South Vietnamese army into a conventional anti-invasion force rather than concentrating on a more flexible civil guard–type response at the village level where the guerrilla war would be fought.

Chau traveled around the country and was appalled by what he saw. The conventional military misbehaved toward the people, acted arrogantly, and sometimes stole their property. American aid was being misused. The appointed governing committees of the villages often comported themselves like little dictators. The communists had not made much headway in the country at this point, but Chau could see that the misbehavior of the military was opening the way for them. He returned to Saigon and wrote a hard-hitting report.

Months passed and Chau heard nothing. He assumed that Diem didn't like his bad-news report or that it had gotten lost in the shuffle at the palace. But it turned out that Diem just took a long time to reach a decision. Diem wanted Chau to try to do something about the situation. He made him a regional commander of the civil guard, the local militia that operated at the village level and was separate from the conventional military. Chau's job was to set up an example that could be followed throughout the country. He was to teach his soldiers how to act toward the people, form a model village committee, and get the local rice farmers involved in a self-defense project. It was the kind of thing that had been advocated by Lansdale. This was early 1961, and Chau's model drew the attention of the Americans. Here was something that worked, and it was created solely by a Vietnamese. CIA station chief William Colby took visitors to see Chau's project. Chau soon met the several American generals assigned to Saigon, including Charles Timmes, head of the military advisory group, who later declared that the group's work in turning the South Vietnamese into a conventional anti-invasion army had been one of the key errors of the war. Chau also met and became the friend of a lieutenant colonel named John Paul Vann, who had arrived to advise a nearby Vietnamese division.

Diem called Chau to the palace to serve as the rapporteur of the national security council, the man who collected all the documents from the various agencies, made a summary of them, and then briefed Diem. Diem was so impressed by Chau's work that he decided to appoint him to govern one of South Vietnam's forty-four provinces. It was now Lieutenant Colonel Chau, chief of Kien Hoa province, to the south of Saigon.

10

VIENTIANE 1959

AMONG THE LANSDALE DISCIPLES who went out to preach the gospel of political action, Rufe Phillips was the Saul of Tarsus. He had undergone a dramatic conversion on the road to Manila. "I was tremendously impressed by what I saw in the Philippines," Phillips said, "and the things that had been accomplished there based on Lansdale's ideas combined with Filipino ideas. And of course Magsaysay was just unbelievably inspiring."

After the Lansdale team was disbanded in late 1956, the Central Intelligence Agency asked Rufe Phillips to go to Laos, to try to work the Lansdale magic there. Phillips accepted the assignment and arrived in Vientiane, Laos's capital, under cover as an official of the organization responsible for administering the aid program. The decision to send Phillips to Laos was, in microcosm, the United States' attempt to fight the communists in that country on a political rather than a military level, which had been all but abandoned in Vietnam after the departure of Lansdale and his team.

Americans who knew Southeast Asia well often preferred the Laotians personally to anyone else in the region. In general, as a people, they had none of the underlying egotism of the Vietnamese or the capacity for brutality of the Cambodians. They were polite, hospitable, cheerful, not very enthusiastic fighters, and—where women were concerned—uninhibited, especially compared to the Vietnamese. There was an old saying that the Vietnamese worked at cultivating rice, while the Cambodians watched it come up, and the Laotians listened to it grow. But the political situation in Laos was something else again. Laos had a king to whom everyone paid lip service, but seldom in its history had the country enjoyed any real form of unity. The gentle Lao were riven by factions and families who disliked each other for reasons indecipherable to the outsider.

Two main opposing groups emerged from the French war. Symbolically enough for the fratricide that followed, the factions were led by half-brothers who were royal princes, sons of the king's viceroy. Prince Souvanna Phouma, the older by eleven years, was rather easygoing, something of a born-again Frenchman, who had agreed to work for gradual independence under the French. Prince Souphanouvong, the younger and more fiery, joined the Viet Minh and became a communist leader in the fight against the colonialists. His guerrilla group was called the Pathet Lao, and they were concentrated in the northern part of Laos, bordering North Vietnam. After the French war ended, the Pathet Lao began agitating to take over the country. They were helped by the North Vietnamese. The extent of Hanoi's aid was a subject of debate and an object of the CIA's intelligence collection effort. The sparsely populated country possessed some of the most rugged terrain of Indochina, and establishing what Hanoi was up to was never easy and always open to challenge.

The 1954 Geneva accords specified that only the French could maintain a military mission in Laos. When the situation, as Washington saw it, began to deteriorate, a plan was got up to circumvent the Geneva accords and supercede the French covertly by sending four hundred American military men, mostly from the Special Forces, to Laos in civilian clothes, ostensibly as technicians to advise the French military mission. Following the American attraction for choosing absurd cover names, the group was called the Programs Evaluation Office, stirring the interest of journalists, who revealed that P.E.O. was headed by a well-known brigadier general whose name had mysteriously disappeared from Pentagon rosters. The group arrived in Laos in 1959, sent by Eisenhower before John F. Kennedy took over.

The Special Forces added muscle to the CIA's political effort, which was not going well. After Rufe Phillips arrived, the Americans encouraged the Laotians to hold parliamentary elections and, in an operation called Booster Shot, brought in a team of CIA officers from Japan and other posts in Asia on temporary duty to get out the vote for the right people. The elections turned out to be a disaster, as the CIA saw it. The pro-Pathet Lao forces won a large number of seats. Then a dispute about whom the United States should support as

Laos's leader developed between the ambassador and the station chief in Vientiane. The CIA thought Prince Souvanna Phouma was not anticommunist enough and started looking around for a right-wing general to replace him as prime minister. The station chief during this dispute was Henry Hecksher, a German whose father had served in the Kaiser Wilhelm government and who was a naturalized American. Ten years later, Hecksher would be involved in a similar dispute with the American ambassador in Chile, when Salvador Allende came to power. Both Hecksher and the ambassador were later removed from Vientiane to clear the way for a new team that included as station chief Gordon Jorgenson, an officer who had served with Lansdale in Saigon. But before that happened, the agency found its right-wing general. The leader of the Pathet Lao was arrested and thrown into jail, but he and some of his followers broke out and headed to the northern mountains, to wage a guerrilla war with North Vietnamese backing. The Americans encouraged the right-wing general to hold elections. The CIA, remembering what had happened in the first elections, rigged these so well that nobody took them seriously. A sturdy little parachute captain named Kong Le decided to put an end to the foolishness by pulling a coup d'état and declaring Laos a neutral country with Souvanna Phouma as prime minister. But the well-meaning Kong Le only added to the foolishness, and fighting broke out among the rightists, the neutralists, and the leftists. The neutralists were sometimes with the leftists and sometimes against them.

Eisenhower emphasized Laos as a major foreign policy concern to John F. Kennedy at the time of his inauguration. Kennedy said that Eisenhower did not mention Vietnam, but portrayed Laos as the key to Indochina and the whole of Southeast Asia in a strategic game of dominos, a view being promoted in Washington by Ed Lansdale, who still had the ear of Allen Dulles. The importance of Laos, as advanced by Eisenhower, was shocking news to Kennedy, as well it should have been considering that Laos was a landlocked country with no industry and three million mostly illiterate peasants whose annual income amounted to a few dollars. Vientiane, the capital city, was a collection of ramshackle buildings splayed along an unpaved main street, with a brothel, Madame Lulu's, discreetly positioned not far from the ministry of defense.

Kennedy took Eisenhower's warning seriously and pondered various options, including that of sending military troops. He ordered the Americans of the Programs Evaluation Office to drop the charade and put on their uniforms as official military advisers. But Kennedy finally concluded that the mess was too confusing to sort out. Luckily, the Russians agreed. Finding they had—in diplomatic jargon—"a coincidence of interests," Moscow and Washington decided to hold a new conference at Geneva to neutralize the country. The coincidence was that neither party wanted to risk going to war over a nation that really wasn't a nation but an assortment of factions whose political abilities were measurable only in terms of their relative cleverness at stealing American aid.

It was at the beginning of this sequence of chaotic events, in the summer of 1959, that an intelligence officer named Stuart Methven arrived in Vientiane. Methven, who was then thirty-two, a slim man nearly six feet tall, with brown hair and a mustache, had a complexion roughened by his passage through youth and clear blue eyes that reflected two seasons, winter and spring. Stu Methven—the name was Scottish—was the son of an army colonel who had retired to New Hampshire. He attended Amherst, where he was interested in journalism. After working a year for U.S. Rubber, he decided to apply to the agency.

Laos was to be the CIA's secret war, and so it was fitting that Stu Methven had been a member of the first class to be trained at "the farm," the agency's facility in the woods at Camp Peary, Virginia, outside Washington, where new recruits learned the craft of intelligence in a nearly yearlong course, followed, for some, by special paramilitary training of the type given to the elite forces of the regular army, and carried out at different places in the United States and Panama. Since the Central Intelligence Agency grew out of the Office of Strategic Services of World War Two, and was staffed by many veterans of the organization, it was predictable that the agency's institutional idea of what constituted the best CIA officer would correspond to what had been considered the best OSS officer: a well-educated man who jumped out of airplanes and spoke several languages. Although it was predictable, it was also in many ways unfortunate that an intelligence agency set up to operate in peacetime formed its ideal based on a world war. And, ironically, the ideal was flawed at its roots. Parachuting from an airplane, which required nothing more than a minimum amount of courage, was a haphazard way to get to a specific point on the ground, and 90 percent of all airborne operations in World War Two had been near disasters, despite the postwar myth that held otherwise. Learning a foreign language truly well, unless one happened to be born into an immigrant family, was a lifelong proposition, and there were fewer good linguists among agency officers than one might have supposed.

But such was the ideal, and Stu Methven fit the profile of the activist CIA officers who were busy around the world from the nineteen fifties through the early nineteen seventies, and he would cap his career by running the CIA's war in Angola from his post as station chief in Zaire. He had graduated from a noted liberal arts college, completed the agency's in-house intelligence and indoctrination program, undergone parachute and paramilitary training, and spoke a foreign language, French, although, at the outset, not particularly well. After Methven moved on from Laos to Saigon, where he lived in a big villa with a menagerie that included a huge boa constrictor that consumed live ducks as hors d'oeuvres, some people saw him as a smoother version of Lou Conein. Though the two men were good friends, Methven resisted the comparison.

"Talk about journalistic license," Stu Methven said. "One time a reporter saw me and Lou Conein in a bar and then described me in a newspaper article as 'Stuart Methven, a dashing Amherst graduate who wears pearl-handled pistols.' I never carried anything but a nine mm, and it was always concealed in a sack or something. That was Conein he was describing. Boy, did I get reamed by my friends about that—'the dashing Amherst graduate with pearl-handled pistols'!"

Whether or not Stu Methven could be considered a cowboy like Lou Conein, there was no question but that he was an effective intelligence officer. Vint Lawrence, a CIA man who followed him to Laos, remembered Methven as being "smart and responsible." On an earlier assignment to Japan, Methven had polished the indispensable technique of getting on well with non-Americans. Rufe Phillips was at the end of his tour in Laos when Methven arrived, and he introduced Stu to his contacts.

"Rufe was very dynamic and knew everybody," Methven said. "He had all these ideas and it was go, go, go. I thought he was excellent. He was the guy doing most of the civic action programs for the agency, but there were also several others, and I joined them."

Partly by chance, partly by personal initiative, Methven became the civic-action contact with a primitive tribe of nomads in the northern mountains widely known as the Meo though they considered the term pejorative and called themselves the Hmong.* No one knew for sure where the Meo came from, but their red-brown skin and high cheekbones declared their Mongol ancestry. Some anthropologists speculated that they were descendants of the armies of Genghis Khan that invaded Southeast Asia seven hundred years before. The Meo, who numbered about a half million, had points in common with Genghis Khan's men. They were fierce fighters and very independent. They scorned the Laotians who lived in the lowlands and valleys, preferring to pass their lives in the high mountains, where they farmed by burning off a mountainside and planting rice, and when the field was exhausted, picking up their village and moving to another mountainside, where the cycle was repeated. Dutch missionaries introduced them to steel knives and flintlock muskets. Every village had a family of metal workers who hammered scrap metal into curved knifeblades and bracelets. They drank rice wine, sometimes staying drunk for long stretches, and butchered a water buffalo in a favorite ceremony. The French had recruited the Meo as guerrilla fighters against the Viet Minh, but after the war ended the tribe went back to its nomadic ways.

Like other CIA officers assigned to Vientiane, Stu Methven worked through a counterpart who was a member of the Laotian army. "I would tell the army what I wanted to do," Methven said, "and they would say, 'Go ahead.' And I would say, 'Okay, who are you going to send with me?' You wanted always to have a Lao officer along, because otherwise you would just get involved in setting up an American program, and that wasn't our objective. We were trying to get government representatives out to the countryside, to say here's your government working for you, bringing democracy to the masses. So I would go along and the Lao officer would say to a district chief, 'What can we do for you?' And the guy would say we need seeds, we need this, we need that. The Lao officer would turn to me, and I would jot it down and say maybe we could help him out. The Lao weren't ashamed to turn to you like that, but we preferred to stay farther out, to let them handle it alone and carry the ball."

The agency had not yet brought in its large fleet of aircraft flying under the cover of Air America, and finding transportation to the

---

*I am using the term *Meo* in this account because the Americans, all of us, with not untypical insensitivity, referred to them this way for the greater part of the war. I mean no offense to the courageous Hmong.

northern part of Laos was difficult. A group of French pilots in Vientiane who were as unsavory as they were charming had a collection of ancient airplanes known informally as Air Opium, and Methven chartered one of them for a trip to the north. The pilot was half-Algerian. He flew Methven to a civilian strip called Opium One. There was a French restaurant nearby, the Snow Leopard Inn, with an old leopard caged outside. Soon one of the agency's small, propeller-driven planes that had been developed especially for its ability to take off and land on short airstrips became available. Called a Helio Courier, it was, along with another plane of the same type developed by the Swiss, the agency's workhorse for moving CIA officers around Indochina. Stu Methven caught a ride to the strategic Plaine des Jarres, which was the focal point for the war in the north against the North Vietnamese–backed Pathet Lao guerrillas, and built the first Helio Courier strip there.

"While I was there I asked around to see if there were any Meo who were part of the Laotian government," Methven said. "I learned that they had a big chief down in Vientiane, a guy by the name of Touby Ly Fong. But he had gone sort of soft and they had him in some kind of ceremonial position. So I didn't feel he was the guy to work with to get the civic action programs going. But we had to work through somebody connected to the government, not just an ordinary Meo, because that was the only way we could get the Vientiane government to support it. Then I heard about a Meo captain, farther north, who was in the Laotian army. I sent word that I would like to meet him, and he came down two days later. He was wearing his uniform, a Chinese-looking guy, very dynamic, by the name of Vang Pao."

Vang Pao had been a sergeant in the French army, and after the war ended he decided to make the military a career, an act that indicated a high degree of determination, for the Meo were discriminated against by the Laotians and his chances for promotion were low. But Vang Pao called attention to himself by his deeds. He was extraordinarily brave, and a charismatic leader. He was also, as Stu Methven discovered to his surprise, remarkably straightforward and honest. They met to talk in a hut belonging to a Filipino medical team that had been sent to Laos at Ed Lansdale's urging, under Operation Brotherhood.

"I asked him if there was any way in conjunction with the Lao government that we could help him and the Meo," Methven said.

"Most people asked for all kinds of things. We had these big radio sets, and people would ask for things like that, or they'd ask for a pistol. But Vang Pao asked for an anvil. 'An anvil?' 'Oui.' The Meo were great at working with metals. So I went back and walked into the station and said, 'I need an anvil.' "

Vang Pao also mentioned that it got cold in the mountains and that the Meo had few clothes. Methven checked around and discovered a military depot that had a stockpile of olive green sweaters left over from World War Two. The military would sell them to the CIA for a nickel a piece. Methven ordered five thousand. He loaded a two-engined cargo plane with the sweaters and the anvil and arranged for a Meo who knew Vang Pao's location to fly with them.

"The anvil went down by parachute, the sweaters we kicked out," Methven said. "As they hit the ground, they fell all over the place. It was a sea of olive drab down there. I later went back to the Plaine des Jarres and walked back up to Vang Pao's position. I think it took two days to get there. And the Meo were lined up along the road waiting for me, wearing those green sweaters."

Over the next few months, Stu Methven saw Vang Pao a half dozen times at different places. One time Methven was on the Plaine des Jarres talking to the regional military commander as they watched Laotian troops clumsily stove a hole in the side of a C-46 while trying to offload a 105-mm artillery piece. Vang Pao was there. The field came under mortar attack. Methven flew Vang Pao and the regional commander in his plane, to make a reconnaissance of the area. The situation was getting worse. This was the summer of 1961, and Kennedy soon reached an understanding with Krushchev about neutralizing the country. Averell Harriman was sent to Geneva to begin negotiations. The Lansdale concept of civic action as espoused by Rufe Phillips had collapsed as a result of the chaos. It was around this time that the CIA decided to try another tactic.

"The station made the decision to start arming the Meo," Stu Methven said, "because the political action program was down the tubes at this point. They told the Lao about this, and they agreed. They also had to work it with Bangkok station, and an officer arrived from there to direct the program."

Stu Methven took the officer from Bangkok, a Texan, to meet Vang Pao. The French had armed the Meo as guerrilla fighters during their war and then had insisted they return their weapons. When Methven told Vang Pao what they were planning and introduced him to the Texan, Vang Pao had one comment.

"He looked me in the eye and said, 'You aren't going to do what the French did, are you? You arm us and then when everything goes to hell, you take back our weapons and leave us.'

"I looked him in the eye and said, 'Listen, this is the United States government you are talking to. When we make a commitment, we keep it. How can you compare us to the French?' I was convinced we'd never let him down."

Afterward, Methven went with the Texan to the first of the sites to be established in the north. A site was a temporary village where the families of Meo fighters collected around a crude airstrip used by the CIA as a forward base from which to wage the war against the Pathet Lao and the North Vietnamese. The number of sites grew until they topped more than sixty. Methven also took part in the first airdrop, which became the standard way of supplying the Meo with rice, as the increasing warfare made it almost impossible for them to farm.

"They'd never seen a rice drop before," Methven said. "We put out a T to mark the spot. The plane came over and the kicker started pushing out bags of triple-sacked rice. The Meo ran out to watch. The first sack hit three and killed them. They had a big party that night. I paid them off and told them to get a buffalo for their ceremonies to make up for the accident."

That was the last time Methven was involved with Vang Pao and the Meo. The Texan and his team took over. Methven was coming to the end of his tour and was looking forward to returning to the States. "Des FitzGerald was the chief of the Far East Division, and he came out to Laos. We were all heroes at the time, because Laos was a big thing, and so FitzGerald says, 'Write your own ticket. What do you want to do?' I said, 'Well, I'd like to take a year off and go back to school.' The agency had all these programs, and I was thinking of going to Harvard or someplace like that. About two months later a message comes in and it says, 'You are going to Vietnam.' I told the station chief, 'There must be some mistake.' And he said, 'Vietnam. No further discussion necessary.' "

As Stu Methven was preparing to leave Laos in late 1961, a twenty-two-year-old New Yorker was completing his training at the Special Forces jungle warfare school in Panama. Vint Lawrence looked the part of the paramilitary specialist, the guy who jumped from airplanes and spoke several languages. He was six-three and weighed one hundred and eighty-five pounds, a handsome, friendly young man with dark hair and brown eyes, whose voice, when he was into his subject, took on such an enthusiasm that it was almost visible, like breath on a frosty morning. After turning in a miserable performance at Exeter, Lawrence managed by hook or family connections to get into Princeton, where, to everybody's surprise, he blossomed into a fine student, majoring in art history and taking part in theatricals. He was in the running for a Rhodes scholarship his senior year. When the Rhodes failed to materialize, he had to make a decision about his future. A faculty member who belonged to his eating club at Princeton and who was a member of the old-boy network that had been in operation since the CIA was formed helped him make it.

"One day he asked me if I would like to serve my country in a different way," Vint Lawrence said. "Like most everybody else, I had a two-year military obligation facing me. He said, 'How about the CIA?' My father had been in the OSS in North Africa during World War Two, and I thought that sounded like an interesting way to complete my military service. Kennedy was running for president. We were all very excited. There was a lot of enthusiasm. About the top twenty-five seniors of my class—that I figured were the top—were asked to come hear a spiel by the CIA, although I was the only one I knew at the time who went. It was like being tapped by a senior society. I felt very honored. So I came down and went through training at the farm and found that to be a marvelous experience, great fun. Here you had forty very bright, very creative, very witty people who were closeted at this farm in Virginia for almost a year, playing imaginary political games. You almost had to have a physical disability to show why you couldn't take the paramilitary training that followed the operational training. And being sort of a gung-ho, quasi-marine type of person anyway, I said, 'Yes, I'll take it.' "

Vint Lawrence was scheduled to work with Tibetans to create an organization to resist the communist Chinese, but at the last minute he was assigned to Vientiane, where he arrived in February 1962. "I spoke high-school French and not very well," Lawrence said, "but that was basically the thing that got me assigned to Laos, because when I arrived I was the only paramilitary officer who spoke it reasonably well." Joe Redick, who was fluent in French, was now the deputy chief of station, but Lawrence rarely saw him. Lawrence lived in an operational safehouse near the airport and did not enter Vientiane but once or twice. He was under military cover. In fact, as was the usual case with young CIA officers, he was simultaneously completing his military service as a second lieutenant in an arrangement worked out between the Pentagon and the agency. He was in ROTC at Princeton, and after graduating took eight weeks of regular artillery training at Fort Sill, before returning to go through training at the farm.

Negotiations in Geneva between Soviet Foreign Minister Andrei Gromyko and Ambassador Averell Harriman had dragged on for months. The competing interests of the rightists, the neutralists, and the communists had to be taken into account. Harriman and the Russians came up with a formula calling for a coalition government, with a neutrality to be supervised by Polish, Canadian, and Indian inspectors from the International Control Commission, which was still located in Saigon, anachronistically, to supervise the long-abused 1954 Geneva accords. There was hesitation by all parties. Nobody really thought it would work. The CIA and some State Department officials didn't want to give up their right-wing general, Phoumi Nosavan, and replace him with Prince Souvanna Phouma, who was suspected of being a little pink. But, finally, on July 23, 1962, the Geneva agreements were signed. All parties were given seventy-five days, until October 8, to put their affairs in order and comply with its terms.

An attitude of bonhomie appeared briefly, which was no more than surface deep. The Russians tried to tilt Prime Minister Souvanna Phouma to their side by giving him nine airplanes and training Laotian pilots; the Americans outleveraged the Russians by footing the bill for Laos's army, in effect paying for the gasoline to fly the Russian planes and picking up the cost of lodging the Russian instructors. Washington made a show of saying that it intended to comply fully with the agreements and withdraw all American advisers from the countryside. The ICC counted each crewcut Special Forces man as he left. The control commission also set up a checkpoint to monitor the withdrawal of the estimated seven thousand North Vietnamese troops in the country. No more than forty were counted as leaving. The Americans had violated the 1954 Geneva accords, which ended the French war. So had the North Vietnamese. Now both parties prepared to violate the 1962 Geneva agreements on Laos.

Vint Lawrence became an instrument of the violation on the American side. Under the Geneva agreements, a small group of Americans were to be left at the Vientiane embassy, including—as Harriman worked it out privately with the Soviets—only two CIA officers. No

American was allowed to operate in the north of Laos, except a middle-aged farmer from Indiana named Edgar (Pop) Buell, a sixty-five-dollar-a-month employee of the International Voluntary Services, a private peace corps under contract to conduct aid projects. Pop Buell, a wiry, balding man about five-four, had arrived in Laos two years earlier, fleeing to a new life after the death of his wife. He began helping Meo refugees in the north and was soon recognized as one of the most effective aid workers in the country. Buell could be crusty, but he was tireless and dedicated, a gift for the Meo, whose name for him, *Tan Pop,* translated into "the man sent from above." Through his personality and competence, Pop Buell developed an influence far greater than his lowly official position. He argued at the time of the Geneva agreements that he had to continue supplying the Meo with rice or else they would starve. The communist side did not readily concede the point. It was known that the Air America planes that carried out Pop Buell's rice drops belonged to the CIA. But it was finally decided that he could remain in the north.

In the summer of 1962, around the time the Geneva agreements were signed, Vint Lawrence flew with Pop Buell to survey the mountainous north where Vang Pao and his troops operated. They were looking for a better base camp for Vang Pao. The one he currently occupied was closely surrounded by mountains and fogged in much of the time, making resupply operations difficult. Lawrence found a bowl-shaped valley, almost deserted, that looked as though it had been created for just the kind of operation the CIA had in mind. It was secure and lent itself to the construction of an airfield. Lawrence gave his superiors the news. It was arranged for Vang Pao and his troops, including their families, to move to the new site, where Pop Buell would feed them. Lawrence had come to the end of his tour in military service. He flew to the States to be mustered out of the army and then returned to Laos as a full-fledged CIA officer, ready to take part in the most closely held secret operation of the war.

The key to keeping the operation secret was found not in Laos but in Thailand. William Donovan, the former head of the OSS, had served as ambassador to Thailand in the early nineteen fifties, and the CIA had developed warm relations with the Thais. One Bangkok station chief, Robert Jantzen, was a drinking buddy of Thailand's prime minister; to compensate for his poor memory, Jantzen sometimes wired himself with a hidden tape recorder for their late-night conversations. The CIA had been particularly effective at helping the Thais create a strong border police, a major concern since Thailand had Malayan communist guerrillas on its southern border and the Pathet Lao backed by the North Vietnamese on the north.

The CIA officers who had worked for years with the Thai border police were assigned to run the Meo operation from Thailand; one of them was the Texan. They first set up at an airbase near Laos's border, not far from the Mekong River, but realized it wasn't secure enough from the curious, so they moved to the large Thai airbase at Udorn, farther south but still within reasonable flying distance of Laos, and made their headquarters in a compound on the base that was impenetrable to journalists. The officers arranged for the Thai border police whom they'd trained earlier to enter Laos secretly and serve as radio operators, training cadre, and support troops for Vang Pao's men. The Thais operated in Laos under the control of the only two CIA officers who were assigned to live with Vang Pao. This way, as the Thais were Asians and more or less merged with the scenery, the agency could keep the number of CIA officers to a minimum and the operation low-key.

Vint Lawrence was one of the two officers assigned to Vang Pao. Anthony Poshepny, known as Tony Po, was the other. It was an interesting mix: Lawrence, a socially adept Ivy Leaguer, quick to develop an enthusiasm for Meo anthropology; Tony Po, about as pure a fighting machine as there ever was, easily bored when he wasn't out on operations. In his forties, a good twenty years older than Lawrence, Po was possibly the best paramilitary specialist produced by the CIA. He had served as a marine sapper in the Pacific during World War Two—the man who went in first and blew up beach fortifications before the others landed—and afterward fought in Korea. He signed on with the agency, and in the nineteen fifties trained Khamba tribesmen from Tibet, and was one of three paramilitary specialists inserted into Sumatra to organize resistance to Indonesia's Sukarno.

Tony Po looked like a block of oak. He had heavily muscled shoulders and arms and a huge head, was about five-eleven, and extremely strong. Fighting was his game, and he carried a boxer's mouthpiece in his pocket when he went to bars. But Po had a cheerful outward disposition. He usually wore a big smile, got on well with Asians, and was always moving his hands to make a point, with a sign language to compensate for his lack of facility for spoken languages, though he eventually learned Lao. One aspect of what made Tony Po tick was never clearly stated. It seemed his father had been a naval officer at

Pearl Harbor and was somehow involved in the scapegoating that followed. Po was ready to fight the war in Indochina singlehandedly if need be to remove the stain, real or imagined, from the family name. He was intelligent and cunning but like many men of action cared little for the drudge work of administration.

Tony Po and Vint Lawrence lived together in a hut in the Laotian mountains for nearly two years, seldom seeing other Americans, flying to Thailand for rest and relaxation infrequently, and never entering Vientiane. This was in the early months after the 1962 Geneva agreements were signed supposedly neutralizing Laos, when the United States was still pretending to be virginal, and they lived an almost fugitive existence, hiding from the white International Control Commission helicopter that circled overhead looking for violators. They were limited by headquarters as to what they could do. Mostly they were in a reporting role, with training the Meo and setting up road-watch teams to monitor North Vietnamese infiltration another duty. Tony Po hated to write. It fell to Lawrence to do the reporting. About fifteen teams with Thai radio operators were located at sites in the mountains. Every night they called in, and Lawrence collated their reports, and transmitted the message to operational headquarters in Udorn.

"Tony Po got increasingly unhappy with me," Lawrence said, "because I was the young kid who in effect was doing all the work and the guy people would come to see when they wanted something done." What Tony wanted was action. "I was far less brave, foolhardy, courageous—whatever you want to call it. Tony had a desire to get out there and mix it up. I got into a couple of dicey situations, but not because I purposefully tried to expose myself."

Tony Po was also subtly being pushed out of the loop with Vang Pao as a result of his inability to speak French. Lawrence and Vang Pao were drawn closer by speaking the common language, though not always grammatically, and by Lawrence's interest in learning about the Meo on a level other than the military. Meanwhile, Tony could be found poring over a copy of the *Wall Street Journal* when he could get it in the irregular mail, sitting on a mountaintop in Laos, a gun by his side, plotting to make a killing in the market—which amused Lawrence, whose father was an investment counselor in New York and who knew the odds on Tony's hitting it big. Not so amusing was when Tony drank, as he did more and more out of boredom, and turned aggressive. It was a relief to both men when Tony Po was reassigned farther north to another mountain tribe, even more primitive, called the Yao, where he could get into the fighting, leaving Vint Lawrence to operate as Vang Pao's case officer.

"My responsibility was basically to hold Vang Pao's hand," Lawrence said. "I ate, lived, and slept with him. I mean, I didn't actually sleep with him, since he had five wives and that wasn't necessary. But I ate every meal with him and talked to him, and was his comforter and friend."

The experience left Lawrence with a deep admiration for Vang Pao. "He was shrewd, bright, and had an extraordinary touch with people," Lawrence said. "He was terribly brave and his exploits had been clearly documented. He could be ruthless when he needed to be, but he was politically very savvy. He did not come from a particularly powerful family, but through a series of good marriages to politically important families he had developed a sort of base. And he had a relationship with the titular head of the Meo, Touby Ly Fong, which was rather similar to my relationship with Tony Po, although I don't mean to compare Tony with Touby."

Touby Ly Fong was the first Meo ever to attend college, and this feat, combined with the backing of the French, who manipulated him for their purposes, consolidated his position as the king of the Meo. The Meo were the largest ethnic minority in Laos. The Vientiane government, needing all the support it could muster against the Pathet Lao, cultivated Touby and made him minister of health and education, not an important position, but flattering. A portly, well-spoken gentleman in his fifties, Touby was loyal to his people, but his French education had broadened his horizons and left him with a desire also to broaden his fortunes. And since the Meo had only one cash crop, Touby became an entrepreneur of the opium business.

A century or so earlier, the British had not only introduced opium to the Chinese but had literally forced it down their throats. British traders, who were buying silk and tea from China, found that they had nothing the Chinese wanted to buy in return, so they brought opium from their colony in India and later fought a war to make sure the Chinese kept using it. After developing a large number of addicts, China started growing its own. Yunnan, a province in the south, was particularly suited for opium poppy cultivation, and from Yunnan it spread across the border into the adjoining Golden Triangle of Southeast Asia—the northern parts of Burma, Thailand, and Laos—where it was grown by desperately poor hill tribes like the Meo as their only means of making money.

In late summer, Meo farmers scattered poppy seeds over their hoed fields. The green plant emerged and grew to a height of three or four feet, with one main stem surrounded by a half-dozen smaller stems, and each stem produced a flower. The flower died and the petals dropped off, leaving a green seed pod the size of a bird's egg. The pod contained a milky white sap. Before daybreak on harvest day, Meo women headed to the fields, wearing small three-bladed knives on finger rings. Slitting each poppy, they left three incisions, from which a milky white sap oozed out. After the sap congealed and turned a brownish-black color, the Meo returned and scraped it off the pod with a dull, flat-bladed knife onto a banana leaf. That was raw opium. The Meo collected the brown sticky stuff into bales and sold it. They got about seven dollars for a kilo of something that, when later refined into heroin or morphine, brought thousands of dollars.

The French had decided on opium sales as a way of defraying the costs of their colonial administration. A former budget analyst named Paul Doumer was appointed governor-general of Indochina, and he reorganized the opium business in 1899 to maximize profits. Doumer's efficiency didn't extend to some of the officials who followed him, and their mismanagement of opium touched off a revolt of the Meo, stirring them to attack the French garrison. Meo production, however, was relatively small at the time. The French were importing from Iran and Turkey 60 percent of the opium that they sold in Indochina. World War Two broke out and trade routes were blocked. The French then pressured the Meo to increase their poppy growing and imposed a tax to insure compliance. Aware that the independent Meo were prone to violence when taken advantage of, the French stopped dealing with the Meo directly and appointed native opium brokers to make their buys. Touby Ly Fong was one of the chief brokers for the French.

At the end of World War Two, the French came under international pressure to stamp out opium smoking in Indochina, forcing them into action. On an official level, the French removed themselves; on a covert level, French intelligence, short of money to finance operations against the Viet Minh, took over the narcotics trade and operated through members of the Corsican underworld.

It was during this period, in 1952, that the CIA was inadvertently implicated in the opium business. The contamination came through the Nationalist Chinese troops of Chiang Kai-shek, who had been chased off the China mainland onto Taiwan by Mao Tse-tung and his communists. Several thousand of Chiang Kai-shek's defeated army couldn't make it to Taiwan but escaped instead across the border into Burma. The Burmese army told the Chinese to surrender their arms or leave and then, when they didn't, launched a military operation against them, forcing the Chinese to retreat to the rugged mountains of the Golden Triangle in Burma, near Thailand. The Burmese were preparing a mopping-up operation at the moment that Washington decided to arm and train the Nationalist Chinese remnants as guerrillas for border protection and harassment of Mao's forces. The CIA flew in paramilitary specialists and opened a training camp. They scoured the area for other Chiang Kai-shek survivors and came up with about four thousand. As the Nationalist Chinese looked around them, they discovered they were in the Golden Triangle and realized they could make more money from smuggling than soldiering, though both were equally as dangerous and required the same skills, as battles were common among competing smugglers. At any rate, using American weapons and supplies to get back on their feet, they became an opium army instead of an anticommunist army; and the CIA operation eventually dissolved, leaving a lethal and well-organized gang of Chinese bandits to make sure that 50 percent of the world's illegal opium reached its overseas markets.

Most Americans assigned to the north in Laos tended to view opium from the perspective of the Meo. The Meo did not use it except to treat sickness. They considered opium the same way an American farmer might look at corn or soybeans. It was their cash crop and one whose prices underwent fluctuations in the marketplace. They had nothing to do with refining it into heroin or morphine. They felt as far removed from its social implications as a farmer whose corn was turned into a bourbon that contributed to the spread of alcoholism. Even Pop Buell, whose work was solely humanitarian, began to see poppy growing from the Meo standpoint after he tried and failed to persuade them to change to another cash crop, such as sweet potatoes. Pop Buell believed that the only answer to the problem lay in buying up the crop and destroying it. The Meo produced no more than a hundred tons of opium a year, which could have been purchased for less than a million dollars, the price of a couple of helicopters. Stu Methven cabled the CIA twice to recommend that the United States do just that, only Methven's idea was to buy it up and dump it on China, to make trouble for the communists. But as usual, when confronted with a moral dilemma, Washington opted to do nothing. Consequently, the word began to spread in news reports that the CIA was supporting dope smugglers and even transporting opium in Air America planes. Much of the speculation centered on Vang Pao; few people had ever heard of Touby Ly Fong.

"I'd get a message every month asking about Vang Pao and the opium," Vint Lawrence said. "And it became a bit of a joke, because I would go down to Vang Pao and say, 'It's that time of month again and I need to fill out the form sent from the agency.' I knew where the opium was stored. It was under his house. He kept one ton there so that when the Americans left he would have some money. It was always the same bales, the same stuff—his insurance. His basic trade-off with Touby Ly Fong was that he did not put pressure on Touby, and Touby was running the opium. Vang Pao needed Touby, because Touby could make a lot of trouble for him in Vientiane. Vang Pao hated Vientiane and didn't like the Lao leadership, which he considered corrupt. So he left Touby alone and the quid pro quo was that Touby left him alone. It was very clear to Vang Pao that we didn't want him to be mixed up with the opium. And he said he understood that.

"Some people said, 'Are American pilots carrying opium?' And I'd say, 'Yes, they are—but they don't know they are.' I never once saw an American pilot make a deal with somebody. But at the airfield, as it grew, you had a runway clogged with three or four hundred people. Some were going to Vientiane, some to another base, and they'd all have these grungy little sacks to carry their possessions. Under the circumstances of war, you didn't exactly have a security check to see who was carrying what before they got on the planes."

Was Vang Pao as disinterested in the opium business as his case officer and friend said he was? That was not easily determined. But it was unlikely that he was the dope smuggler as portrayed in other accounts, some of them emanating from the family and supporters of Touby Ly Fong, who were jealous of Vang Pao's power and saw him as a usurper. Vang Pao was, of course, a Hmong who had grown up around the crop. The fact that he kept a ton of opium as "insurance" indicated that he was not entirely innocent of the business. But Vang Pao was aware of Washington's sensitivity about the matter, and everyone who knew him remarked on his responsibility. Moreover, opium required extensive cultivation, and as the war expanded the Meo had less opportunity to grow it. The biggest poppy crop was grown farther north, in the tribal area of the Yao, where Tony Po was assigned. And Vint Lawrence was convinced that Tony Po stood as firmly against the opium business as anyone. "Tony was a fighter who wanted more action, more troops," Lawrence said. "And opium destroys people."

It was not likely either that Air America was involved in transporting opium beyond the inadvertent way recounted by Lawrence. It was difficult to describe to Americans who were used to controls at their own airports what an airport in wartime Asia was like. Masses of people crowded into airplanes that generally landed on no particular schedule, carrying everything from crying babies to squealing pigs. There were no smiling hostesses—it was load 'em up and go. To make sure no one was secreting a kilo of opium—2.2 pounds—under his rice or chickens would have been impossible. Also, there was other transportation around for the dope smugglers. The signing of the Geneva agreements ended for all practical purposes Air Opium as flown by French mercenaries; and they retired to a life of restaurants and hotels in Vietnam. The opium trade was taken over by Laotian generals who had their own transportation or who could make a deal with members of Vietnam's air force to move it.

Yet, from whatever angle one examined it, the American involvement with opium in Laos, no matter how inadvertent or peripheral, was an ugly business, and one that had disastrous consequences as a result of Washington's refusal to face the issue squarely. It was only a matter of time before other people realized, as Pop Buell and Stu Methven had, that the answer lay in cornering the crop. But they were people on the other side, and their intention was closer to Methven's than to Buell's. They bought it up and dumped it on the Americans. By 1970, Vietnamese children were selling American soldiers a highly addictive heroin that cost practically nothing.

Not long after Tony Po left, the restrictions resulting from the quasi-adherence to the 1962 Geneva agreements were lifted and Vang Pao's men began increased operations under CIA direction. More Americans arrived in Vientiane. The ambassador, William Sullivan, believed the charade of neutrality should not be dropped entirely. He was convinced that the situation would only be made worse by bringing in regular American troops, and he spent much of his time trying to head off a formal militarization of the conflict. Ambassador Sullivan supervised the situation so closely that he became sort of an ambassador/field marshall, responsible for diplomacy and for coordinating military action, of which Vang Pao's men were the great hope.

The crude hut where Vint Lawrence and Tony Po passed nearly two years was replaced by more substantial buildings. Lumber was brought in from outside. A marketplace was built. The floodgates opened. Power generators came first, then air conditioners, paved roads, recreational clubs. An office building as impressive as any to be found in South Vietnam was constructed as a joint command for Vang Pao and the CIA and their Thai agents. More refugees and families of guerrilla fighters crowded into the CIA base, and Long Tieng—as it was known—grew to forty-five thousand inhabitants, the third largest town in Laos.

Still, a degree of secrecy was maintained from journalists. This was partly due to Pop Buell and his refugee operation, which inadvertently provided a safety valve for the CIA. Pop Buell left Long Tieng and moved to another base seventeen miles away, called Sam Thong, where he established a hospital, a school, and supply facilities, with its own airfield. Buell took a position with the Agency for International Development at a better salary. He was never employed by the CIA, though Vint Lawrence did much of the work coordinating his Air America rice shipments for the Meo. Pop Buell's base at Sam Thong was open to journalists and to anyone who wanted to drop in, whereas the CIA base a few miles away was off-limits. As a result, newspaper stories out of Laos focused on Pop Buell, who was colorful and quotable, taking some of the pressure for publicity off the CIA operation.

Anointed by the CIA, Vang Pao moved up in rank, lingering for a while at colonel and then promoted to general and placed in charge of the military region in upper Laos, an unheard of advancement for a Meo. Vang Pao's dream was to capture Sam Neua province in the northeast, which was taken from the French in 1953 and had been under communist control ever since. Sam Neua City, a road-junction provincial capital, was the headquarters of Pathet Lao leader Prince Souphanouvong. Sam Neua and another province, Phong Saly, whose northernmost border was only eighty miles from Hanoi, were the key staging areas for North Vietnamese operations in Laos. For a while it appeared Vang Pao's dream might come true. His guerrillas spread out through the mountains and attacked the North Vietnamese when they least expected it, using hit-and-run tactics. During three years, from 1962 through 1965, they won one engagement after another.

"We turned the tables on the communists in the north of Laos," Vint Lawrence said. "They were concentrated in the towns and had to use the roads, which were subject to ambush by Vang Pao's guerrillas. It was almost a reversal of the situation that existed in South Vietnam between the Americans and the Viet Cong."

The guerrilla war of this period stood as the CIA's most successful undertaking in Southeast Asia. Not coincidentally, it was also the only CIA operation that looked like an OSS operation taken straight out of World War Two. There was nothing morally or politically ambiguous about this particular part of the Indochina conflict. And the fight had nothing to do with stopping infiltration down the Ho Chi Minh Trail, as was commonly thought; the trail was farther south. The North Vietnamese, not unlike the Germans of World War Two, were invaders bent on conquering the homeland of the Meo and installing a puppet regime in Vientiane. The Meo were motivated not as anticommunists but as a people fighting for their survival. Their resistance movement was led by a strong and charismatic native commander. The movement was supported by a minimum number of American operatives; at the guerrilla war's height, no more than eight or nine CIA officers were assigned to northern Laos, ensuring that the Meo developed their own leadership and self-reliance.

Vang Pao was brought to Washington and feted by the CIA. He was one of the best field commanders in Indochina, and the agency's director wanted to make sure he understood he was appreciated. Stu Methven was assigned as his escort. "Just tell us where you would like to go, what you would like to see," the CIA director told Vang Pao, "and Mr. Methven will take you." Stu had visions of lounging around poolside in Florida or California with Vang Pao, sipping a cool drink and enjoying the scenery. But Vang Pao already knew what he wanted to see. "Detroit," he said. "Thank you." The Meo from the hills of Laos who had asked Methven for an anvil when they first met watched with fascination as metal went in one end and came out the other as an automobile.

Soon, however, the shine was lost. It started with what seemed like a practical idea. The air war against North Vietnam began in March 1965, and many air force planes flying the bombing runs were based in Thailand, some of them at Udorn, headquarters of the Meo operation. Sometimes the planes aborted their missions because of bad weather or battle conditions and dumped their bombs on Laos's jungles on the way back to Thailand. Instead of dumping, why not use the bombs to support Vang Pao's operations? An air force officer was assigned to work with the CIA men to provide Vang Pao with air support. But giving guerrilla fighters air support was the first step in turning them into conventional forces. As the air war expanded, the air force wanted to install a radar station in northern Laos, a few miles from North Vietnam, to guide their planes to attack Hanoi. The Meo were assigned to guard the radar station, reducing them to the role of ordinary foot soldiers. They were hit-and-run guerrillas, not soldiers trained to hold a static position, and when the North Vietnamese attacked in force, they fled. The radar station was captured, shaking the confidence of everyone involved.

"Vang Pao started to go down a slippery slope," Vint Lawrence said. "We pushed him more and more into a conventional military mode, which I felt was death to his people. The pressure to do this came from various directions. The agency and the State Department didn't want the U.S. military back in Laos, and I think they were right. Sullivan was there and very effective at brokering, moving back and forth. But this put pressure on Vang Pao to do more—to go in and hold the Plaine des Jarres, for example. And some of it came from Vang Pao. He'd had three years of pretty good success, and he saw this as an opportunity for himself. So he stubbed the toe of the North Vietnamese, and they started wheeling in the big boys. From the summer of nineteen sixty-five till I left in the spring of 'sixty-six, it became clear that the North Vietnamese were not about to let the northern provinces of Laos go. I think they realized that all their southwest country bordering Laos was completely populated by tribal people, and they saw Vang Pao as a threat to their back door, among other things. They were determined to put in whatever forces were necessary to keep it."

Vint Lawrence left Laos before the destruction of the Meo began. Looking back, he did not know what he would have done if he had been assigned to Vang Pao later in the war, when the guerrillas were being turned into a conventional force. "I would have strongly recommended against it," he said. "It's easy to say I would have resigned from the agency, but I don't know what I would've done."

Correctly or not, the CIA officer associated with the destruction of the Meo in the minds of many of the old hands who served in Laos in the early days was Ted Shackley, who took over as Vientiane station chief in 1966. The Meo operation was run from Thailand, but the responsibility belonged to the Laos station chief, and Ted Shackley was known as a take-charge guy. It was under Shackley's direction that the Meo became a conventional army. In providing them with air support, he worked closely with an air force officer named Richard Secord. The day Lawrence left the CIA base, there were five American employees of the agency assigned there. Six months later, after the agency agreed to let the air force use the base as a forward staging area, four hundred air force men moved in and took over Long Tieng, ending what had been the Vietnam War's only OSS operation.

It was oversimplifying, Lawrence knew, to put the blame on Ted Shackley. From what he understood, Shackley was a superb intelligence officer, but one of his first chores when he returned to CIA headquarters was to brief Shackley, who was on his way to Vientiane, and Lawrence had instinctively disliked the man on first meeting. Shackley seemed to lack a sense of human connections; and the Meo needed someone who could understand and sympathize with them. It was one thing to be hardnosed, another to be callous, and Vint Lawrence was not sure that Ted Shackley perceived the difference. There were others who would share Lawrence's sentiments when Shackley became involved in the Chau case.

When Vint Lawrence left Laos, he was undecided whether he would return. He had put in four years and was recovering from an illness. He talked it over with William Colby, his division head. To Lawrence, Colby was the opposite of Ted Shackley—a man interested in human beings.

"Colby called me in and said, 'Do you want to go back?'

"I said, 'Of course, a part of me wants to go back. I'm very fond of these people.'

" 'You realize, if you do go back, you aren't going to come home.'

" 'What do you mean?'

" 'Well, a lot of you guys haven't made it through'—the attrition rate was high just from downed airplanes and helicopters—'and those who have don't want to come back at all. I want you to think about it, and we'll talk next week.' "

At their next meeting, Colby had already made up his mind. "I'm not going to let you return to Laos," he told Lawrence. "I want you to work for me for a year. If you're going back into the agency, you've got to figure out what you want to do and where you want to go. You'll see everything that goes on in the Far East as my assistant.' "

"Colby was great to work for," Lawrence said. "He was a hardworking and dedicated guy. I arrived at five-thirty every morning and culled his messages. I was basically his eyes and ears. I toted his bags and played special assistant. Then I made a movie about Laos for the CIA, to explain the Meo operation."

As he readjusted to the United States, Vint Lawrence realized that his future did not lie with the CIA. For one thing, on a professional level, he had been virtually a co-commander of a twenty-five-thousand-man guerrilla army at the age of twenty-six. How could he ever top that? or equal it? The old hands at the agency advised him to get out. When he reentered the system, they warned, there would be people waiting to cut him down to size. He also realized he was not very good at the techniques of foreign intelligence. He didn't like the idea of suborning people.

"I talked it over with Colby," Lawrence said, "and he said, 'God, get another career.' He believed strongly in working for the government, but also believed you needed something else, so when the government pissed you off you could leave. Washington will chew you up, he said, unless you have another place to go. That happened to intelligence officers who'd only been intelligence officers for twenty or thirty years. A CIA officer was practically unemployable by the time he left—nobody would touch him."

So Vint Lawrence decided to quit the agency before he turned thirty. He considered going back to school to get a doctorate in anthropology, but gave himself over to the harder struggle of becoming an artist. As the years passed, he appreciated Colby's advice more than ever. Colby was right: some guys came back dead or didn't come back at all. Tony Po married a native and settled in Thailand. He'd been in the bush too long, Tony, and America no longer made any sense to him.

The attempt by the United States to oppose the Pathet Lao and the North Vietnamese in Laos ended in defeat. But the methods chosen to oppose the communists, first the use of political action and then the launching of an OSS-style guerrilla operation, at least had the effect of helping prevent the introduction of U.S. combat forces. Had the same attitudes prevailed in Vietnam, the country might have been spared a wider war. On the other hand, the Laotian experience did have a certain influence on the evolution of the Vietnam conflict. A number of CIA paramilitary operatives were transferred to Saigon after their political action programs failed in Laos, and among them was Stuart Methven, who was to become Chau's contact with the agency.

11

SAIGON 1961

WILLIAM COLBY WAS THE MOST EFFECTIVE American political action operative to serve in Vietnam, and though his work as the CIA station chief in Saigon and later as head of the pacification program with the rank of ambassador involved him in many aspects of the war, his major areas of concern paralleled the programs developed by Chau. Early on, Colby realized the war had to be fought at the village level, where the South Vietnamese army's conventional anti-invasion force was the least effective, and so he spent his next years trying to promote the training and arming of a local militia that could combat the communists in the villages both politically and militarily. Like Chau, Colby also realized that the most important target in the country was not the guerrilla fighters but the political and administrative apparatus of the Viet Cong. Falling into the bureaucratese so beloved by Americans, he called it the "Viet Cong Infrastructure" (VCI), which made the communist functionaries sound rather like bridges and roads, and usually left outsiders confused as to what he was talking about.

The striking facet of William Colby was his approachability and his willingness to consider another point of view. If you wanted to argue, for example, that the CIA was the creation of a few bored Ivy Leaguers from the OSS who were suffering a predictable letdown after World War Two and that without a war, in peacetime, the agency inevitably turned into a sort of secret police with liberal arts degrees eager to promote and protect the interests of a multinational capitalism while ex-OSS officers recaptured a little of the old excitement by playing cowboys and Indians with the Soviet KGB, William Colby would not flare up in anger but would listen calmly, perhaps concede the validity of a point or two, and then conclude that your argument was based on a superficial analysis and a misunderstanding of international affairs. His openness was not a clever device to hide an intractability but extended to relations with his children; his son Paul remembered his father during the most controversial days of the war as being someone they could always talk to, even if their views differed.

Men as approachable and open as Colby often had subsidiary traits—a sense of humor, say, an appreciation of irony, perhaps a tendency to introspection. But that did not describe Colby. His sense of humor was thin and awkward, and he communicated human interest rather than human warmth. He was at bottom a shy man.

Born in St. Paul, Minnesota, in 1920, Colby was an only child. His father, an army officer with a Ph.D. in English from Columbia who retired as a colonel, served as the editor of various post newspapers and wrote a dozen or so books, ranging from a study of English Catholic poets to a compilation of army slang. His father, Colby said, was too intellectual for the military and a maverick who never fit in. His mother he described as a "charming Irish lady, very warm, very pleasant." The Colbys moved from post to post, and young William did not have time to put down roots. The three years he spent in China, beginning at age nine when his father was assigned to the Fifteenth Infantry, he recalled with pleasure, and he hoped some day to go back. He attended an excellent British school while in China, which put him a grade or two ahead of his contemporaries in the States. When the family moved to Burlington, Vermont, his father insisted that Colby enter a regular high school, believing it would be good for him. After that he applied to West Point—"made a perfunctory stab at it," he said—but was turned down because of his vision; he had worn glasses since childhood. He enrolled instead at Princeton. At sixteen, he was two years younger than most of his classmates, an only child who had spent his youth on the move, something of an outsider who worked in the dining halls at Princeton to help pay his tuition.

He majored in political science and excelled in the military training of ROTC. An influential moment of his college career came in his junior year, when he spent the summer in France, and he remembered it as the time he began to develop his approach to understanding and dealing with non-Americans, which he would use as an intelligence officer.

"I always thought it really doesn't pay for Americans to be telling other people how to do things," Colby said. "You get more done by asking a set of Socratic questions to make your point. It went back to my summer, when I was trying to understand why the French did things the way they did. You brought it out by being sympathetic, curious, interested."

Colby's technique—the soft approach—went well with his shyness and his physiognomy and was likely a virtue born of necessity. He lacked the presence to overwhelm anyone with bluster or blarney the way some intelligence officers did. He was five-eight, with brown hair, and wary blue eyes behind the glasses. He kept his naturally slim frame trim by doing exercises in the bathroom every morning, but was not an athlete. He smoked during World War Two and then quit. He was a moderate drinker, preferring when he was in Vietnam a couple of gin and tonics in the evenings. The sum of his parts was unimpressive, and he could add as well as anyone.

"I said in my book that there's the traditional gray man, the intelligence officer who is so unobtrusive, so unnoticeable that he can't catch the eye of a waiter in a restaurant," Colby said. "And that's a little bit of my character—I have a hard time catching the eye of a waiter. So it's not a deliberate pose or anything. It's natural."

People who knew Colby remarked on his devotion to Catholicism. "I think religion meant a great deal to him," Vint Lawrence said. "It helped him through a lot of tough times, made him a good soldier, because he believed in what he was doing." While in Saigon, Colby attended six o'clock mass each Sunday morning, going by himself when his family was not there, sometimes to the redbrick cathedral, other times to the chapel of Brother Crawford, a priest who had been a missionary in China and lived for years in Asia. Colby did not discuss his religion or display any proselytizing tendencies. It was a private matter. As for his attending weekly mass while fighting a war, he said, "I did it. I sort of assumed it was part of the rules."

Most men who possessed great physical courage, even discreet and sophisticated men, tended to show it through a certain swagger—if not with words, then by a subtle body language. But Colby's swagger count was almost zero. He could have been a bank clerk afraid of his own shadow for all one could tell by looking at him or listening to his conversation. It was only after talking to people who had seen him in action and examining his career that one realized Colby was not only brave but also enjoyed exposing himself to danger. He did not wear pearl-handled revolvers, but he and Lou Conein were of a brotherhood.

It was as OSS commandos that Colby and Conein first met, Colby showing even then the school-drudge determination mixed with the quiet courage that would turn him into one of the key Americans— "the most effective," Ed Lansdale called him—to serve in Vietnam. After the war, where he served in France and Norway, he graduated from Columbia Law School and went to work in the firm headed by William Donovan, the former head of OSS. But Colby was not so much interested in making money as he was in engaging himself in a worthwhile cause. He had developed a passion for politics. Not the politics of speeches and backslapping, but the politics of ideas and action. He left New York to serve as an attorney for the National Labor Relations Board. Like Dan Ellsberg, he considered himself a liberal, a supporter of unions and civil rights at home, an anticommunist in international affairs. Years later, when James Schlesinger, a former secretary of defense and director of Central Intelligence, told him, "Bill, you are the only liberal ever to head the CIA," Colby repeated the remark with pride. The Central Intelligence Agency was attracting men who considered themselves liberal in the same way that Colby did, and when one of his former OSS chiefs asked if he was interested in joining them, he did not hesitate long. His assignment to Stockholm was interesting, but it was in Rome that he began to call attention to himself.

"I worked very hard in Rome, was always working, because we were in a battle," Colby said. "That was the thing. It wasn't an easy post where you let the world go by. We were right in the middle of a very serious fight with the communists. So I was on the phone and going out at night making contacts all the time. I was working very hard indeed and enjoying every minute of it."

Colby spent five years in Italy and performed so well that he confidently asked for reassignment to the Far East. "They came back and said, 'Will you go to Saigon?' And I said, 'Fine.' I really wasn't plotting it from a career point of view. I thought it would be an interesting place to work, to go to an action spot. I wouldn't have asked to go to a dull, dead place. Sending me to Belgium, for example, would have disappointed me a great deal. My chief of division rather apologized to me that he couldn't make me chief of station in Saigon. I went out as deputy chief. It didn't bother me. I would do whatever I was told. But it turned out that I became chief of station when the other fellow left after about a year."

The split within the CIA among the different types of intelligence officers reflected the split that had existed within the OSS. Basically it boiled down to the men of action and the men of thought. The latter included the analysts who shuffled papers and wrote reports and took no part in operational matters. The men of action were subdivided into two groups. There were those, on the one hand, who collected information by recruiting agents, which often amounted to bribing local politicians, experts in FI—Foreign Intelligence. They considered themselves to be "pure" intelligence operatives. On the other side were covert officers usually with paramilitary training or OSS experience who were adept at doing such things as training guerrillas or organizing a coup d'état. The two types sometimes overlapped, in the sense that a paramilitary officer could fill an assignment involving classical intelligence work.

By background, William Colby should have belonged to the paramilitary types and been a better educated and smoother version of Lou Conein, as perhaps Stu Methven was. By temperament, though, he was drawn not to the politics of guns but to the politics of ideas and organizations, an attraction enhanced by his tour in Italy, where he was involved in manipulating—"supporting," he would have said—political parties of the center to stop the advances of political parties of the left. From Colby's personal thesis and antithesis arose a synthesis that converted him into an advocate of what he sometimes called "covert nation building."

The agency's proponents of nation building were the only new kind of intelligence officer to emerge from the old OSS structure. The idea behind them could be traced to the Marshall Plan after World War Two, when massive foreign aid was injected into Europe, to speed the recovery of the countries devastated by the war. The Marshall Plan was so successful that in the early nineteen fifties academic thinkers proposed that the same concept be applied to nations breaking free of their colonial bonds. It was a liberal and democratic translation of Britain's earlier rationale of the need to shoulder the white man's burden. The United States should help the less fortunate countries modernize, help them build their nations, and provide at the same time a democratic alternative to Soviet-backed communism. The concept attracted many supporters in Congress and the academic community and appealed to CIA officers like Colby who considered themselves liberal. They saw it as a way of adding the most generous instincts of their political idealism to the sometimes brutal secret war against communism.

Colby's evolution into a nation builder did not come overnight. After he took over as the chief of the Saigon station in 1960, one of the first things he did was to plan a program of OSS-type commando operations to be used against North Vietnam, including saboteurs to be inserted into the country and harassing raids to be directed against coastal installations. It was the sort of thing Lou Conein would have thought of, and, as a matter of fact, Conein served as a liaison with the commando group after he returned to Vietnam. Three years later, when Colby was chief of the Far East Division, his assistant Bob Myers helped persuade him that such OSS throwbacks were ineffective in a political war.

Morever, even in his most political moments, Colby never entertained the idea of Lansdale that the communists could be defeated by tactics built around psychological warfare. Colby represented the mainstream of the CIA's nation-building theorists, while Lansdale was forever the maverick. "Lansdale thought if you got a good image going it could have a substantial political effect," Colby said, "that in fighting the ideological challenge of the communists you could turn to, oh, fables, folk songs, things like that. And this is where we differed. The folk songs were fine. But I thought they needed some guns to go with them."

Colby felt a closer kinship to Robert Thompson, the British counterinsurgency expert, who was in Malaya during the communist-inspired guerrilla war; and they had long private conversations about the proper approach to the Vietnam problem. "He and I got along extremely well, with a nuance of difference," Colby said. "We thoroughly agreed on the importance of building up the police. That's something Americans never understand—the role of the police. We sort of look at it as the flashing lights. But in a primitive society the police are always one of your big things."

William Colby was not a man who relaxed easily. Occasionally he lunched at the Cercle Sportif, but he wasn't much of a tennis player and didn't adapt to the French style of leisurely living in Saigon, as other American officials had. If Colby had anything that might be called a hobby, it was traveling. He enjoyed moving around, getting a feel for the different parts of a country. Even as overworked as he was in Rome, he managed to take his family on trips around Italy. Perhaps it stemmed from his rootless childhood. At any rate, as soon as he reached Saigon, he grew restless to get out in the field, to see for himself. These early trips were critical in forming his approach to the war. For Colby realized that if the communists were to be beaten, they would have to be beaten in the villages, not in Saigon. A new leadership arising from the countryside was the only answer. In their way, the born-again Frenchmen of the urban centers constituted as big a problem as the Viet Cong. Colby learned that President Diem and his brother Nhu felt the same way.

Nhu admired the way the communists controlled their areas by placing highly dedicated cadres in key positions. He thought he could overcome the influence of the French-trained Vietnamese elite by inserting his own loyal Can Lao cadres throughout the Saigon government and operating in secrecy, as the communists did. As discreetly as possible, Colby let Nhu know that he thought the control mechanism was a bad idea.

"I was saying that you've got to get your political system so that it works a little more openly," Colby said. "And the place to develop it is in the rural community. You had to count on new leadership coming from there and bringing authenticity to the country."

Colby handled Nhu delicately. He made his suggestions through questions that often came at the end of a long monologue by Nhu exposing in numbing detail his near paranoia about French intrigues against the Diem government. Colby would report on his trips to the field and ask for Nhu's comments. He believed he was having an influence on Diem's brother.

"Yes, I'm sure I did," Colby said. "I wasn't telling him what to do. I was just helping him think through the issues."

Colby began experimenting with different projects to oppose the communists. His inclination from the first was to arm the farmers of a village so that they could defend themselves from the highly successful Viet Cong tactics of forcible recruitment, propaganda, and tax collection, which were usually carried out not by large units but by only three or four armed guerrillas. Logical as Colby's plan may have sounded, he did not find it easy to persuade Diem of its value. Diem was afraid the farmers might turn their weapons on him. He felt more comfortable about the support of the Catholic refugees from the North, and Colby was able to establish some self-defense groups in the delta. By agreement, the CIA station chief worked with Nhu and the ambassador with Diem, and Colby spent a great deal of time encouraging Nhu to take a look at some of the villages where self-defense projects had been started.

"Out of these experiments, Nhu began to think in larger political terms than just self-defense," Colby said. "He began to see it as a community base for a new kind of political system."

The United States Special Forces were formed several years before Colby arrived in Saigon. Their purpose was to develop resistance organizations of Asians to be ready in the event the Chinese or the Soviets overran the region. The Special Forces were the Pentagon's bow to the OSS, divorced from the OSS's political function, which the CIA had taken on. With the mission of organizing Asian resistance groups, Special Forces training teams were sent to Taiwan, Thailand, and South Vietnam. Their role was soon expanded, however, to include other assignments that split three ways into special unit, clandestine, and paramilitary projects. In Laos, Special Forces men were used in the Programs Evaluation charade to wrest responsibility away from the French for training the Laotian army. In South Vietnam, they were attached to the military advisory group as members of—another remarkable cover name—the Combined Studies Group, which was directed by a CIA officer, an army colonel, who reported to Colby. In this program Colby started when he took over as station chief, the Special Forces men of the Combined Studies Group trained Vietnamese commandos to penetrate Laos in cross-border operations and to carry out sabotage and harassment raids against North Vietnam.

While Colby was looking for ways to provide self-defense for the villages, the CIA officer who directed the Special Forces came upon an International Voluntary Services worker, a younger Pop Buell, who was teaching agricultural techniques to mountain tribal groups in South Vietnam's central highlands. Called Montagnards—French for "mountain people"—they were divided into a number of tribes resembling but often more primitive than Vang Pao's Meo in Laos. The young worker of the private peace corps, whom Colby later hired away to the CIA, spoke the local tribal dialect and had established good relations with the mountain people. Through him, Colby was able to get a promising self-defense project started in a Montagnard village, using a Special Forces team to train and arm the villagers. Trying to emphasize that it was a self-defense project and had nothing to do with the Saigon army, Colby named the Montagnard units the Citizens Irregular Defense Group, or CIDG.

Colby thought he was on the right track. "CIA and Special Forces made a good team," he said. "It paired Special Forces paramilitary expertise with CIA sensitivity to political content." But not long afterward, in the wake of the Bay of Pigs disaster in Cuba, most large-scale paramilitary operations, except the one in Laos, were taken away from the CIA and transferred to the Pentagon's control, including the Special Forces in Vietnam. Without the CIA political head, the Special Forces military body began to duplicate every mistake the French had made in Indochina with their static defense system.

It started with an attempt to improve upon Colby's original idea. The Special Forces decided to use CIDG units, which the CIA was funding, to provide security for a camp they intended to develop as a base to train other self-defense units of nearby villages. From this first camp grew the concept of establishing more Special Forces camps and using the CIDG as a mercenary force for operations against the communists along South Vietnam's borders with Cambodia and Laos. The CIA's self-defense plan, which Colby had hoped to turn into a political program, evaporated and was replaced by the Pentagon's assumption of border control duties, a purely military chore. According to the Pentagon, the Special Forces camps were "astride and controlled" North Vietnamese infiltration routes into South Vietnam. In reality, the barbed-wire enclosed camps controlled nothing a few meters from their perimeters and were sitting ducks for communist attacks, which were launched with relative ease in the isolated surroundings and provided the communists with propaganda gains in their long-war strategy. News reports of yet another Special Forces camp being attacked, if only by a few mortar rounds, added to the public perception that the United States was hopelessly bogged down.

But all that was ahead, and in the early days it looked as though Colby and the CIA were onto something. From the various self-defense experiments grew the strategic hamlet program. The French had tried and failed at a similar program, but American optimism was undimmed. The most controversial aspect of the strategic hamlet program was its contention that if security could not be brought to the villages, then the villages should be brought to security. This meant uprooting some of the rice farmers from their ancestral lands and forcibly relocating them in newly created and more secure hamlets.

As usual, there were sharply differing opinions in Saigon over the effectiveness of the program. As usual, also, the best way to judge whether or not it was making progress was to examine the Viet Cong's response to it, and they were taking the project as a serious threat and doing their best to disrupt it.

IN TRYING TO GET the strategic hamlet program moving, it became apparent that the Americans were as disorganized as the Vietnamese assigned to administer it. Washington started looking around for someone who might pull everything together, and Rufe Phillips emerged as an obvious possibility. Phillips had quit the CIA and joined his father's airport engineering business, which, as a Yale history major, he was learning by osmosis. He was no longer the dashing Lansdale operative but a settled man with family considerations. He had married an attractive Chilean named Barbara, and they had two young children. Moreover, his father was ill with cancer and needed Rufe's help with the business. But a Lansdale disciple of civic action he still was, and he agreed to return to Saigon in late 1962 on a temporary basis, to make a study of how the aid program could be reorganized.

"Nhu had gotten interested in the strategic hamlet program from a political point," Rufe Phillips said. "He had some zany ideas, some of them really horrible, but here he had grabbed something good. One place he went wrong, of course, was by saying we've got to create strategic hamlets by moving a lot of people. But the basic idea was good, to start some sort of program of self-help. I examined the aid program and said, 'Look, we've got to decentralize it and put the money out in the provinces.' Everything was tied up in Saigon, not so much on the American side as the Vietnamese. A province chief would tell me, 'I can't even go out and buy three mosquito nets without sending a request to Saigon. By the time I get the approval, prices have changed and I can't buy them.' He had no funds to draw from to help the rice farmers with war damage or floods. So I said, 'Well, let's try to break this logjam.' "

Rufe Phillips recalled that a joint Chinese-American organization had been created on Taiwan to oversee the use of aid funds at a local level. He suggested the Americans do the same thing in Vietnam. They would place an American aid representative in each province as a member of a committee consisting of him, the American military adviser, and the Vietnamese province chief. The two Americans would act as guarantors that the money, which would be available immediately for Vietnamese use, was spent on legitimate projects. Phillips decided to stay on to put his plan into effect. He was appointed the first head of the rural aid program. He became the father of a bureaucracy that underwent numerous name changes and grew into CORDS—Civil Operations and Revolutionary Development Support—a name that suggested the program's bulk.

Phillips sought and got Diem's approval for his new version of the pacification program and then unveiled it at a strategy meeting on Vietnam in Honolulu called by Secretary of Defense Robert McNamara. He returned to Saigon and began developing an assistance plan for each of the country's provinces. Using the Lansdale technique of trying to let the Vietnamese do it themselves, Phillips called in each province chief and built the program around his problems and needs.

"There was this one province chief," said Phillips, "a wonderful guy with great ideas—Tran Ngoc Chau. He came to Saigon to see us and in effect said, 'I don't want any help. I'm doing just fine. I don't want you Americans coming down to Kien Hoa and screwing up my program.'

"I said, 'Wait a minute. We're not here to change your program. We'd like to know what it is you are doing. We want to shape what we're doing to support you.' "

The more Phillips thought about their conversation, the more he liked Chau. "I'd never met anyone so highly motivated," Phillips said. "If you wanted someone who had an instinctive understanding of how to generate popular support in a province, this was the man, Chau. He impressed me as being a very proud, very intelligent guy who obviously had a clear idea and sense of purpose in what he was doing." As head of the rural aid program, Phillips was concerned with such things as getting fertilizer to the rice farmers, digging wells, and providing health care. Some of Chau's projects were political, outside the scope of Phillips's aid mission.

"One day I ran into Stuart Methven, whom I'd known from Laos," Phillips said, "and I told Stu about Chau. I said, 'He's got some terrific ideas, and some of them are not the kind of thing my organization can support.' "

Stu Methven was interested to hear about Colonel Chau. He was looking for a new project. So far, Methven's tour in Vietnam had not worked out the way he had expected. After he left Laos, he spent a few months at Langley headquarters and arrived in Saigon in mid 1962. Since he had dealt with the Meo in Laos, it seemed natural that he should try to get something going with the mountain tribesmen, Montagnards, in Vietnam. He and several other CIA officers who had served in Laos worked on a mountain scout program, in which they recruited twelve-man teams of Montagnards to operate along South Vietnam's borders. The mountain scouts were different from Colby's CIDG. But after the Bay of Pigs, large-scale paramilitary operations were taken away from the agency, which meant that Methven had to give up his project.

Methven got angry when he learned he had to leave the Montagnard program. John Richardson had come from the Philippines to replace William Colby, who had been promoted to headquarters in Virginia, and they got together to decide what he was going to do. Methven didn't tell Richardson, but he wanted to avoid, if possible, getting involved in any program he might later have to turn over to the military, and that was the reason he suggested that Richardson allow him to follow up Rufe Phillips's idea of working with Chau.

There were two separate aspects of the pacification program at the time Methven went to meet Chau. One part of the program, which was staffed by civilian foreign service officers of the Agency for International Development, was pointed toward bringing economic improvement to the rice farmers. The other part, which was run by the CIA, was concerned with establishing local security for the farmers through paramilitary organization and propaganda. Chau's program was unusual and showed promise because it brought both aspects of pacification into a coherent whole. Chau had what the Americans with their splintered programs lacked: an overall plan. Borrowing ideas from the communists, he set about to involve every citizen in some type of productive organization that would glue them together in support of the local and then national government—whether farmer, merchant, or housewife. To find out what the average citizen thought about the government, Chau established a census grievance program, which involved sending his assistants to talk to the villagers and write down their complaints, so he could act on them.

Like Ed Lansdale and Rufe Phillips, Chau believed that democracy could be created in the countryside and that the best policy was to win the communists over to the government, not to kill them. This was why he established an amnesty program, to make it easy for the Viet Cong to change sides. Chau believed the real threat from the Viet Cong lay in their political/administrative organization, which was composed of highly dedicated functionaries who were usually referred to, even by the communists, as cadres, a French term that originally meant "frame" or "framework" but which had evolved into a name for the order-givers and decision-makers of an organization. Here, too, Chau's response to the threat was subtle. He would not send military units into a village after the cadres because the soldiers might destroy the village and kill innocent people during their search. Instead, he would use three-man counterterror teams to capture or kill the hard-core communist functionaries.

Stu Methven was quick to realize that Chau was probably the most forward-thinking pacification specialist in the country, and he offered CIA help. Chau went to Saigon to see President Diem. Chau told Diem that an American who seemed to be from the CIA—Chau wasn't sure and Methven didn't say—proposed to finance his program in Kien Hoa, and he wanted to know if Diem approved. Diem telephoned his brother Nhu and told him about Methven's offer. Nhu said it sounded okay and added that the CIA was already funding a similar program in another province, apparently referring to a civic action project Lou Conein had set up on his return. Diem knew nothing about Conein's program and was angry he hadn't been informed. But Diem told Chau that he trusted him and that Chau could accept the CIA offer so long as he made sure he remained in control of the program.

Stu Methven intended to spread Chau's program to nearby provinces, and he was looking for a place he could train cadre. Methven was covering six provinces for the CIA. The Saigon station was still relatively small, with only thirty or forty men, and he was given a great deal of leeway with his operations. He was showing the same kind of personal initiative that had drawn the attention of his superiors in Laos. As he traveled around, he heard about a private army run by a businessman who was close to Diem. The businessman used his army, which had Diem's tacit approval, to protect and broaden his financial interests. He was particularly keen on keeping the road that ran forty miles from Saigon to the seacoast at Vung Tau open, because he had a monopoly on selling shrimp in the city—his men were called the Shrimp Soldiers—and it was necessary that he keep the coast road free of communist blockades, something the Saigon army seemed incapable of doing. So the businessman opened a camp near Vung Tau and trained his men in not only military tactics but also civic action techniques, based on the premise that a happy and noncommunist citizenry was good for business.

Methven decided to give some of the CIA's financial support to the businessman too. He was thinking that the Vung Tau camp would make a fine place to train people for Chau's program. The businessman already had a training staff in operation. Thus the seeds were sown for a new approach to pacification. Yet the promise shown by Chau's work was largely based on the energy, dedication, and honesty of Chau himself, and finding other Vietnamese to match him was difficult. In reality, the easiest part of his program for the CIA to develop came from his idea of establishing small counterterror teams to fight the Viet Cong on their own terms. It was a tactic that appealed to a paramilitary specialist like Stu Methven, and from this crude beginning were to grow the deadly beak and claws of the Phoenix program.

IN LATER YEARS, William Colby and Edward Lansdale would argue that real progress was being made in pacification during those early years. There was a degree of support for their contention, some of it coming from the Viet Cong, who admitted through their sympathetic reporter Wilfred Burchett, the Australian communist journalist, that 1962 belonged to the Saigon government. Colby and Lansdale would further argue, with not a little bitterness, that the progress of pacification was halted by the United States' blunder of overthrowing Ngo Dinh Diem.

Ngo Dinh Diem made a number of mistakes from the moment he took office, but none was as costly to him in the long run as his decision to arrest and jail Dr. Phan Quang Dan. Dan was attending Harvard Medical School in 1954 when Washington was looking for a man to put in power in Saigon. There were some in the Central

Intelligence Agency who preferred Dan to Diem, but the doctor was not as well known as Diem and was not picked. The following year, as Ed Lansdale was helping to install Diem, he returned home and became a leader of the opposition. It was too much to say that Dr. Dan was a born-again American, but he had a faith in democratic principles and was a clear-cut alternative to the usual run of born-again Frenchmen who made up most of the political opposition in Saigon. He was an appealing figure both to American government officials and to journalists. Perhaps because of Dr. Dan's attractiveness to the Americans, Diem and Nhu considered him their biggest threat. Dan was arrested before the first National Assembly elections and forced to give up his medical post at the University of Saigon. After he was elected by the largest plurality of any candidate in the country in the 1959 National Assembly elections, he was arrested again and disqualified from taking his seat by a Diem-controlled court.

Until this point, Diem's acts of political repression might have been excused, especially by those who had in mind what they considered the larger strategic interests of the United States, as unfortunate but necessary moves to consolidate his power in a newly formed and factionalized country. But Diem's treatment of an honest, pro-American politician like Dr. Dan was too much for some officials to stomach, and they began to make their distaste for the Ngo family known. Even Wolfe Ladejinsky, the CIA agent who replaced Lansdale as Diem's adviser and who lived in the presidential palace compound, joined with Ambassador Eugene Durbrow to urge Diem to let Dr. Dan take his seat. Diem refused.

Diem's repression of an American favorite, an obvious error to everyone, emboldened the opposition. A few months later, in April 1960, eighteen political figures formed the Bloc for Liberty and Progress and issued a manifesto calling for greater freedoms. The group met at the Caravelle Hotel in the center of Saigon, a modern, overly air-conditioned structure smelling of plastic. Diem and Nhu rejected their petition and contemptuously labeled them "the Caravelle Group," painting them with the mark of the born-again Frenchman. Diem continued to arrest his opponents.

At the same time, the communists were making their first gains on the battlefield. In early 1960, they attacked a regimental headquarters of the Saigon army. The Ho Chi Minh Trail was opened, and some of the ninety thousand southern communists who had gone north in 1954 began to reinfiltrate into South Vietnam. A month after the

Caravelle Group made public the political divisions that existed in Saigon, Hanoi's Central Committee decided the time had come to get rid of Diem and take over the country. The National Liberation Front was formed at the end of the same year, on December 19, 1960, made up in part of nationalists, as the Viet Minh had been, but controlled by the communists.

The convergence of these two factors—Diem's political repression and communist gains in the countryside—set the American bureaucracy to squabbling in Saigon. It pitted some of the civilians, who thought a change of tactics was needed, against the military advisory group, who thought everything was going fine and resented civilian interference in their area of expertise.

Ambassador Eugene Durbrow believed that either Diem had to change his political ways or the United States should look for a replacement. He asked to be allowed to take a hard line, and the State Department agreed. Durbrow met with Diem, urged him to undertake political reforms, and recommended that he pack his brother Nhu and one of his chief henchmen off on a diplomatic mission. Diem reacted coolly to Durbrow's suggestions for reforms and dismissed the idea that he separate himself from his brother.

The lid had been kept on the Saigon military since Lansdale smothered the Hinh coup attempt. None of the generals wanted to go out on a limb without American support. But as it became clear that some Americans were dissatisfied with Diem and that the Saigon politicians were against him, one of the most impetuous of the Vietnamese military officers decided to take matters into his own hands. Airborne Colonel Nguyen Chanh Thi had served as a corporal under the French but did not qualify as a born-again Frenchman. From a poor farm family, courageous, and personable, Thi was authentically Vietnamese. Thi's problem was that he had more guts than brains.

At 3:30 A.M., November 11, 1960, Colonel Thi began his attack on the presidential palace. Ngo Dinh Diem was having a sleepless night and had risen to get a soft drink from his bedroom refrigerator when the firing broke out, saving him from being killed by the machine-gun bullet that skimmed over his bed and slammed into the wall. William Colby's house, one block away, was hit by stray bullets. Colby got his wife and children under the stairwell, the safest place in the house, and walked after sunrise nearly a mile to the embassy.

Lansdale's idea of training a presidential guard showed results. The bodyguards, numbering only sixty men, held off a battalion of paratroopers. When the fight bogged down, Diem used the time to try to muster support among his army commanders outside Saigon, working the telephones. Colby put two of his men with the rebel forces, George Carver, a thirty-year-old operative who disliked Diem, and Russ Miller, a former World War Two paratrooper. Carver dealt with the rebel leadership, while Miller handled the military end.

Some station chiefs tried to bypass their ambassador, but Colby wasn't one of them. "Ambassador Durbrow's position was that we would not sign up in support of Diem," Colby said. "I thought he made a mistake, but he was the ambassador." Durbrow, a gravel-voiced foreign service professional, talked to Diem on the phone while the coup attempt was in progress and told him the United States intended to maintain an even-handed approach and encourage both sides to negotiate. Durbrow instructed Colby to have his two men, Carver and Miller, persuade the rebels to negotiate. George Carver, who wanted Diem overthrown, argued with Colby, who replied, "George, I know your position. I don't agree with you, and we haven't got time to discuss it now." Miller followed orders without comment.

The coup bogged down. Realizing that American support was being withheld, Colonel Thi's rebels agreed to negotiate. Diem pretended to work out an agreement with them, stalling for time until his loyalist troops could reach Saigon. Durbrow saw through Diem's ruse. He telephoned and emphasized that Diem should keep his word and carry out the agreement. Diem promised he would see what he could do. But loyalist troops soon arrived with tanks and dispersed the rebels. Colonel Thi and his fellow coup leaders fled to Cambodia, where they were given asylum.

The failed coup took place a few weeks after Ambassador Durbrow had given Diem what amounted to a dressing down and urged him to get rid of his brother Nhu. As Durbrow later said, "I was pretty damn tough on him. He didn't like a goddamned word I said." Diem and Nhu, not unreasonably from their point of view, concluded that the Americans had encouraged the coup. If more proof were needed besides Durbrow's cool attitude during the fight, there was the presence of George Carver and Russ Miller with the rebel leadership. Hurt and angry, Diem and Nhu wanted to retaliate for this presumed breach of faith. But their dependence upon the United States was too great for anything other than a symbolic showing of their displeasure, and for this, George Carver was chosen. When William Colby met Nhu after the coup attempt, Nhu said he knew Carver had encouraged the rebels, and he hinted that relations between the two countries would be improved by Carver's departure from Vietnam.

Carver was under cover as an aid worker, and Colby denied his connection with the CIA, knowing that Nhu didn't believe him. Anyway, Colby added, Carver had served as a reporter for the embassy, not as an inciter of the coup. A few days later, Carver received a threatening note purported to be from the failed rebels, accusing him of betraying them. Colby believed the threat was Nhu's handiwork and saw in it a way to break the impasse. Colby took the note to Nhu and said, "One of our officers has had this terrible threat from the people who used to be in the rebellion. We've decided to move him and his family out of the country." George Carver, who later became a Vietnam specialist at CIA headquarters, left Saigon. "Everybody's face was saved," said Colby.

Diem and Nhu turned their fury on the Saigon politicians who supported the rebels. The luckless Dr. Phan Quang Dan, who had thrown in with them, was arrested and imprisoned once more, as were members of the Caravelle Group, who were agitating for Diem's removal.

As these events were taking place, little noticed by the public in the United States, whose attention was focused on the election of John F. Kennedy, Ed Lansdale decided to reinsert himself into the controversy. Now a brigadier general, Lansdale was working in the Pentagon's Office of Special Operations, the military contact point for covert work involving the Central Intelligence Agency. Lansdale had two CIA officers on his staff who served as a liaison between the two organizations. Lansdale was interested in taking a fresh look at Vietnam. He was also anxious to remove himself from Washington and any connection with the operation the CIA was planning to launch against Fidel Castro's Cuba. Lansdale, the political action specialist, believed the Bay of Pigs invasion was going to turn into a disaster, and he didn't want his fingerprints to show up on the planning in the aftermath. Besides, a change of administrations always offered possibilities to the ambitious, and Lansdale's interest in influencing Vietnam policy had not diminished. On his own initiative, he scheduled a trip to Saigon during the first two weeks of 1961.

When Colby's station heard Lansdale was on the way, some CIA officers assumed he was coming to make a grab for a larger share of intelligence operations on behalf of the Pentagon. Nevertheless, Colby laid on a detailed briefing for Lansdale, concealing nothing. Colby believed the briefing went badly and wrote in his memoirs that

Lansdale "obviously thought he was being subjected to some form of shell game and hardly said a word during the whole evening." Colby was wrong. According to Lansdale, and as confirmed by Joe Redick, who came from Laos to attend the briefing, he was impressed by Colby and his station. "To my mind," Lansdale said, "William Colby was the best they had."

In fact, after talking to Diem, Lansdale had his harpoon out for bigger fish than Colby's station. Lansdale wanted to get Ambassador Durbrow fired. He believed that Durbrow's actions during the failed coup had ended his effectiveness with Diem. Lansdale thought there was a pressing need to give the ambassador's job to someone who had a special sensitivity for dealing with the Vietnamese—someone like himself, for instance. Lansdale returned to Washington and wrote a sky-is-falling memo, saying that Vietnam needed "emergency treatment."

The Lansdale memo wound up on the desk of the new president, who read it with concern. In one of the first major meetings after his inauguration, John Kennedy scheduled back-to-back discussions on Cuba and Vietnam and asked that Lansdale attend. McGeorge Bundy, Kennedy's national security adviser, sent a memo to Secretary of State Dean Rusk, Secretary of Defense Robert McNamara, and CIA director Allen Dulles, saying, "The president's interest in Cuba needs little explanation. His concern for Vietnam is a result of his keen interest in General Lansdale's recent report and his awareness of the high importance of this country." At the meeting, which took place on January 28, 1961, Kennedy and his advisers discussed a new counterinsurgency plan for Vietnam. Kennedy approved the plan two days later, writing on the flyleaf, "Why so little?"

During the meeting, Kennedy turned to Lansdale and said, "Did Dean tell you I want you to go to Vietnam as ambassador?"

"No, he didn't," said Lansdale.

Lansdale wondered if Kennedy was making a serious job offer. But he never had time to find out. The bureaucracy heard of Kennedy's comment and mobilized to kill the appointment. The assistant secretary of state with responsibility for Vietnam went to Dean Rusk and made his opposition known, asking Rusk whether the United States' image might not suffer if the well-known CIA operative was put in such a prominent ambassadorial position. More of Lansdale's enemies emerged from the Pentagon and other agencies brandishing ice picks. Nothing more was said about his going to Saigon. Kennedy did take his advice about removing Durbrow, however, and two months later Frederick Nolting, another foreign service professional, was appointed as ambassador.

Ed Lansdale became Robert McNamara's assistant for special operations. The job potentially offered him a great deal of influence in formulating Vietnam policy, but his dislike of bureaucracy had become almost obsessional by this time, and he continued to make enemies left and right. Chairing the Vietnam task force, he opened a meeting by announcing to State Department officials: "We will begin with a ten-minute session for you to say what a dirty bum I am." Lansdale was unable to develop a good working relationship with his boss, Robert McNamara. Returning from Vietnam, he went to McNamara's office to brief him on his trip, carrying some Viet Cong weapons he'd collected to start a museum of guerrilla warfare at Fort Bragg.

"He told me on the phone that I had five minutes to give him a briefing on Vietnam," Lansdale said. "I went in and he was sitting at his desk, and I put all these dirty weapons down—crude looking, and including those big spikes that they had as punji stakes, with dried blood and mud on them. I put them on this beautiful mahogany desk—I just dumped them on that. I said, 'The enemy in Vietnam used these weapons, and they were just using them a little bit ago before I got them. The enemy are barefoot and wear sandals. They wear black pajamas, usually, with tatters or holes in them. I don't think you'd recognize any of them as soldiers, but they think of themselves that way. . . . Always keep in mind about Vietnam, that the struggle goes far beyond the material things in life. It doesn't take weapons and uniforms and lots of food to win. It takes something else, ideas and ideals, and these guys are using that something else. Let's at least learn that lesson.' Somehow I found him very hard to talk to. Watching his face as I talked, I got the feeling he didn't understand me."

General Maxwell Taylor believed he understood Lansdale too well. Taylor, who was Kennedy's personal representative, had about as much in common with Lansdale as did J. Lawton Collins, who was Eisenhower's personal representative during Lansdale's first tour in Vietnam. Taylor had been called out of retirement three days after the Bay of Pigs debacle to report on what had gone wrong. Taylor, who had commanded the 101st Airborne Division at its near disaster in Normandy during World War Two, enjoyed a reputation as the military's guy who jumped out of airplanes and spoke several languages, and was presumably, in Kennedy's view, just the officer to investigate the failures of the CIA's men of the same type. Kennedy was influenced by Maxwell Taylor's book, *The Uncertain Trumpet,* published the year he was elected, which attacked the Eisenhower administration's defense policies of relying on the strategy of massive nuclear retaliation and called for a doctrine of flexible response. Taylor's book had no apparent connection to Vietnam, however, and over time he would show no greater facility for dealing with the problem than had General Collins. But he did share Collins's distaste for Ed Lansdale.

"Lansdale was an idea man," Maxwell Taylor said, "and he could turn out ideas faster than you could pick them up off the floor, but I was never impressed with their feasibility."

Nevertheless, Max Taylor had to treat with Ed Lansdale. For if Taylor's stock had gone up with the Kennedys as a result of the Bay of Pigs fiasco, so had Lansdale's. Jack Kennedy and his brother Robert were impressed that Lansdale had opposed the operation and had distanced himself in such a way that he was not implicated in Taylor's investigation, which caused CIA director Allen Dulles and others to lose their jobs. So when Kennedy dispatched Maxwell Taylor on an important mission to Saigon on October 15, 1961, Lansdale was also on board. Taylor was determined to keep Lansdale from stealing his show, and told him before they landed that he would not be among the mission members visiting Diem.

"Well, I'm an old friend of Diem's," Lansdale said. "I can't go to Vietnam without seeing him. I'll probably see him alone. Is there anything you want me to ask him?"

Max Taylor, like Lightning Joe Collins before him, was exasperated beyond words with Lansdale and refused to discuss the matter further. Diem's secretary was at the airport to greet the delegation, and he invited Lansdale to dinner at the palace. While Taylor was talking to reporters, Lansdale told White House assistant Walt Rostow about the invitation and slipped away. Lansdale was surprised by how assertive Nhu had become since he had last seen the two brothers. Nhu frequently answered for his brother, causing Lansdale to ask Diem, "Can't the two of us talk together? Your brother can be in on this, but is he running things or are you?" The question obviously had no clear answer.

The next day Maxwell Taylor and Walt Rostow met with Diem, who ambiguously circled the question of bringing in American troops, leaving Taylor with the impression that Diem wanted a defense treaty and preparations for the introduction of combat forces. Taylor himself was persuaded of the need to put more Americans in the country, which he thought might be done, at low political risk, under the ruse of sending a flood relief task force composed of logistical and engineering units, as well as combat troops. Taylor conceded that his proposal had disadvantages, but concluded: "The risks of backing into a major land war by way of SVN are present but not impressive. NVN is extremely vulnerable to conventional bombing, a weakness which should be exploited diplomatically in convincing Hanoi to lay off SVN."

President Kennedy was not enthusiastic about Maxwell Taylor's recommendations to send combat forces. He was more impressed by Lansdale's ideas about political action—but not in terms of Vietnam. Kennedy, who had developed his own obsession, was interested in seeing if Lansdale could use his techniques to get rid of Fidel Castro, something Lansdale had accurately predicted couldn't be accomplished by military action alone. After the meeting in which the Taylor mission presented its report, Kennedy pulled Lansdale aside and told him, "Drop everything else you're doing. I want you to work on Cuba"—removing from the policy-making scene the one man in Washington who fearlessly opposed an increased conventional military presence in Vietnam, and also removing perhaps the only man who could have turned Diem, who was now under growing attack from a small group of young American journalists, away from some of his damaging policies.

12

SAIGON 1963

DAVID HALBERSTAM, whatever his faults, was never accused of being excessively subtle. The night he arrived in Saigon in 1962 he attended a going-away party for *Newsweek*'s François Sully, a Frenchman who was being kicked out of the country for offending Madame Nhu. "The most striking quality about that gathering," Halberstam recalled, "was an atmosphere which reminded me strongly of my working days as a reporter in Mississippi: we all seemed to be outsiders. There was no one there from the mainstream of the American embassy or the American military mission—just as in Mississippi comparable gatherings of reporters never included the leaders of the Chamber of Commerce, the mayor or a local legislator." Halberstam quickly got the feeling that Saigon was another case of reporters versus rednecks. This seemed to be verified when he talked to officials at the American embassy and discovered, he wrote in *The Making of a Quagmire,* that "they were not a bit unhappy to see François go. He was, as one of the highest embassy officials at the time told me, just a *pied noir,* a derogatory phrase implying that he was something of a half-breed."

Actually *pied noir* didn't mean that at all. The American official was really implying that François Sully was a redneck and that embassy staffers were the good guys. Halberstam's misinterpretation, though, of what itself was a misinterpretation by the official, was symbolic of the situation that existed between the press and the American mission, with both sides considering the other the redneck, and neither side understanding very clearly what it was trying to define. With *pied noir* (black foot) meaning a Frenchman who was born in Algeria—his foot in Africa, so to speak—one could be a *pied noir* and a redneck, or a *pied noir* and a Nobel Prize winner like Albert Camus.

The press, in this case, measured in terms of influence in the United States, mainly consisted of three reporters—Halberstam of the *New York Times,* Malcolm Browne of the Associated Press, and Neil Sheehan of United Press International. They were relatively young—Halberstam and Sheehan were in their mid-twenties, Browne a little older—and largely untested. How three young reporters came to play such a major role in the evolution of the Vietnam War could be attributed to one of the quirks of the trade. In the business world, assignments fraught with financial danger and needing considered judgment were usually handled by older, seasoned executives. But in journalism the reverse was often true. Reporting a fast-breaking story involving personal hardships and separation from families called for the kind of energy and enterprise that a journalist over forty could seldom muster.

Few young reporters, however, ever had as much power to influence events as did Halberstam, Browne, and Sheehan. Until they arrived, the story had been covered by the over-forties from their bureaus in Hong Kong and other settled places, or by locals like François Sully, who had lived in Vietnam for seventeen years and who started as a part-time reporter. The old Asia hands would fly to Saigon, interview their contacts at the American embassy and among Vietnamese politicians, and return home to write their stories in tranquil surroundings. The visiting journalist was not liable to become personally involved with the story, and his work usually reflected the viewpoint of the American embassy officials who were his chief contacts and, in effect, his bread and butter. But after Colonel Nguyen Chanh Thi's aborted 1960 coup, followed five months later by the Bay of Pigs disaster in Cuba, interest in Vietnam stirred the journalism establishment to open Saigon bureaus with regular staffers.

If Halberstam, Browne, and Sheehan were young, they also had unusually good academic credentials for three reporters assigned to cover what was still considered a backwater story. David Halberstam graduated from Harvard, where he was managing editor of the *Crimson;* Neil Sheehan had also gone to Harvard, on an academic scholarship; Malcolm Browne attended Swarthmore. They were, in a sense, the best and the brightest of the young American reporters in Saigon, and they had great confidence in what they were doing, the most can-do of reporters who were seldom anything but enthusiastic—and all realized they would be replaced, their careers stymied, if they failed to nail the coonskin to the wall: *A Damn Good Story.*

By virtue of the fact that the Associated Press serviced most of the daily newspapers in America, Malcolm Browne, who was personally though not professionally shy, with an idiosyncratic dressing style, preferring bright red socks to go with his limp khaki slacks, should have held the top position of influence. Second place should have belonged to the other wire service reporter, Neil Sheehan, an affable Irishman who projected an air of distraction that made him seem vaguely off-key. In reality, though, it was David Halberstam who dominated the threesome.

David Halberstam arrived in Saigon at a confluent moment in the history of the war and the *New York Times.* John F. Kennedy had rejected Maxwell Taylor's recommendations on introducing combat troops, but had given the go-ahead to increase military aid in a piece-meal fashion, providing the Vietnamese with thirty or so banana-shaped CH-21 helicopters and pilots to ferry them into combat, along with a few aging fighter-bombers for air support. To handle the buildup, a new military organization was formed—the Military Assistance Command, Vietnam (MACV)—with General Paul Harkins as its head, a few months before Halberstam arrived.

At the same moment, the *New York Times* was approaching the height of its influence, owing to a ripple effect that washed over to the television networks, which were expanding their news coverage. Several years later, the situation would begin to reverse itself, and it would become not uncommon to see *Times* reporters huddled around the tube, taking notes. But when Halberstam arrived in Saigon, it was the *Times* that greatly helped set the news agenda for the networks, and thus for America. If the men who had their hands on America's communications levers did not exactly believe the *Times* emanated from a burning bush, they did treat it with the utmost respect as the country's newspaper of record.

In David Halberstam, the *Times* had a reporter who was not afraid to set his own agenda. Well over six feet tall, with a broad-shouldered angularity that made him seem even taller, the bespectacled Halberstam was capable and energetic. While the average journalist was distinctly not meek, Halberstam was propelled by an ego as bright as a strobe light. He had talked his way into the Vietnam assignment after reporting from the Congo and was not easily intimidated by anyone. He set out to cover the Vietnam story with complete independence.

The thrust of Halberstam's reporting, and that of Browne and Sheehan, was not antiwar by any means. Basically what they were saying was that the fight was going badly. In fact, they were exercising the critical function of modern journalism, which held the implicit belief that anything going well did not merit much reporting. This brought them into intellectual conflict with men like William Colby and Stuart Methven, who were equally as well-educated and knew as much about Vietnam as the journalists, and who believed, despite all the problems, that the fight against the communists was progressing, and that too much criticism might turn into self-fulfilling prophecy. Reduced to the essentials, whether the war was going well or not at this point was a matter of interpretation, since facts could be accumulated to support either point of view. But the point of view that was going to receive the widest attention, as all but the most naïve knew, was that of the journalists.

It was in this atmosphere that government officials launched a campaign to discredit the reporting of Halberstam, Browne, and Sheehan. The easiest charge made against them was that they were young and inexperienced and "trying to make a name for themselves," which, of course, they were. No one would have questioned a young businessman's ambition to make money, and making a name for oneself was the journalistic equivalent of making money and should have carried no implication of a lack of integrity on the part of the reporters, as government officials clearly intended.

More infuriating, as the newsmen saw it, was the campaign that was begun to call into question their courage. Taking the lead from Ngo Dinh Diem, who had earlier ridiculed his opposition as "the Caravelle Group," embassy and military officials suggested that reporters got their stories in the ninth-floor bar of the Caravelle Hotel, from the French-tainted Vietnamese who hung out there, and that they seldom ventured to the countryside, where they might find themselves in harm's way. The theme was picked up by older visiting newsmen such as Washington columnist Joe Alsop and relayed to journalists back home.

Being a reporter in a war and having the military cast aspersions on your courage was like being a piano player in a brothel and having the girls suggest you were impotent, with all the winks and smirks that involved. The fear of being so labeled drove some reporters to take such chances that they wound up in body bags, thereby making the point moot; and few journalists, no matter how self-assured, took the question of courage lightly. The matter finally reached a head when *Time* magazine, directed by its hawkish managing editor Otto Fuerbringer, ran a press story supporting the Caravelle charge against the reporters, prompting *Time*'s own correspondent in Saigon, Charles Mohr, along with another friend of Halberstam's, to quit in protest. Mohr was not against the war; in fact, he continued to believe, long after many of his colleagues had changed their minds, that the cause was just. As his resignation from *Time* indicated, the vicious fight going on between the press and the mission cut across ideological lines.

In David Halberstam's case, the word was passed that he had actually cried on an operation when he saw dead bodies, presumably the ultimate put-down from the military point of view. Halberstam, an urban Jew who had already covered two reportorial macho stories—civil rights in the South and the war in the Congo—might not be expected to take such aspersions lying down—and he didn't. For every charge made against him, he reported the story ever more aggressively, and he wore it as a badge of honor when John F. Kennedy asked the *New York Times* publisher to transfer him out of Saigon, which the *Times* refused to do.

"We all personalized the struggle," Neil Sheehan recalled. "But Halberstam personalized it more than anyone else."

There was truth to the charge that the reporters spent an inordinate amount of time in Saigon and not in the countryside, where the war was going on. That had to do, at least in part, with the nature of the conflict. In World War Two and Korea, newsmen had been assigned to major American units and left there. They were bound to be in on the action. But how did one cover a guerrilla war that was fought with sporadic incidents? It was a question that reporters would be asking long after Halberstam was gone. Moreover, newsmen covering the war in the early days were without the helicopters and planes for ferrying journalists around the country that accompanied the big buildup in 1965 and were left to their own means of securing transportation. Sensitive to the charge that they were not getting out of Saigon, which government officials suggested was due to cowardice, and forced to fend for themselves on matters of transportation in a country without much transportation, the Saigon reporters hit on their own expedient.

"In those early days of my Vietnam assignment I was trying to decide how to evaluate this perplexing war," David Halberstam recalled in *The Making of a Quagmire*. "How do you add up thirty minor engagements each day, almost all of them in places you've never been to, and with no substantive information to cast light on the significance of the situation? It was very quickly obvious to me that the story could not be covered from Saigon briefing rooms, despite all the multicolored arrows on the maps. The Seventh Division struck me as being as good a litmus paper of the war as any: the problems were all there, the Government had a fair chance and it was unlikely that things could go badly there and well elsewhere, or vice versa. Besides, My Tho, the division headquarters, was only forty miles south of Saigon on a good road, and we reporters could drive down, talk with friends and participate in operations."

The American adviser to the Seventh Division was Lieutenant Colonel John Paul Vann. So it was almost a coincidence derived from the technical difficulties of covering the war and the need, both personal and professional, to get out of Saigon that the young reporters, especially David Halberstam and Neil Sheehan, fell under the influence of Vann, one of the bravest and smartest men to serve in the war. John Vann was as close to an Ed Lansdale as the army produced, and he had the same fearlessness in seeking to promote his point of view. But whereas Lansdale was relatively closemouthed with the press, John Vann was determined to use newsmen as his weapon against the bureaucracy.

And what John Paul Vann had to say made a damn good story. Almost alone of the military careerists, Vann contended that the war was being fought badly and as a consequence being lost. Like Ed Lansdale, John Vann believed totally in the justness of the cause. He was probably more conservative than Lansdale and certainly less flexible. Vann simply wanted to change tactics and policies to conform with his own ideas—good ideas, indeed—about how the war could be won. The Saigon reporters made sure he was heard loud and clear, which drove General Paul Harkins, the commander of MACV and the jut-jawed picture of can-do optimism, up the wall. In journalistic terms, as always, by the nature of a business that responds to salients and not subtleties, the key point of Vann's thinking reflected by the newsmen was *things were going badly,* not *things had to change.*

Six months after he arrived in Saigon, David Halberstam was one of several reporters who got together over lunch with Senator Mike

Mansfield, who was on a fact-finding trip, to give him an informal briefing on how they saw the situation. "Mike already had his doubts," Halberstam recalled, "and, of course, by then we were all very, very discouraged and pessimistic and we had become the enemies of the mission and of the regime. . . ."

Several weeks later, on January 2, 1963, a battle occurred that the newsmen covered with all the resources at their command. It involved John Paul Vann and the division he advised. The operation began as an attempt to knock out a communist radio transmitter and what was thought to be a company-sized force guarding it. From the moment the first helicopters took off, everything went wrong. The communists apparently had been tipped off and were waiting in battalion strength, armed with heavy machine guns and mortars. John Vann displayed his usual courage, but the battle of Ap Bac was lost and five helicopters were downed, three Americans killed, largely because of the incompetence and cowardly behavior of Saigon army officers who were supposedly leading the operation.

Major General Charles Timmes arrived at the scene with his boss, General Paul Harkins, about the same time as newsmen from Saigon. Timmes, a gentle man who had jumped into Normandy with the 82nd, liked John Vann, whom he considered "sometimes brave beyond good sense, but highly effective." Harkins was already outraged by critical comments in the press that could be traced to Vann.

"The difficulty at Ap Bac," Charles Timmes said, "began when Vann yelled to Harkins when he saw him, 'Those bastards didn't fight worth a ————.' He was very critical that the Vietnamese were cowards. A lot of press people were around when Vann yelled this out, and they heard him. Harkins, as I recall, relieved him. He was going to send him back to the States. I said, 'Don't do that. It will give you a black eye with the press. Let me take care of this.' I made Vann my special assistant, and sent him around the country. He left not long afterward and then resigned from the army."

The battle of Ap Bac, examined in isolation, was militarily significant and indicated the serious problems facing the Saigon army, with the Viet Cong now standing and fighting in battalion strength. But it didn't necessarily signal the end of the world. Nevertheless, the press portrayed the battle as being truly earthshaking, not in small part because it involved John Vann, who was ready to speak his mind about it to reporters like David Halberstam and Neil Sheehan, to whom he had become a hero. The newsmen believed they had found ultimate proof of how ineffective were Diem's forces and thus Diem himself. In a biography of Vann written many years later, Neil Sheehan all but admitted as much. "Ap Bac was a big picture that discredited the big picture [General] Harkins and [Ambassador] Nolting were projecting," Sheehan wrote. "We exploited the battle as much as we dared for this reason, and when Vann, out of his anger and a shared interest, tacitly offered an alliance afterward, we entered it eagerly."

The newsmen were made all the more determined to advance their view after the press conference held by General Paul Harkins and Admiral Harry Felt, Harkins's superior from Honolulu. Harkins looked the newsmen in the eye and called Ap Bac a victory for the Saigon army. But Harkins's fatuity was merely banderillas to the bull. It was left to Admiral Felt to act as the picador. He urged the newsmen, particularly Malcolm Browne, "to get on the team." That exhortation, as it continued to reverberate among journalists in Saigon over the years, lost none of its power to enrage, which probably bewildered Admiral Felt, who was simply asking the newsmen to return to the way it used to be in the old days.

After Ap Bac, the focus of the story shifted to the political situation, the Buddhist crisis, and a critical examination of Diem's policies, deepening the feud between the reporters and the American mission, which had become bitterly personal. It was the Buddhist crisis that brought Diem down, and Neil Sheehan had a few candid words about the role the press played. "Halberstam and I and the other correspondents had seized on the Buddhist crisis as we had on Ap Bac," he said. "We had been holding it up as proof that the regime was as bankrupt politically as it was militarily."

Barry Zorthian, a government official generally liked and respected by reporters, who was later brought in to smooth relations between the press and the mission, believed that the newsmen were closer to the truth in describing the situation than were the embassy and the military. But Zorthian believed too that Halberstam, Browne, and Sheehan played what amounted to an extrajournalistic role in the destruction of the Diem regime—which almost every government official, including some who forgot how they felt about Diem at the time, came to regard as the crucial error of the war.

"They were characters in the story," Zorthian said. "They were so involved and so intense about it that they became, if you will, actors on the stage. I don't mean to say they did that maliciously. They almost were dragged into it, almost forced into it."

MIKE DUNN HAD SPENT more time in school at the army's expense than any officer in the Pentagon. Dunn, who graduated from Harvard, attended Yale, MIT, and Cornell, and took a Ph.D. in political science from Princeton. After he left Princeton, a lieutenant colonel, he was assigned to the office of the army chief of staff. One of his jobs was to brief Henry Cabot Lodge, a reserve major general who came to the Pentagon every summer, as Dunn put it, "to refurbish his skills and impart wisdom to segments of the general staff." Lodge had been a United States senator, a delegate to the United Nations, and the Republican vice presidential candidate in 1960.

Mike Dunn and Henry Cabot Lodge were from the same state, Massachusetts, but from entirely different social worlds. Dunn, a darkly handsome man of medium height who was blunt-spoken and quick with a wisecrack, affected the manner of an Irish pub crawler and talked in accents far from patrician, as though determined, whatever success life brought, not to forget where he came from; and that, mixed with the educated intelligence and obvious sophistication, made for an interesting personality that evidently appealed to Henry Cabot Lodge. Lodge hated to be bored, and whatever might be said about Mike Dunn, he was seldom boring. So when Lodge became the new ambassador in Saigon, replacing the foreign service professional Frederick Nolting, he asked Mike Dunn to go with him. Lodge said that if Dunn accepted he would arrange his transfer to the foreign service, with a salary equivalent to that of a lieutenant general.

Mike Dunn believed that Henry Cabot Lodge, who had earlier made his availability known to President Kennedy, got his job, at least in part, through the *New York Times*. "Halberstam, Sheehan, and Browne just didn't report what was going on over there," Dunn said. "They influenced it in mark and measure. And they influenced Lodge's appointment." Dunn believed that Kennedy and his aides thought they could deflect some of the press-inspired criticism of the war that was growing in the Congress by making a political appointment of Lodge, a national Republican figure, as ambassador and portraying the war as a bipartisan effort.

The precipitating events that brought Henry Cabot Lodge to Saigon in August 1963 began when Vietnam's Buddhists joined the ranks of the dissatisfied and launched antigovernment demonstrations. The controversy started in Hue, Diem's hometown, over a question of whether Buddhists could fly their religious flags to celebrate Buddha's birthday. Diem said no. The Buddhist action caught everybody by surprise. Never in the country's modern history had Buddhist monks played a political role. As seen from Washington, the crisis appeared to have stunning implications. Kennedy had fought a domestic religious issue to win his election to the presidency, and now it seemed that his Catholic client in Saigon had made an enemy of all the country's other religious adherents. For Vietnam was a Buddhist country, wasn't it? That made it sound as though Diem was like a Catholic in America who was opposed by every Baptist, Methodist, Presbyterian, Episcopalian, Lutheran, Mormon, Jew, and Moslem. Diem, on the other hand, was treating the Buddhists as though they were just another dissident sect like the Cao Dai or Hoa Hao, with which he would have to deal firmly.

Neither Washington nor Diem had a grasp of the situation—nor, as it turned out, did the journalists. While the Buddhists as a religious group had undeniable grievances, they were not the monolithic force they appeared to be and were portrayed as by the press. Diem knew his country and undoubtedly realized this. What he failed to credit was the Buddhist monks' ability to mobilize and channel the general discontent of an impoverished country at war to make it appear to be a religious uprising. In retrospect, "the Buddhists" really meant a few monks who started out with legitimate grievances and turned them into an attempt to grab political power, without having any specific program. They were typified by one of the leading monks, Tri Quang, an instigator of the first demonstrations against Diem, who was taken seriously for years by journalists and embassy officials and who, besides revealing himself to be a political agitator with delusions of grandeur, made no sense at all. Tri Quang's success floated on American cultural ignorance: he was able to cloak his incoherent political ideas, vaguely founded on neutralist and third force principles, with a gobbledegook that was taken for Buddhist mysticism—and therefore

Tran Ngoc Chau shortly before
he was arrested and dragged
from the National Assembly,
February 26, 1970. *Courtesy
Tran Ngoc Chau.*

Chau's brother, Tran
Ngoc Hien. A communist
intelligence officer, Hien
tried to open communi-
cations with the U.S.
ambassador in Saigon
on behalf of the National
Liberation Front in 1965
but was turned down.

Tran Ngoc Chau
after his arrest. South
Vietnam president
Nguyen Van Thieu
accused Chau of being
a communist spy for
seeing his brother Hien.
UPI.

Edward G. Lansdale and South
Vietnam president Ngo Dinh Diem.
The CIA dispatched Lansdale to
Saigon in 1954 after the French
defeat and he became Diem's
adviser. *Courtesy Pat Lansdale.*

THE TWO FACES OF PACIFICATION

ABOVE. Rufus Phillips, a member of Edward Lansdale's CIA team, accompanies Vietnamese farmers on the first American-backed pacification operation—September 1954. *Courtesy Rufus Phillips.*

BELOW. Thirteen years later, in 1967, Vietnamese farmers are forced from their homes by an American soldier during a massive U.S. military operation. *Dana Stone.*

Ed Lansdale in action with the Vietnamese. *Courtesy Pat Lansdale.*

Pat Yapcinco Kelly and Madame Nhu at Vung Tau in 1956. Ms. Kelly married her longtime friend Edward Lansdale nearly twenty years later.

President Ngo Dinh Diem and CIA station
chief William Colby. Edward Lansdale called
Colby "the most effective" American to serve
in the Vietnam War. *Courtesy William Colby.*

Ambassador Henry
Cabot Lodge. CIA man
Colby considered Lodge
a "disaster" as Saigon
ambassador.

Henry Cabot Lodge and
his chief of staff, Mike
Dunn. *Courtesy John
Michael Dunn.*

Ngo Dinh Diem on a Lansdale-inspired trip to the countryside. *Courtesy Rufus Phillips.*

Diem (right) and his brother Nhu were murdered during an American-backed coup in 1963. *UPI.*

Rufus Phillips and Stuart Methven—Laos 1959. Methven later became Chau's CIA contact and helped develop counterterror teams used in the Phoenix program. *Courtesy Rufus Phillips.*

Lucien (Lou) Conein in retirement after a long career as a CIA operative. *Brian Smale/1988.*

Edward Lansdale and Barry Zorthian, chief of public information in Saigon. Zorthian believed Lansdale, the political action specialist, became "irrelevant" after the 1965 military buildup. *USIS.*

Barry Zorthian briefing selected newsmen in his Saigon office. Other spokesmen briefed the entire press corps at the daily "Five O'Clock Follies." *Courtesy Barry Zorthian.*

David Halberstam, Malcolm Browne, and Neil Sheehan were accused by some government officials of playing an extrajournalistic role in the destruction of the Diem regime. *Life.*

Robert Shaplen, Keyes Beech, George McArthur, and Wendell (Bud) Merick were considered the old hands of the Saigon press corps and had the best contacts at the U.S. embassy and CIA. *Courtesy George McArthur.*

Ambassador Ellsworth Bunker
and South Vietnam president
Nguyen Van Thieu.
(Background, center) John
Hart, Edward Lansdale, Barry
Zorthian. *USIS.*

ham Xuan An and Nguyen
ung Vuong, circa 1955, when
ey worked for Lansdale's
IA team. An, later a *Time*
rrespondent, admitted after
e war he was a Viet Cong
lonel and communist spy all
ong. *Courtesy Rufus Phillips.*

Theodore (Ted)
Shackley, nicknamed
"the blond ghost," ran
the CIA's secret war in
Laos and then was
assigned to Saigon.

Daniel Ellsberg with wife, Patricia Marx, after revealing that he gave the *New York Times* the secret Pentagon Papers. *New York Times.*

Tran Ngoc Chau with wife, Bich Nhan, and their children, circa 1963, when he was governor of Kien Hoa province.

John Paul Vann, pacification expert and, along with Edward Lansdale, the most controversial American to serve in Vietnam. Vann got many of his pacification ideas from his friend, Tran Ngoc Chau. *Dick Swanson.*

Tran Ngoc Chau in 1980
after he escaped from
Vietnam by boat. *Neil
Sheehan/New York
Times.*

Zalin Grant (author) in
Cambodia at the time of
the American invasion,
May 1970.

worthy, Americans thought, of respect and consideration. This had the effect of increasing his influence with the Vietnamese, who took seriously anyone the Americans took seriously.

The only thing clear at the time, however, was that Diem was handling the situation badly. The embassy leaned on him to negotiate with the monks, and some headway was being made until Madame Nhu, who was never able to keep her mouth shut, issued a resolution denouncing Buddhist leaders as communist dupes. Four days later, on June 11, 1963, the Buddhists pulled one of the most dramatic publicity stunts in history, outmaneuvering Diem. After phoning American newsmen that something interesting was going to happen at a busy Saigon intersection, two monks drenched a third, the seventy-three-year-old Quang Duc, with gasoline, whereupon he assumed the lotus position and lit a match. In case anyone missed the point, a monk intoned over a public address system, in English: "A Buddhist monk burns himself to death. A Buddhist monk becomes a martyr." Malcolm Browne of the Associated Press was there to take the photographs that appeared around the world. Madame Nhu dismissed it as a "barbecue." Washington reacted by ordering the embassy to threaten Diem that if he didn't meet the monks' demands, the United States would publicly disassociate itself from his Buddhist policy. Diem knew that would be an open invitation for his enemies to mount a coup d'état, and he signed a compromise with the Buddhists.

The crisis had gone too far, though. The Buddhist movement was increasingly dominated by younger and more radical monks, and it was doubtful that Viet Cong operatives were looking on with disinterest. The Buddhists continued to agitate, and Diem, under the influence of his brother and sister-in-law, became more intractable. On August 21, 1963, as Henry Cabot Lodge, on his way to Saigon, was meeting in Honolulu with outgoing Ambassador Nolting and Assistant Secretary of State Roger Hilsman, they received word that Diem had ordered an attack on the Buddhist pagodas. At first, it was thought that the raids had been conducted by the Saigon army. But it became known that they were carried out by police and Vietnamese Special Forces units controlled by Nhu.

The pagoda raids, which were scheduled to take place when there was no American ambassador in Saigon, outraged most officials in Washington, but probably none so much as Roger Hilsman, the assistant secretary of state for far eastern affairs. An abrasive intellectual,

Hilsman had fought with American guerrilla units against the Japanese in Burma and thought himself an expert in guerrilla warfare, often recalling his experiences at ho-hum length in meetings. Hilsman had developed a distaste for Ngo Dinh Diem's leadership and was persuaded that if Diem were to continue in office, his brother, at minimum, would have to go. Hilsman had a formidable ally in the person of Averell Harriman, the under secretary of state, who not only shared Hilsman's political assessment, but went further by holding a personal animus for Diem, who had made the mistake of acting imperiously with Harriman, himself a bit imperious, during a trip to Saigon, when Harriman was trying to get the balky Vietnamese to sign the Geneva agreements on Laos.

At any rate, two days after Henry Cabot Lodge reached Saigon, Roger Hilsman and Averell Harriman sent him a cable that was the beginning of the end for Ngo Dinh Diem. There was a certain amount of dodging and ducking after the fact about how the August 24 cable was cleared and who had a hand in drafting it, for the message turned out to be breathtakingly close to a warrant for a coup d'état that led to Diem's murder. It mainly expressed outrage about Diem's brother Nhu. "U.S. Government cannot tolerate situation in which power lies in Nhu's hands," it said in part. "Diem must be given chance to rid himself of Nhu and his coterie and replace them with best military and political personalities available." Then the drop kick: "If, in spite of all your efforts, Diem remains obdurate and refuses, then we must face the possibility that Diem himself cannot be preserved."

The cable caused William Colby to stop what he was doing and fly to the West Coast to brief CIA director John McCone. He and McCone were against any efforts to remove Diem. So were Robert McNamara, the Pentagon, and General Harkins in Saigon. But on lower levels the bureaucracy was split, as were Vietnamese officials. Even Nguyen Dinh Thuan, Diem's chief of staff, was secretly talking to Rufe Phillips about the need to get rid of Nhu.

As William Colby saw it, the biggest shareholder in indecision was John F. Kennedy. "There were pro-Diemists and anti-Diemists in the administration, and too bad to say it but President Kennedy essentially vacillated between the two," Colby said. "He didn't definitively say we're going to follow this line, to do this or that. What he would do was send somebody out to take a look, to bring home a new assessment. That was a way of avoiding a decision. 'Let's get a new assessment.' He couldn't help it, let's face it. If you've got the big guns of the press denouncing your policy out there, you've got to be a little nervous about it."

Two weeks after the Harriman-Hilsman cable was sent to Ambassador Lodge, President Kennedy decided to get a new assessment. He chose as his two reporters one man from each of the bureaucratic camps of pro-Diemists and anti-Diemists. Marine general Victor Krulak, McNamara's choice, not surprisingly, was convinced the war could be won with Diem. Joseph Mendenhall, the Harriman-Hilsman choice, had served in Saigon with Ambassador Durbrow and had become outspokenly disaffected with Diem around the time he kept Dr. Phan Quang Dan from taking his National Assembly seat. Krulak and Mendenhall didn't like each other personally and exchanged no unnecessary words during the trip, which lasted ninety-six hours, including forty-six hours of flight time from Washington to Saigon and back. On September 10, 1963, they presented their findings to President Kennedy and his advisers. Krulak said that militarily things were going well; Mendenhall said that politically things were going to hell. Their briefing offered Kennedy an opportunity for a quip that made the meeting famous: "Did you two gentlemen visit the same country?"

Rufe Phillips spoke after Krulak and Mendenhall were through. He had flown back with them, although not with the intention of briefing Kennedy. His father, ill with cancer, had taken a turn for the worse, and Phillips was making plans to leave Saigon and government service, to be with his dad and assume management of the family business. Mike Forrestal, a Kennedy aide and Harriman protégé whom Phillips stopped by to see, asked him to take part in the briefing at the last moment. Phillips's reporting from Saigon had turned pessimistic, and the Harriman-Hilsman forces probably thought of him as supporting their assessment. Phillips was convinced that Nhu had to be separated from Diem and, in fact, had influenced the Harriman-Hilsman cable to Lodge with a negative cable of his own about Nhu the day before. But Phillips saw the briefing as an opportunity to try to persuade President Kennedy to send Lansdale to Saigon. Diem, who felt misunderstood and isolated from the Americans, had asked Phillips to see if he could arrange for Lansdale to return as his adviser. Phillips took the request to Ambassador Nolting and told him that Diem didn't intend it as a slight to him, but that he simply believed Lansdale could help him in dealing with the Americans. When Lodge arrived, Phillips told him the same thing, and thought he had got Lodge's approval for Lansdale's return.

In his briefing, Phillips told Kennedy that he did not agree with either Krulak or Mendenhall. The military situation was worse than Krulak portrayed it, he said, because Saigon troops had been withdrawn from the countryside to defend Diem against a possible coup attempt and the Viet Cong were moving into the vacuum. The Buddhist problem was serious and undermining the government, he said, but it wasn't the only problem and should be kept in context. The big problem, he thought, was Nhu, and Phillips concluded by telling Kennedy, "I think we should make every effort to save Diem. If we can get Nhu out of the country, we can get some kind of compromise with the Buddhists. And there's only one person I can think of who can do this. That's General Lansdale over in the Pentagon. I recommend that you send him out to Vietnam as soon as possible."

Kennedy said, "Thank you very much. What you've said has been very useful, and I thank you for your recommendations, particularly in regard to General Lansdale."

The news of Rufe Phillips's suggestion that Lansdale be sent to Saigon spread through Washington offices concerned with Vietnam. Lansdale himself heard about it from his own sources within an hour of the meeting. So did his enemies. They emerged once more to kill the idea in the cradle. Instead, two weeks later, President Kennedy decided to get a new assessment. This time he sent a delegation that included Maxwell Taylor and Robert McNamara, plus William Colby, Mike Forrestal, and William Sullivan. The six-day trip was unproductive. Taylor and McNamara found Diem to be distant and, to them, inexplicably serene in the face of the crisis; both officials left with less sympathy for him and his brother than they arrived with. What the trip revealed was that Henry Cabot Lodge had taken over in Saigon and was acting with the assurance of a national political figure who had his own power base and who was not about to tip his hat to anyone but the president. And if Kennedy was not ready to act decisively, the man he had beaten in two major political contests was.

"He turned out to be a shrewd, tough operator, very much a match for the Ngo family," David Halberstam said of Lodge. "He was absolutely single-minded, he worked hard and did his homework, and he had no illusions about the task facing the United States."

"Lodge was a disaster as an ambassador," William Colby said. "He had no concept of running a mission. He was a total lone wolf, and couldn't waste his time on administration. He took an instant dislike to Diem, and considered him out of touch and not a very political animal. Why? I don't know. I really don't. It baffled me."

"I loved Lodge," Mike Dunn said. "I make no bones about it. I don't think there was ever anybody in my life I liked as much. I got very close to him and lived with him in the same house for six or seven months over there. He was a patrician, but that's all right if a guy handles it well, and he did. His ability to laugh at himself was unparalleled in my experience. The thing about Lodge that got him in trouble in Vietnam and kept him, in my judgment, from being vice president of the United States was that he just didn't suffer fools gladly—and he reserved the right to define who was a fool. And he was a little abrupt and not a workaholic either. It's true. I would be the last to deny that. But some of those hard workers over there would have benefited their country and the Western world immensely if they had slowed up.

"I don't think Lodge was anti-Diem from the beginning," Dunn added. "Certainly not anti-Diem to the extent he became. But he saw himself as a practicing politician, not as a diplomat, and he was annoyed that the Ngo Dinh Diem regime couldn't understand they were making grievous political errors, as indeed they were."

To help correct Diem's errors, the practicing politician called upon the talents of a practicing intelligence officer. They made an odd couple, to say the least, Cabot Lodge and Lou Conein.

WHEN WE RETURNED TO VIETNAM in 1961, Saigon was less French and more American. But the food was as good, and all my old friends were still there. The embassy said we would be given an allowance to rent a house. I chose a beautiful villa and sold my mink stole so I could decorate it the way I wanted. Lou was always busy. I knew if I was to spend any time with him, I would have to make sure we had the best food and everything at home so his friends and business contacts would come there. I turned one room into a place for entertaining, designed by a French decorator and done in reds and greens, with a bamboo

*bar as a centerpiece. Then I hired a cook and helper. At the time of
the Diem coup, lots of Vietnamese generals were coming to our house.
Tran Van Don was there; Le Van Kim, a very dear friend of Lou's and a
brilliant officer; also, Ton That Dinh, who was crazy. The Vietnamese
are worse than the French about gossiping, and the talk was about
Madame Nhu. I don't know whether it is because of our French influence,
but the Vietnamese always seemed to make things bigger than they
were.*

LOU CONEIN got into the coup business on July 4, 1963. The leading Vietnamese generals, after attending an American Independence
Day reception at the embassy residence, decided to go to the Caravelle Hotel, and Tran Van Don invited Conein to have a drink with
them. Don was acting chief of staff for the Vietnamese armed forces.
Conein had first met him in Hanoi in 1945, when Don was a lieutenant
in the French army. Don was born in France and held a French passport. Le Van Kim, who happened to be his brother-in-law, was Don's
deputy. Kim also held a French passport. He had worked as an assistant to film director Marcel Pagnol and was about as French as a
Vietnamese could be and still have almond-shaped eyes and yellow
skin. He was a courteous, soft-spoken man, and considered the
brightest of all the generals, though a little indecisive, by Americans
who knew them. Le Van Kim was a friend of Rufe Phillips. He had
directed the first reoccupation—pacification—operation in 1954,
which was how Phillips got to know him. Tran Van Don and Le Van
Kim were brighter and more sophisticated, but lesser known than
another general who had also served in the French army, Duong Van
Minh. As a colonel, Duong Van Minh had gained a measure of fame
and received a professional boost from Ed Lansdale for his role in
helping put down the Binh Xuyen rebellion, when Diem was trying to
consolidate his power over the sects. Much of Minh's stature with the
Vietnamese seemed to be based on his height: he was extraordinarily
tall for a Vietnamese, nearly six feet, and admiringly called Big Minh
by those he towered over.

As the best known of the generals, Big Minh should have been
chief of the armed forces, but Diem and Nhu feared he might turn his
fame against them, and they assigned him to a harmless job, where
they could keep an eye on him. They appointed instead a loyalist to

the top military post, but he fell ill, and the next best choice seemed to be Tran Van Don, whose cautious treading through the political swamps of Saigon had led Diem and Nhu to believe he was no more than a skirt-chaser and a yes-man who could be counted on to do what he was told. Don had a way with women, and it was rumored by Saigon gossip, which was always tilted toward the lascivious, that he had charmed Madame Nhu.

After the Buddhist crisis and Diem's inept handling of it began, the embittered Big Minh made bold noises among the generals about the need to be rid of the two brothers, which influenced the normally cautious Don and Kim to start thinking about it too.

Tran Van Don thought Lou Conein drank too much, but then again, a lot of Americans drank too much, especially measured in terms of the Vietnamese, who drank little and then some ungodly concoction of Coca-Cola and scotch, and Don did not believe Conein's taste for whisky diminished his trustworthiness. Besides, he had known Lou Conein longer than any American in Vietnam, and Don, a subtle intriguer, understood that Conein did not care for Diem and Nhu either. So after the Independence Day reception, Don told Conein over a drink about the discontent among the military, particularly with Nhu, trying to get a feel for how the United States might regard a coup. The generals were worried about the country, but also concerned because they believed Nhu capable of terminating any of them on a whim. As dissatisfied and worried as they were, it was unlikely they would move if they thought Washington might prune them afterward.

Lou Conein listened to what Tran Van Don had to say and reported the conversation to his station chief, John Richardson, who relayed the word to Washington. The night Conein was drinking with the generals, John F. Kennedy was meeting with his advisers the same day on July 4th and trying to decide what to do about Diem. As usual, the meeting reached no decision. Tran Van Don's talk of a coup was not encouraged. Still, tensions continued to rise between Diem and the Buddhists. The first protest by immolation drew such attention that on August 5 another monk burned himself, followed by a third eleven days later. Then Diem and Nhu launched their raids on the pagodas.

Two days after the pagoda raids, Tran Van Don got in touch once more with Lou Conein to discuss the possibility of a coup. At the same time Don was talking to Conein, Le Van Kim went to see Rufe Phillips. The generals were upset that Nhu had tried to put the blame on the army for the pagoda raids. Kim said that Nhu and his wife had to go, and that if the United States took a clear stand against them, he and his fellow generals would oust them. Nguyen Dinh Thuan, Diem's chief of staff, also met with Phillips and added to the chorus against Nhu.

Rufe Phillips's cable to Washington reporting on his conversations with Kim and Thuan fed the already sizable antagonism of the Harriman-Hilsman forces arrayed against Diem and Nhu, and a day later—two days after Henry Cabot Lodge arrived in Saigon—the famous cable was sent suggesting that Diem might have to go if he couldn't be separated from his brother. Lodge said later that he was surprised by the cable, but, if so, he recovered quickly enough to send a reply saying he was in agreement with the policy.

Later William Colby would say, "I considered the Diem coup to be *the* key error of the war. Out of the overthrow of Diem came the essential collapse of the South Vietnamese, which was remedied only by Johnson's sending in the troops." Therefore Colby was not cheerfully disposed to anyone on a policy level connected with the coup, least of all to Henry Cabot Lodge. But he realized the impact of the Harriman-Hilsman cable of August 24. "The tough thing about this telegram," Colby said, "was that Lodge took it as a directive to find a coup—and he sent the station out to find one."

The Saigon station immediately queried Colby and his boss John McCone for instructions. "My reply," Colby said, "was that you stay close to the ambassador. You do exactly what the ambassador says. We don't want CIA out there on its own. And even though I disagreed with what the ambassador was doing, still the station had to be part of his organization."

The CIA followed up by instructing Lou Conein and another officer to get things moving by contacting two other generals in addition to Tran Van Don and Le Van Kim. The two generals, Tran Thien Khiem and Nguyen Khanh, had helped save Diem during the 1960 coup attempt but had since grown disaffected. Neither man was ready to move, however, and Henry Cabot Lodge, fresh to Vietnam and ready to get started with a bang, was exposed to a peculiar aspect of the Vietnamese military officer's character that other Americans already knew so well. Hesitant and indecisive about fighting the Viet Cong, the generals were the same when it came to launching a coup against Diem. Before it was over, Henry Cabot Lodge and Lou Conein would have plenty of time to get to know each other.

AFTER THE LANSDALE TEAM broke up in late 1956, Conein returned to the States and asked to be transferred back to the army. The Pentagon told him he had been on special assignment too long and stood no chance of being promoted to lieutenant colonel unless he returned to the mainstream and started acting like a soldier. His assignment was to the newly formed Special Forces, a unit that still left him outside the regular army, and he continued to be worried about his promotion. But it finally came through, and he settled down, relatively content, at Fort Bragg. "I played cowboys and Indians and had a lot of fun running around jumping out of airplanes," Conein said. He was selected to develop a free-fall parachute program for the Green Berets, and from his experiments grew the Golden Knights, the army's precision skydiving team. The Special Forces unit he commanded was sent to Laos in 1959. Because the Green Berets were going under civilian cover, it was decided that Conein should not accompany them, since he was known in Indochina as an intelligence operative. Instead, he was reassigned to military intelligence and dispatched to Tehran, where he was not known. "I stayed in Tehran from 1959 to 1961," Conein said, "and then retired and came right back to the cookie factory—the CIA." He had put in twenty years in the army and knew he was going no higher than lieutenant colonel. "About that time, the units I'd formerly been connected with in the Special Forces were transferred from Laos to Vietnam. And they were running this big program for the bare-ass Montagnards. So I was sent over as a CIA contact with Special Forces." Typically, Conein told no one that he wasn't any longer in the army, not even his friend Rufe Phillips. He enjoyed wearing his pearl-handled pistols and a camouflage uniform, and later, when his role in the Diem coup became known, he was usually referred to as Lieutenant Colonel Conein.

When he began his assignment as Lodge's agent for pulling off a coup, Lou Conein was uncomfortable. "At first I didn't talk to the ambassador," Conein said. "I was scared of him. The rumor had it you couldn't smoke in front of him, all kinds of things. Once I got to know him, though, he wasn't all that bad. He was very in love with his position, and he was going to knock that American team together, even if he had to fire everybody."

It turned out well that Lodge and Conein were able to communicate in person, for Lou wasn't much of a writer. One day John Richardson, the station chief, walked past Conein and Stu Methven shortly after Conein had finished reporting to him. Said Richardson as he passed: "Lou, what you really need is an amanuensis."

Conein turned to Methven. "Amanda *who*?"

Part of the problem was Conein's inability to type because he was missing the top joints of the first two fingers of his right hand. His car developed engine trouble one night in Germany when he was assigned to drive a CIA officer, a woman, from one base to another, and as he was under the hood fiddling with the fan belt and the generator pulley, she tried out her own mechanical knowledge by stepping on the starter. So Conein usually took notes and read them to his chief.

Conein saw Lodge for the first time after he returned from a meeting with Big Minh. Lodge came to the CIA office to listen to Conein's verbal report to Richardson. Conein gave his notes to Richardson or Lodge, written in longhand, and they composed the reports that went to Kennedy and his advisers. After a while, Conein began to relax around Lodge and grew to like him.

It appeared the feeling was reciprocated. "The secret to success with Lodge," Mike Dunn said, "was to be amusing, in the French sense of the word. One of the things we did was put on a lot of acts for him, and Conein was one of the stars. He was very entertaining. Besides, you had to talk to Conein in person to have any hope of believing what he was going to tell you. It would have been very hard to understand some of the maneuvering that was going on without seeing this fellow in the flesh. I think Conein carried out his instructions up to a point. I mean, everybody was playing their own game. Lodge had no illusions about bureaucratic loyalties and the way the lines really ran."

"Lou was worth his weight in gold over there," Stu Methven said. "I think he was a great officer. His role in the coup was instrumental. Without him, I don't think they could have pulled it off. Or at least it would have been much clumsier."

Yet, despite Lou Conein's efforts, the embassy could not get the generals to move against Diem. By the end of August 1963, Ambassador Lodge realized that the matter was going to be difficult and drawn-out, and he began looking for other ways to bring pressure on Diem. Policymakers in Washington, too, drew back from counting on a coup and searched for another method of bringing the Diem regime into line. The focus was still on removing Nhu. Ed Lansdale had his own idea about how this could be done, which he revealed to Averell Harriman and John Kenneth Galbraith, the ambassador to India and a Kennedy friend, over breakfast in Washington. Lansdale thought Harriman and Galbraith should get in touch with their friends at Harvard and establish an important-sounding policy group on Vietnam and then invite Nhu to become a member. "Kick him upstairs," Lansdale said. "Tell him he's an intellectual. Listen to him and give him a job there. He'd come, and Diem would let him go." Lansdale explained that Diem had given his father a deathbed promise that he would take care of his younger brother. "And we Americans have come in and bluntly told him to get rid of Nhu," Lansdale said. "Well, his father's wishes mean more to him. He's a family man. Instead of that, if we had gone in and said, 'We have a real good job for Nhu and want you to help us convince him to go,' he'd do it. You know, he'd think it was good for his brother, which it would be." Lansdale's idea was given little consideration. The policymakers in Washington were in a mood to use muscle, not subtle persuasion, although a long and complicated plan of action drafted by the Harriman-Hilsman group suggested that Lansdale head a reconciliation effort with Diem, if that option were chosen. It was not.

On October 5, 1963, President Kennedy decided on specific measures for applying pressure on Diem. The same day Lou Conein met with Big Minh, at Minh's request. The generals, Big Minh said, had finally gotten together on a plan for a coup. The easiest way, said Minh, was to assassinate Nhu and keep Diem on as a figurehead. Conein reported to Lodge what Big Minh said. The station recommended that the ambassador not set himself against an assassination plot, because the other two alternatives Big Minh had discussed might lead to protracted bloodshed. But CIA director John McCone quickly cabled the station to withdraw the recommendation to Lodge, saying the agency "certainly cannot be in the position of stimulating, approving, or supporting assassination, but on the other hand, we are in no way responsible for stopping every such threat of which we might receive even partial knowledge. We certainly would not favor assassination of Diem. . . . Consequently believe best approach is hands off. However, we naturally interested in intelligence on any such plan."

There were signs that John McCone and William Colby were growing exasperated with Henry Cabot Lodge. If there was going to be a coup, it was going to be Lodge's coup, not the CIA's. They were particularly angered by Lodge's decision to fire John Richardson as station chief and send him back to the States, which was suggested by Mike Dunn. Richardson's recall, which took place on October 5, 1963, was supposed to put pressure on Nhu, the station chief's contact. Whether the tactic worked or not, it did have the effect of making more enemies for Lodge and Dunn. At the time, Dunn was engaged in his own maneuvers to become the ambassador's chief of staff over his only rival, a CIA officer and friend of Lodge's son, who had arrived in Saigon as part of the Lodge team. Dunn's exuberant willingness to serve as Lodge's hatchet man did not hurt his cause.

Later, the CIA went after Mike Dunn by having Lou Conein invite him to his home for drinks and secretly tape their conversation while trying to lead Dunn into making indiscreet comments about Lodge. Then the CIA sent the tape to the ambassador. "McCone did that," Dunn said. "I mean, they were playing high-stakes poker over there. The top guys. They wanted to get me out of there, because they thought I was a real hindrance to the local station. Well, I was just in too solid with Lodge for that to make a lot of difference, and I was guarded in what I'd said. If they had cut and spliced the tape a little bit, it certainly would have been helpful to them." Dunn didn't hold the betrayal against Lou Conein. It was just business.

The machinations led Lodge himself to deceive General Paul Harkins, who had been a family friend since they served together at Fort Bliss in the nineteen twenties. He cut Harkins out of the cable traffic about the coup and began sending his own military assessments to Washington without showing them to the general. The State Department finally told Lodge to share the message traffic with Harkins, and when the general learned what was going on, he filed a strong protest against the coup.

"In my contacts here," Harkins said, "I have seen no one with the strength of character of Diem, at least in fighting the communists. Clearly there are no generals qualified to take over in my opinion."

Paul Harkins had few admirers for his understanding of how to fight a political-military war. But he was a professional officer who had extensive dealings with the Vietnamese generals, and it appeared that Washington paid little attention to his negative assessment of Diem's possible successors—which William Colby found inexplicable.

"A fascinating point to me is that I don't remember a serious conversation at policy levels at which we discussed *who* might succeed Diem," Colby said. "It was always *the generals.* You don't run a country like that, with *the generals.* You've got to find a *who.* Nobody thought Big Minh would ever do it. He was hopeless. I knew Duong Van Minh, and thought he was a total blowhard, without a useful idea in his head."

Where Lodge was getting his information was not entirely clear. Some of it came from the younger foreign service officers in the embassy who had turned against Diem. There was even a split in the CIA station. And some of it, according to Mike Dunn, came from the newsmen who were acting as Lodge's eyes and ears.

"I don't care what they say now," Mike Dunn said. "But they used to come into my office at the embassy and tell me what was going on. They weren't sitting out there as neutral observers. They were players. I think it's fair to say that Ambassador Lodge depended upon them very heavily as sources of information, not from just what they were sending home in their dispatches, but from what they told him in private."

Still, said Dunn, this did not mean Lodge was irrevocably committed to the overthrow of Diem. "You see, this is the thing everybody misses about Lodge. He looked to be tricky and devious simply because he was so open. He wasn't afraid of anything or anyone. He respected the office of the president. But nobody, in his mind, was giving him passing or failing grades. He was operating on his own. That's the big risk a president takes in making a political appointment. Yet he spent the weekend before the coup with Diem and spoke to him at great length about including more diverse elements in his cabinet. There were three Americans involved in this meeting—the ambassador and his wife and myself. I was with him all the time, and Lodge just wasn't able to dissemble enough to fool me. So I think he sincerely believed at that late date that the Diem regime could be made to work. And he certainly didn't have a great opinion of the triumvirate waiting in the wings."

Actually, Lodge's messages to Washington revealed that he was building a Pontius Pilate strategy for a coup. Having wound up the generals and set them to marching, he now recommended to John F. Kennedy that the United States not instigate a coup but not try to stop one either. "First," Lodge said, "it seems at least an even bet that the next government would not bungle and stumble as much as the present one has. Secondly, it is extremely unwise in the long range for us to pour cold water on attempts at a coup, particularly when they are just in their beginning stages. We should remember that this is the only way in which the people of Vietnam can possibly get a change in government. Whenever we thwart attempts at a coup, as we have done in the past, we are incurring very long-lasting resentments, we are assuming an undue responsibility for keeping incumbents in office, and in general are setting ourselves in judgment over the affairs of Vietnam."

Lodge's maneuver of trying to wash his hands of responsibility for a coup had the effect of forcing the indecisive White House to commit itself, simply to try to prevent things from possibly falling into chaos. The anti-Diemists in the State Department evidently realized what Lodge was up to and sent him a green-light cable, authorizing him to tell the generals the United States would not oppose a coup, which, as William Colby saw it, was "a straight-out endorsement" for Diem's removal. But two days later, on October 29, 1963, McGeorge Bundy, speaking for Kennedy, told Lodge: "We reiterate burden of proof must be on coup group to show a substantial possibility of quick success; otherwise, we should discourage them from proceeding since a miscalculation could result in jeopardizing U.S. position in Southeast Asia."

The White House was so nervous about Lodge's suggestion that he bail out and let the plane crash wherever it might that Kennedy sent him detailed coup instructions, for the first time, on October 30, 1963, probably the last communication Lodge received on the subject before Diem was overthrown two days later. The anxiety of Kennedy and his staff about an ambassador who was "operating on his own" was obvious in the cable's first point, hammered home once again: "We do not accept as a basis for U.S. policy that we have no power to delay or discourage a coup." With that said, the White House laid down guidelines for a coup. The United States would not intervene directly on either side, or commit its military resources, and would give asylum to those involved in case the coup failed. "But once a coup under responsible leadership has begun, and within these restrictions," the White House said, "it is in the interest of the U.S. Government that it should succeed."

Whether he planned it that way or not, Lodge, in playing Pilate, had forced the hand of a president who was playing Hamlet.

A WEEK BEFORE THE COUP the White House grew skittish about Lou Conein's role. Kennedy's advisers suddenly realized that practically everything they knew about the coup was coming from one intelligence operative who had a controversial reputation. White House worries about Conein were intensified when General Harkins, who was trying to stop the coup, suggested that Conein was a liar and that his chief contact, Tran Van Don, was playing a double game. After Lodge fired John Richardson, leaving Dave Smith, his stolid deputy, as acting station chief, Conein became, for the moment, the most important CIA operative in the world. Lodge defended his agent, assuring the White House that Conein "has carried out my orders in each instance explicitly."

As Conein told it the generals had not set a definite date for the coup, but it would probably take place before November 2, 1963. This undoubtedly reflected, to an extent, the generals' inability to put their plans in order. They were suspicious and distrustful of each other. But passing on tentative dates to Conein also could have been another way of trying to get a clear policy stand from the White House. Was it a coincidence that the generals decided to move two days after John F. Kennedy finally committed himself by sending detailed coup instructions to Lodge? Or did Lou Conein signal with a wink and a nod to Tran Van Don that the word from Washington was go?

Lou Conein thought it came down to choosing sides. There were a number of other coup plots being hatched in Saigon. Nhu himself was rumored to be planning a preemptive coup to flush out the various plotters. "My estimation," Conein said, "was that even if the generals were disunited in certain things and had petty jealousies between them, they at least controlled the forces. And it was better if a coup was going to happen, as it definitely was, that they do it."

On November 1, 1963, the morning of the coup, Ambassador Lodge accompanied Admiral Harry Felt, who was on a visit from Honolulu, to pay a courtesy call on President Diem. Felt knew that a coup was in the works, and he asked Lodge how it was coming. Lodge wasn't giving anything away. "There isn't a Vietnamese general with hair enough on his chest to make it go," he told Felt. After Felt and Lodge met with Diem, the Vietnamese asked Lodge to stay behind for a private talk.

"I know there is going to be a coup," Diem said, "but I don't know who is going to do it." Diem complained that American agents were conspiring against him. He told Lodge he would give the embassy their names.

"I said that I hoped we would get the names," Lodge reported later, "and he could be sure if any American committed an impropriety, I would send him out of the country." Such casually stated duplicity was enough to make anyone whistle.

Lodge was scheduled to return to Washington for consultations. Diem told him he ought to talk to William Colby and former ambassador Nolting about his brother. They would tell him, he said, how much he needed Nhu's help and advice. Nhu's problems started, Diem said, when Colby was station chief in Saigon in 1960. Colby came to Diem and told him that Nhu should not live in an ivory tower but should get out more into the countryside. Nolting agreed with Colby, and it was "due to their pressure" that Nhu had taken a more active role in government. Then, Diem said, people had begun to accuse Nhu of usurping power, and he became unpopular.

As Lodge got up to leave, Diem said, "Please tell President Kennedy that I am a good and frank ally, that I would rather be frank and settle questions now than talk about them after we have lost everything. Tell President Kennedy that I take all his suggestions seriously and wish to carry them out, but it is a question of timing."

Rufe Phillips's father had died several weeks before and he had come back after the funeral and arranged for his wife and children to return to the States. He was planning to leave Saigon in a few days, after helping the new chief of rural development get settled into the job.

"Early in the morning on the day of the coup, before it started, I got a call from Lou," Phillips said. "He said, 'Would you mind staying with Elyette and the kids? I think the balloon is going up today.'"

One of Tran Van Don's aides told Conein to go to the Vietnamese military headquarters at the Saigon airport. Although he was retired from the army, Conein did not want to risk being captured wearing civilian clothes during a coup, which might get him shot on the spot as a spy, so he put on his lieutenant colonel's uniform and topped it off with his Special Forces beret. He put forty-two thousand dollars worth of piastres in a brief case, to give to the generals. The money was supposed to be used to buy food for the troops taking part in the coup, or to pay off death claims to the families of anyone killed. Whether or not it was actually used this way, it wound up with the generals. Conein loaded his jeep with grenades and a submachine gun and sped to military headquarters, arriving there shortly after noon, before General Don returned from the airport terminal, where he was seeing off Admiral Felt.

Big Minh, the coup leader, looked surprised to see him, but when Conein said that Don had told him to report to headquarters, Minh assigned him a desk and a telephone in a large office. The generals were in the next room with their communications net, and from time to time they visited Conein and told him what was going on. The coup started at 1:30 P.M., beginning with a brief fight next door to headquarters with the Vietnamese Special Forces, who were Diem loyalists. The Special Forces commander and his brother were arrested by the coup troops and shot later the same day.

"I had a voice radio," Conein said. "Nine-nine was the prearranged code word to say that the coup was on. So I established communications with the embassy and gave them my telephone number in case they wanted to get in touch with me. Big Minh came over and said, 'Conein, if we fail you are coming with us.' If the coup failed, they planned to fight their way to Cambodia. We had nine armored cars, extra gasoline and everything. We were going to shoot our way out."

Diem reacted the same way he had reacted to the 1960 coup. He got on the telephone and started trying to find some support among his military commanders. But this time it was different. The generals who had saved him before were members of the cabal. Three hours after the coup began, Diem phoned the embassy to see what the Americans could do for him. He talked to Henry Cabot Lodge, who recorded the conversation and cabled it to Washington.

DIEM: Some units have made a rebellion and I wanted to know what is the attitude of the U.S.?
LODGE: I do not feel well enough informed to be able to tell you. I

have heard the shooting, but am not acquainted with all the facts. Also it is 4:30 A.M. in Washington and the U.S. Government cannot possibly have a view.

DIEM: But you must have some general ideas. After all, I am a chief of state. I have tried to do my duty. I want to do now what duty and good sense require. I believe in duty above all.

LODGE: You have certainly done your duty. As I told you only this morning, I admire your courage and your great contributions to your country. No one can take away from you the credit for all you have done. Now I am worried about your physical safety. I have a report that those in charge of the current activity offer you and your brother safe conduct out of the country if you resign. Have you heard this?

DIEM: No. [*And then after a pause*] You have my telephone number.

LODGE: Yes. If I can do anything for your physical safety, please call me.

DIEM: I am trying to reestablish order.

Most written accounts of the coup, though differing in minor details, agree on what happened next. Diem and Nhu refused to give up. They continued to try to muster support by phone. That night, under cover of darkness, they slipped away from the beseiged palace and took refuge with a Chinese businessman in Cholon, Saigon's Chinese quarter. Around seven on the morning of November 2, they agreed to surrender at a Catholic church. The generals sent an armored car to pick them up, and on the way to coup headquarters they were shot and killed by Big Minh's bodyguard.

And what was Henry Cabot Lodge's role in Diem's surrender? According to the Pentagon Papers and other accounts, he had none. His conversation with Diem the previous afternoon, the Pentagon Papers said, "was the last that any American had with Diem. Lodge, as was his custom, retired that night about 9:30 P.M." Such accounts seem implausible if one remembers that Lodge had emphasized to Diem that he was worried about his safety. *"If I can do anything for your physical safety, please call me."* Why would Diem, who knew he was liable to face death if taken by the generals, not bother to get back in touch with Lodge?

It didn't make any sense because it wasn't true. Diem made another phone call to Lodge around seven in the morning, after he decided to surrender.

"Lodge talked to Diem twice," Mike Dunn said. "Once in the afternoon and once the next morning. That morning Diem asked if there was something we could do. Lodge put the phone down and went to check on something. I held the line open. I was the last American to talk to Diem alive, although I guess Lodge came back on the line to say goodbye. Lodge told Diem he would offer them asylum and do what he could for them. I wanted to go over—in fact, I asked Lodge if I could go over and take them out. I said, 'Because they are going to kill them.' Told him that right flat out. He said, 'We can't. We just can't get that involved,' and so forth. I was really astonished that we didn't do more for them."

Could anything have been done to save Diem and Nhu?

"Yeah," Dunn said, "I think we could have forced the issue."

Diem and Nhu were killed between seven and nine o'clock on the morning of November 2. The tales told by Tran Van Don and Lou Conein about this time period were interesting in their divergencies. Don's account, given in his published memoirs, had Diem calling General Khiem at 6:45 A.M. and agreeing to surrender. Don made it sound as though Diem was positively anxious to be taken by the generals. "He told Khiem his whereabouts at the church in Cholon," Don wrote, "and asked for transportation to pick them up because he felt insecure there." Don and Khiem then told Big Minh Diem's location, according to Don, and Big Minh sent the armored car to Cholon to get them.

Conein's version, given for this book, disagrees with Don's account. According to Conein, Diem made three calls to the generals that morning. In the first, he refused to speak to the acknowledged coup leader, Big Minh. He spoke with another general instead. Diem wanted to make a deal whereby he gave up power and and left the country with full honors. He was told he would have to talk to Big Minh. He called back and spoke to Minh and made the same proposal. Big Minh turned Diem down, and the conversation was broken off in anger. A little later, Diem called Big Minh again, requesting only safe conduct to the airport and departure from Vietnam. About this time, according to Conein, Big Minh asked if the embassy could supply an airplane to take Diem and Nhu out of the country. Conein called the station and was told that it would take twenty-four hours to get a plane with sufficient range to fly the brothers nonstop to a country of asylum. Washington had decided in advance that Diem should not be allowed the chance of getting off at a refueling stop in a nearby Asian country, where he might try to mobilize support for a countercoup against the generals. Conein informed Big Minh of the problem.

Lou Conein's account followed the lengthy after-action report he sent to CIA headquarters within several days of the coup, which was turned over in 1975 to the Senate subcommittee investigating assassination plots against foreign leaders. During an interview for this book, Conein added several significant details to his after-action report and his testimony before the Senate committee. According to Conein, the generals had cut the telephone lines in the Saigon area, leaving open only selected lines such as those to the embassy, to the palace, to Conein's house, and to various military command posts. Therefore, although there had been reports to the contrary, Big Minh and the other generals thought Diem was still at the palace and using the telephone there. Unknown to them, Diem had earlier run a line from the home of his Chinese friend through the palace switchboard for use in case of just such an emergency. During the 1960 coup attempt, the conspirators had also left the palace switchboard line open. The palace had been bombarded and was surrounded, but Diem's presidential guards were holding out. It was one of Big Minh's terms that Diem order a ceasefire, which was supposed to take place at 7:00 A.M.

According to Lou Conein, two groups headed toward the palace at seven to pick up Diem. One group, which included Big Minh, drove jeeps from the airport through the golf course in a back approach to the palace. The group with the armored car escort was sent down the main road. Conein included in his 1963 after-action report that an escort showed up at the palace around 8:00 A.M., but that Diem was not there.

Then how did Big Minh learn the real location of Diem and Nhu in the following few minutes? There, Lou Conein stopped and returned to his original declaration of 1963. He said that an "informant" must have seen Diem and Nhu and called coup headquarters. When closely questioned for this book, he said, "It was simple. Somebody spotted them." Although Conein was a collector of details and a connoisseur of gossip, he refused to speculate about who that "somebody" was.

No documents were turned up by Pentagon Papers researchers or anybody else reporting on Diem's call to Lodge around seven that morning. There was little reason to doubt Mike Dunn's account, however. Not only did Dunn like and respect Henry Cabot Lodge, but he also continued to feel indebted to him years after his death. Several months after the coup, the American military in Saigon, like the CIA, tried bureaucratically to slit Dunn's throat, and Lodge saved him. Court-martial charges were brought against him by General Paul Harkins, co-signed by General William Westmoreland, on the grounds that Dunn had made false statements, particularly in regard to what Harkins had been trying to tell Lodge, though not necessarily only during the coup period. Lodge threatened to go public with his support of his chief of staff, and the charges were dropped. It was testimony to Dunn's agility, and to Lodge's support, that he wound up as a major general, and later served as an assistant to both Spiro Agnew and Gerald Ford when they were vice presidents.

So it was not farfetched to speculate that Diem called Lodge after Big Minh's refusal to provide him with safe conduct out of the country and asked to be allowed to surrender to the Americans instead. Neither was it farfetched to speculate that he would have given his real location to Lodge, not to Big Minh. Lodge left the line, according to Mike Dunn, to "check on something," which would have given him time to get in touch with Lou Conein.

By his own account, Lou Conein left coup headquarters at 7:15 A.M., a few minutes after Big Minh headed to the palace. He decided, he said, to go home, because the generals were preparing for a post-coup press conference and he didn't want newsmen to see him there, wearing a uniform and carrying a weapon. It would have taken Conein about twenty minutes to drive home through the deserted streets. He lived several blocks from the palace. Yet, with two radios, he somehow lost contact with the CIA station long enough that the acting station chief told Stu Methven to go to coup headquarters and find Conein. Methven drew no conclusions about Conein's absence and appeared years later never to have discussed it with him.

"I lived on the outskirts of Saigon in Gia Dinh and was the closest one to the airport," Stu Methven said. "So they wanted me to go out and get Conein. They were trying to get in contact with him and couldn't. I don't know why they wanted to get in touch with him. Anyway, I got there about the time they were bringing the bodies in, and there was a sea of reporters around. I just decided that the best thing for me was to get the hell out of there."

On the other hand, there was no way of disproving Conein's story that he simply decided to leave at 7:15 and went home. It was, however, his opinion that Diem and Nhu had been killed on Big Minh's orders because of their final act of duplicity in agreeing to surrender but not telling Big Minh their location.

"I have nothing to base this on," Conein said, "but I think Big Minh thought all the time that Diem and Nhu were at the palace, and when he got there and found they were not, he became extremely peeved."

According to Tran Van Don, Conein himself became rather peeved when they got a report during the night that Diem and Nhu might not be at the palace. "About 3:00 A.M. I was informed that Diem and Nhu were no longer at the Gia Long Palace so I gave orders for security personnel to search for them, not knowing whether to believe this report or not," Don wrote in his memoirs. "Conein seemed to be irritated by this news, saying that Diem and Nhu must be found at any cost."

The hypothesis that Lodge gave Diem up that morning was not inconsistent with the position he later took with a third Ngo brother, who was the de facto ruler of central Vietnam. Ngo Dinh Can asked for asylum at the American consulate in Hue three days after his brothers were killed. Can departed Hue in an American plane, escorted by a vice consul, a lieutenant colonel, and two military policemen—all Americans. When they reached Saigon, Can was turned over to Lou Conein and then to the coup leaders on the orders of Lodge. Don said in his memoirs that Lodge stipulated that Can was to be treated in a legally correct way. He was jailed and executed a few months later, while Lodge was still ambassador.

"So I left and went home that morning," Lou Conein said. "I was tired. I smelled like a she-goat in heat. All I wanted was to take a shower. The Special Forces team guarding my house had drunk all the beer. Not long after I got there, the telephone rang.

" 'Hello.'

" 'Lou, you have to come to the embassy.'

" 'Look, I'm tired.'

" 'Right now.'

" 'Okay.'

"I went to the embassy and was shown a message from Washington: 'Where is Diem and Nhu?' I said, 'I don't know. They went to get them at the palace.'

" 'You know where this message comes from, don't you?'

" 'Yeah.' I could tell it came from the highest authority. 'Okay, I'll go find them.'

"I returned to general staff headquarters, and went up to Big Minh's aide. 'I got to talk to Big Minh.' And of course it was complete chaos, with all the former government ministers running around. I gave Big Minh some messages from the ambassador; then I said, 'Where is President Diem and Nhu?' He said, 'They committed suicide.' 'Where?' 'The Catholic church. The one out in Cholon. You want to see them? They're here.' "

Conein told Big Minh that he definitely did not want to see the bodies, because he didn't believe for a second the story about their committing suicide and didn't think anyone else would either. He did not want to involve himself further in the coup. He reported to the embassy and then went home but was too keyed up to sleep. A few days later Big Minh invited Conein and his wife Elyette to headquarters and gave him a decoration. "It was like the Legion of Honor but Vietnamese," said Elyette, who was pleased.

As the years passed, the Diem coup did not recede in the minds of many government officials but loomed even larger, as they reassessed the war and came to consider the coup one of the key errors. No one blamed Lou Conein for his role. It was Henry Cabot Lodge who came in for criticism—and also the newsmen who were in Saigon during that period.

"The newsmen had prejudices that prevented them from seeing the truth," Ed Lansdale said. "Halberstam I believe was somewhat responsible for Diem's death. He came out and interviewed me when he was writing one of his books—*The Best and the Brightest*—and I told him, 'Why don't you write a book about what you did in Vietnam? You are a historical figure, really.'

"He said, 'What do you mean?'

"I said, 'I won't tell you who told me this, but an American who was there, a friend of yours, told me that after Diem was killed, you said, 'I told you I was going to get that sonofabitch.' That means you were influencing people about Vietnam tremendously, and you ought to confess to all that in a book.'

"He got mad at me. He didn't deny it. But he stayed mad the whole interview. It shows up in his book. I'm a good guy in one part, and a bad guy in the other. I guess he went back and said, 'The sonofabitch. I'll get him too.' "

THE OVERTHROW OF DIEM had disastrous consequences for Chau's pacification work. Nothing could be accomplished without political stability in Saigon, and for the next several years one coup would follow another, as the generals who toppled Diem engaged in a struggle for power. Security deteriorated in Chau's province, and most of his programs were abandoned by his successor, who also consolidated Chau's three-man counterterror teams into platoons and then company-sized units, turning them, as they were being turned all over the country, into murderous bands of mercenaries who operated as the enforcers for corrupt province chiefs.

II

BLOOD IS THICKER

13

WASHINGTON-SAIGON 1970

IN FEBRUARY 1970, as Chau was hiding out in Vietnam's delta, Dan Ellsberg, in Los Angeles, was air-expressing two packages of secret documents on the war to Senator J. William Fulbright, Democrat of Arkansas and chairman of the Senate Foreign Relations Committee. The documents, known as the Pentagon Papers, were addressed not to Fulbright but to Norvill Jones, Fulbright's longtime assistant and contact point on matters concerning Vietnam. Worried that Fulbright might be politically compromised if it became known that he was the recipient of such a massive file of illegally obtained secrets, Jones told no one, not even the committee's chief of staff and his nominal boss, Carl Marcy, that Ellsberg was sending the stolen documents. Shortly after he put them in the mail, Ellsberg telephoned Jones.

"They're on the way," Dan Ellsberg said.

"Wonderful," Norvill Jones said. "Can we reimburse you for the expense?"

Ellsberg had spent his personal savings on photocopying the documents, and he told Jones that he appreciated the gesture. "It comes to about fifteen hundred dollars," Ellsberg said.

"Oh, no, we don't have that kind of money," Jones said. "I meant for the postage."

"Forget it," Ellsberg said. "It's only forty-five dollars."

Dan Ellsberg and Norvill Jones got on well, but the confusion about the reimbursement pointed to a larger misunderstanding that separated the two men. As Ellsberg saw it, he and Jones were on the same side of the fight; both were trying to end the war, and Fulbright and his committee had become the vanguard of the crusade in Washington. But to Norvill Jones it wasn't quite that simple. The antiwar movement was not an ecumenical gathering of the church; there were numerous sects and self-proclaimed knights riding off in various directions—usually in the wrong direction, as Jones saw it. He thought that only his leader, Fulbright, carried a splinter of the true cross. It was part of the committee's responsibility, Jones believed, to provide an outlet for the people who felt strongly about the war, and he had helped set up hearings for a range of antiwar spokesmen. But he and other committee staffers were concerned also with keeping the less desirable elements of the movement away from Fulbright, who privately considered them to be idealistic but misguided. Dan Ellsberg could not be lumped with the usual fervent protesters, that was obvious, but he appeared to Jones to represent something potentially more dangerous.

"I thought he was a firecracker ready to explode," Jones said. "I wanted to keep my distance and the committee's distance from him."

Norvill Jones believed the Foreign Relations Committee's position on Vietnam to be politically fragile. Though the outspoken dove Frank Church was a committee member, the committee's thrust was based largely on Fulbright's opposition to the war, which had contributed to the downfall of Lyndon Johnson. Never in recent history had a sitting president been opposed so forcefully by a Senate committee chairman, moreover, by a senator from the president's own party, once a loyal and close friend. And Jones, from a poor family in Princeton, Arkansas, had played a significant role in bringing about this state of affairs. Acting as Fulbright's lieutenant to marshal congressional support to end the war, Jones had put his own career on the line.

Jones had been with Fulbright his entire working life, starting as a messenger when he was fourteen in the summer of 1944, when Fulbright, a congressman, was running for his first senate term. After Fulbright won, Jones went to Washington, where he attended Capitol Page School from six-thirty till nine-thirty each morning and then worked as a doorman in the Senate. He soon transferred to Fulbright's office as a clerk and enrolled at George Washington University night school until the Korean War, when he flew helicopters off aircraft carriers as a naval officer. Back in Washington, he completed college and entered law school, finishing in time for the reshuffle in Fulbright's office that made him the senator's legislative assistant.

Jones became Fulbright's traveling companion during re-election campaigns, and only the administrative assistant was as close as he to Fulbright over the years. The frequent contact seemed made for a father-son relationship to develop.

"Between us it was always 'Senator Fulbright,' " Jones said. "We never had a close personal relationship. He was a very formal man, a gentleman from the old school, not so much introverted as inner directed. Though he wanted quality work from his staff, he was not the kind of manager who could direct them to that end. He was impatient to some extent but too reserved and self-controlled ever to show much in the way of temper or exasperation. He was never a back-slapper, but he had the ability to make people in Arkansas and elsewhere respect him for his mind. He came across as a decent, straightforward sort of man. He didn't pussyfoot around, wasn't mealymouthed as many politicians are. The staff had great respect for him, because, I think, they looked upon him as being so superior to themselves, as I did."

Jones became the Foreign Relations Committee's staff man for Vietnam by chance. He was tired of what he was doing in Fulbright's office, and when a friend left the committee he asked Fulbright if he could have the job. He had no specific duties at first. "I didn't want to be known as Senator Fulbright's man, looking over the shoulders of everybody else," Jones said. "I wanted to join the collegial atmosphere of the staff, so when the guy who covered Asia left in 1964, I was able to take over his job without knowing anything about Asia." Courteous and low-key, with prematurely graying hair that offset blandly handsome features, Jones had always been a bookworm, and he undertook to read everything he could find about Vietnam.

It was not difficult to top Senator Fulbright's knowledge of Vietnam. Fulbright, a former Rhodes scholar, acclaimed by many to be one of the most brilliant minds of the Senate, probably knew less about the war, in specific terms, than a college student who followed the back and forth of the battles in the press. If Fulbright had ever read a book about Vietnam, it didn't show in his conversation. Fulbright seemed aloof from Vietnam as Vietnam, seemed to see it rather as an abstract principle in foreign affairs. He had never visited the country. The closest he came was a stopover in Thailand. There was debate among the staff as to whether Fulbright should make a trip to the war zone, if only for appearance's sake, as scores of other politicians had done. Jones, as sensitive as cat whiskers to the senator's preferences, came down on the side of those who opposed the trip.

Fulbright himself grumpily dismissed the idea of going to Vietnam. "I was invited to go," Fulbright said. "But do you remember George Romney's experience? There was nothing you could do but listen to their briefings. You had no possibility of learning anything except what they were willing to tell you."

Still, one was left with the impression that Fulbright did not really care to see for himself. He disliked details. He was opposed not simply to Vietnam but to the kind of thinking that had led the United States to get involved there in the first place. His record revealed that he had spoken out and even voted for foreign intervention in Asia. But his zigzags represented more the maneuvers of a practical politician with one eye on a conservative constituency in Arkansas than an ambivalent mind. In truth, Fulbright had not changed his ideas since the nineteen fifties, when he began to consider America's China policy ridiculous. Unlike many members of Congress—*most* members—Fulbright had evolved a firm but subtle philosophy about America's role in the world. To him Vietnam was not the disease but a manifestation of the disease, a form of cancer that might show itself and then go into remission only to recur a few years later. So Fulbright did not speak against the war with the moral fervor of a liberal arts professor, or a George McGovern, nor in the apocalyptic terms of a student protester. He seemed almost coldly detached from the emotions stirred by the war and the daily facts of Vietnam. He was a doctor who believed it his duty to treat the root cause of the disease, not just this recent infection of American foreign policy, and the best medicine, he believed, was education, to be injected slowly, with great patience, into the rump of Congress, from whence it would spread through the body politic.

Fulbright had gently nudged the Foreign Relations Committee to oppose the war. He was not very good with his personal office staff, never socializing with them, limiting his contact to two or three aides, politely distant to everybody; but he was excellent with his colleagues on the committee, always accommodating, sympathetic to their political needs, scrupulously fair. At first, he met privately with members of the administration and sent Johnson memo after memo listing his concerns about Vietnam. When it appeared he was getting nowhere, Fulbright and his staff began looking for a way to bring pressure on

Johnson. The obvious answer was to hold Senate hearings on the war, but the hearings would have to possess a legitimacy, some legal basis, not be simply a self-generated inquisition of administration policies.

When a funding bill for Southeast Asia came up in January 1966, Fulbright decided to use it as a way of questioning administration officials about the war in public hearings, which generated so much interest that they were carried live by the television networks. After taking a battering for several days, President Johnson tried to steal the headlines away from the committee by cooking up a meeting in Honolulu with South Vietnam's Premier Ky.

Lyndon Johnson did not take opposition to his policies philosophically, and he turned against Fulbright, whom he had often called, when he was Senate majority leader, "my secretary of state." "I was sitting over there at a big Democratic dinner, in the armory, I think it was," Fulbright said, "and I was about ten feet from Johnson when he began referring to me as a Sunshine Patriot and a Nervous Nellie and all those things. Before that, I used to be invited to the White House to meet with him privately. But afterward I saw him only with the leadership of the Senate and House." The estrangement was not easy for the Fulbrights. Fulbright's wife had been a close friend of Johnson's wife, sometimes doing Lady Bird's Christmas shopping for her.

Observers in Washington assumed there was an element of a vendetta in Fulbright's opposition to Johnson. It was known that Fulbright believed that he had been deceived by Johnson into being the floor manager for the Gulf of Tonkin Resolution, which Johnson then used as a quasi-declaration of war to continue the military buildup and to start the bombing of North Vietnam. The resolution was passed in August 1964, after the administration charged that North Vietnamese patrol boats had attacked American destroyers without provocation on two separate occasions.

It was Fulbright's sore point about the Gulf of Tonkin Resolution that Dan Ellsberg decided to massage as his opening for enticing him to release the Pentagon Papers in a dramatic Senate hearing that would, if not end the war, severely damage the effort. At his first meeting with Fulbright, on November 6, 1969, Ellsberg brought along not the Pentagon Papers but notes from the secret command-and-control study conducted by the defense department, which suggested the likelihood that the second Tonkin Gulf incident never occurred, leaving the inference that Johnson had lied to Congress to get the resolution passed.

Nothing was ever simple with Dan Ellsberg. Trying to sort out the chronology of his thinking during this period was like trying to rear-range sand on a beach after a pounding by many a wave. But it seemed he first planned to release the Pentagon history in conjunction with the Vietnam Moratorium on October 15, 1969, and the antiwar march on Washington a month later, hoping the documents would trigger an uprising that would force Richard Nixon's hand. But Nixon, cannily holding out the promise of a secret plan to end the war with honor, diffused the impetus of the protest movement; and it was then that Ellsberg turned to Fulbright, in a meeting arranged by Jim Lowenstein, a staff investigator for the Foreign Relations Committee, whom Ellsberg had met in Vietnam.

In that first meeting, on November 6, 1969, as Jones later remembered it in a confidential memo prepared for Fulbright, "He talked generally about how Congress and the public had been deceived on the war, and offered to provide materials but not specifically the Pentagon history. He turned over an envelope with notes on the command-and-control study (this was something we knew existed, done by the Institute of Defense Analysis on what happened during the Gulf of Tonkin incident, which we had been trying some time to get) and perhaps a portion of the Pentagon Papers about the Tonkin Gulf incident. You [Fulbright] told him to work with Jones and Lowenstein."

"The first thing I did was hand the Tonkin Gulf papers to Fulbright," Ellsberg said. "I wanted to make sure the people in the room didn't develop a bad memory and later say that Fulbright had never seen this stuff."

Ellsberg believed that releasing the Pentagon Papers through senate hearings like the ones Fulbright held in 1966 would have a greater impact than leaking the documents to a newspaper. There was also a personal consideration at stake. He made it plain that he was prepared to go to jail if necessary but that he was not enamored of becoming a martyr and had no desire to enter prison, the odds of which his doing seemed lighter if he gave the documents to a senate committee rather than to a newspaper. When he sought legal advice, he was told that the chances of his going to jail were about 50 percent if Congress brought the papers out, perhaps 70 percent if the *New York Times* released them, and 95 percent if anybody else did it.

But Ellsberg's ploy of presenting the Tonkin Gulf documents to Fulbright as a teaser to get him interested in releasing all the Pentagon Papers was flawed. To begin with, he misread Fulbright's nature. "I mostly thought not that they had lied about Tonkin, but that Johnson had lied about his own intentions," Fulbright said. "I felt misled as to his intentions, what he had in mind." The fact that Ellsberg's Tonkin papers revealed lies and deceptions did not titillate Fulbright, as it might have easily hooked a journalist. The lies were just a detail to him. More important were Johnson's overall actions of using the Gulf of Tonkin Resolution to enlarge the war, and Johnson, under tremendous public pressure, had decided not to run again for president. Besides, Fulbright had already conducted hearings on the Tonkin Gulf incidents, after a naval officer got in touch with him and said that the Pentagon was lying.

Ellsberg also misread Norvill Jones, whom he considered "a nice guy, a bright guy with right thinking on Vietnam." Jones was certainly that, but he was also, from head to foot, a political animal, as sleek as a lynx. Behind the cover of a soft-spoken voice and an easy smile, his cool eyes were taking in Ellsberg and were not overjoyed at what they saw. "In the first meeting he was articulate but nervous and worried," Jones said. "He spoke fast and made jerky movements. He seemed to be a harried man."

To Jones the dangers were many. First there was the propriety of getting Fulbright involved in trafficking in stolen secrets. Leaked documents were as common as rain in Washington, but there was no precedent for releasing such a massive file as Ellsberg possessed. There were also the other committee members to consider. What would they think of Fulbright and Jones involving them in this controversy? Fulbright had worked hard to maintain unity, to keep the senators who still supported the war from splitting off in acrimony. Fulbright, as Jones knew, did not hanker for a confrontation with President Nixon at this particular moment for several reasons. Nixon claimed to have a secret plan to end the war and had been in office for less than a year. Fulbright believed the president should be taken at his word and given time to carry out his plan. There was also another less noble, more practical reason for his reluctance. Fulbright was in political trouble at home, partly because of his outspokenness against the war. He had won his re-election in 1968 against a rabid and inconsequential segregationist by only a surprising 54 percent, sending a chill through his staff, who realized he would go under in the next election, in 1974, unless he did something to stem the tide.

Henry Kissinger, Nixon's national security adviser, made a point of courting Fulbright during his first months in office, and Fulbright responded unblushingly. The two men had a lot in common intellectually. Both examined the world with a grand vision. Kissinger was a Europeanist, as was Fulbright, whose years at Oxford were a formative experience. Some on Fulbright's staff distrusted Kissinger, but their grumbling about the relationship with Nixon's agent was tempered by the realization that their boss, who was, after all, a shrewd politician, had something up his sleeve. While Kissinger was angling to moderate Fulbright's criticism of Nixon's war policies, Fulbright was angling to get the increasingly popular Kissinger, a well-feathered hawk, to make speeches on his behalf in Arkansas, to help shore up his falling support.

As this tacit quid pro quo was being played out with Kissinger, Fulbright was content to remain relatively quiescent and let the Foreign Relations Committee's two investigators, Jim Lowenstein and Dick Moose, stir up the press against the war. Lowenstein and Moose had used Vietnam to carve out a public role for themselves in a job that normally called for anonymous staffers. Few people had ever heard of Norvill Jones, for example, which was the way publicity hungry senators preferred it; and there was some muttering about all the ink Moose and Lowenstein were getting as they bounced back and forth to Vietnam, writing critical reports about the war effort and cultivating reporters; but everybody had to admit they kept the spotlight on the committee. They made a good team and complemented each other—Lowenstein, conservative, cautious, the archetypal foreign service officer; Moose, the opposite, emotional, an activist. They were self-starters whose work Fulbright looked upon with benign detachment.

Jones, a neural extension of Fulbright, needed none of the factors that influenced the senator's thinking to be spelled out to him. Almost by instinct, Jones decided on a plan for handling Ellsberg that would not put Fulbright or the committee at political risk and at the same time would sound like a logical step to Ellsberg, solicitous of his wishes to make public the Pentagon Papers in hearings. Instead of releasing the stolen secrets and perhaps getting Ellsberg in trouble, Jones suggested, why not let Fulbright first write Defense Secretary Melvin Laird and formally request that the Pentagon turn over the study to the Foreign Relations Committee. Whatever Laird's response, as Jones knew, the committee would benefit.

226

"During that whole period there was a kind of ping-pong game going on between the executive branch and the committee," Jones said. "We were using every weapon we could find to try to make it appear that we were not getting access to information, trying to show that the committee was cut off from very important information to use in the decision-making process."

Without realizing it, Dan Ellsberg, the fast-talking Harvard intellectual, had been downshifted into first gear by a slow-talking Southern pol. Predictably, Secretary Laird refused to turn over the classified study to the Fulbright committee, despite the four letters requesting it that went out over the senator's signature. Ellsberg, growing impatient as the months passed and there were no hearings, decided to drop his effort at what he considered a subtle enticement of Fulbright and offered to send most of the documents of the Pentagon study directly to Norvill Jones in February 1970.

"I didn't know what I had, really," Jones said. "They were not in any formal order—just hundreds of Xeroxed documents. I took some home and put myself to sleep reading them."

AS DAN ELLSBERG MAILED the Pentagon Papers to the Fulbright committee, Tran Ngoc Chau was sending word to Keyes Beech of the *Los Angeles Times* that he wanted to see him. Chau trusted Beech. He had hid out at Beech's home from Thieu's police before John Paul Vann and Ev Bumgardner spirited him out of Saigon to Can Tho, in the delta, and now Chau wanted Beech's advice about he should do.

Keyes Beech (his first name rhymed with *skies*) was at the other end of the spectrum in the Saigon press corps from the young reporters who followed in the footsteps of David Halberstam and Neil Sheehan and were often critical of the war effort. Beech, fifty-seven years old, a trim man in hornrimmed glasses, balding, with a scythe of white hair, was one of the over-forties who had been covering Vietnam for many years as a commuter when Halberstam and Sheehan, in their twenties, arrived as two of the first permanent staffers. From Tennessee, Beech had served in the marines as a combat correspondent, seeing action on Tarawa and Iwo Jima, and after World War Two had become a Pulitzer Prize–winning correspondent for the *Chicago Daily News,* later moving to the *Los Angeles Times.*

"I knew Dave and Neil in the early days before the war got big," Keyes Beech said. "I was commuting between Tokyo and Saigon, and they were pleasant and helpful. They kept a file of stories in their office that was open for any reporter to use, and indeed other correspondents were encouraged to come in and use the file, which was shrewd of them, because that way they had the whole press corps working for them. Mal Browne was the other resident American correspondent, but Dave and Neil were working very closely together. They were persuaded that Diem had to go. Halberstam was always very decisive about such things, and he was very emphatic in that respect.

"I said, 'Well, I'd like to remind you of one thing. I was writing nasty stories about Ngo Dinh Diem when you guys were still at Harvard. On the other hand, if there is anything I've learned in all these years in Asia, it is that you don't overthrow a government unless you have something as good or better waiting in the wings to take over.' That was my position. If not Diem, who? He was a true nationalist. He had that going for him.

"There's no question but that I was quite conservative," Beech added. "But where I differed from certain other correspondents, many of whom were young enough to be my sons, was in this respect: I knew that war was hell long before I got to Vietnam."

Beech was tough and blunt-spoken but amiable and generally well-liked in the press corps. He always looked in excellent shape, and he took the same chances as other newsmen. He was a pleasant companion over drinks or dinner, although inevitably, as the war became more controversial at home and newsmen began to drop the pretense of being "objective" observers—at least among themselves—there were arguments with some of the younger reporters.

"Oh, we had arguments," Beech said. "I'm sure many of them considered me an old fogey. I took a much longer view of the war than they did. At the end of one evening, a *Washington Post* reporter, a very cool young man, said, 'I don't give a goddamn about your generation. I just want to get my generation out of here.' My feeling was that if we could get the war under control, get a hold on it, then there would be a good chance for changing the Saigon government for the better. But if the communists were allowed to win, there would be no second chances."

While Beech's conservatism didn't win him many points with the Saigon press corps, it did help open doors to sources in the American mission. He was one of the handful of journalists who had ready access to the ambassador and the CIA station chief. Frank Snepp, the CIA analyst who was close to station chief Ted Shackley, believed that Keyes Beech and a few other journalists were manipulated by the embassy and particularly by the CIA.

"There were three journalists—Bob Shaplen, Keyes Beech, and Bud Merick—who had an inside track at the embassy you wouldn't believe," Snepp said. "I'm not suggesting they weren't good journalists. But after talking to Shackley, they would go to another embassy—the British, say. What they didn't know was that we held regular briefings for these embassies, so they wound up getting our information from them too. Shackley had a genius for making a journalist think he was being taken into his confidence."

Snepp's charges, made after the war, caused bad blood with the journalists he criticized. "Snepp said we were unwitting dupes," Beech said. "Snepp and I—well, I consider Snepp an immoral, lying sonofabitch. He knows how I feel about him, and I know how he feels about me."

Keyes Beech's relationship with Ted Shackley, though perhaps unusual for the Vietnam War, was not a divergence from the relationship many of the older journalists had maintained with the CIA and other government officials. An unspoken give and take existed on both sides, which neither side was unaware of. Older journalists such as Beech also tended to be less ambivalent than their younger colleagues about a possible conflict between the demands of patriotism and the requirements of journalism. Robert Shaplen, for example, *The New Yorker* correspondent and author of several influential books on Vietnam, a member of Beech's generation, revealed after the war that he had secretly involved himself in an unsuccessful attempt to free American prisoners of war in 1966, at the request of roving ambassador Averell Harriman.

"I had a professional relationship with Ted Shackley," Keyes Beech said. "He was helpful to me. I've heard a lot of people criticize Shackley, and a lot of them hate his guts, but I've never heard anyone accuse him of being stupid. He was the best intelligence man I've ever known. Not that I'm an authority on the subject, but I did know nine different station chiefs in Saigon, starting with Bill Colby and ending with Tom Polgar. There were three or four times when I know Shackley tried to use me, in the sense of having me write a story a certain way, with a certain point of view. And I said, 'I'm not writing for you. I'm writing for my newspaper.' At the same time, I don't doubt that Shackley figured I was a useful person for him to know. But I was fully aware of what I was doing. Very often we had strong disagreements, in particular about Chau, which almost ruptured our relationship."

Beech first met Chau when Chau was chief of Kien Hoa province. The only thing he remembered about the encounter was that there was friction between Chau and his American adviser, an army lieutenant colonel. The American colonel disagreed with Chau's tactics and told Beech, "Chau thinks the way to win the war is to win the people over, not to shoot at them." It wasn't until the late nineteen sixties that Beech really got to know him.

"I liked Chau," Beech said. "I thought he was one of the few original minds who really wanted to do something about the war. He was obviously a difficult man to deal with, being from Hue, upper class and all that, but he was worth paying attention to and making good use of."

When Ev Bumgardner, an official in the pacification program who was secretly helping Chau, got in touch with Beech and asked if he could provide Chau with a refuge for a few days, Beech readily agreed. Who could think of a better hideout? Beech's home at 10 Alexandre de Rhodes was right under Thieu's nose, a half-block from the palace. Ted Shackley was a frequent guest for lunch, and not even the suspicious CIA chief was likely to guess Beech's secret.

"One day Shackley came to lunch when Chau was there," Beech said, "and I was amused to have Chau hiding in the next room, where he could have eavesdropped on our conversation if he wished."

Beech began to write articles based on his talks with Chau. "He told me how two guys from the CIA had offered to finance a political party for him providing he would support Thieu—and he refused to do that," Beech said. Chau revealed other information about the CIA to Beech, who felt he was telling the truth. "The CIA had some very definite ideas on what they wanted him to do, and those were things he did not necessarily want to do," said Beech.

Beech went to the embassy to speak privately with Ambassador

Bunker and Shackley. "I pointed out that of course Chau had a brother who was a communist agent. No question about it. But I argued that if everybody who had a brother or sister or father or mother on the other side were put in jail, there wouldn't be enough jails in South Vietnam to hold them all. I also argued that there was nothing to indicate that Chau himself was an agent, although he did have a feeling for his brother. I don't think I made much of an impression on them.

"Some of the stories I wrote, though, particularly the one about the CIA trying to enlist Chau in forming a political party, got a reaction in Washington, and Senator Fulbright picked it up and ran with it. This created a lot of headaches for the CIA and particularly for Shackley. He was quite upset with me. But that was irrelevant."

Beech was beginning to feel the heat, however. Other journalists in Saigon were getting rockets from their home offices asking why they weren't on top of the story. Terry Smith of the *New York Times* phoned Beech and said, "You seem to have a monopoly on Chau. I wonder if I could borrow him." Beech laughed and said, "Well, if you promise to send him back." But he knew that if other journalists had figured out he was hiding Chau, it would not be long until Thieu and the embassy realized the same thing.

"I began to get a little concerned," Beech said. "Not because of worries about myself, although they could have theoretically kicked me out of the country. But I was not harboring a fugitive, because charges had not been lodged against Chau. I was more concerned about my cook, his wife, and eight children, who lived in the back of my house. Thieu's police could have done all sorts of things to them. So I called up Ev Bumgardner and told him they would have to come get Chau."

After Bumgardner and Vann hid the Vietnamese in the delta, Chau got in touch with Beech and asked him to fly to Can Tho. Vann knew that Beech was coming. "I was not one of Vann's fans," Beech said, "because Sheehan, Halberstam, and Browne had already adopted Vann as one of their own, and when that happened I didn't want any part of him." Nevertheless, Beech had to admit that Vann was about as audacious as you could get. Vann had hidden Chau in the American compound—two doors from the CIA base headquarters in Can Tho. Vann briefed Beech on the plan for getting Chau out of Vietnam.

Vann was ready to help Chau get away, but he doubted whether that was the best course, and Chau wanted to ask Beech what he thought. "Chau said, 'Mr. Vann told me he doesn't want me to leave,' " Beech said. " 'If I leave now,' he said, 'I'll become just another dissatisfied exile, and I'll be quickly forgotten. On the other hand, if I stay and fight I could be executed or imprisoned. Of course, it's my life and my choice.' "

" 'That's right,' I said. 'It is your choice. Nobody can make it for you. It's very simple. Either you stay or you go.' "

AS CHAU PONDERED HIS CHOICE, he thought of the day in 1965 when it had started, the day that his brother Hien appeared at his office in Kien Hoa. His visit came as a bolt from the blue. Chau hadn't seen Hien since the time Chau slipped away in the jungle from the Viet Minh sixteen years before and left the communist side. Solemn, unsmiling Hien. He was a man of integrity, impeccable in his actions, worthy of respect. But a true believer. Marx and Lenin were his gods. Chau had no idea what he wanted, but he tried to see the situation from Hien's perspective and to prepare himself as best he could.

The timing of Hien's visit was probably no accident, Chau thought. It came after the arrival of American combat troops in 1965 had blunted the momentum of the communist forces. The Viet Cong no longer enjoyed the prospect of seeing South Vietnam fall into their hands like a rotten mango, in the wake of the political and military chaos that followed the Diem coup. Was Hien exhausted by the pounding of the Americans and ready to give up?

The two brothers greeted each other with emotion. Hien wore a pair of slacks, a white shirt, sandals. He could have been any middle-class Vietnamese visiting the province chief to discuss a problem; Chau was known for his open-door policy. Tea was served. Chau spoke first. He had prepared what he wanted to say. His first concern, he said, was that Hien uphold the family dignity. He should never forsake his pride. If Hien had grown tired of the war, Chau wanted to help him. He would see to it that Hien was sent to the United States or France, where he would have time to recover, to relax and study. But Hien must not act like any other Viet Cong who surrendered, some of whom lowered themselves into obsequiousness and showed a readiness to betray their former comrades. Chau believed that both Hien and himself had been true to their convictions. Both had a reason to fight. Hien had no cause to suffer a feeling of humiliation. If you are tired, Chau ended, quit quietly. I will help you.

Hien received his brother's speech coolly. He pulled out a letter and handed it to him. It was from the former chief of cadres whom Chau had worked for as a Viet Minh. He was now a high official in the National Liberation Front. The NLF, though made up largely of Southerners, some of them noncommunists, was controlled by communists who reported to Hanoi. The Front was an adaptation of the political camouflage first used by the Viet Minh against the French to conceal their true colors. Hien did not speak of his rank, but Chau deduced that his brother was a colonel in the intelligence section of the defense ministry in Hanoi and assigned to COSVN, the command headquarters in South Vietnam. Officers at his level would operate on instructions passed down from the defense ministry, if not the ruling Politburo. A brother of Hien and Chau was the English translator for the Politburo.

Chau returned the letter to Hien without reading it. He wanted to receive Hien as his brother, Chau said, not as a representative of the Front. But Chau realized that he had come on an official mission. Hien had no intention of giving up. Indeed, he was more determined than ever. Hien began by saying that they had observed Chau for years. The Front had compiled a thick dossier on his career. They had decided that Chau was not like the others. Hien wanted to recruit Chau but knew better than to try to give him a sales pitch about communism. Instead, he told him he wanted to speak about what they both could do for their country. Not for the communists, he emphasized, but for the country. If you believe you are fighting for a good cause, Hien said, you should look around and ask how many people like yourself have been appointed province chiefs. If you are not interested in money or position, why are you fighting against us?

Chau answered that he was not fighting against Hien because he was a communist. For a Vietnamese, he said, it was not an ideological question of who was a communist or an anticommunist. They were not the United States confronting the Soviet Union. For them the question was who could best help Vietnam. And that was what he was fighting for, Chau said—the country. Of course he was unhappy with the Saigon regime, he said; he was unhappy with many things. But he was dedicated to the cause of freedom. Nevertheless, he was not

233

against the Viet Cong as individuals. They were good Vietnamese. But they were wrong.

Chau was disappointed that they wound up debating politics instead of talking about family matters. He hungered for news of his relatives in the North. Was Hien a brother first and a communist second, or vice versa? Was bronze made of tin and copper, or copper and tin?

Another reason for Hien's sudden appearance became apparent after further talks. He wanted to meet personally with Ambassador Henry Cabot Lodge in Saigon, to open up a channel of communications between the National Liberation Front and the Americans. He suggested that Chau arrange for the meeting through John Paul Vann. There was no doubt in Chau's mind that Hien was operating under instructions from Hanoi, but when Chau tried to question him about the purpose of the proposed meeting with Lodge, Hien replied that he was not allowed to state the reason, even to his brother, although he could tell him that the war had to be solved in talks between the Front and the Americans. But why in Saigon, Chau asked? Surely you have other channels. Hien replied that every channel had a specific objective, which was all he was prepared to say.

When Hien's request was considered, it made sense to believe that Hanoi might want to open communications with Ambassador Lodge, who had already demonstrated his clout by overseeing the removal of Ngo Dinh Diem. A man who could get rid of a leader like Diem could also push aside a Vietnamese general or two and make way for a coalition government in Saigon. Nobody, of course, could be sure that was what the communists had in mind. Hien's mission could have been that of an agent provocateur, designed to stir up trouble between the Americans and the Saigon government. But the timing suggested otherwise, for Hien appeared at the moment the communists realized the Americans had an overwhelming technological superiority. These were not the road-bound French they were fighting, but an enemy who could leapfrog a battalion or a brigade with its supporting artillery to a new position within a matter of minutes by helicopter. Comments by communist leaders after the war revealed that this was indeed a moment of crisis in their confidence that the Americans could be defeated. No one could doubt the resiliency and tenacity of the gritty little guerrilla in black pajamas—but a B-52 attack could shake anybody's faith.

Chau told John Paul Vann about Hien's request. Vann said he would carry the message to Ambassador Lodge. Chau also told his CIA contact, Stu Methven. He did not know Methven as well as Vann and he omitted the information that Hien was his brother, identifying him as a Viet Cong intelligence officer.

"He said he had this source on the other side and could make these contacts," Methven said. "I encouraged him to do so. I said we would be more than happy if we could get in touch with these guys. That all is true. But I'll be damned if I remember his saying that it was his brother he was talking about."

John Paul Vann, who knew Hien was Chau's brother and so informed Lodge, returned from Saigon with the word that the ambassador refused to meet with the National Liberation Front's representative. Lodge suggested instead that Hien talk to another embassy official. One could see a reason for Lodge's caution. If Hien turned out to be an agent provocateur and Hanoi chose to publicize the meeting, the ambassador would be compromised with the Saigon government, which he was trying to coax into some form of stability. On the other hand, if the United States were truly interested in trying to bring about a negotiated settlement of the war, then opening discussions with Hanoi through Hien would be a risk well worth taking. The fact was that Hien's feeler came at a time when the Americans were at their most optimistic. A light had been glimpsed at the end of a tunnel. As a further indication that Hien's mission was probably of substantial importance, he refused to see anyone but Ambassador Lodge. If the communists could not talk to the pro-consul who was talking to the president of the United States, they would talk to no one.

Hien appeared once more after the 1968 Tet offensive to offer Chau a position as a cabinet minister in the National Liberation Front if he would defect from the Saigon side. Chau looked at his brother incredulously. How could he make such an offer after their long hours of talks. Hien shrugged. He said he was following instructions from the Front. After that, Chau lost contact with Hien. He did not tell anyone in the Saigon government about his meetings, fearing that the government, which had undergone a half-dozen upheavals, was so unstable that the secret would get out and compromise everybody concerned. And neither the embassy nor the CIA informed Vietnamese government officials about Chau's contacts. The secret lay in the files for nearly five years.

14

SAIGON 1965

ED LANSDALE WAS UNAWARE of the communist attempt to communicate with Ambassador Lodge. Had he known of it, he would have taken it as further proof that the war could still be won by political rather than military means. In 1965, as Hien was getting ready to visit Chau, Lansdale was packing his bags to go to Saigon as Lodge's special assistant for pacification.

While Lansdale had lost none of his enthusiasm for Vietnam, the previous nine years, after the Saigon Military Mission was disbanded and he returned to Washington to work in the Pentagon, had been a frustrating period for him. The first disappointment came with President Kennedy's backing away from the offer to make Lansdale his ambassador to Saigon. Then Kennedy saddled him, in late 1961, with the job of trying to get rid of Cuba's Fidel Castro. Just what the Kennedy brothers, Jack and Bobby, had in mind when they said "get rid of Castro" later became the subject of press speculation and a congressional investigation; and Lansdale joined other officials in the public denials to protect the Kennedys (and themselves), but in private he was subtle enough to understand what they were calling for and honest enough to put it in words—which got him in trouble after he took over as operations chief of the secret project to overthrow Castro, code-named MONGOOSE. Lansdale used the phrase "liquidation of leaders" in a memorandum listing the possible courses of action to be taken against Castro, and what a flurry that caused! One did not put such specifics on paper, he was told by a CIA and former

FBI agent, who was perfectly willing to help knock off the Cuban leader, so long as "deniability" was maintained.

But even without the gaffe, it was clear that Lansdale was unsuited for the Cuban job. He was a specialist in creating governments, not in overthrowing them. He tried gamely to get in the swing of it, calling for "boom and bang" in Cuba, but it was obvious to the CIA paramilitary men who worked with him that he understood little about sabotage and over-the-beach operations. What's more, he was not allowed to be his usual freewheeling self but was kept under tight rein by a supervising structure headed by General Maxwell Taylor, who was not a Lansdale admirer. Lansdale developed a six-phase plan for overthrowing Castro, but was given permission by Taylor to advance no farther than the first phase, devoted mainly to intelligence collection. The sabotage and espionage operations that went off under his direction were either mere pinpricks or out-and-out bungles. His critics claimed that Lansdale's ever bountiful cornucopia of ideas was heavily on the nutty side.

Yet his presence on the Cuban project was largely irrelevant to its success or failure. The fact was that Fidel Castro was not going to be dislodged by anything short of military invasion—or by assassination. Since an invasion was out of the question, it began to look as though the alternative offered the best hope of getting rid of him, and nobody thought Lansdale would be good at carrying out an assassination plot. When the Cuban missile crisis occurred in October 1962, President Kennedy and his attorney-general brother, who'd both grown impatient with Lansdale's lack of progress against Castro, decided to close down his operations, to avoid exacerbating the tense situation at hand, which looked as if it might lead to a nuclear war. After the crisis was over, Lansdale was replaced as head of the Cuban project by Desmond FitzGerald, chief of the CIA's Far East Division. FitzGerald's old job was taken over by his deputy, William Colby. On the day Kennedy was killed in Dallas, FitzGerald was in a Paris hotel room encouraging a Cuban agent to erase Castro, after the CIA had tried but failed to get the Mafia to do the job. The new president, Lyndon Johnson, believed that the attempts against Castro were somehow linked to Kennedy's assassination and halted the project.

With the failure of his Cuban job, Lansdale was at loose ends. He tried to write a role for himself as a specialist on South America, but the State Department, worried that he would display his penchant for independent action, succeeded in limiting his influence on Latin American policy. Nor did he work out as an assistant to the secretary of defense. He had reached an impasse in his career. Churlishly, the Pentagon cut orders for his immediate retirement while he was out of Washington on a trip to Bolivia. The order was modified on his return and the retirement postponed for five months, and he was promoted to major general as a consolation, but Lansdale was in despair. He was cleaning out his desk at the Pentagon on November 1, 1963, when a friend from the Associated Press called to tell him about the coup d'état in Saigon. Other military men might have accepted the news with resignation and used a barbecue-and-golf-filled retirement to put Vietnam behind them. But the Diem coup made Lansdale, who was fifty-five, more determined than ever to try to influence American policy.

He moved into the Executive Office Building, next to the White House, as a consultant to the Food for Peace program. It was volunteer work, an unpaid position for a good cause, with a direct benefit accruing to Lansdale by putting him in proximity to the national leadership. One rising figure in Washington was a senator from Minnesota by the name of Hubert Humphrey, who had been the motivating force behind the Food for Peace program, and who took a paternal interest in its success. Humphrey, the Senate majority whip and a friend of Lyndon Johnson, was a strong anticommunist who shared the same buoyant optimism of Lansdale that international problems could be resolved by political means. It was said that Kennedy lifted the idea for the Peace Corps from Humphrey. In any event, the two of them, Humphrey and Lansdale, the politician and the political operative, seemed as natural as a June wedding; and Rufus Phillips got in touch with William Connell, Humphrey's chief of staff, to set up a meeting. Connell was impressed by Rufe Phillips and quickly converted to the Lansdale philosophy.

"Clearly, Lansdale wanted to direct the war into a much more political role and apparently was being blocked by the National Security Council at the White House and by the Pentagon," William Connell said. "So I think he decided to make an end run, to come at Johnson through Humphrey."

Hubert Humphrey became Lansdale's chief supporter in Washington and a conduit for his ideas to President Johnson. "The process was delicate," said Humphrey in his memoirs, "since, in effect, I was challenging Maxwell Taylor, for whom Johnson and I had esteem growing in part from Taylor's close association with President

Kennedy." But Humphrey believed in Lansdale. "Instinct said Lansdale was right—at least more right than Taylor—but my military knowledge was limited," he said. "Johnson listened to what I had to say, but he understandably did not consider me an expert, even bolstered by Lansdale, whose views deserved being on par with Taylor's, Bundy's, Rusk's or McNamara's."

President Johnson, who did not know a great deal about foreign affairs, the domestic side being his primary area of expertise, depended for advice on the Kennedy holdovers in his new administration, and he circulated the memo Humphrey wrote about Lansdale to them. On June 25, 1964, Major General Chester V. Clifton, Jr., Johnson's (and formerly Kennedy's) military aide and a Taylor supporter, iced Humphrey's suggestion that Lansdale and Phillips be sent to Saigon. In his memo to Johnson, Clifton said, ". . . fine as these men are, they have a reputation for using the 'lone wolf' approach rather than being men who can participate as part of a team effort. I do not recommend that you inject Lansdale-Phillips into the action at this time."

Humphrey, who was about to become Johnson's vice-presidential running mate, did not push the Lansdale appointment, but he continued to speak out, appropriating Lansdale's ideas. In September 1964 he wrote: "We should not attempt to take over the war from the Vietnamese. The present struggle is between Vietnamese of various political beliefs. No lasting solution can be imposed by foreign armies. We must remember the struggle in Vietnam is as much a political and social struggle as a military one. What has been needed in Vietnam is a government in which the people of Vietnam have a stake."

Johnson was unimpressed by Humphrey's hoisting of the Lansdale banner, but he apparently suffered a twinge of doubt about having dismissed with little consideration the political strategy espoused by Lansdale on the advice of General Clifton and the Kennedy holdovers. The twinge was caused by the poor showing in Saigon of the hero himself, Maxwell Taylor. In June 1964, when Henry Cabot Lodge decided to return to the States to take part in the presidential campaign, Johnson sent Taylor to Saigon as his ambassador. Here was a chance for the man who had given such unequivocal advice on Vietnam over the years to show what he could do. Instead of making an in-and-out trip to Saigon as he had done so many times, Taylor now had the opportunity to live there, breathe the air, and deal with the Vietnamese on a day-to-day basis.

Admittedly, Taylor arrived in Vietnam at one of the worst periods of the war. The Diem coup, instead of solving the problem, opened the door to political chaos. In one of his last acts before quitting Saigon as CIA station chief, William Colby had drafted a list of possible successors to Diem in case something happened to him. Heading Colby's list was a general named Nguyen Khanh. And for a while, after Khanh, on January 30, 1964, overthrew the generals who had overthrown Diem three months earlier, Washington thought it had found a strongman who could prosecute the war. Robert McNamara, whose demeanor was not normally suggestive of personal warmth, flew to Vietnam and embraced Khanh with a buddy hug, a signal to all that he was America's boy. But Colby's assessment of Khanh's abilities soon appeared to be woefully shortsighted.

"I may be a little too defensive, a little too tolerant of Khanh," Colby said. "But the thing he became erratic about after he took over was the Buddhists. Khanh knew that the Americans had turned on Diem because he couldn't get along with the Buddhists. Now, if I were the one who took power thereafter, I would be very careful in my relations with them, because the Americans might turn on me too. Of course by that time we were disgusted with the Buddhists, so we became annoyed at his tolerance for them. It was a turnabout that in a curious way led to the break between ourselves and Khanh."

Whatever the case, Khanh's emotional distress, caused by his confrontations with the Buddhists and sundry other crises, appeared so great as to call into question his stability. His mood shifts were frequent, his statements edgy and unpredictable. A carnival atmosphere developed at the Joint General Staff headquarters, where newly minted colonels and generals elbowed each other for position on the merry-go-round. All that was missing was the cotton candy and a booth for guessing the date of the next coup d'état.

Taylor was given high marks for bringing order and discipline to the American mission. He acted like the general he was and told everybody to shape up or ship out. The problem started when he demanded that the Vietnamese do the same. Taylor was usually tactful with Khanh and the generals, but his growing exasperation with their shenanigans was finally tipped over by an incident that involved Lou Conein and got the CIA man kicked out of Vietnam. After working for months to encourage political stability, Taylor and the embassy had engineered a semblance of a civilian government, made up of a High National Council headed by two distinguished but aging civilians of no great competence. Khanh and the younger officers wanted the council to sign a decree retiring all the older generals who had been involved in the Diem coup, thus removing them by fait accompli from the power struggle then going on among the so-called Young Turks. When the new prime minister and chief of state refused, Khanh's generals arrived in the middle of the night and told the council that it was dissolved. Ambassador Taylor, irritated by this puff of wind at his house of cards, advised the civilian council to defy the generals and refuse to be disbanded. This angered Khanh and his men.

Taylor called the generals to the embassy for a dressing down. Khanh refused to come and sent four emissaries, including Nguyen Van Thieu and Nguyen Cao Ky, who were rising powers among the younger generals. Taylor greeted them coolly.

"Do all of you understand English?" he asked. "I told you all clearly at General Westmoreland's dinner we Americans were tired of coups. Apparently I wasted my words. Maybe this is because something is wrong with my French because you evidently didn't understand. I made it clear that all the military plans which I know you would like to carry out are dependent on government stability. Now you have made a real mess. We cannot carry you forever if you do things like this."

During the discussion, one of the Vietnamese, Cang, the navy commander, flared back at Taylor: "It seems as though we are being treated as though we were guilty. What we did was good and we did it only for the good of the country."

Taylor tried to persuade them to support the civilian regime and to restore the High National Council. The generals refused. Giving up, Taylor ended the meeting by saying, "You people have broken a lot of dishes and now we have to see how we can straighten out this mess."

When Khanh heard what happened, he began to steam. Not only had Taylor caused the emissaries to lose face by dressing them down, but he had also put Khanh in the position of looking like an ineffectual leader if he did nothing to counter this American insult of treating them, as Ky put it, like a bunch of second lieutenants.

Several days after the meeting, Khanh, who was in the mountain resort of Dalat, phoned Lou Conein and asked to see him. After getting his station chief's okay, Conein took an Air America plane to Dalat to talk to the general. Khanh was in an irascible mood and angry with Ambassador Taylor. Conein made notes of his criticisms of Taylor and carefully asked if Khanh was certain that he wanted Conein to relay his comments to the ambassador. When Khanh said he did, Conein flew back to Saigon and went to the ambassador's residence, where he found Taylor playing tennis with Alexis Johnson, his deputy ambassador. Conein read his notes to the two men. Taylor looked at Conein sternly and said, "You sure you understand French?" Taylor decided to go immediately to Dalat to see Khanh, but the airport had become fogged in and he had to turn back. By the time Taylor talked to Khanh, several days later, the mood of the Vietnamese had changed completely. He was cheerful and said that everything was fine. Meanwhile, Khanh's brother-in-law had told Beverly Deepe, a reporter for the *New York Herald-Tribune,* what Khanh had told Conein—that he considered Taylor persona non grata. Taylor probably believed that Conein had given Deepe the story. At any rate, after it appeared, Taylor called Conein to his office and said, "Colonel, I'm afraid you have outlived your usefulness. I'm going to ask for your recall." He showed Conein the message he was sending to the director of the CIA. Conein requested thirty days to get his family out of the country, and Taylor agreed.

Taylor's dustup with the generals hurt him at the White House. He was no longer the awesome figure above criticism he had once been in the eyes of Johnson and his staff. A week later, on December 30, 1964, Johnson, who had read the *Herald-Tribune* story, sent Taylor a personal cable expressing his worry about the lack of progress ". . . in communicating sensitively and persuasively with the various groups in South Vietnam. . . . In particular, I wonder whether we are making full use of the kind of Americans who have shown a knack for this kind of communication in the past . . . even if they are not the easiest men to handle in a country team. To put it another way, I continue to believe that we should have the most sensitive, the most persistent, and attentive Americans that we can find in touch with Vietnamese of every kind and quality. . . ."

Lansdale! No question about it. Lyndon Johnson was telling the proud Taylor that Lansdale and his adherents could do a better job with the Vietnamese. It was a slap in the face, and taken as such. According to General Westmoreland, Taylor was "stung" by Johnson's implied criticism. And although he never admitted it straight out, Taylor was coming to believe that Lansdale had been right and himself wrong about a number of things, particularly about the advisability of introducing American combat troops into Vietnam. It was a startling about-face to those who knew him.

"Ambassador Taylor objected to bringing in American ground troops," General Westmoreland recorded in his memoirs. "Although some years earlier while in Washington he had recommended bringing in U.S. Army Engineers primarily to help in flood relief but also to provide an American ground presence, he had come to the conclusion by early 1965 that once the United States assumed any ground combat role, the South Vietnamese would try to unload more tasks. Sending the first U.S. ground combat troops would be a foot in the door leading to ever-widening commitment. He saw problems for the 'white-faced' soldier trying to adjust to an Oriental environment, probably unable to adjust to the exigencies of guerrilla warfare in the same way the French had failed to adjust."

In fact, although Westmoreland was careful to speak of it in the modulated tones of an-officer-and-a-gentleman in his memoirs, Taylor's change of heart caused something of a break between them. This was all the more remarkable as Westmoreland was a Taylor protégé, and, like Paul Harkins, the first MACV commander, had been selected for the job partly at his recommendation. Taylor, Harkins, and Westmoreland looked as though they were cast from the same ingot of stainless steel. Stiff-backed, jut-jawed, overflowing with medals, the three of them cut terrific figures in uniform. (The Taylor-Harkins-Westmoreland record in Vietnam suggested that all generals should be subjected to the Ulysses S. Grant dress test: the better a man looks in uniform, the more skeptical one should be of his abilities. This would have identified Creighton Abrams, who was slump-shouldered and as rumpled as a charter passenger, and Fred Weyand, who looked like a tall, rawboned clodhopper, as the most capable commanders to serve in Vietnam—as indeed they were.) Before Taylor's arrival, an ambiguous relationship had existed between the military commander and the ambassador. Paul Harkins considered himself at least coequal and not subordinate to the ambassador. In this case, Johnson made it clear, probably at Taylor's behest, that the ambassador would be running the show.

Yet in the early months of 1965, after Taylor's dispute with the generals, President Johnson began to look to Westmoreland for advice. The momentum for greater intervention was growing in Washington. Knowing that Taylor was against bringing in combat troops,

Westmoreland hit on a way of getting around him, by asking for marines to be sent as guards to protect the Da Nang airbase, as opposed to their coming as combat troops. Westmoreland later asserted that he was worried about the security of the airbase, which was used for bombing attacks on North Vietnam, and that his request for marines was not a strategem to pave the way for a further military buildup. In any case, to Westmoreland's relief, Taylor bought it. But Taylor had begun to exhibit the same symptoms of testiness with the top-ranking American general that he had shown with the top-ranking Vietnamese general. The landing of the marines at Da Nang on March 7, 1965, touched off his temper once again. Westmoreland told of it:

"Circumstances of the landing led to the only sharp exchange I ever had with Ambassador Taylor. Word of the time of the landing got to me from the Joint Chiefs before it reached the embassy, and even though I notified the embassy, the word apparently failed to get to the ambassador in advance. He was visibly piqued, his upset accentuated because the marines had arrived with tanks, self-propelled artillery, and other heavy equipment he had not expected. 'Do you know my terms of reference,' Ambassador Taylor demanded sharply, 'and that I have authority over you?' 'I understand fully,' I replied, 'and I appreciate it completely, Mr. Ambassador.' That ended the matter."

Actually, it didn't. Westmoreland and Taylor disagreed again, though with tempers under control, about the most important question of military strategy: how the troops would be used once they were in the country. Taylor, in another nod to the Lansdale philosophy, did not want American troops roving around destroying the countryside and creating more Viet Cong. His attitude was influenced by his deputy, U. Alexis Johnson, a career diplomat, who was more sensitive than most officials to the ramifications of bringing in conventional troops. Taylor wanted to lock the Americans into specific areas—called enclaves—on the densely populated coast of South Vietnam, with their backs to the water, limiting their forays on offensive operations in towns and villages. Taylor's recommendations were kept secret by the White House, but another famous airborne general of World War Two, James Gavin, went public less than a year later with a similar proposal for an enclave strategy. As its supporters saw it, the enclave strategy would allow the Americans, along with their South Vietnamese allies, to bring long-term security to a specific area, which in turn would facilitate pacification in the form of economic improvement projects for the rice farmers and the winkling out of the Viet Cong's political/administrative organization by selective police action in a program like Phoenix.

Westmoreland strongly opposed the enclave strategy. His influence as the field commander on the scene was growing with President Johnson, and he was able to beat down the proposals of Taylor and Gavin. "I disagreed with the enclave strategy," Westmoreland said. "As my staff study put it at the time, it represented 'an inglorious, static use of U.S. forces in overpopulated areas with little chance of direct or immediate impact on the outcome of events.'" Westmoreland devised instead what he considered a more glorious strategy based on the traditional mission of the conventional infantry in searching out and destroying the enemy, sometimes called in the case of Vietnam the "attrition" or "meatgrinder" strategy—meaning kill enough of them and they would give up, theory had it.

The small group of political action operatives such as Ed Lansdale, John Paul Vann, and William Colby recognized from the outset that Westmoreland's decision to concentrate on moving around to kill the Viet Cong would mean that pacification would fail because of a lack of stable security for the villages. Why should the rice farmers commit themselves to the Saigon government if they faced the prospect of the Americans coming in, shooting up their villages, and then leaving the area several days later for the Viet Cong to take over once again? As long as the Viet Cong village chief was able to escape them and remain active, he could recruit more guerrilla fighters to replace those the Americans had killed.

Though Maxwell Taylor had moved toward the Lansdale position, he was by no means ready to embrace the guru of political action. After he received the stinging cable from President Johnson following his flap with the Vietnamese generals, Taylor replied with a politely acerbic cable of his own, telling Johnson that he didn't need any help in dealing with the Vietnamese.

Nevertheless, with his lack of political finesse exposed to the world, and his private disagreements with Westmoreland over strategy common knowledge at the White House, it was evident that Taylor had outlived his usefulness. Johnson decided to get rid of him. The explanation for his leaving was fuzzed over, and his new job description was that of a powerful-sounding White House adviser, but his influence had all but evaporated, and Taylor was never to play another major role during the war. His quiet departure from Saigon, in

July 1965, raised the curtain for the second coming of Henry Cabot Lodge.

ED LANSDALE MADE USE OF his relationship with Hubert Humphrey to penetrate the Senate Foreign Relations Committee. He published an article in the October 1964 edition of *Foreign Affairs,* entitled "Viet Nam: Do We Understand Revolution?" which reiterated his philosophy and attracted some attention; and the following month his lieutenant, Rufe Phillips, circulated a prescient memorandum among Washington policymakers. The Lansdale-Phillips memo predicted that Washington would soon have to adopt one, or a combination, of four approaches to the war: (1) the bombing of North Vietnam; (2) sending combat troops to South Vietnam; (3) negotiating a withdrawal; or (4) undertaking a "positive, politically-oriented, integrated program." The memo opposed the first three options and concluded that "Only the last course of action offers real hope of an outcome consonant with United States national objectives, principles, and honor." Senator Humphrey decided that it was time to put Lansdale and Phillips in touch with the Foreign Relations Committee, and in January 1965 he arranged for an informal session with Fulbright, himself, and Senator John Sparkman.

"What I'd done was get in very close to Hubert Humphrey," Lansdale said. "He then took me up and introduced me to the senators on the Foreign Relations Committee. I talked to Fulbright for a while, and he said, 'You sure you are a general? Generals scare me. They have brass buttons and all these decorations.' He looked at me for a minute. 'But you understand what the score is.' Humphrey said, 'Yeah, and we want you to back him.' "

Fulbright tried, but when he spoke to Lyndon Johnson about Lansdale, he said, he received "a very cool reception." Moreover, the administration reacted with spite after Lansdale's session with Fulbright. Lansdale and Phillips had brought along a couple of pacification officials who had flown from Saigon to brief the senators. One of them, Bert Fraleigh, who had worked with Phillips around the time of his tour as head of rural development, echoed the Lansdale line about

247

Vietnam being a political war. After Fraleigh's boss at the Agency for International Development learned that he had talked to the committee, he was fired for "disloyalty."

Hubert Humphrey fared no better with Johnson. When the Pentagon ignored both the strategy of pacification by political action and the military enclave strategy for limiting the destruction in the countryside, Humphrey became disillusioned with the way the war was being fought, but he quickly lost whatever influence he had left with Johnson.

"By 1965 Humphrey had really begun to question the efficacy of the bombings and the big battalions and the heavy artillery," said William Connell, his chief of staff. "Much of his questioning was due to his exposure to Lansdale. Johnson said to Humphrey, 'Tell me anything you want to say as long as it's done in private. But don't cross me in a meeting.' He knew Humphrey was garrulous, and he was paranoid about the possibility of his leaking something. Then one day in a National Security Council meeting, Humphrey opposed the president on the question of the bombing of North Vietnam. Johnson was furious. He froze him out. He didn't want to hear any more of Humphrey's views on pacification and nation-building."

Having decided, however, to get rid of Maxwell Taylor, Johnson picked Lodge as his replacement with the idea of deflecting republican criticism of the war, and Lodge saw the possible value of taking Lansdale with him. To grease the way for Lodge's return to Saigon, Johnson sent him to Vietnam on a fact-finding trip nearly two months before it was announced that Taylor would be leaving. Afterward, he appeared before the Foreign Relations Committee to report on his trip. Lodge had a shrewd understanding of what would play well with Fulbright and what would help get him through his confirmation hearings as ambassador, which he knew would be coming up in a couple of months. Speaking before the committee Lodge sounded as though he had undergone an organ transplant from Lansdale and Colby, calling Vietnam a "politico-military" war. Fulbright was suitably impressed by his attitude, and he emphasized to Lodge how taken he and other senators had been by Lansdale when he appeared before them four months earlier.

It might have been at this point, after realizing that Lansdale had the support of some formidable political powers, that Lodge decided to ask Lansdale to accompany him to Saigon. He would not have made the offer without the president's approval, but the decision was probably takcn in a shorthand discussion between the two politicians that lasted no more than seconds. Neither of them needed a calculator to add and subtract the pluses and minuses of the appointment. Beyond the politics of the matter, however, Lodge truly believed that Lansdale might help him get the pacification program restarted, after it had lain dead in the water during the two years of political chaos following the Diem coup. On his first tour, Lodge had backed a plan for trying to turn a province close to Saigon, called Long An, into a showcase for pacification. He believed that if he could pacify this one province and demonstrate that it could be done, the techniques developed in the process could be used to pacify other provinccs, in the fashion of a spreading oil slick. Lodge's project had failed, and he was interested in having Lansdale try his hand.

His doubts about recruiting Lansdale were diminished further by the attitude of the Foreign Relations Committee at the session called to act on his confirmation as ambassador. The hearing took place on the morning of July 27, 1965, and Fulbright braced him again on the question of taking a political rather than a military approach to the war, referring once more to Lansdale's meeting with the committee. With foresight, Lodge had invited Lansdale for lunch that same day, after he finished with the committee.

"Lodge asked to see me for lunch," Lansdale said. "I'd known him when he was a senator and met him a couple of times when he was ambassador to Saigon. He said, 'The president has asked for you to go to Saigon. I've wanted to see you back there for a long time, because you are the real expert on pacification.' He told me he'd tried to pacify Long An province but hadn't succeeded. Hc said hc couldn't get any Vietnamesc officials to stay overnight in the villages. I said, 'There's something more than military security we should be generating. We've got to have a political effort.' I asked him to let me work on the political end as well. He said that the embassy already had a political man for that. He wanted me to come to Saigon by myself as his assistant for pacification. But I insisted on taking a team with me, and finally he agreed."

Lansdale thought there was still a chance to win by political means if only he could set the thinking of Johnson and Lodge on the right track. He drafted a memo, which Lodge sent to the president. "The enemy in Vietnam understands thoroughly the political nature of the war he is waging," Lansdale wrote, in part. "The enemy sees his every act as a political act, and uses psychological, military, and socio-economic weapons to gain his political goals. This is a strict rule the enemy borrowed from Clausewitz. Lenin, Mao, Ho, and Giap have been clear and firm on this basic rule. The Viet Cong have obeyed it amazingly well. Our side has broken this rule over and over again. It is being broken daily right now.

"Thus, when you ask my help to get a Counter-Subversion/Terrorism program moving, you are really asking me to help you to get our side to start obeying and applying the prime rule of the war in Vietnam. It isn't separate from the other programs. It is the basis upon which the war in Vietnam will be won or lost. The psychological, military, and socio-economic programs are its instruments, not ends in themselves. Political bankruptcy in Vietnam and the direct use of U.S. combat forces complicate your task vastly. (A U.S. commander, tasked to attack a suspected enemy position, is going to clobber it first by bombing or artillery to cut his own U.S. casualties to a minimum when they attack; casualties of Vietnamese noncombatants must be secondary to his responsibility to his own command and mission.) I point this out to underscore the fact that something brand new, perhaps of considerable difference from anything previous, will have to be worked out in Vietnam to put the war on the essential political footing."

McGeorge Bundy read Lansdale's memo and passed it on to President Johnson, adding a note: "Lansdale appears quite ready to take over MACV—and yet he's not all wrong. Can we afford some creative tension?"

Whether or not Lansdale's methods would have won in Vietnam, the logic of his memorandum was irrefutable. He fully realized that American military tactics would result in tremendous civilian casualties among the rice farmers, the very people the United States was supposed to be winning to the Saigon government's side. He wasn't trying to blame the military but simply to point out the reality of the use of conventional combat troops. But Lansdale's memo appeared not to have made a dent in White House thinking, except to gain him a little indulgent tolerance from McGeorge Bundy, Johnson's reputedly brilliant national security adviser. Having consistently supported an integrated political-military approach to the war his entire career, Lansdale, finally, was heading back to Saigon once again. He was returning at the precise moment Lyndon Johnson decided to launch a massive ground war in Vietnam.

On July 28, 1965, the day after Lansdale's lunch with Lodge,

Johnson announced at a televised news conference that he was sending fifty thousand more troops to Vietnam. What he didn't say was that he intended to send an additional fifty thousand four months later and to raise their number by a hundred thousand in 1966. The secret debate over whether to send large-scale combat forces had begun with General Westmoreland's request on June 7, 1965, for a buildup of troops—three months after the marines arrived to protect the Da Nang airbase. Westmoreland believed that American forces would have to be used to prevent the collapse of the Saigon army, which was suffering one defeat after another on the battlefield, and whose will to fight, never strong, was declining with each passing day. Johnson's advisers first reacted by saying that his request went too far, but most of them agreed that he should be given enough troops to insure a military stalemate on the battlefield. A stalemate, they believed, coupled with the bombing of North Vietnam, would either force Hanoi to negotiate a settlement or stop the North Vietnamese from supporting the Viet Cong in the South.

Not that the president showed any hesitation about sending the troops once it came down to, in the opinion of his military commander and his advisers, the possibility that South Vietnam might go under without them. His decision, he said in his memoirs, was based on two factors. The first had to do with his belief in the domino theory, the idea that if South Vietnam fell "all of Southeast Asia would pass under communist control, slowly or quickly, but inevitably, at least down to Singapore and almost certainly to Djakarta." "Second," Johnson said, "I knew our people well enough to realize that if we walked away from Vietnam and let Southeast Asia fall, there would follow a divisive and destructive debate in our country . . . about 'who lost Vietnam' . . . even more destructive to our national life than the argument over China had been."

Dominos and China were on Johnson's mind, not any fancy theories about how to fight the war coming from a maverick like Lansdale.

ANOTHER CRUCIAL CHANGE could be pinpointed as occurring around the time of Lansdale's return to Saigon. It had to do with the kind of news the American public would receive about the war from that point onward. On August 3, 1965, the day Lodge passed to Johnson Lansdale's memo that warned that the American military could suppress the communists "but cannot defeat them short of genocide unless our side puts the war on a political footing," a U.S. Marine company was moving from the Da Nang airbase to the village of Cam Ne. The mission of the marines had been changed without public announcement from one of protecting the airbase to making combat sweeps. This attracted the intense interest of journalists, who wanted to show the first scenes of American troops engaged in combat. The marines moving into Cam Ne were accompanied by CBS television reporter Morley Safer and his cameraman and sound technician.

The perspiring Morley Safer who walked into Cam Ne that day was not the picture of mellowed-out urbanity that he would appear to be twenty years later on CBS's *60 Minutes.* Safer, a Canadian, was, at thirty-four, a rough-seamed ball of aggression. An Anglophile who shared the not uncommon Canadian ambivalence about American culture, he seemed especially skeptical of Americans who wore uniforms or were spokesmen for the government. Most reporters had, as it might be gently described, an adversarial relationship with military flacks. But Safer appeared to enjoy rattling their cages for the sheer hell of it.

Only three weeks earlier, in mid-July 1965, Safer had gotten into a verbal fight with Arthur Sylvester, assistant secretary of defense for public affairs, who was on a trip to Saigon with Robert McNamara. Press relations, never good, had deteriorated shortly before the arrival of the marines in Da Nang over the question of access to the airbase, which was being used for bombing raids on North Vietnam. A group of reporters met to discuss their grievances with Sylvester, a gritty ex-newspaperman. When Sylvester tried to lecture his former colleagues on what he considered to be their patriotic duty, Safer retorted, "Surely, Arthur, you don't expect the American press to be the handmaidens of the government." Safer was jabbing Sylvester with the old exhortation of Admiral Felt for reporters to get on the team, which had been pinging around the press corps since the Halberstam days. "That's exactly what I expect," Sylvester replied, and the meeting broke down in acrimony. "I don't have to talk to you," Sylvester said. "I'll talk to your editors."

Thus, in a sense, Morley Safer the television journalist replaced David Halberstam the print journalist, who had left Vietnam the year before, as the target for the American mission's discontent with how the war was being reported. And Safer, like Halberstam, an aggressive journalist with the same abundance of self-confidence that sometimes spilled over into arrogance, was not going to back away from the fight. Safer's status as the reporter the mission loved to hate was confirmed by the story he filmed at Cam Ne. It showed American marines burning the thatched homes of the villagers, whom they believed to be Viet Cong.

Safer's Cam Ne story outraged the mission. General Westmoreland was furious. During the Halberstam days, the embassy and the military had tried to discredit reporters by calling into question their courage and by charging that they spent most of their time in Saigon. But the 1965 buildup brought helicopters that newsmen could use to move around the country. No one could accuse Safer of sticking to the city. Nor could anyone accuse him of lacking courage, for he had proved on numerous occasions, along with his cameraman Jerry Adams, that he was ready to put himself on the line to get the story. The only charge left to be made against him was that he had somehow stage-managed the burning incident. Years later, after hundreds of villages had been torched by American troops, General Westmoreland still maintained that Morley Safer had handed the marines a Zippo lighter and urged them to do the job for his camera.

Yet the Cam Ne story cut to the heart of a larger question, one that was lost in the controversy over whether it was real or staged. How did a TV reporter cover Vietnam? In trying to evaluate what he called "this perplexing war," David Halberstam asked, "How do you add up thirty minor engagements each day, almost all of them in places you've never been to, and with no substantive information to cast light on the situation?" Morley Safer's answer (though not Safer's answer personally of course but television's in general) was that the availability of helicopters and the military buildup now made it possible to cover a minor engagement each day and that the drama of the filmed incident could stand for its own meaning. One could, in effect, substitute action for evaluation in telling the TV version of the war. And that action often portrayed the brutality of war as it issued from the American side, as no camera crews covered the communists.

TV journalists might have reported the kind of political action stories Lansdale and Colby and Chau were concerned with, but such stories could not be told in forty-five to ninety seconds with dramatic effect. Network officials such as Richard Salant of CBS made periodic trips to Saigon and vowed to put more substantive stories on the tube. But the least cynical TV reporter was ready to admit the truth: it was a film clip of a helicopter, the most visually exciting instrument of warfare since the plumed knight, mixed with the dramatic sounds of rifle or artillery fire as grunts humped through jungle and rice paddy, that moved the goods to the public.

Not that the print journalists didn't get caught up in the same superficial technique. "As the American buildup proceeded," said Jason McManus, then a *Time* writer, "there was a tremendous fascination with the hardware and the exotic aspects of the war. I think, in retrospect, that kind of starry-eyed technological approach influenced the overall tone of the magazine." Another major aspect of the print story, McManus pointed out, "was the endless spinoffs of human interest stories." And of course there was the daily scorecard of battles and body counts showing the Americans piling up the most points but not really winning.

When newsmen wanted to write about the political aspects of the war, they found themselves turning increasingly to Barry Zorthian, the civilian head of the Joint United States Public Affairs Office, which, among other things, was responsible for putting on the briefing for journalists at five each afternoon in an air-conditioned, theaterlike auditorium in the heart of Saigon. Zorthian, who was short and swarthy, looked like the maitre d' of some vaguely Byzantine restaurant who was ready to sing the praises of the week-old moussaka. In fact, he was of Armenian descent and born in Turkey, arriving in America at age three. But appearances were deceiving in the case of Zorthian and at variance with the deeper reality. Zorro, as he was called, was one of the shrewdest and most sophisticated government officials to serve in Vietnam.

Zorthian had attended Yale, where he was a member of Skull and Bones, and served as a captain with the marines in the South Pacific during World War Two. He had newspaper and radio experience, but his career had been devoted mainly to government information, first with the Voice of America, then as public affairs officer at the New Delhi embassy. In early 1964, Zorthian was assigned to Saigon as part of the shake-up in the mission that followed the Diem coup. Ambassador Lodge, who considered himself an expert on dealing with newsmen, ordered Zorthian to steer clear of the press corps and concentrate on routine public information programs. But Lodge as well as Westmoreland soon recognized Zorthian's special talents, and they urged Washington to appoint him the overall policy coordinator for the media, making him, as his role was often described, the information czar in Saigon.

"A clique grew up around Zorro," said Frank McCulloch, *Time*'s Saigon bureau chief. "I was part of it. We could get information other reporters couldn't. He would invite six or eight journalists to his villa every Thursday evening—someone from either of the newsmagazines, the wire services, the *New York Times, Washington Post,* and a TV network or two. He'd serve us drinks, and then we'd listen to whatever key figure from the mission—or occasionally someone from Washington—he had arranged to brief us. What the official told us would often be off the record. Other times it would be on background, meaning we could use the information but without revealing the source."

After the Thursday backgrounders, Zorthian further narrowed the insider field by inviting a few of the reporters to stick around for an all-night poker game, at which many a dram was downed, as Zorthian relieved the newsmen of sums that presumably did not appear on their expense accounts. While there was a definite element of manipulation to Zorthian's modus operandi, he was genuinely interested in journalists and understood them on a personal level.

To win the respect of journalists such as Frank McCulloch, a former *Los Angeles Times* editor and ex-marine who was one of the best to cover the war, Zorthian obviously had to be more adept than the usual run of government officials who were always, in one way or another, with varying degrees of exasperation, urging newsmen to get on the team. McCulloch and other insiders were under no illusions about what Zorthian was trying to accomplish. "His employer was the U.S. government, and his duty was to present that government in the best possible light," McCulloch said. "Given that criterion, he was a pretty good public servant." By leaning on reluctant mission officials to talk to journalists, by arranging transportation for newsmen at difficult moments, and by presenting himself as the voice of sweet reason in an otherwise hostile mission, Zorthian won the gratitude and trust of the press corps and accumulated the kind of media influence that he could use selectively against his own targets in the bureaucracy—targets such as Ed Lansdale.

While Barry Zorthian was the reference point for political stories on the American side, local legmen hired by Saigon news bureaus served as the reference point on the Vietnamese side. To understand the importance of the Vietnamese legmen, one needed to compare an American journalist metaphorically to a Tibetan journalist, which, under the circumstances prevailing in Saigon, was not as farfetched as it might sound. If a Tibetan journalist who spoke no English came to the United States and hired an American legman who could read the newspapers and understand as a matter of course the basics of his own culture, one might not be surprised to find that the Tibetan journalist tended to accept his American legman's information and opinions as the received truth. So it was with American journalists and their Vietnamese legmen in Saigon.

The two most influential Vietnamese legmen were Nguyen Hung Vuong and Pham Xuan An, both of whom began their American-oriented careers as employees of Lansdale's intelligence team in the mid 1950s. Vuong, who was short, thin, and exceedingly fragile, was the more cerebral of the two. Pham Xuan An, who was taller than the average Vietnamese but who grew stooped as the years passed, was the more direct in his political assessments. Ostensibly a collaborator with the Americans, Pham Xuan An was in fact a secret agent for the communists and, by his own admission after the war, had been a spy since he worked for the Lansdale team.

After the Lansdale team was disbanded and withdrawn from Saigon, Vuong and An became legmen for American journalists. Vuong worked for *The New Yorker*'s Robert Shaplen, Lansdale's best journalist friend. An worked first for the *New York Herald-Tribune*'s Beverly Deepe and then for *Time* magazine, where he later became a staff correspondent.

The influence of Pham Xuan An and Nguyen Hung Vuong stretched far beyond the borders of *Time* and *The New Yorker.* They were either brighter, older, or more self-assured than the other Vietnamese legmen; and so it was left to them to hammer out the general line about Vietnamese politics at Givral's coffee shop each afternoon, which was then relayed to practically every American journalist in Saigon. Pham Xuan An provided, directly, at no extra charge, his interpretation of the political situation to a number of influential American journalists outside of *Time.*

Pham Xuan An was seen in the uniform of a colonel after the fall of Saigon. This went over rather badly with Murray Gart, who, as *Time*'s chief of correspondents, had hired An as a full-fledged staffer, making him the first known case of a communist agent to appear on the masthead of a major American publication as a correspondent.

256

"An, that son of a bitch," Gart said later. "I'd like to kill him."

No doubt Gart was speaking a bit hyperbolically out of personal embarrassment over the matter. Actually, many journalists who had known An did not seem perturbed that a communist agent had been a major source, direct or indirect, for many of the political stories filed out of Saigon. Some of them were titillated to have known a Viet Cong colonel, and others were, to a degree, in sympathy with the communist victory—although a few of the most committed persisted in thinking of it as a victory for the National Liberation Front, long after the northern communists had chewed up and spit out the noncommunist remnants of the southern movement. Journalists such as Morley Safer and David Greenway sought out Pham Xuan An on trips back to Saigon after the war, and they usually viewed his deceptive career with sympathy. Perhaps the journalists figured that between Barry Zorthian, the American information expert, and Pham Xuan An, the Vietnamese communist agent, the political story as reported by the U.S. media had averaged out.

In any event, American newsmen seemed little disappointed that the main focus of the story shifted from murky Vietnamese politics to the military buildup in 1965. Yet the question remained: what did it all mean? The only thing clear was that Ed Lansdale wasn't going to get much help from journalists in trying to give his answer.

JOE REDICK was the least flamboyant member of the Lansdale team who had served in Saigon in 1954, and he was the first to try to point out to Lansdale in 1965 the change in circumstances brought about by the American buildup.

"Lansdale asked me to go back with him," Redick said, "and I told him, 'This is a mistake. We shouldn't go. It's too late.' He said, 'That may be true. But it'll be fun anyway.' I was in a job with the CIA that I liked, but I felt I should go, that he needed me, a bureaucrat, along."

Rufe Phillips wasn't very optimistic either. "All of us were lobbying for Ed to go. I think it was through the efforts of Vice President Humphrey that he was sent back. It came down to a tough choice for me, because I would have to give up an active business. If I had felt the chances were pretty good we could have succeeded, maybe I would've dropped everything. But I'd already gone through a very disappointing exercise out there." Phillips agreed to take off a month from his business to help establish the new team in Saigon.

Not even Lou Conein was enthusiastic. After Ambassador Taylor demanded his recall from Saigon, Conein had returned to CIA headquarters and been offered a covert job in Latin America. He was attending the Foreign Service Institute to learn Spanish when he received a message from his boss telling him that Taylor was being replaced by Lodge, who had requested that Conein be among those going back to Saigon with him. Conein asked about his scheduled assignment to South America, but was told he couldn't refuse Lodge's request and was ordered to attend a briefing at the State Department on the change of regimes at the Saigon embassy. When he got to the meeting, he was surprised to see Lansdale and other members of his old team there.

Dan Ellsberg was also heading to the meeting at State. After working as a consultant to Rand on defense matters and impressing his contacts at the Pentagon, he had been hired the year before as an assistant to John McNaughton, the assistant secretary of defense for international security affairs. McNaughton was Robert McNamara's chief deputy for Vietnam and was spending 70 percent of his time on the problem. He told Ellsberg he wanted him to take some of the pressure off. Ellsberg jumped into the job with his usual intensity and in a short time, by working long hours seven days a week, had established himself as an influential player among the bright young men surrounding the secretary of defense. He was attending the meeting at State as the Pentagon's representative in lieu of McNaughton.

"Colby introduced Lansdale at the meeting," Ellsberg said. "He began by saying, 'I should explain that General Lansdale was once a member of CIA but he has retired. He is now returning to Saigon on a State Department mission.' Lansdale got up and described what he was going to do. He said he would work with the Vietnamese on the political side. After the meeting was over, I went up to him and Conein, and told him I had been impressed by his article in *Foreign Affairs*, and that I was interested in going to Saigon as a member of his team. I said I was a GS-18 but would volunteer to go at any rank, so long as I had enough money to pay my alimony.

"Lansdale said, 'How would you characterize yourself?'

"I said, 'Well, I have a side that is somewhat crazy.'

258

"He and Conein said, 'Give us an example.'

"I told them I had already looked into the possibility of going to Vietnam as a marine captain."

Several months earlier Ellsberg had gone to see his former company commander, who was then assigned to the personnel branch at marine headquarters. The officer told him he would be accepted back into the marines and probably given the rank of major. But a commission as a major would have meant a staff position, and Ellsberg wanted to command a rifle company in combat, with the rank of captain. Since he was a GS-18—the civilian equivalent of lieutenant general—accepting such a low rank would have appeared strange, and he was worried that if anyone at the Pentagon learned of his position he might be yanked out of the line and assigned to write speeches for a general. Meanwhile, he fell in love with Patricia Marx, a freelance journalist and antiwar activist from a wealthy family, and gave up his idea of going back into the marines.

Lansdale told Conein to check out Ellsberg's story. "I had never heard of Daniel Ellsberg until that time," Conein said. "Dan was an extremely intelligent man, maybe a little flaky at times, but he could talk, and he could really write."

"I liked Ellsberg," Lansdale said. "But I had a sort of underhanded motive for putting him on the team. I wanted somebody to keep the bureaucrats off my back in Saigon, and here was this bright young man who could talk a mile a minute."

The power struggle in Saigon had begun to sort itself out by the time the Lansdale team arrived. Chaos had followed the overthrow of Diem, and from November 1963 until Nguyen Cao Ky took over in June 1965, the government changed nine times, but the political situation was not nearly so complicated as it might have seemed to anyone reading press accounts. Part of the problem was that American journalists understood little about the country and therefore were unable to comment very clearly on what was happening. In retrospect, the political situation evolved along bumpy but simple lines. Lou Conein's friends, the top-ranking generals who overthrew Diem, were older men who were heavily influenced by the French. Two of the key conspirators, Tran Van Don and Le Van Kim, held French passports. Beneath them was a body of younger officers, generals and colonels, who had been trained by the French but had not been under the colonial influence long enough to become born-again Frenchmen. Though they had no strong cultural identity as Vietnamese patriots, their chief outside influences were split between French and American, with neither side predominating. (In the latter stages of the war a young officer class of born-again Americans would develop, but not soon enough to make a major difference.) Thus, while the younger officers were not purely Vietnamese in outlook, they were self-conscious about maintaining their independence and skeptical about becoming too Americanized.

The Diem coup was only the first stage of a two-part process to decide who would rule South Vietnam. The second stage, which followed on the heels of the coup, was the move by the young officers to get rid of the upper layer of generals like Don and Kim who had been in power since Diem took over the government in 1954. After this was done, the real weeding out began. In the eighteen months following the Diem coup, two officers, both in their mid-thirties, emerged with the most support among their fellow generals. One of the officers, Vice Air Marshal Nguyen Cao Ky, discovered, almost to his surprise, that his position as commander of the air force, with its capacity to bomb opposition groups into submission, gave him a pivotal role in changing, or not changing, the government by the usual means of coup d'état. The other officer was Brigadier General Nguyen Van Thieu, whose growing power was based, not like Ky's on command of an important military unit, but on the fact that he was one of the smartest generals and canny in his moves to gather influence.

Neither Ky nor Thieu emerged as the uncontested leader of the generals. The other officers, jealous of their prerogatives, were unwilling to grant anyone the kind of power that Diem had held. A third general, Nguyen Chanh Thi, had ambitions of his own that made him wary of Ky and Thieu, whom he considered upstarts. Thi was the officer who led the abortive 1960 coup against Diem. He returned from exile after Diem was overthrown and took command of the military region in the northern part of South Vietnam, which included the country's second and third largest cities, Hue and Da Nang, a fiefdom that he ruled like a warlord, his chin outthrust at Ky and Thieu. He was eventually removed by force, during an uprising that broke out in the spring of 1966.

The generals toyed with the idea of putting civilians in charge of the government, and thanks to the frantic efforts of the embassy and CIA even tried it a few times, but the temptations of power were too great for them to relinquish. Under American pressure to form some kind of stable government, they finally got together and after the usual emotional wrangling, during which each of them portrayed—no doubt believed—himself to be a self-denying patriot interested only in the good of the country, they ratified the choice of Ky as prime minister and Thieu as president, an arrangement that gave the airman the most power.

Nguyen Cao Ky was not unknown to the Americans. Trained as a transport pilot by the French, he had distinguished himself in Saigon's fledgling air force as an officer with style and courage, both of which tilted toward flamboyance. When CIA station chief William Colby began his commando raids on North Vietnam, it was Ky who volunteered to be his pilot; when Washington launched the first overt bombing attacks against the North in 1965, it was Ky who insisted on leading the contingent of Vietnamese planes. Although plenty of Vietnamese officers were as courageous or more so than Americans, having physical courage was not a prerequisite for becoming a Vietnamese general, and Ky's bravery made him popular with both the Americans and his own people. Moreover, the Americans liked him because he was open and friendly; and the Vietnamese, a people with little facial or body hair, admired his handsomeness, which was accentuated by a rare and luxurious mustache.

William Colby conceded Ky's courage but was not overly impressed by his intelligence or his tendency to impetuosity. Ky could not restrain his tongue, and this got him into trouble. He expressed admiration at one point for the strong leadership of Hitler, an example, some American press accounts suggested, of his incipient Nazism, when, in fact, it was another indication of how poorly educated and unsophisticated he was, at least in Western terms, for Ky was a young man of decent instincts who happened to like gambling on cockfights, beautiful women, flashy clothes, and flying airplanes more than he loved sitting at a desk poring over documents of state. It was said that in comparison to Thieu he was lazy when it came to government work, and in comparison, he probably was. If he lacked a broad education, he possessed a self-confidence that allowed him to pick aides who did not, men such as Bui Diem and Nguyen Ngoc Linh, both of whom could have easily slid into jobs at the State Department on C Street.

One might have assumed that an American ambassador would be appalled to find a Captain Midnight, as Ky was dubbed as a consequence of his preferences for purple-colored costumes and six-guns, in charge of the Saigon government. But such was not the case with Henry Cabot Lodge. "Lodge liked Ky because he was dashing, he had a beautiful wife, and he flew in combat," Mike Dunn said. "Ky had a rakish air about him that Lodge enjoyed. Lodge thought that all soldiers ought to wear whipcord britches and snap a crop. Ky was not too smart, of course."

Lansdale also liked Ky. Ky did not have Diem's stature as a nationalist, but neither did he have his dogmatism. He was young and unformed, potential clay in the hands of someone who might wish to try to mold him into a strong political leader.

"I liked Ky personally, and he used to talk to me so frankly that it hurt," Lansdale said. "But he talked too much, particularly when reporters were around. I said, 'Zip your lips. You are being quoted and putting all these black marks against you.' He would talk to the press and I'd sit on the sidelines. Suddenly he'd look at me and make the motion of zipping his lips, knowing he had talked too much, and I'd motion back, 'Yeah, let's get out of here.' "

Lansdale had no trouble establishing rapport with the young generals. Besides his personal touch, his reputation had grown to mythic proportions. "I had been dealing with the country so long that some of the people who were now ministers and generals were just kids when I'd first gone to Saigon," Lansdale said. "They gave me a dinner one night, and Ky and Thieu and all the generals were there. They asked me to tell them about the early days, about Diem and how I met Trinh Minh The. They were sitting around me on the floor, and I almost started off by saying, 'Once upon a time . . .' They were asking for their history from a foreigner."

Since the Vietnamese were ready to give Lansdale the kind of benefit of the doubt that they were unprepared to give other Americans when it came to assessing his motives, he was able to talk to them in a frank way without alienating them, even about such a sensitive matter as corruption, although he was having trouble bridging the rift between Ky and Thieu. The two officers were separated by differing personal styles and by a struggle for power that took on the aspects of a guerrilla war. Ky was the more open of the two, and Lansdale worked hard to get him to take the first step to resolve their differences, which grew as time passed.

"I'd tell Ky, 'Come on,' " Lansdale said. " 'It's only a couple of steps to Thieu's office. I'll bring you two together and get out of the room.' But Ky wouldn't do it. He said, 'That sonofabitch. I'm not talking to him.' "

Nor would Thieu deal with Ky. Their fight never turned into an overt confrontation where cards could be thrown on the table. The Vietnamese, by nature, hated the kind of confrontations that Americans thrived on. Their fight took the form of a long and debilitating underhanded struggle. At one point, Ky was landing his helicopter at the palace and disturbing Thieu, who liked to sleep late. Thieu would never complain to him about it. Finally, Thieu's wife politely asked Ky to stop, saying that his helicopter was bothering her plants. Whether Lansdale could have brought the two leaders together was problematical, but, in any event, he did not get the chance to try with the full backing of the mission, for shortly after arriving in Saigon he ran into his own power struggle within the American bureaucracy.

WHILE IT WAS WIDELY BELIEVED that the United States government had grown too large after World War Two, no situation had arisen to measure how well the multiplicity of government organizations would work together under pressure to achieve a specific foreign policy goal, until Vietnam came along. It might be argued that the war was an unfair test of performance, but the jealousies and incompetence that emerged in Vietnam clearly resulted from a birth defect, not the war.

"There wasn't a hell of a lot of teamwork in the mission," Barry Zorthian said. "You get under that kind of strain, things not going well, and everybody is ready to blame the other guy. There were lots of mutual suspicions and old enmities that never got completely overcome. The CIA thought the military was too conventional, and the military thought the CIA had a lot of cowboys running around getting into its business. The Agency for International Development, trying to do its job of nation building, believed the military was a disaster and tearing up the country. The U.S. Information Service was regarded as a puny bunch of people playing as psychological warriors."

The bureaucracy seemed united only on one question, and that was the need to cut Ed Lansdale and his team off at the knees before they were able to mobilize the kind of power and influence that might threaten the primacy of each organization on its operational turf. As Lansdale was interested, naturally, in establishing his influence at the top of the Saigon government, his first major conflict arose with Lodge's chief political officer at the embassy, Philip Habib. About Habib it said little to note that he was bright. The State Department brimmed with intelligent and sophisticated people, but their bureaucratic caution often seemed to congeal after a few years into something a little squishy. Rare it was to find someone at State as direct and forceful as Phil Habib, someone fully prepared to give you his opinion on a subject, eyeball to eyeball, without hedging it six different ways. Not only was Habib tough-minded, he was also as nimble a bureaucratic operator as ever hit Saigon.

"Phil Habib didn't like Lansdale one bit," Barry Zorthian said. "He regarded Lansdale as a meddler and, in Vietnam terms, almost as irrelevant. Phil belonged to the establishment—the conventional, standard machine structured to carrying out State Department missions. He regarded Lansdale as an unprogrammed loose cannon, a maverick upsetting things without discipline, without acceptance or commitment to Washington direction."

The Lansdale appointment, as Zorthian saw it, was a mistake that had come about "because Lodge was pressured." "I was back in Washington for consultations just prior to Lodge's second tour, and I had lunch with Lansdale," Zorthian said. "I was not only shocked but amazed at what Lansdale thought he was getting into, what kind of role he thought he was going to have. He had the impression he was coming out to run the counterinsurgency program, as he had in the Philippines. But that whole phase had ended, or was in the process of ending. Troops were pouring in. With the military came all the hardening of the arteries—the superstructure, the support tails, the command setups, the staff meetings—everything that Lansdale stood against. So Lansdale ended up—some of it by deliberate pushing, some of it due to the facts of life—on the outside with his nose pressed against the windowpane looking in."

The operator besides Phil Habib who gave Lansdale the shove outside was Zorthian himself. Lansdale considered Zorthian less than adequate in his dual role as chief of the psychological warfare program as well as head of the information bureaucracy; he wasn't the only one who suspected that Zorthian, though tops at press relations, might be out of his depth in psywar. Lansdale had brought his own psywar expert with him, and, as usual, when it came to dealing with his own countrymen, his subtlety turned into a reversible jacket—good with the Vietnamese, bad with the Americans.

"I thought U.S. psychological warfare operations were kindergarten stuff," Lansdale said. "I wanted Zorthian to do more. I had one of the top USIA people with me, Hank Miller, who had been senior to Zorthian back in Washington. Zorthian used to invite the two of us over to his house in Saigon, and we fought like cats and dogs. I was trying to get him to do more with his information program, and he was trying to tell me I didn't know anything about it."

"I thought Lansdale was one of these—what's the phrase?—unrealistic, fuzzy-headed guys who were living in the past," Zorthian said. "If Lansdale had come two years earlier, right after or before the Diem coup—maybe. But by the time he got back out there he was irrelevant. He didn't think so. But I did."

It was likely, as Zorthian said, that Lansdale had been overtaken by events before his arrival. Still, it didn't make things any easier to have two colleagues as formidable as Habib and Zorthian against him. Habib was a jowly, overweight American of Lebanese descent, and reporters in Saigon joked that he and Zorthian, operating together, looked and talked like two rug merchants of the Levant who had just received their latest shipment of "genuine" Persian carpets. Zorthian, who had journalists figured out, would have never gone after Lansdale with a meat cleaver. Rather, he would take a deep drag off his cigarette, look pensively out the window of his upstairs office, release a sigh of resignation with the smoke, and then speak to a reporter, softly, reluctantly, off-the-record and in all confidence of course, about poor Ed Lansdale, the hopeless romantic. There was always enough about Lansdale to provide evidence that he might be a well-meaning but slightly nutty soul, and Zorthian's interpretation of him found its way into the works of David Halberstam and Frances FitzGerald, who were, ideologically, not overly resistant to the idea, and into the writings of other journalists. While Zorthian worked the media, Habib made sure that Lansdale got nowhere in the bureaucracy.

"We clashed very definitely, Phil Habib and me," Lansdale said. "Zorthian and Habib didn't understand the war. Beyond that, they were pushing themselves for promotion. I got in very close to Ky's staff. After a few weeks, one of the Vietnamese officials told me, 'Habib has come to me and said he doesn't want me to see you any more.' Imagine that with a war going on."

Despite his fight with the bureaucracy, Lansdale, in one of his early accomplishments, was able to enhance Ky's position with Lyndon Johnson. The president flew to Honolulu in early 1966, in an attempt to shift attention away from the Fulbright hearings on the war, and Lansdale was involved in preparing the prime minister for the conference. President Johnson was pleasantly surprised to find at Honolulu that Ky sounded like an American politician—a Texas democrat, as a matter of fact. Lansdale had gone through Johnson's speeches and suggested to Ky's speechwriter that he work some of the president's sentiments into the remarks prepared for Ky to give at the meeting.

Lodge looked the other way as the fight went on between Habib and Lansdale. "Lodge liked unconventional people, and Lansdale was that," Mike Dunn said. "But he soon decided that Saigon had become a bureaucratic environment. Lodge was the most unimpeded fellow I've ever known, someone who just went with people who were useful. Lansdale was a kicker who didn't make field goals, and so he cut him. To be useful was all that was necessary—whether you were blue-eyed or brown-eyed, Lodge didn't care. Habib was not the best-looking man in the world, but Lodge thought he was wonderful. Habib was sharp in a bureaucratic environment and got the job done."

Yet, despite the forces arrayed against him, Lansdale chalked up a remarkable accomplishment that was not attributed to him and not widely known by the Americans in Saigon. More than any other official, he was responsible for imposing the American-style electoral system on South Vietnam in the midst of a war. Lyndon Johnson, like others in Washington, was interested in demonstrating that South Vietnam was a democracy, and therefore worthy of American support. But bringing it about was easier said than done. And many questioned whether it should be done at all.

"In my judgment," Mike Dunn said, "Lansdale wanted the reality of elections, while Lodge was convinced we needed only the appearance of a democracy in order to do what we had to do. Which wasn't the same thing."

Lansdale brought Rufe Phillips to Saigon in 1966 to help him construct an electoral system. Lansdale wanted first to create a constituent assembly that would give way to presidential and parliamentary elections. He and Phillips set out to find Vietnamese who would consent to run for office, and they began conducting classes for candidates at Lansdale's house. One of the first names that came to Phillips's mind was Tran Ngoc Chau, and he and Lansdale encouraged Chau to run.

This was not to suggest that there were no Vietnamese who were independently pushing for a democratic system. There were indeed, and Lansdale was their ally and catalyst. Everything considered, though, Lou Conein, who was by then, he said, "sick of Vietnamese politicians," believed that Lansdale almost singlehandedly brought about the system of elections. "Lodge knew a lot about politics, but I think he was baffled by the Vietnamese type of politics," Conein said. "Lansdale was not. He realized he had to make the Vietnamese think they came up with the idea of holding elections."

While Lansdale was occasionally able to operate effectively on a political level by the force of his reputation and his personality, his team found themselves blocked at every level in the bureaucracy. Even the CIA station chief Gordon Jorgenson, who had served with Lansdale in 1954 and liked him, was politely but firmly determined to keep the interlopers off his turf. A big handicap for the team was that it had not been given a budget, although the State Department had said that funds would be waiting in Saigon. This led Lou Conein to believe that their mission had been sabotaged by Lansdale's enemies even before they left Washington.

"For about a month we had hopes we would get somewhere, that we would establish a role for ourselves," Dan Ellsberg said. "It's hard for me to judge what Lansdale might have done had he had more of a position and Lodge's confidence. But the bureaucrats worked very quickly to fence him off once we got there. I saw a very isolated and frustrated and beaten man. In that context Lansdale was depressed, and he drank a great deal. He stayed up late telling endless stories about his past exploits. It was during that period that I developed a strong affection for him."

Lansdale also came to like Ellsberg very much, although he looked upon him as a slightly wayward son who needed protection from his own naïveté. With time on his hands, Ellsberg was able to devote energy and enterprise to chasing women. His favorite was an attractive young lady of French and Vietnamese blood who happened to be the mistress of the reputed Corsican underworld chief in Saigon.

Lansdale believed that Ellsberg was unbuttoning himself into a dangerous situation.

"The Corsican was going to slit Ellsberg's throat," Lansdale said. "I had to go to the Corsican, whom I wouldn't have otherwise touched with a ten-foot pole, and ask for Ellsberg's life."

Ellsberg thought Lansdale was exaggerating, but he began to pay attention when Conein came to him and said, "Listen, my friend. You are in much more trouble with the Corsicans than with the Viet Cong. You know what they do when somebody fools with one of their women? They'll get you down on the pavement and whip your face with barbed wire."

Lansdale was not happy either with Ellsberg's attraction to combat. "Ellsberg would ask for a week's leave, which I would give him," Lansdale said, "and he would grab a rifle and go out against the Viet Cong. I told him that was wrong. I said, 'We're here to make friends with the people, to win them over to our side, and you don't do that by throwing a grenade at them.' "

Ellsberg's forays into combat as a civilian, revealed after he released the Pentagon Papers, made him an unsatisfactory candidate for canonization by the antiwar movement; this, combined with an intensity that often left him sounding pompous and self-righteous when he got wound up on a subject, added to his image as something of a pariah, if not an out-and-out flake, to both sides, prowar and antiwar. Just why he wanted to go into battle was not entirely clear to Ellsberg himself, who, after his return to the States, sought an answer to the question through psychoanalysis.

Ellsberg did not tell Lansdale everything he was doing on operations. He knew that Lansdale would be upset with the risks he was taking and worried that he might get the team in trouble. After a while Ellsberg began to draw closer to John Paul Vann. Ellsberg shared a couple of enthusiasms with Vann, whom he looked up to. Neither man was much of a drinker, but Vann was a womanizer of such boundless energy and indiscriminate tastes as to make Ellsberg seem like a shy celibate. And both men liked taking risks.

Ellsberg tried to bring Vann and Lansdale together. Both Vann and Lansdale had their circle of admirers among the young Americans who worked in pacification. They were two men who preferred to operate outside of the bureaucracy. But their styles were different, and it developed that they became two different poles of attraction.

While Lansdale's reputation with the press was declining because of his lack of effectiveness and the battering he was taking from Habib and Zorthian, Vann's reputation was rising as a result of the perception that he was a man who could get things done and was someone who wasn't reluctant to talk to the press about what he was doing.

"I brought Vann over to the house one night to show Lansdale the pictures he had taken of the effects of the American bombing in the delta," Ellsberg said. "Vann, like myself, was totally antibombing, and Lansdale hated it too. Vann pulled out the pictures, but Lansdale was very reserved and said, 'You shouldn't show these to anybody.' Vann left and Lansdale said, 'What's this guy doing?' I thought Lansdale would share Vann's feeling, but the idea that Vann was taking photos like that and showing them around shocked him."

Perhaps there was jealousy on Lansdale's part, but, if so, it was minor, and he was convinced that Vann in turn wished him well. They had known each other in the Pentagon, and Vann had expressed an interest in joining the Lansdale team, until he realized it wasn't going to work out. Lansdale thought Vann was very sincere and dedicated to helping Vietnam. "But he had his own ideas about how it should be done," Lansdale said, "and he wanted the Vietnamese to do it his way. He was very fond of them but also very critical. He would tell me, 'I know this guy is a friend of yours, but against the VC he was a jerk.' On the other hand, he would do anything he could to help a Vietnamese who was in trouble. Vann was a strange personality."

Lansdale did not oppose Ellsberg's defection to Vann. Without admitting it in conversation, he knew that he was beaten but thought he might find some effective way to operate even if his team could not. Lou Conein and the others were drinking, idling on heavy fuel, and he knew it was only a matter of time before he lost their interest. Conein, in fact, was one of the first to go. He asked if he could transfer back to the CIA. The station put him in charge of the base at Bien Hoa, outside of Saigon. In terms of working with the Vietnamese, it was an excellent choice, but like Lansdale Conein was often better with the Vietnamese than he was with his own countrymen. "I had my dissatisfactions with Bien Hoa, and I let them be known to anybody who would listen," said Conein. Following an incident where Conein, having had a few scotches, tried to drop either a flower pot or a bag of water—depending upon who was telling the story—on the head of an

American official walking below, he was transferred to an isolated province called Phu Bon. Discovering that all the Vietnamese officials there had, like himself, been exiled, he started calling the province Phu Elba. After doing not much of anything for a year or so, Conein left Vietnam and retired from the CIA. Other team members dribbled out of Saigon unnoticed. Lansdale was still there, but only Dan Ellsberg had adapted to the new situation.

DAN ELLSBERG MET CHAU through John Paul Vann, and, as with Vann, Chau became the most important influence on his thinking about pacification. Chau loved to talk theory, and so did Ellsberg. But it wasn't just that. Ellsberg was impressed by the Vietnamese's calmly stated belief that democracy could work in Vietnam. Ellsberg was impressed because, oddly enough, that was not what the majority of the Americans he knew believed. Though they paid lip service to free elections and democratic principles, most of them believed that, to work, democracy needed a higher degree of education and sophistication than the Vietnamese possessed. This led some of them to private thoughts that the Viet Cong, who, after all, were nationalists fighting against a foreign presence, would establish the best government for the country after their victory. Chau considered such thinking another form of Western condescension, almost unconscious on the part of Americans, who, either prowar or antiwar, were convinced they knew what was best for the Vietnamese; and he explained his belief that the rice farmers, given a choice, would prefer to remove their corrupt officials by ballots rather than by bullets used by the Viet Cong. Ellsberg was persuaded by Chau's arguments, and he decided that democracy might have the kind of universal applicability that many Americans, democratic as they were themselves, were not ready to concede.

Dan Ellsberg was a strange combination of an imaginative intellectual who was infatuated by ideas and a bureaucratic maverick who liked to fire guns. Had Ellsberg's former colleagues at Harvard known of his extracurricular activities, they might have dismissed him as a serious thinker on Vietnam. Pursuing women and having an itch for combat, however, were not to be held against someone by the Americans who were serving there. Both enthusiasms, in fact, ranked as better credentials than an advanced university degree. Personal recklessness, which might have translated into flakiness in academia, was not only not bad in a war environment but even rather admirable. So Ellsberg was accepted by the men running the war with a readiness they might not have accorded other intellectuals. Moreover, his desire to emulate his hero, John Paul Vann, caused him to risk driving the roads of Vietnam instead of going by plane or helicopter, as most Americans did. Consequently, Ellsberg probably saw more of the country and talked to more people than any other official in the pacification program at the time.

During his travels Ellsberg sought out a small group of younger officials in the pacification program who had gained a reputation for their unconventional thinking. Most of them were admirers of Lansdale and Vann.

"I met a half-dozen guys who thought of themselves as the good guys in Vietnam," Ellsberg said. "They believed they were different from other Americans. They had Vietnamese friends, and some of them spoke the language. They didn't believe in the use of air power, but believed we should be engaged in small political operations. They were contemptuous of the French, and anxious that Americans not imitate them. Above all, they had a view of the way the war was going which was totally at odds with the official view."

The bright young men that Ellsberg sought out were not only intelligent and energetic but also—though he did not include this description of them—ambitious and very impatient to correct matters now, today, but not in two, five, ten years, which seemed verging on a lifetime to a bright young man in a hurry. At this point, their pessimism was not based on the belief that pacification could not be accomplished, but on the fact that it was not being done expeditiously, and that their leaders did not seem to know how to go about it. But their pessimism was hardened to the point of impossibility by the first results of General William Westmoreland's strategy of attrition.

After the war was lost it became open season for any sort of attack on Westmoreland. There were grounds enough for criticism, to be sure, but not for reasons of doubting his integrity. Rather, there was a serious question about the suppleness of Westmoreland's mind and his aptitude for commanding the American side of a political-military war.* Even there, one had to look at the situation in which he found himself when he took over MACV to complete the picture.

Westmoreland arrived in Saigon shortly after the Diem coup, when the country was in chaos, as it would remain for the better part of his four-year tour. "Stepping from the plane," he said, "I received a less-than-impressive introduction to Vietnamese leadership." The general sent to greet him was a born-again Frenchman, who "frequently urged that I assume command of the Vietnamese military forces and do the job for them." Moreover, noted Westmoreland with contempt, "On two occasions during attempted coups d'état he was to try to take refuge in my quarters."

His formative experience with his allies, however, occurred five months later when he tried to launch a pacification operation in the area surrounding Saigon. Westmoreland had two motives for putting his prestige behind the operation. First, he wanted to defeat the Viet Cong. Along with that, he was using the operation as the beginning of a series of moves to take responsibility for pacification away from the civilian bureaucracy. This was not because the military considered itself more expert on the subject, but because Westmoreland, who commanded the largest organization in the country, wanted jurisdictional control over all programs. It was the major turf fight of the war among the Americans, which was to last from 1964 until 1967, when a compromise was reached that gave the military control of pacification but left the real power in the hands of a civilian, first President Johnson's assistant Robert Komer and then William Colby.

The pacification operation, which Westmoreland named "Cooperation" in Vietnamese, turned out to be a disaster. There was, he found,

---

*Westmoreland had an excellent memory. He was very good at handling the technical details of a problem. He did a masterly job of logistically installing a half-million Americans in a country a half-world away. What he seemed to lack was intuition of the kind that could not be measured by intelligence test or enhanced by formal education. Housewife or general, you either had it or you didn't—and he did not. In 1970 I met the historian then helping Westmoreland write his memoirs, and we began speaking about him. I'd had a number of contacts with the general in Vietnam, at a low journalistic level. We came from the same state, and I wished him well. The historian and I agreed about Westmoreland's many fine qualities. "Westy's problem," he said, "is that he's not very bright." He did not mean it harshly, rather as a statement of fact, and we both knew he was talking about something more subtle than a lack of basic intelligence. That was the way officials such as Ellsworth Bunker and William Colby felt about Westmoreland too—though, out of a personal regard for him and an appreciation of the tactical restraints imposed upon him by the White House, they would have never admitted it publicly. Others, Dan Ellsberg, for example, who liked their villains black and their heroes white, saw him as a duplicitous force for error or evil.

precious little of that commodity. His allies were too engulfed in their power struggle to pay much attention to what he was trying to do. As Westmoreland saw it, the failure of Operation Cooperation could be "summed up in two words: political instability." From that point onward, he praised the valiant efforts of the Vietnamese people to the media at every chance, smiled his way through meetings and ceremonies—and largely ignored them.

During his first year, as the Viet Cong grew stronger and the situation worsened, Westmoreland became more optimistic that he could win if he were given enough troops. The theories of guerrilla warfare as propounded by the Vietnamese communists, available for anyone to read, showed that they proposed to achieve their victory by moving into successive stages of military activity, from small unit to large unit operations. By 1965, when he requested American troops, the Viet Cong were attacking in battalion strength. Rather than seeing that as a disaster, Westmoreland took it as a tactical opportunity. The Viet Cong seemed to be setting themselves up to be knocked off by the overwhelming firepower and new helicopter mobility of American troops. And what other strategy, from Westmoreland's perspective, seemed viable, if not that of trying to kill enough of the Viet Cong to make them give up? He had already lost faith that the Saigon army was capable of helping him take on pacification operations. No stable government or single leader existed in Saigon.

Maxwell Taylor had learned enough during his tour as ambassador to realize that American troops would probably wind up destroying the countryside and making Viet Cong out of rice farmers who might have been won over to the Saigon government side. This idea seems not to have occurred to Westmoreland, probably because the Vietnamese as a people never came into focus for him, and because, unlike Taylor, he was not surrounded by civilian aides more politically sensitive than he. Westmoreland's private attitude about the Vietnamese could be glimpsed through an anecdote he told of his and his wife's encounter with the country's food.

"Kitsy and I both had some difficulty adjusting to Vietnamese food, notably to *nuoc mam,* a pungent fermented sauce made of drippings from suncured fish, which the Vietnamese eat on their rice as a basic source of protein," Westmoreland said. "As Kitsy put it, you ate it in self-defense as the only way to be able to tolerate the odor of it on everybody else. A bottle of *nuoc mam* once broke on my plane, and we almost had to don gas masks in order to survive."

Vietnamese food, with its Chinese influence, was regarded by gourmets as one of the world's more notable cuisines; and *nuoc mam,* strong, but not strong enough to warrant a gas mask, was a condiment that many Americans who spent any length of time in the country came to enjoy. The character of *nuoc mam* (fish sauce) gave rise to G.I. humor, though, an understandable reaction on the part of, say, a nineteen-year-old private from South Carolina who had been taken out of his environment for the first time, but perhaps less understandable as a cause for giggles by his commanding general. There was no need to hurl epithets at Westmoreland; he was, inescapably, a product of his place and generation. The average Vietnamese were, in a manner of speaking, as author Ralph Ellison put it in another context, invisible to him.

The problem was, so were the Viet Cong. If his strategy of attrition was to work, he had to find them in order to kill them; and the communists began to play a game of hide and seek. Several months after the arrival of U.S. combat troops in 1965, Hanoi sent the first of its regular combat units to South Vietnam, beginning the seven-year transition that changed a guerrilla war carried out almost entirely by poorly armed southern Viet Cong into a conventional war conducted with tanks and artillery and rockets by the North Vietnamese. It is doubtful that the communists, who always looked at Vietnam as a political war, ever thought they could defeat American forces in any consistent way on the battlefield. Rather, their strategy revolved around both conducting a long war to wear down American domestic opinion, as they had done against the French, and, more immediately, drawing the American troops into the jungles and away from the heavily populated coastal areas where they were needed to provide stable security if pacification were to succeed.

Whatever their true strategic intentions, the North Vietnamese were nevertheless surprised by the first major battle of the war between their conventional forces and the Americans, which took place in the mountainous jungles of the Ia Drang in November 1965. Hanoi discovered in that battle just how effective the Americans' helicopter mobility could be. Whole brigades, the sub-unit of a division, could be moved from one position to another with amazing speed. The French had not possessed such startling mobility, and it was obvious to the communists that they had to readjust their tactics. They could not afford to go against the Americans head-to-head except under the most advantageous conditions, or out of sheer desperation for political purposes. Their answer was to try to avoid combat unless they could surprise the Americans with an ambush. Most American casualties were suffered in ambush attacks that usually lasted no more than a few minutes and in the explosions of boobytraps that were often laid by women and children. Combat of the World War Two type, with prolonged fighting between opposing units, was rare. To counter the communists' chief tactic of laying ambushes, the Americans tried to strip away their jungle cover by defoliating possible ambush sites with an airsprayed chemical known as Agent Orange, which turned out to be a self-inflicted ambush itself, for the chemical was believed to have caused cancer among some American soldiers who came in contact with it.

It was the difficulty of finding the communists, except when they wanted to be found, that drove Westmoreland toward tactics that resembled a scorched earth policy. After spending a year looking through the haystack and not finding enough to make his attrition strategy work, he began to burn the haystack. Fire bombs were dropped on forests where the communists were thought to be operating. When the humid jungle refused to burn efficiently, Westmoreland ordered giant bulldozers designed to uproot and plow under their base areas. His tactics, combined with the air and artillery bombardment, caused a population shift, as rice farmers and their families fled from the countryside to the towns. Creating refugees, which began as an inadvertent byproduct of the search for the enemy, came to be looked upon by some of Westmoreland's officers as a valid tactic in itself, since every rice farmer who fled the countryside was one less potential recruit for the communists.

In the basic American unit, the rifle company, composed of around two hundred men, most of them barely out of their teens, the search for the enemy took on a routine. In populated areas, the Americans moved through villages, upending things in their search. In most cases, the enemy had already fled, possibly leaving behind hidden weapons and ammunition and rice. One hiding place was the thatched roofing of their hutlike homes. The Americans first began to burn the huts to destroy hidden ammunition; but then, in many areas, it became a standard practice that left thousands of innocent civilians homeless. In unpopulated areas, the Americans were landed by helicopters on isolated mountaintops, firing as they came in, so as to spoil any ambush attempts, which were frequent. They set up temporary fire bases to be used for patrolling the jungle in the unceasing search.

With a strategy based on killing an enemy who usually retreated at the approach of the Americans, leaving behind boobytraps or a few snipers, officers who were worried about promotions became anxious to demonstrate that they were performing well. The pressure on them traveled downward from Westmoreland. The demands for a "body count" became cruder and more specific with each descent in the chain of command. Officers at field level tried to create incentives for their troops. In some units, soldiers were given a three-day pass for every Viet Cong they killed. It was a system bound to lead to brutal excesses, and one in which a dead civilian was automatically counted as a Viet Cong.

Westmoreland seemed oblivious to what was happening in the countryside. He expressed astonishment in his memoirs that the term "search and destroy" had taken on unpleasant connotations in the public mind. His staff had come up with the description as one of three terms to be used during the first pacification operation with the Vietnamese that had failed. They would begin by searching out and destroying the Viet Cong, then "clear" the area for pacification, and finally "secure" it for the future. "Since it is always the basic objective of military operations to seek and destroy the enemy and his military resources," Westmoreland said, "I saw nothing contradictory or brutal about the term, yet as the months passed, many people, to my surprise, came to associate it with aimless searches in the jungle and the random destroying of villages and other property. Some even labeled American strategy in Vietnam a 'search-and-destroy strategy,' when in reality 'search and destroy' was nothing more than an operational term for a tactic." Westmoreland confessed that he was unaware of how "twisted" the meaning of the term had become until early 1968, when former TV personality John Charles Daly, a friend of Westmoreland, then head of the Voice of America, told him, "General, you are your own worst enemy to perpetuate a term that has been so distorted." Westmoreland then dropped "search and destroy" for several more innocuous terms, including "reconnaissance in force," but didn't change the nature of his operations.

By 1968 even some supporters of the war were putting *search and destroy* in ironical italics, and one might have found Westmoreland's comments about his surprise to be disingenuous, if not incredible, unless one happened to know him. Given his level of intuition, no doubt he *was* surprised. There was also a question as to how much he really knew about what was going on. Looking back, John Chaisson, a Harvard-educated marine general who worked for Westmoreland, said that one of the major errors of the war "was the failure of American generals to get their boots muddied." The nearest most of them came to combat was a few thousand feet above the battlefield in a helicopter that had usually been remodeled for their comfort. Westmoreland devoted several paragraphs of his memoirs to describing his closest call of the war, which occurred when his plane came under fire on an airstrip near the Laotian border. If he had accompanied an operation through an area filled with civilians, smelled the fear sweat and experienced the frustration of troops who were losing their buddies to boobytraps, then watched as they wiped out a village with air or artillery after receiving a few sniper rounds, he might have lost a little of his surprise at how "twisted" the meaning of *search and destroy* had become. Certainly his subordinates, who were trying to respond to his demands for a body count, were not going to tell him. This was not to suggest that Westmoreland and the other generals lacked courage. But the nature of the war converted them into managers who appeared after battles to award their troops bonuses in the form of ribbons and medals, rather than turning them into leaders who were closely attuned to their men.

Still, one could make too much of their lack of perception. Westmoreland chose to put on blinders when his own service tried to show him his strategy was wrongheaded. The army chief of staff, Harold K. Johnson, who was considered a military intellectual, ordered a team of officers to conduct a study of Westmoreland's operations. The study, completed after nine months, in March 1966, concluded that the focus should be on rural construction instead of on fighting a war of attrition. This was an astonishing vote of no-confidence in the military commander in Vietnam. But Westmoreland, at the height of his influence with the public and the White House, managed to get the study reduced from a planning document to a "conceptual" document, in effect emasculating it. The study was treated with such sensitivity that army officers were forbidden to discuss its existence outside the walls of the Pentagon.

Westmoreland, in fact, believed that his strategy was working and that no valid alternative existed. The first battle at Ia Drang had convinced him he had spoiled Hanoi's strategy of trying to cut South Vietnam into two halves that could be isolated and taken piecemeal.

Thereafter "spoiling" operations became the order of the day, especially during the dreaded period of the expected "monsoon offensive," which seldom materialized.

Remarkably, the only general who questioned Westmoreland's clearly questionable assumptions about North Vietnamese strategic intentions turned out to be a marine. Remarkably, one says, because in terms of carrying out military operations the marines, as courageous as they were, seemed poorly suited to fight in Vietnam, bringing with them a mentality that dictated numerous amphibious landings (as if Vietnam was another Iwo Jima or Guadalcanal), and being slow to adopt the army's new and effective helicopter mobility tactics. But the first marine commander, Major General Lewis Walt, blue-eyed, barrel-chested, and sensitive, had much more first-hand contact with the Vietnamese than did Westmoreland, as his troops were assigned to the coastal areas in the upper part of South Vietnam; and he realized that in the end the most important factor in winning the war was gaining the allegiance of the population, an allegiance that could be won only through pacification programs, which, if they were to work, needed his troops to bring long-term security to the area. General Walt believed that Hanoi's sending of its regular troops into South Vietnam in late 1965 was just a ploy to draw his marines away from the populated areas where they were making progress in removing the Viet Cong and were experimenting with pacification projects. What was the point of chasing the North Vietnamese through the jungles? Walt asked Westmoreland. That was just giving them the advantage. But Westmoreland ordered Walt to begin "spoiling" operations, and thenceforth the marines engaged in a lot of meaningless and costly battles in isolated jungled areas, winding up almost trapped at Khe Sanh, itself meaningless and quickly abandoned, until they were saved by massive airpower and their own grit. As Walt had predicted, the only thing "spoiled" was pacification on the heavily populated coastal areas.

ALTHOUGH WESTMORELAND was convinced that his strategy was hampered only by a lack of additional troops and by the White

House's refusal to let him pursue the enemy into Laos and Cambodia, Lyndon Johnson himself began to show a concern about pacification operations. At first his interest was merely cosmetic, a reaction to the pressures brought about by those who opposed the war and opposed, in particular, Westmoreland's search-and-destroy operations. Johnson found it expedient to rehabilitate his vice president, Hubert Humphrey, and to send him to Saigon in early 1966 as a cheerleader for what Johnson called "the other war." His description suggested that Lansdale's declarations that the political and military aspects of the war were inextricably linked had made little impression. Johnson understood the nature of bureaucracy, though, and he realized in 1966 that Saigon was the lair of a hydra-headed monster.

White House pressure prompted two studies on reorganizing the pacification effort. One, run by the military, concluded not surprisingly that pacification should be put under the control of Westmoreland. The other study was conducted by the civilians. Ambassador Lodge called in his assistant, George (Jake) Jacobson, and told him to organize a task force to examine the problem. Jacobson was the embassy's mission coordinator, the connecting link between the various agencies of the bureaucracy. An army colonel who appreciated the whisky of Scotland and a well-turned ankle of any nationality, Jacobson had pulled a tour in Vietnam as early as 1954 and had wound up making the country his life's work. His hearty personality and straightforward efficiency created the perfect embassy functionary. Jacobson seemed to have never met an ambassador he didn't like, and he worked for all of them, from 1965 until he fled at the side of Graham Martin in 1975. As he put it, with no small pride, "Fate charged me with emptying the wastebaskets and sharpening pencils for a helluva lot of great Americans."

Though he liked Lansdale, Jake Jacobson had joined with the others in the bureaucracy to cordon off his team, which he considered made up of "a bunch of odd characters." The exception, he thought, was Dan Ellsberg, "head and shoulders the best of the lot." Jacobson, who was John Paul Vann's best friend, was impressed by Ellsberg's courage. "Ellsberg was a brave man," Jacobson said. "He walked with the infantry on many a mission to find out what was going on." So when Lodge told Jacobson to pick a task force to study pacification, Ellsberg was the first of eight officials he chose. "Ellsberg was one of the most productive and maybe the brightest fellow on the whole task force," Jacobson said. For three months, Jacobson's investigators traveled about the country, looking at all aspects of pacification, now, in an effort to avoid the French term, called "revolutionary development."

The importance of the Jacobson study was that it coincided with the disillusionment of Robert McNamara, which, in the latter months of 1966, was breaking out of its chrysalis. McNamara, who had first thought that Hanoi could be frightened, and then bludgeoned, into making concessions by an air war, had decided that the bombing was ineffective and that Westmoreland's search-and-destroy operations were leading, at best, to a stalemate. When he visited Vietnam in October 1966, a few weeks after the Jacobson study was completed, McNamara was ready to consider any alternative to the Westmoreland strategy. As for the air war, he wanted to build an electronic barrier across South Vietnam to try to stop infiltration, while curtailing the bombing of North Vietnam. McNamara's disillusionment was nurtured by his deputy, John McNaughton, Ellsberg's former boss at the Pentagon; and it was natural that Ellsberg should be brought into the defense secretary's consultations. Ellsberg flew back to Washington on McNamara's plane. During the trip, the secretary asked for an extra copy of a vividly pessimistic report Ellsberg had written, entitled "A Visit to an Insecure Province."

Robert McNamara's report to Lyndon Johnson on October 14, 1966, represented a major shift in the strategic thinking about the war. He recommended to the president that air and ground operations be stabilized and that emphasis be placed on pacification and on the development of self-government in South Vietnam. In his report to Johnson, McNamara paraphrased the Jacobson study, including Ellsberg's contributions to it. Undersecretary of State Nicholas Katzenbach, who had accompanied McNamara to Saigon, turned in a separate report. He agreed with McNamara and recommended that Lodge's deputy ambassador, William Porter, be put in charge of pulling the pacification program together, and that Porter be given an army general as a deputy to make sure the military cooperated. The Pentagon admitted that pacification wasn't going well, but made a counter-proposal that all programs be placed under Westmoreland.

Johnson had taken McNamara's advice about strategy at the start of the air and ground war, and he was still ready to listen to him when he began to backtrack. Johnson seemed, in fact, to have few ideas himself about how to fight the war. Neither was he an Abraham Lincoln, ready to fire generals left and right to find someone who seemed to know what he was doing. Johnson tightly controlled the war, but it was a control derived from assuming what he considered to be the moderate position between the two extremes of the advice he was receiving. Ambivalent from the start, and never the warmonger that he was often portrayed by his critics as, Johnson indicated by his decisions that he believed the role of the commander in chief was not to get out in front but to dominate the middle. If McNamara was now recommending increased pacification instead of increased military operations, it followed under Johnson's leadership principle that there should be a little more of both.

The idea of putting Lodge's deputy, William Porter, in charge of all pacification programs had been around for months. It was, of course, the job Lansdale should have held, had he not undergone defenestration by the bureaucracy. Porter was a competent and easygoing careerist who was unlikely to make waves. There was a collective shrugging of the shoulders when he was put in charge of pacification as head of the Office of Civil Operations. Dan Ellsberg, who was losing some of his enthusiasm for the war but none of his taste for power and influence, had cut himself off from Lansdale. He became Porter's assistant in 1966 and one of the top investigators to evaluate and establish whether pacification was working under the new reorganization. Ellsberg concluded that it was not. But he was beginning to realize it wasn't simply a matter of getting the bureaucracy properly organized. The problem lay with the whole American approach to the war, just as Lansdale had prophesied. The country was being destroyed by massive military operations. What would be left to pacify? As Ellsberg got to know the country better, he saw another serious problem. There were not enough Vietnamese officials who were as honest and dedicated as his friend Chau.

THE ONLY NEW APPROACH to pacification that took root after the Diem coup was derived from Chau via Stu Methven and the CIA, and it involved the training of cadres and counterterror teams. After Diem was overthrown, his businessman friend, the owner of the private army called the Shrimp Soldiers, was jailed, and Methven asked Nguyen Van Thieu, the Saigon army commander in the Vung Tau area, if the CIA could take over the training facility used by the Shrimp Soldiers. Thieu agreed, and Methven got in touch with Ralph Johnson, a CIA officer with whom he had worked in Laos and then on the mountain scout program in South Vietnam, and told him about Chau's ideas. Johnson had a talent for training and organizing. He had discovered a very capable Vietnamese lieutenant by the name of Le Xuan Mai, and recruited him for the mountain scout program. Though technically still in the Saigon army, Mai in reality became one of the key CIA agents of the war. Since the mountain scout program had been turned over to the military, it was arranged for Mai to go to Vung Tau to take charge of the small cadre-training program. Chau had been assigned as mayor of Da Nang and wasn't involved with the program at the moment. Methven and Johnson and other CIA officers would drop by Vung Tau from time to time to check on Mai's operation, but no Americans were permanently assigned there.

It looked as if that was about as far as Chau's ideas would go, especially after it was learned that Peer de Silva was to replace John Richardson as the CIA station chief. De Silva was known to dislike political action and paramilitary operations, so there was little likelihood that he would be interested in Chau's programs. De Silva considered himself a classical intelligence officer and early in his career had served as a security officer for the atomic bomb project of World War Two.

One could almost hear the abacus clicking in the mind of William Colby, the Far East Division chief, when he picked Peer de Silva. The paramilitary specialists at the agency, the old OSS types, had been tarnished by the Bay of Pigs, and their star was in decline. Peer de Silva, a classical intelligence officer, was not likely to engage in paramilitary operations, which had been assigned to the Pentagon after the shakeup. As the advisory effort increased, and the military's influence grew, it was now necessary more than ever for the CIA to get along with those who wore uniforms, and it didn't hurt that de Silva was a West Point graduate. Also, though his formative experience was in Europe, he knew Asia and was currently serving as the Hong Kong station chief.

William Colby, with CIA director John McCone's concurrence, decided to wait until mid-1964 before shifting de Silva to Saigon. Dave Smith had taken over as acting chief after Lodge got Richardson removed, and Smith, who was competent and colorless, appeared able to get along with the ambassador. Colby thought there was no rush in making the transfer. Lyndon Johnson heard about the delay, however, and with irritation ordered McCone to put de Silva in Saigon immediately. If de Silva was the best man for the job, demanded Johnson, why wasn't he already there?

McCone took de Silva to meet President Johnson before he departed for Saigon, and Johnson warned him that his first job was to get along with Henry Cabot Lodge—not the easiest man in the world, Johnson said. After the meeting, McCone reemphasized the need to get along with Lodge. "He can be abrupt and ruthless," McCone said. To smooth the way for de Silva, McCone and Colby accompanied him to Saigon, where they were going to introduce the new station chief to Lodge in a relaxed social setting over lunch, to which Dave Smith was also invited.

Lodge was hardly into his first course when he began to complain to McCone that he neither wanted nor needed a new station chief. He said he was content to have Dave Smith, whom he knew and liked, continue as the acting chief. He gestured at de Silva and said he was an unknown quantity who could only be a bother. "Dave and I were both dismayed as we were talked over like competitors at a dog show," de Silva recalled. Neither McCone nor Colby liked Lodge, and finally McCone, wearing a tight smile, told the ambassador that unless he had a definite reason for refusing de Silva's assignment, then he, as director, felt he must insist on the new chief for the position.

The next day Lodge called de Silva to his office. He waved him to a chair and began to pace back and forth before a window while he spoke. "I'm sure you remember our luncheon yesterday at my house and I want you to understand I have nothing against you personally," Lodge told de Silva. "I simply do not want a new station chief, but that's now beyond arguing. There are, however, two things I want you to do without delay, although I know you're about to return to Hong Kong to collect your family. First, you will have noticed on the door of your office there is a large brass plaque bearing the title 'Special Assistant to the Ambassador.' I don't want to see that plaque on your door when you get back from Hong Kong. Second, you have inherited from your predecessor a very large and long black sedan. That car is newer and longer than my official car. Get rid of it."

To succeed in an embassy setting a station chief first had to gain the confidence of the ambassador. Lodge had made it clear that he didn't regard de Silva very highly, and Mike Dunn, Lodge's chief of staff, moved to limit his access to the ambassador. Was it a coincidence, then, that less than six months after he arrived in Saigon, Peer de Silva, the self-proclaimed classical intelligence officer, became a convert to paramilitary operations conducted outside the embassy? Stu Methven and Lou Conein thought it such a remarkable case of a tenderfoot joining the cowboys that they looked upon his conversion with skepticism.

"De Silva came to Saigon as the big intelligence officer and said, 'Let's knock off all the bullshit,' " Methven said. "So the intelligence guys were back in the saddle, and all of us political action types were out. Then de Silva went for a briefing in Quang Ngai province on the political teams operating there and found religion. He came back and told us all about it. I said, 'Well, we've been doing the same thing down in the delta for months, you know.' " Methven was referring to the programs developed by Chau.

The political teams in Quang Ngai were created by a police official who was an old acquaintance of CIA agent Mai at the Vung Tau camp. The Vietnamese official attracted the support of one of the bright young men who was an admirer of Lansdale. His name was Frank Scotton, and he had no connection with the CIA but was an employee of the United States Information Service. Scotton spoke Vietnamese, had good ideas about political motivation, and was skilled at attracting publicity to his project.

Le Xuan Mai encouraged de Silva to fly to Quang Ngai to take a look. Back in Saigon, de Silva called Methven and other case officers to a meeting to discuss taking over the project and expanding it countrywide. De Silva's deputy suggested that the forty-man teams be called "people's action teams," usually shortened to PATs. With Colby's enthusiastic approval, the station set about to expand the Vung Tau facilities into a five-thousand-man training camp. De Silva assigned three CIA officers to the installation. The course of study was heavily weighted on the side of political motivation, but the PATs were also to be armed. They would wear the simple black cotton pants and shirt of the rural Vietnamese without any insignia to distinguish them from the common people, would live and work among the villagers, giving them political indoctrination against the communists, while helping them with farming and educational techniques and defending them at night from the guerrillas.

The CIA's new involvement with paramilitary operations, coming at a time when the agency was supposed to be giving them up, did not make General Westmoreland happy. Westmoreland was already trying to bring the large, non-CIA pacification organization under his control, which had grown from the early efforts of Rufus Phillips as an economic improvement program, and the CIA was now going off in another direction. After tiptoeing around the problem for a while, de Silva brought it up directly with Westmoreland. The general delivered some compliments about the CIA's role in developing the PATs, and then got down to what he really thought. "Two questions come out of this," Westmoreland told de Silva. "Manpower for the PAT program must be carved out of somebody else's hip. Okay, whose? Then, and this may be the toughest question of all, which American element is best suited to support the Vietnamese in their development of the PAT program? CIA or MACV? These are problems bothering us and I'm sure they're bothering you as well."

Realizing he was going to have trouble with Westmoreland, de Silva tried to outmaneuver him by making a trip to Washington to give his version of what the CIA was trying to do. He briefed officials at the Pentagon and State Department and made a pitch to members of McGeorge Bundy's staff at the White House. As it turned out, the showdown he anticipated was postponed by the decision to send combat troops to South Vietnam and to begin the air war. Westmoreland and his staff at MACV, though decidedly unenthusiastic about the agency's new paramilitary operation, had little time to wage a turf fight at this time, and de Silva was left alone.

After de Silva found religion, as Stu Methven put it, he was ready to spread the gospel of paramilitary operations to all parts of South Vietnam. One operation that drew his attention was the use of counterterror teams, the idea Methven had taken from Chau and begun to develop on a small scale. The counterterror teams, later changed to the more euphemistic but no less murderous provincial reconnaissance units (PRUs), became an arm of the Phoenix program, and there was always confusion about who they were, where they came from, and what they did. Chau's idea, to use counterterror units as a last resort for eliminating the Viet Cong shadow government and as an integrated part of his political action program in Kien Hoa, was converted by the CIA into a separate operation to stand by itself. The change did not come about by any conspiratorial or cynical design, but, like other programs, grew haphazardly during the period of political chaos after the Diem coup. The CIA was constantly trying to develop techniques to identify the Viet Cong who were working as committee chiefs, recruiters, province representatives, and tax collectors. Once they were identified, the National Police arrested them or the counterterror teams were sent to kill or capture them at night. Since the counterterror teams were under the control of province chiefs less scrupulous than Chau, they were sometimes used to terrorize innocent Vietnamese for purposes of political or financial extortion, and their reputation as CIA-trained thugs began to spread throughout the country.

Chau had also developed what he called census grievance teams, people who were sent into a village to talk to the farmers and record their complaints. A responsible government was a government that worked for the villagers, he believed, no matter how poor or uneducated they were. The CIA adopted his idea for census grievance teams, but again converted it into a separate operation and took it out of the context of his original intentions.

By early 1966 the pacification program was characterized by a staggering disorganization. The PATs were being trained at Vung Tau, census grievance teams in Saigon, counterterror units at various places. The economic improvement arm of the pacification program, staffed by civilian AID workers and foreign service officers, was operating as a separate entity in every province. All had their own concepts and staffs, and all were jealous of each other.

THE CIA WAS HAPPY with its thriving training center at Vung Tau, and black pajama–clad people's action teams were being turned out and dispatched to the countryside like clockwork, where they were meeting with varying degrees of success, usually depending upon how effectively they were directed by the province chiefs who exercised operational control over them. Vung Tau became a showplace where every visiting American congressman and senator was taken to see what the CIA was claiming to be the biggest success of the pacification effort. The politicians seemed to accept as normal that the exhortatory slogans and signs that bedecked the center were in English.

It was with no pleasure, therefore, that CIA officers assigned to Vung Tau learned that the Saigon government had decided to take over the training center and put Chau in charge. Chau was known to be an independent-minded Vietnamese, different from Le Xuan Mai, the present commander of the center, who was a capable officer and who never forgot who was paying his salary. With Chau in charge, the CIA men knew they would have to salute him, not vice versa.

A few months earlier the Saigon government had created a ministry of rural construction as the controlling agency for pacification on the Vietnamese side. Lansdale was the senior adviser to the minister in charge, Nguyen Duc Thang, who, like Chau, was incorruptible. Opposed to the Americans running anything, Lansdale thought the Vietnamese should always be out in front, with the Americans standing behind the curtain, whispering. How large a role he played in encouraging the Vietnamese to take the Vung Tau training center away from the CIA was not known. Nguyen Cao Ky and his pacification chief undoubtedly needed little encouragement, because they were sensitive to the growing American involvement in every facet of Vietnamese life, and gossip was spreading throughout the country that the Vung Tau center was a CIA operation, tainting the people's action teams.

In any event, the Vietnamese and the CIA got into a fight over who would control the Vung Tau center, with Chau taking a battering and making enemies who would never forgive him. Peer de Silva's tour had been cut short, and he was not in Saigon. De Silva was looking out his office window one morning, talking on the phone, when he noticed an old gray Peugeot sedan being pushed by a Vietnamese near the embassy. He spotted a detonating device, a time pencil, stuck in the back of the driver's seat, and he began to fall to the floor, but a split-second too late. He was seriously wounded by the explosion; one of his secretaries was killed and many others injured. He tried to go back to work, but his vision began deteriorating and he was transferred out of Saigon. A new embassy was built in another part of town, surrounded by a high fence. The station chief who replaced de Silva did not want a fight with the Vietnamese about Vung Tau, but neither did he want to give up control of the CIA's biggest program.

The dispute took place at the Vung Tau center. It started when a decision was made to change the PATs into fifty-nine-man teams called "revolutionary development" (RD) cadre. This was to be done by grafting on nineteen specialized cadre, including census grievance workers. The CIA had changed Chau's original idea of census grievance into a covert program of putting secret informers in villages and hamlets to identify members of the Viet Cong organization, who could then be eliminated by counterterror teams. Now it was decided to return to Chau's old concept and add census grievance cadre to the RD teams as overt workers in the countryside. Chau, who was assigned as a colonel to the ministry of rural construction, arrived in Vung Tau to help write the training program for the new cadre.

Caught in the middle of the dispute was an army major by the name of Jean-André Sauvageot, who was serving with the CIA on temporary assignment. Sauvageot, the son of a doctor and himself a philosophy major at Ohio University, had arrived as a district adviser and, studying on his own in the evenings, had become the best Vietnamese linguist of the war. His work brought him to the attention of John Paul Vann and Ev Bumgardner, who urged him to take a job at Vung Tau because they were not totally pleased with the way the CIA was running the center. After Jean Sauvageot moved to Vung Tau, he began to change the tone of the American effort. He gave up his military uniform for the black pants and shirt of the rural Vietnamese. He refused to live in a separate compound with the Americans. To the surprise of his CIA boss, he turned down an air conditioner for his room. He ate Vietnamese food, slept on their hardwood beds with a thin bamboo mat, and insisted on living no differently from any Vietnamese student at the center.

Sauvageot liked Chau personally, found him to be highly competent, and welcomed his presence at the training center. "But the CIA didn't seem to like to have him there," Sauvageot said. "They wanted to do it by themselves. They felt they had a good operation going with Le Xuan Mai, and why have Chau and his people from the Saigon ministry mucking around?"

After negotiations, it was worked out by the embassy and the Saigon government that the Vietnamese would take over the Vung Tau center, and Chau was assigned as the new commander. "Chau was coming to take over as a real commandant, not as a CIA employee like Le Xuan Mai," said Sauvageot. But on the day he was supposed to arrive the instructors at the center rebelled and demanded that the CIA not relinquish control. Sauvageot was dumbfounded. The Vietnamese staff formed a "struggle committee" and threatened to prevent Chau from assuming command by armed force if necessary. They wanted to keep CIA agent Mai as commandant.

For the next few days Sauvageot acted as the intermediary between the CIA in Vung Tau, the CIA in Saigon, and the Vietnamese struggle committee. The Americans found the situation embarrassing, and the CIA cooperated in trying to end the impasse. Finally, Sauvageot was able to smooth the way for Chau to assume command.

The CIA's fears about Chau were soon realized. The Vung Tau camp was constructed so that visitors had to pass through the office of the CIA adviser in order to get to the office of the Vietnamese commandant, which naturally made the Vietnamese look like a flunky. Chau's first act was to have two separate entrances built, one of them giving direct access to his office. This did not endear him to the CIA.

Yet, despite his moves to turn Vung Tau into a Vietnamese-controlled operation, Chau was not personally hostile to the CIA and admired many of its officers, particularly William Colby. His point was that he did not wish to become a CIA agent. Ironically, as word spread that Vung Tau was run by the CIA, the Saigon gossip circuit began to say that he was just that.

Chau did not last very long at the Vung Tau center. At the urging of Frank Scotton, another talented Vietnamese officer, Nguyen Be, was brought in from Binh Dinh province to work with Chau. The two men, both of them former Viet Minh, both honest, and both with strong personalities, did not get on well. There was also tension with whoever headed the Saigon government, since the cadre program offered anyone politically ambitious an obvious way of creating his own power base in the countryside. Lansdale, by this time, had been able to persuade Nguyen Cao Ky to hold constituent assembly elections; and Lansdale, along with Rufus Phillips, who arrived on a visit, encouraged Chau to resign from the army and become a politician. Nguyen Be took over the Vung Tau center and was credited by William Colby and other government officials in their historical accounts as being the imaginative force behind the cadre program.

Chau's name was conveniently forgotten.

15

SAIGON 1967

IN 1967, CHAU WAS BECOMING one of the most successful politicians in the country. He returned to his old province of Kien Hoa and won a stunning percentage of the vote in a fair election to the National Assembly. As he was completing his transition from army officer to civilian politician, the pacification program was going through its final reorganization. Tired of the squabbles between the military and the civilian bureaucracies, President Johnson sent Robert Komer, his White House assistant for pacification, to Saigon with the rank of ambassador and told him to do whatever necessary to beat the program into shape. Komer asked Johnson to assign William Colby, who was at CIA headquarters, as his deputy, and Colby took leave from the agency to take up a post once again in Vietnam. Colby was impressed with the clever scheme that the irrepressible Komer, who routinely left tales of outrage in his wake, had come up with to glue together the jagged pieces of the pacification program.

"Komer knew that if you put pacification under the military it would be lost, because the military would go out and shoot everybody," Colby said. "But Komer also understood that the military would never accept anything but a unity of command. Therefore the only way to make it work was to put pacification under the military, in civilian hands. He had the genius to see that. He drove the military crazy, of course—did for years."

The reorganization left General Westmoreland as head of the pacification program, with Komer doing the day-to-day work as his deputy. Although Westmoreland had developed a military strategy that seemed the antithesis to carrying out a successful pacification program, he had fought for years to bring the civilian bureaucracies under his control, and he was ready for the compromise that gave him a civilian deputy. The civilian he got in the form of Robert Komer, however, was not what he had expected.

Westmoreland was usually a paragon of courtesy and discretion when describing his colleagues in his memoirs, but he seemed barely able to contain himself when speaking of Komer. "The Lord knows the president handed me a volatile character in Bob Komer," Westmoreland wrote. "The nickname 'Blowtorch' was all too apt." But Westmoreland conceded that, for all the trouble Komer caused him, he was the right man for the job of pulling the different rigid bureaucracies together as a team.

The new behemoth was called CORDS—Civil Operations and Revolutionary Development Support. A key point of the reorganization was that half of South Vietnam's provinces would have senior advisers who were military, with civilian deputies, and the other half would have civilians in the top position, with military deputies. Most of the civilian advisers were foreign service officers; five or six came from the CIA. Their provincial staffs were further integrated between military and civilians. John Paul Vann was given one of the top jobs outside Saigon.

This, then, was to be a major triumph of the war: two years after a massive buildup, the Americans finally organized themselves into a relatively coordinated bureaucracy.

CORDS may have been working as a bureaucracy, but there was still doubt, at least by journalists, as to whether pacification was working. Much of the controversy surrounded the computerized program Robert Komer installed after he took over to measure the progress of CORDS' efforts, which was based on a monthly questionnaire CORDS' field reps were required to fill out. It was called the "Hamlet Evaluation System" (HES). Komer believed that the press overplayed the use of computers in pacification and that this in turn made the American public and the Congress skeptical of the entire program.

"Most of the critics take off on the HES without having been informed," Komer said in 1968. "John Tunney, for example, the California senator. I'm not criticizing John, but he said, 'How the hell can American advisers who are here only a year and don't speak Vietnamese analyze the hearts and minds of the hamlet farmer?' I said, 'John, give us a little credit. We're not entirely idiotic. We designed the system to measure objective phenomena, not hearts and minds. We told these guys to measure what they can measure. They know when a mortar shell gets fired into the hamlet, or when there's been a shooting incident at night. They know whether a bridge has been built, whether the hamlet school is functioning, whether the village well is bringing up potable water.' So he immediately came back to me with the one question out of thirty on the form that's not objective: 'Has the Viet Cong infrastructure been seriously disrupted?' I said, 'John, you've got me on the hip. That question is the most difficult to analyze, I grant you.' "

It was the question about the continuing existence and success of the Viet Cong political and administrative organization—or the Viet Cong infrastructure, as Komer insisted on jargonizing it—that drove him to create the Phoenix program.

SINCE ROBERT KOMER'S DEPUTY William Colby was a well-known CIA official, and since Phoenix was organized by the CIA, Colby was usually regarded as the father of the Phoenix program—which gave Chau a pang of remorse when he later heard people criticize Colby, because Chau knew that Phoenix had evolved from his efforts with the counterterror teams and that in fact *he* was the father of Phoenix, even if it had grown into the kind of operation he had never dreamed of.

Actually, far from being the mysterious operation that it came to be thought of by the public, Phoenix was, in effect, another bureaucratic reorganization, pushed through by the force of Komer's personality, not long after he did the same with CORDS in 1967. In this case the reorganization involved the multitude of intelligence organizations that were operating with little coordination. During Colby's early tour as station chief, he had helped establish a Vietnamese version of the CIA called the Central Intelligence Organization. The CIA also supported and worked through the special branch of the National Police. Military Intelligence operated through its counterpart organization, the Vietnamese Military Security Service. Then came various operations run by the staff G-2s of military units, and anybody else with enough money to set up an agent net. Intelligence in Vietnam was a morass of disorganization, with each unit jockeying for power and jealously guarding its secrets.

The idea behind Phoenix was to bring all the different intelligence units together at the province and district levels in an attempt to identify and eliminate the political and administrative organization of the Viet Cong. Colby and others had long tried to emphasize that the Viet Cong officials who indoctrinated the rice farmers, collected taxes, and recruited guerrillas should be considered the crucial targets. It seemed obvious that if one man had the skill to recruit hundreds of guerrillas, his value to the war effort was greater than that of one man who carried a rifle and did what he was told. Obvious it seemed, that is, to everybody but the American military, whose strategy was still based on piling up bodies, and one body in black pajamas looked the same as another. Komer undertook to thump the idea into the military's head that the war could never be won without first eliminating the Viet Cong political organization.

Colby asked the CIA for the loan of a few officers to get the program started, and intelligence centers were established in districts throughout the country. The Phoenix program, as Colby often tried to explain, was a coordinated intelligence collection service. Once the Phoenix staff identified a member of the Viet Cong political organization, they passed the information on to someone else for action, to either the National Police, the provincial reconnaissance units, the Saigon army, or the American military. The Phoenix staff, in other words, did not run operations to eliminate the Viet Cong. Moreover, if a VC official was killed on the battlefield during a regular military operation and identified afterward, his name was reported to the intelligence center and listed in the statistics as a victory for Phoenix.

From the start Phoenix was controversial and a magnet for attracting antiwar protest in the States. Some of the suspicion about the program grew from its very name. In Vietnamese folklore, the giant tortoise stood for longevity and the carp symbolized wisdom, but it was the phoenix that was truly wondrous, a heroic and powerful bird that could regenerate itself from the ashes. The myth of the phoenix had existed for centuries. In early Egypt, the phoenix was the embodiment of the sun god, fabled to live for five hundred years, then to be consumed by fire, only to rise once again fully restored to youth. To use the name of the world's best-known symbol of regeneration and life for a program specifically designed to eliminate the Viet Cong political/administrative organization by coldblooded killing if necessary suggested that the Americans were engaged in a sort of German concentration camp "Work Will Make You Free" cover for their operation. On the other hand, the Americans had an innocent knack for choosing names that were inappropriate or faintly ridiculous, and no devious motives seemed attributable to the obscure army officer who gave Phoenix its tag.

Much of the controversy grew from Colby's and Komer's insistence on describing Phoenix in bureaucratic terms that were clear only to themselves. As they described it, Phoenix was designed to "neutralize" the Viet Cong "infrastructure," in which an "agitprop" cadre, say, was a more important target than a guerrilla soldier. Neutralize—was that another euphemism for assassinate, similar to "terminate with extreme prejudice"? Infrastructure? And what in God's name was an agitprop cadre, anyhow? The failure to explain themselves in simple English contributed to a widespread belief that they were out to assassinate the largely innocent opponents of the Saigon government and trying to cover up their immoral acts with bewildering obfuscations.

Robert G. Kaiser, Jr., a *Washington Post* reporter who was skeptical of the war, felt impelled to try to strip away some of the confusion surrounding Phoenix, and in a lengthy article published on February 17, 1970, captioned "U.S. Aides in Vietnam Scorn Phoenix Project," he began by noting that the public perception of Phoenix in the United States did not match the reality of the operation in Vietnam.

"Some war critics in the United States have attacked Phoenix as an instrument of mass political murder," Kaiser wrote. "Such sinister descriptions are not heard in Vietnam, where Phoenix has the reputation of a poorly plotted farce, sometimes with tragic overtones. The contradiction between Phoenix's lurid reputation as a sort of Vietnamese Murder, Inc., and the scorn with which it is widely regarded here typifies one of the most popular grievances of American officials in Vietnam: 'They don't understand at home what's going on out here.' " Kaiser went on to report that "Many of the accusations against Phoenix cannot be verified here. Some seem to be based on misunderstandings of Phoenix terminology and statistics." The next day James Sterba of the *New York Times* published a critical article on Phoenix that backed up Kaiser's interpretation of the program.

To a great degree, Phoenix's dark reputation was based on the earlier murderous operations of the provincial reconnaissance units

(PRUs), which had evolved in an undisciplined fashion from Chau's counterterror teams during the political chaos following the Diem coup. As Kaiser pointed out, the PRUs had been brought under stricter control and most of their excesses ended. But their reputation persisted and made good copy for reporters looking for a punchy angle.

During the same month that Kaiser's and Sterba's articles appeared in the *Post* and the *Times,* the normally staid Georgie Anne Geyer, a close friend of the conservative Keyes Beech, published an article in *True* magazine entitled "The CIA's Hired Killers," which began: "As the war becomes more political and less military, targets shift from the enemy's army to its civilian leadership. To get the job done, the U.S. has trained an elite corps of assassins to eliminate the Viet Cong's 'shadow government.' " Using the hardnosed prose favored by men's magazines, Geyer told how she had accompanied a PRU group on an operation in the delta, in which eight members of the "Viet Cong infrastructure" were killed and twenty-six captured. But nowhere did she indicate that the PRUs had attempted or engaged in assassination. Rather, from her account, the Viet Cong appeared to have been killed or captured after an armed fight that was typical of any military operation in Vietnam.

Stories like Geyer's about the PRUs added to the impression that the CIA was running an assassination program, and William Colby inadvertently provided ammunition to the bump-off theorists when he publicly reported that around twenty thousand VC officials had been eliminated by Phoenix. It was widely assumed that they had been rubbed out by the PRUs. Actually the largest percentage had been killed on the battlefield and then identified as VC officials after the fact. Their inclusion in the statistical column of Phoenix was valid but also a way of fulfilling the quotas levied by Saigon and making the program look more efficient than it was in reality.

"Phoenix wasn't all that effective," said Colby. "It was like many programs in that it never worked the way it was supposed to. But it did focus on a key element and a necessary one—i.e., the fight against the secret apparatus. That made the communists feel under pressure. As they lost their connections with the population and were driven out of areas, they attributed their problems to Phoenix, when they really should have attributed them to the growth of self-defense forces and that sort of thing. So when the communists now talk about Phoenix as the reason they had a hard time during that period, I believe they make the same mistake as the Americans who heard so many horror stories about Phoenix that they think it was what pacification was all about."

Colby admitted that some of the horror stories were true. "There were excesses in the program," he said. "I knew things had gone on that shouldn't have happened. I never denied it, and that's what got me in trouble, because I didn't deny it."

There was little doubt as to Colby's sensitivity to the pitfalls inherent in the war's most controversial program. He was open about Phoenix's flaws—surprisingly open, in fact—and evidently sincere in his attempts to correct excesses. Yet his was the view from Saigon. As always, the perspective was different in the field, where directives from headquarters were seldom followed to the letter and reports flowing back to Saigon did not tell the whole story. In some respects, not much had changed since the days of Pat McGarvey, a CIA officer who worked on an early version of the program in 1964.

"One guy who was a source of information about the VC relieved his family of three generations of debt," Pat McGarvey recalled. "He turned in phony reports fingering as Viet Cong people his family owed money to."

The controls instituted by Colby helped end the more blatant abuses that McGarvey saw in the early days, but no one could figure out how to stop the other forms of intimidation and extortion that Phoenix opened to Saigon government officials. By threatening to brand an innocent civilian as a Viet Cong unless he paid up, a corrupt official could turn Phoenix into a profitable shakedown. There was also a question about the value of many of the Viet Cong officials targeted by Phoenix. They were broken down into different lettered categories of importance and listed as A, B, or C on color-coded files. Frank Snepp went on operations with the PRUs a few times, though as a CIA analyst that was not his job.

"The orders were that no Americans were to be in on the hit or the snatch," Snepp said. "It was to be only the PRUs. In this one particular exercise, we went out and stopped at the edge of a hamlet while the PRU people went in. I'd helped make up the target list and I was so proud of having identified a Viet Cong suspect. He was a hamlet-proselytizing cadre, an agitprop person. They brought this guy out and he must have been eighteen or nineteen. It was such a letdown. 'So this is our enemy,' I thought. He had nothing to offer."

Ultimately, of course, the problem with Phoenix was that it had been taken out of the context of Chau's original intentions. It simply wasn't enough to kill the Viet Cong officials. The Saigon government had to counter the communists' programs with something better. And to do that, more dedicated Vietnamese like Chau were needed.

Nevertheless, by 1970, pacification had made its most impressive gains of the war. While the antiwar movement was growing in the United States and pressure for a total military withdrawal increasing, American officials such as Ellsworth Bunker and William Colby in Saigon were beginning to feel that finally they were on the right track and winning.

III

ALL THE NEWS

16

SAIGON 1970

JOHN PAUL VANN'S PLAN to smuggle Chau out of Vietnam, in order to remove him from Thieu's grasp, was coming unraveled by late February 1970. Chau's hesitation about whether to flee had given the president's agents and the CIA time enough to get a fix on his location, and it was reported to the embassy that Vann was hiding him out in Can Tho. Ambassador Ellsworth Bunker was furious. He ordered Vann to appear at his office.

Speaking in his usual quiet manner, Bunker told Vann that he would be dismissed from his job and removed from the country if he continued to involve himself with Chau. Bunker took the position that the affair was a matter for the Saigon government to resolve and strictly between the Vietnamese. He said he knew that Vann had powerful friends in the media and that his dismissal might cause a few problems, but, said Bunker, he was prepared to face them.

"John Vann came to my office after his meeting with Bunker and said, 'By God, that was a frightening thing,' " said George Jacobson, who worked for the ambassador and was Vann's friend. "It was the only time I ever saw Vann shaken. He was white and sweating."

Yet, despite Bunker's warning, Vann refused to give up Chau and proceeded with the plan to help him leave the country. But Chau learned of Bunker's threat, and the news pushed him into making a decision. He would not be responsible, he decided, for ruining Vann's work and ending his career. Chau told Vann he wanted to return to Saigon.

Chau refused to believe, however, that the embassy and the CIA

301

would let Thieu put him in jail. He had worked with the Americans for such a long time that he did not think they would abandon him, especially since they knew the truth about his contacts with his communist brother. It was all a mistake, he thought.

On his return to Saigon, Chau got in touch with Jean Sauvageot, who had left the Vung Tau training center and was now William Colby's representative at the prime minister's office. Colby had been promoted to head the pacification program after Robert Komer was assigned to Turkey as ambassador in the final days of the Johnson administration. Chau asked Sauvageot for help in clearing up the misunderstanding about his contacts with his brother.

Chau's call distressed Sauvageot, who agreed to meet the Vietnamese for breakfast at the Continental Hotel. Not only did Sauvageot work for Colby, whom he admired, but Colby had shown him every courtesy and even invited him to live at his private villa. Sauvageot frequently served as Colby's translator on trips out of Saigon. Sauvageot suspected that Colby would not be happy to hear that he was meeting with Chau, but if anyone in Saigon outside of Ambassador Bunker had the clout to help, Sauvageot knew, it was Colby.

"I told Colby how concerned I was about Chau," Sauvageot said. "He replied that it was very unfortunate but that we had our relations with the Vietnamese government to consider and had to be careful. I think he believed I would take the hint and quit associating with Chau without his having to tell me directly. But I felt a sense of moral obligation."

William Colby felt a sense of the impending success of the pacification program. Years had been lost, he believed, because of the stupidity of overthrowing Diem. Nothing could be accomplished without the political stability of the Saigon government. Now stability had been achieved, the Viet Cong had been decimated by the Tet offensive, and the nature of the war had changed into a conventional battle with North Vietnamese regulars, which the Americans were good at fighting. Victory was possible, he thought. Colby knew that Chau had probably contributed more to pacification than any other single Vietnamese. But which took priority in terms of winning the war—helping Chau or doing nothing to threaten the political stability of the Thieu regime?

Sometimes Chau phoned Sauvageot at Colby's villa, using the code name Billy, and they spoke in Vietnamese while Colby was in the next room. Sauvageot told Colby that Chau had done a lot for the United States. The embassy and the CIA had been happy at the time, he reminded Colby, for Chau to provide the information about his brother Hien without sharing it with the Saigon government. Sauvageot said that he believed all of them had a moral duty to work the matter out with Thieu and not let Chau be arrested or abused.

Shortly after his conversation with Colby, Sauvageot received a phone call from the CIA asking him to come to their office at the embassy that night. When he got there, he was met by a CIA officer who didn't waste words. "We understand you've been saying we have some obligations to Chau," he said. "Yes, I think we do," replied Sauvageot, who listed his reasons. The CIA man called another officer in and asked him to go through the file on Chau.

"Major, we have no connections with Tran Ngoc Chau," said the CIA man with the file. "We have no obligations to him and never have. You've been misinformed. So stay away from him. Forget about him. Do you understand?"

"Yeah," Sauvageot said. "I think it's wrong and I don't agree. But I understand." He left.

Sauvageot kept seeing Chau, but more discreetly, asking him not to call Colby's house anymore. Then one day Chau phoned him at the prime minister's office and with a note of urgency asked to see him as soon as possible. Sauvageot suggested that they meet at a restaurant. To avoid surveillance, he rode a bicycle through back alleys where no car could follow.

Chau had begun to believe he was in real danger, and he asked Sauvageot if he could help him. "There's only one possibility I can think of," said Sauvageot. "If you want to get in the trunk of my Falcon sedan, I'll drive you across the Cambodian border and let you off. Once in Cambodia, you'll be on your own." But Chau had already decided against fleeing to Cambodia under the plan devised by John Vann, and he thanked Sauvageot, saying, "No, I don't think I'll do it."

"I got back to the office at about three in the afternoon," Sauvageot recalled. "My secretary said, 'It's Mr. Colby on the phone for you.' I picked it up and Colby very coldly said, 'How about not seeing that fellow anymore—ever. Is it clear?'

" 'Yes, sir,' I said. He hung up. I never knew till years later how they learned that I met with Chau that day. The CIA bugged my phone."

ELLSWORTH BUNKER, OF ALL THE AMBASSADORS to serve in Saigon, seemed the least likely to be involved in the abandonment of a friend of the United States such as Chau. When the affair was over, even his admirers admitted that it had not been his finest moment. In fact, it appeared that someone wished the whole thing forgotten, for after Bunker's voluminous reports to the president were declassified and made public, it was discovered that the only page missing from the files concerned his comments about Chau. The Chau affair, and Bunker's tenacious support of Thieu, was emblematic of the shift in the ambassador's thinking in the three years he had been in Saigon. He had arrived with the idea of ending American involvement in Vietnam as quickly as possible. And now he, like Colby, had begun to believe the war could be won after all.

Lyndon Johnson's private instructions to Bunker when he appointed him ambassador in 1967, as later recounted by Bunker after Johnson died, were so astonishing as to leave many of the ambassador's former associates incredulous. Yet there was little reason to doubt that what Bunker told his wife, Carol Laise, and his friend Bruce Palmer represented the truth of his conversation with President Johnson.

"His mission was to make it possible for the Americans to get out of Vietnam," Carol Laise Bunker said. "There was no question about that. And yet it wasn't really known."

Bruce Palmer and Bunker served together in the Dominican Republic during the 1965 crisis and formed a friendship that continued in Vietnam. "Years later, in June 1981," General Palmer recalled in his memoirs, "Ambassador Bunker told me that in January 1967, when President Johnson asked him to go to Saigon, the president said that Bunker's mission would be to wind up the war for American troops as quickly as possible. The president apparently did not elaborate on what might constitute an acceptable South Vietnamese security posture which would allow U.S. troops to return home. It was a private conversation with only the two men present."

Whether that was an indication that Lyndon Johnson had already given up on an American victory by the beginning of 1967, or whether it was just another manifestation of the president's ambivalence, it went a long way toward explaining why Ellsworth Bunker, seventy-three, was chosen to follow Maxwell Taylor and Henry Cabot Lodge. Nothing in Bunker's career suggested that he would perform well in the role of a pro-consul charged with leading American troops to victory in a war. To the contrary, everything pointed to his talents as a negotiator. Bunker had gone into diplomacy at the urging of Dean Acheson, his Yale classmate, during the Truman administration, after a long career of running the family business, the National Sugar Refining Company, and had served as ambassador to Argentina, Italy, and India. His touch as a diplomat could be seen by the way he handled Ed Lansdale, who might have presented the ultimate test for any ambassador.

"Lodge told me, 'Bunker doesn't want you,' " Lansdale said. " 'I've talked to him. You'd be smart to return to the States with me. I can protect you.' I don't know what Lodge was going to protect me from. I didn't give a damn anyhow. I said, 'No, I still have work to do. I'll stay and let Bunker kick me out of the country if he wants.' I went to the airport the day Bunker arrived. He asked me if I would ride in his car to his residence. He told me on the way that he thought I could be very useful in keeping the United States knowledgeable about Vietnamese desires."

Lansdale remained in Saigon a few months longer and was treated courteously by Bunker though given no more power than he had held under Lodge. When Lansdale finally decided to leave in 1968, he carried with him the opinion that Ellsworth Bunker, along with Donald Heath in the nineteen fifties, was the best ambassador to serve in Vietnam.

Bunker realized that the Saigon press corps held the power to influence the success or failure of his mission, and in June 1967, two months after he arrived, he called six of the top newsmen in for a confidential briefing. The *Time* bureau chief considered Bunker's comments so potentially explosive that he took the precaution of filing his report to the magazine's editors from Hong Kong rather than entrusting it to his Saigon wire. Bunker told the journalists that he saw the presidential elections, scheduled for September, as a step in the process that could lead to negotiations, but asked them not to attribute his speculation to an American official. He told them he had called Thieu and Ky to his villa the previous Monday and given them a talking to for the way they were jockeying for power. His remarks, he said, were directed mainly at Ky, who was using his position as prime minister to try to insure that he would be elected president.

Bunker's session with the journalists was a remarkable display of candor and calculated to win them to his side. It soon became apparent, however, that the tactic, as he saw it, had not worked. Taking newsmen into his confidence had no visible effect. Press reports out of Saigon continued to reflect pessimism about the way the war was going. *Stalemate* was the description frequently used.

"He became gun-shy of the press," said Bunker's son, Samuel. "It was maybe the first time in his experience, really, that what the press was saying was so terribly important. And he just didn't think they were doing a responsible job. He expressed frustrations about this all the time."

Ellsworth Bunker was, by nature, a formal man who played his cards close to the vest. His disappointment with the press corps added to his caution. This became increasingly apparent after the media described the 1968 Tet offensive as a victory for the communists, which Bunker believed, given the fact that the Viet Cong had been decimated during the attack, to be wrong. There were a few journalists he trusted, such as Keyes Beech and Robert Shaplen, but the rest he treated with an Edwardian courtesy and reserve that could stop dead the most impetuous questioner. He was much too wise to let his frustrations with the press show. He continued to be accessible and often hosted informal dinners, to which he invited small groups of journalists. The newsmen were charmed by his taste. He gave the best dinners in town, and whether he appeared in a lightweight tropical suit, a black tie and tux, or his frequent uniform of well-pressed chinos and a short-sleeved shirt, no one was better dressed. At the end of an evening he would swirl his cognac around in his glass and say, "Okay, boys, I've told you a lot. Now how about you telling me what I should know. What's going on in the country I don't know about?" More than one journalist departed in a mellow mood, preferring not to mull over the thought that Bunker had given much less than he had received. For in truth he spoke less and less on the record, and, except for official cables and reports, wrote practically nothing about Vietnam. After he left the war, he worked on his memoirs but declined to have them published.

Bunker's only confidant was his wife, Carol Laise, a career foreign service officer who was nearly twenty-five years younger than he.

Laise had fought her way up through State Department ranks when it was explicitly no advantage to be a woman. She met Bunker in New Delhi, and after his first wife died some years later they decided to get married, only a month before, it turned out, Lyndon Johnson wanted to send him to Saigon. Laise was then ambassador to Nepal.

President Johnson assigned Bunker an airplane, and during his years in Vietnam he would go to Katmandu to visit Carol or she would come to Saigon. On Bunker's long weekends in Nepal, Carol would pack a picnic and drive the two of them, alone, without a security detail, in her convertible to a valley where they had a view of Mount Everest. It was the only place in the world where they could enjoy true privacy. There, and perhaps on the Vermont farm outside Brattleboro that Bunker loved so much. Though from New York, he preferred to be known as coming from Vermont. "I think he was very pleased when the press started describing him as the tall, taciturn Vermonter," Samuel Bunker said. He had an earthy sense of humor that those who knew him thought a surprising and pleasing contrast to his old-world formality.

"Bunker's strong point was that he could control and impose his will on diverse personalities like Colby, Shackley, and Creighton Abrams—simply, I think, out of force of his grace," Frank Snepp said.

"Bunker was absolutely number one among the ambassadors," William Colby said. "He was clear, simple, strong, and decisive; also subtle."

Bunker and Colby liked and admired the third member of the power triumvirate—Creighton Abrams, who replaced Westmoreland in 1968. Someone remarked that Abrams was so good that he deserved a better war. Part of his reputation was built on the chance of being able to profit from his predecessor's mistakes. Another part grew from his personal style, which seemed more appropriate to a nonheroic war than did Westmoreland's Eagle Scout manner. Stocky, rumpled, stoop-shouldered, Abrams could joke about military absurdities and himself as he puffed at a cigar and drank a gin and tonic, his stereo blasting out Beethoven or Mozart from his large collection of classical music. Westmoreland worked hard at cultivating journalists and was always accessible and accommodating, while Abrams hardly bothered to conceal his contempt for them. But it was Abrams who came off with the better press. Yet his reputation was not entirely the result of chance and style. Abrams had in abundance the one thing that Westmoreland lacked: intuition.

Instead of asking his commanders about body counts, Abrams might question them about Viet Cong tax collection efforts in their area, or about their success in identifying members of the Viet Cong shadow government. He moved away from Westmoreland's massive search-and-destroy operations and put new emphasis on cordon tactics, whereby his troops sealed off a sector and waited for Vietnamese police to comb the hamlets looking for Viet Cong. At the same time, he began using huge B-52 bombers like artillery pieces to hit suspected enemy forces, a heavy-handed tactic difficult for journalists to observe, thus difficult to criticize.

Colby liked Abrams because he had finally found a general who understood that the war could not be won on the basis of racking up body counts so long as the political apparatus of the Viet Cong continued to operate. Bunker liked him because of his devotion to helping the South Vietnamese improve their military forces, which was a prerequisite to the ambassador's original instructions from Johnson to get American troops out of Vietnam as soon as possible. The White House changed hands in 1969, but Richard Nixon indicated that he intended to follow the Johnson administration's negotiating track, which was developed in 1968 after LBJ announced he would not run for a second term as president. Though the policy of "Vietnamization" was Nixon's, Bunker and most everyone else thought that Abrams would do a better job with the South Vietnamese military than Westmoreland, who had been soured by Vietnamese incompetence and disorganization during his first months as commander.

With Abrams as military commander and Colby handling pacification, Bunker could turn his attention to cementing the power of the Saigon government, headed, since the 1967 elections, by Nguyen Van Thieu. There was little doubt that Bunker faithfully executed his instructions from the State Department and the White House. He was no Henry Cabot Lodge, tap dancing on his own, making policy. If Bunker had a flaw, his critics believed, it was one not infrequently attributed to ambassadors who spent long tours in the same country: He began to identify himself too closely with the success or failure of the head of the Saigon government. Some thought Thieu became Bunker's bridge on the River Kwai.

"Ellsworth felt that Thieu was able and that he grew on the job," Carol Laise Bunker said. "And he believed that within the constraints of the situation Thieu did remarkably well. When I say constraints, I mean that Thieu had two audiences to deal with, his own public and the public in the United States. Ellsworth thought at times that Thieu was too cautious. But there was a canniness to his caution that he understood."

The presidential elections, four months after Bunker's arrival, fell into place with his conception of how diplomacy should be conducted. By nature he was uncomfortable with making demands of anyone or using the force of threats to accomplish his mission. The election of Thieu by constitutional means, as he saw it, precluded such tactics. He stressed the legality of the Saigon regime and refused to order Thieu to do anything. Instead, he established the habit of consulting with Thieu, almost as if he were dealing with the head of the British government during wartime. He traveled the half-mile from the embassy to the presidential palace several times a week.

"Bunker wrote out notes to himself on three-by-five cards before he went to see Thieu," said George Jacobson, who sometimes accompanied him. "He memorized what was on the cards; then we drove to the palace. The Vietnamese were very polite. You'd never find someone like Thieu sitting behind his desk. After everybody shook hands, we gathered around the coffee table, where tea was served. Bunker used the same gentle tone of voice at all times, no matter whom he was talking to. His approach was soft, yet never wishy-washy. The conversation between him and Thieu developed as it would between any two people who knew each other well."

Bunker's good manners and mild sternness captured the Oriental imagination. He stood in sharp contrast to the military directness of Maxwell Taylor, the arrogance of Henry Cabot Lodge. "He sits up straight and listens, never showing signs of impatience or nervousness," a Vietnamese journalist said. The Vietnamese nicknamed him "The Ice Box." The man innately unqualified to be a pro-consul was considered by the Vietnamese public to be the most powerful American ambassador of all. Bunker's perceived power and his unstinting support of Thieu stopped the coup plotting in Saigon.

As Thieu blossomed under his benign tutelage, Bunker, in private, glowed with pride, telling journalists that Thieu had become "an astute politician." Thieu's progress was made even sweeter by the fact that Bunker and Westmoreland were almost alone in promoting him as America's choice. Others, from Lodge to Lansdale and Ellsberg, had supported Ky.

"Bunker didn't want John Vann or anyone else in the official family to get too close to Chau during the time he was having trouble with

309

Thieu," George Jacobson said. "Chau was a sound military guy and a good administrator on the civilian side. Bunker had no particular dislike for him. But he did have an interest in stroking Thieu—certainly not in ruffling him. Bunker was interested in getting Thieu to do what he recommended, and he considered that a hell of a lot more important than a squabble between the government and Chau. It was as simple as that."

PEOPLE WHO MET NGUYEN VAN THIEU for the first time were usually surprised. They arrived expecting to see an Asian hardcase who had slashed and hacked his way to the top of the heap in Saigon, a beribboned general wearing a bulletproof vest under his tunic, a pistol stuck in his waistband. Instead they were greeted by a physically unimpressive man about five-five, stockily built, conservatively dressed, with not a medal showing, who politely served his guests tea, all the while speaking with charm and animation in moderately fluent English, occasionally fumbling for a word or phrase to fit into the overworked present tense. Yet the impression of Thieu as an amiable politician was not entirely correct either. He was tightly wound. He chain-smoked Kool cigarettes as he talked, tearing off the filter and stuffing the remaining part into a gold Dunhill holder. He was a loner. Though he had a keen mind, well organized, he was not an intellectual; he read magazines and newspapers, seldom a book. He worked hard but was a relatively late riser. He found relaxation on his boat searching for tuna off the coast of Vung Tau, where he had a vacation home, although he was not a notable fisherman.

Thieu's rise had been slow and unspectacular, that of a cautious survivor rather than a charismatic leader. By early 1970, however, he was approaching the peak of his confidence in his ability to rule South Vietnam and to deal with the Americans. It was a confidence that had grown with Ambassador Bunker's careful nurturing of his ego. But an even larger and publicly unknown reason for his new forcefulness was based on his perception of the debt he thought Richard Nixon owed him. Simply put, Nguyen Van Thieu believed that he had made Richard Nixon president of the United States.

Thieu wasn't alone in assigning a crucial value to the role he played in the 1968 presidential election. William Connell, Hubert Humphrey's chief of staff, also believed that Thieu's blockade of the peace negotiations in the last three days of the campaign was probably decisive in determining the outcome of the election. So did Theodore White, the political journalist, who documented the '68 campaign in his *Making of the President* series.

"Johnson's stopping of the bombing a few days before the election gave a tremendous surge to the idea that we might be able to get out of Vietnam," William Connell said. "That began to turn the election around. Our polls showed Humphrey pulling even with Nixon. Then the withdrawal of Thieu at the last minute from the peace process just took the edge off it. I was present, on the plane, when Humphrey got the word that Thieu was refusing to send a negotiating team to Paris. Humphrey did not get angry very often. He was a happy fellow. But that day he was enraged. He said, 'By God, when we land I'm going to denounce Thieu. I'll denounce Nixon. I'll tell about the whole thing.' And the staff said, 'Nobody will believe you. They'll figure you are pulling this out of a hat because you are desperate. It's just too awful. Nobody will believe Nixon made a deal with Thieu to undercut the negotiations.' Humphrey said, 'That's right. I won't do it. But we'll take care of those bastards when I get elected.' He knew, though, that Thieu's move was possibly going to ruin him."

Thieu was certainly trying to do that. He had become Humphrey's implacable enemy the year before, in November 1967, when the vice president had journeyed to Saigon as Washington's representative to the inauguration of Thieu and Ky as president and vice president of South Vietnam. One of Ed Lansdale's supporters briefed Humphrey aboard Air Force Two before he reached Saigon about the widespread corruption among the Vietnamese, and several journalists with his party assured him that official reports of how the war was going were inaccurate and that American policy was failing. Humphrey was in a mood to speak plainly with Thieu and Ky when he arrived.

Accompanied by Bunker and a staff member, Humphrey went to the presidential palace, where he took on Thieu, bluntly warning him that the Vietnamese would have to make significant changes if U.S. support was to continue.

"Thieu listened," said Humphrey, "delicately holding a cigarette, its smoke drifting up and away from him. He broke the pose to flick the ash from his cigarette in a manner that suggested that he was also flicking away what I had said.

"Then he spoke: 'No, you will be here for a long time. We are aware of what you say, but we realize that your support will have to continue, and perhaps increase for the next five or six years.' He seemed ready to go on and I interrupted: 'Perhaps I haven't made myself clear.' Then I repeated with greater detail and even more firmly what I had just said, and concluded, 'What we are doing to Vietnamese society is not healthy for you or us.' "

When they left, Humphrey asked Bunker if he had been "undiplomatically harsh." Bunker, who himself would never have spoken to Thieu like that, ever the diplomat, said, "No, I think it was just what he needed to hear. That was fine." Had Ed Lansdale been along, he would have told Humphrey it wasn't fine at all. Humphrey was expressing Lansdale's sentiments but did it in a way guaranteed to make enemies of Thieu and Ky. Lansdale talked to them about corruption and the need for changes, but he never lectured them and never used words like "Perhaps I haven't made myself clear." Ironically, Hubert Humphrey, having become a Lansdale disciple concerning the substance of Vietnam but without having adopted the Lansdale style of dealing with the Vietnamese, quite possibly ended his chances of being president of the United States.

When Nixon's operative Anna Chennault, the Chinese-born widow of General Claire Chennault, commander of the Flying Tigers in World War Two, urged Thieu to hold on and not commit himself to Johnson's peace negotiations, the Vietnamese president was more than ready to agree. Anna Chennault was in close contact with John Mitchell, Nixon's campaign manager. "A Humphrey victory would mean a coalition government in six months," Thieu explained. "With Nixon at least there was a chance."

Thieu got a feel for Nixon's well-rounded duplicity shortly after the election, when the new president leaned on him to take part in the peace negotiations. Thieu wasn't happy with Nixon's change of attitude but believed it a tacit confirmation of his worth to the Republicans in refusing to cooperate with the Democrats on the eve of the national election. Yes, Thieu decided, he had made Nixon president, and Nixon owed him one.

Early in 1969, fortified by the belief that Nixon and Bunker were behind him, Thieu decided to attack one of his two major sources of political opposition. He had shown little hesitancy in trying to neutralize his individual opponents, but this time he was attacking a whole class, Saigon's intellectuals. It was a Diem-like move, and, in fact, as Thieu had settled into the presidency, he had begun to identify with the former dictator. Thieu had led the assault on the presidential palace during the 1963 coup and been promoted to general on the basis of his participation, but he had come to believe that Diem had done a far better job than he was given credit for and that he himself faced Diem's old enemies, the intellectuals who had criticized the government in power since South Vietnam was founded. Thieu was, it appeared, developing something of a fetish about Diem. He often told visitors that his large ornate office was Diem's bedroom, and he insisted on using Diem's old Mercedes as his official car long after he could have taken a newer one.

The intelligentsia included roughly anyone who had a higher education, quite often received in France and, increasingly, in America. As a class, the intellectuals were fiercely nationalistic, disdainful of Americans, utopian-minded, and antiwar. They wanted peace but had no plan for bringing it about. They rejected communism but were accepting of the communists. They were contemptuous of their own military, not that they or their sons would deign to serve; and over a café filtre or a Rémy Martin could hold forth eloquently about how the repressive Thieu government was trampling individual liberties and antagonizing the youth of the country. Though much of what they said was correct, they were not people who inspired much trust or sympathy.

It was the case of Nguyen Van Lau, the English-educated publisher of the *Saigon Daily News,* which set Thieu off. His agents discovered that the influential Lau was holding conversations with a friend from his childhood who was now a communist intelligence officer—Chau's brother, Hien. When asked why he had failed to report his contacts with Hien, Lau replied, "As an intellectual, I cannot report a friend to the authorities." After Hien was picked up by the police, Thieu had Lau arrested, along with twenty-six other professional people, including doctors and pharmacists.

Speaking to a training class of hamlet administrators at Vung Tau, Thieu sounded like Diem in his attack, saying, "You are more patriotic than these intellectuals who drink four glasses of whisky a day and eat only Western dishes. Although they are well educated, they are slaves to the communists."

The speech was declared by Bunker's embassy to be one of the best Thieu had ever made. When he followed up by censoring or closing a number of newspapers and arresting more people, there was hardly a murmur of dissent from the Americans, who had become as irritated with the intellectuals as they had with the Buddhists. Emboldened by his successful attack on the intellectuals, Thieu decided to take on his second source of opposition, Lansdale's creation, the National Assembly, and along with it, Tran Ngoc Chau.

IN 1949, WHEN CHAU WAS DECIDING to leave the Viet Minh, Thieu was on his way to the French infantry school at St. Cyr. Thieu had come to the attention of the French the previous year, when they had asked for volunteers to their new officer candidate school, which was accepting Vietnamese students. Thieu graduated as a second lieutenant and was selected for further training at St. Cyr, the French West Point. One of his classmates, also picked to go to France, was Dang Van Quang, who, in personality, was the opposite of Thieu. Quang was light-hearted and voluble, always laughing and joking.

During the long boat trip to France, Quang showed Thieu a photograph of his distant cousin, Nguyen Thi Hai Anh, an attractive nineteen-year-old Catholic and daughter of a prosperous practitioner of Oriental medicine in the delta town of My Tho. Lonely and homesick, Thieu asked Quang for her address, and began a correspondence that lasted the eight months he was at St. Cyr. When he returned to Saigon, they met face-to-face and began a courtship. They were married on July 18, 1951.

Thieu and Quang went their separate ways as army officers but stayed in touch. Thieu did not make friends easily. He was reserved, a loner. But Quang was an exception. They had gone through basic training together, shared the experience in France, and, most important, were linked by a family connection through Thieu's wife. Thieu and Quang rose in rank to become generals. Thieu was considered by the Americans to be capable and honest—with the caveat of course that honesty in Vietnam was a relative matter. There was no relativity where Quang was concerned, however. He gained the reputation for being the most corrupt general in the country.

When Thieu started taking money could not be established, but the momentum picked up after the Americans could take no more of Quang's blatant corruption and forced him out of his army command of the delta. Thieu reluctantly acquiesced to Quang's firing—and then made him his chief adviser at the presidential palace. It was not a friendship he was going to give up. From then on, when the Americans wanted to talk to Thieu about corruption, they had to set up the appointment through Quang, who often sat in on the meetings.

"Thieu was not nearly as corrupt as others, but corrupt enough, I'm afraid," said Mark Huss, an AID official with many years in Vietnam. "I think in the latter part of the war he and his wife, particularly his wife, came to the conclusion that things were just a little too dicey not to squirrel away something overseas. If you've got a guy like Quang who's willing to do all the dirty work and never bother you with the details, it makes life easier and pleasanter for you. That was basically their relationship."

Rather than making an issue of Quang with Thieu, the Americans, especially the CIA, tried to use him. "You didn't buy him because you couldn't control him," said Frank Snepp. "But he was very useful to have an open line to, and he afforded us access at will. Actually, Quang finessed us, because it meant we couldn't report on a major source of corruption in that government. Who is controlling whom, finally?"

Whatever Quang's status with the CIA, William Colby was ready to make use of him but was not enamored either. "Quang was a son of a bitch," Colby said. "He was just no good. I always thought in a way that he was a court jester. He was always bubbling around, talking."

Colby prided himself on what he considered his ability to make a realistic assessment of a situation and then work toward a goal despite a variety of negative factors. As he saw it, "Corruption in that part of the world existed. There was not a helluva lot you could do about it. You obviously had to keep it from going too far. And you could certainly keep your own people away from it. But it was like other things—you had priorities, and the priority on my mind was the villages. The first problem in the world was to win the war. Then you could work on corruption later. I didn't see it as adversely affecting the work that was going on."

With an American attitude toward corruption that was ambivalent at best, Thieu and his associates took little trouble to conceal their use of bribery to subvert the National Assembly. Thieu had grown exasperated with this American creation that had been foisted upon the country in the middle of a war. Despite his and the CIA's attempts, Thieu had never been able to develop a strong pro-government party. Nor was there a united opposition. The National Assembly reflected the usual brand of political machinations and intrigue. Thieu's way of handling the problem was to invite the assemblymen to the palace for a reception and run them through the next room almost in single file, where they were handed envelopes of "Tran Hung Dao vitamins," so called because the ancient leader of Vietnam, Tran Hung Dao, appeared on the stacks of piastre notes, given to them by Thieu's chief bagman, a wealthy pharmacist.

By corrupting the National Assembly Thieu was almost able to bring it under control. Almost, but not quite. There were still a few independent and honest legislators who were ready to oppose him on matters of democratic principle. Chief among them was Tran Ngoc Chau. Thieu knew that if he could break Chau, the National Assembly would be his.

17

WASHINGTON-SAIGON 1970

THE STATE DEPARTMENT, realizing that Thieu was out to destroy Chau, began to urge Ambassador Bunker to head him off. Under Secretary of State Elliot Richardson was the official most concerned, his interest in the case stimulated by his assistant, who had served in Saigon and who knew Chau and many of his supporters. Richardson's assistant made a trip to Vietnam in late 1969 and talked to Ev Bumgardner and John Paul Vann, who outlined Thieu's strategy against Chau. Using Chau's contacts with his brother to accuse him of procommunist activities, Thieu was trying to get the National Assembly to strip him of parliamentary immunity so that he could be arrested and imprisoned by a military court. Thieu's bagman, Nguyen Cao Thang, the pharmacist who passed out the Trung Hung Dao vitamins, was in charge of the immunity question, with Thieu's friend, Dang Van Quang, plotting the moves.

On December 27, 1969, Elliot Richardson sent Ambassador Bunker a cable politely ordering him to stop Thieu. "I leave it to your discretion how to bring this problem to Thieu's attention," Richardson said. "I think he should know that arrest of Deputy Chau would not be helpful to administration efforts to retain the support of American people for our policy in Vietnam." Richardson told Bunker that Chau had a number of devoted supporters in Washington both in and out of government. "They are convinced," he said, "that GVN's move against him is not because of any alleged communist activities but because he is an effective and vocal critic of the shortcomings of the GVN." Moreover, said Richardson, "Several reports have indicated

317

that GVN's case against him is weak in terms of his having aided communists in contrast to his having admittedly associated with them."

Four days later Bunker replied to Richardson, politely declining to bring up the matter with Thieu. "Personally I doubt that Chau is or ever was a disciplined communist," Bunker said, "but this does not mean 'GVN case against him is weak in terms of his having aided communists.' " Bunker told Richardson that seventy members of the National Assembly had voted that day to lift Chau's immunity but that the number wasn't sufficient to carry the motion and that it appeared there would be no trial. Bunker ended by saying that his demurrer was "not to suggest that I in any way disagree with the conclusions of your message. I shall continue to remain in close touch with the situation and if necessary raise it with Thieu in the terms that you have suggested."

But Bunker did not raise it with Thieu, not even after the Vietnamese president showed that he was determined to ruin Chau, whose case was linked with two other assemblymen accused of pro-communist activities. When Thieu failed to have Chau's immunity lifted by constitutional means, he ordered his bagman to circulate a petition in the National Assembly to reconsider the question. By bribery and threats, he intended to get the 102 needed signatures so that he could arrest Chau. Simultaneously, he launched a propaganda campaign to portray Chau as an agent of the CIA and the communists.

The story written by Keyes Beech, when Chau was hiding out in his home, caused a strong reaction in Washington. Beech said that the CIA had offered Chau money to form a political party but that the deal had fallen through because the agency wanted him to support Thieu. Chau preferred to maintain his independence. Chau, unlike Thieu, believed that the Saigon government should open direct negotiations with the National Liberation Front. When Thieu used Chau's contacts with his brother as a pretext for trying to destroy him, Beech wrote, the CIA refused to help clear his name. Beech quoted Chau as saying, "If this is a sample of the way the Americans treat their Vietnamese friends, I wonder about the future of thousands of other Vietnamese who have cooperated with the Americans." Beech's story was followed within days by other pro-Chau stories, filed by Robert G. Kaiser of the *Washington Post* and Terence Smith of the *New York Times.*

Senator J. William Fulbright had been aware of the Chau case for three months. Dan Ellsberg, while trying to encourage Fulbright to release the Pentagon Papers, had brought up Chau's troubles with Thieu; and the Foreign Relations Committee's two investigators, Richard Moose and Jim Lowenstein, had taken an interest in the case. Moose had attended a Saigon dinner party with Ambassador Bunker in December, at which, he later said, Bunker claimed there was irrefutable proof that Chau was a communist, an accusation that Bunker denied making. In any case, Fulbright had already formed the opinion that the Saigon embassy and the CIA were not doing enough to help Chau. Keyes Beech's story confirmed his belief, and Fulbright decided to make a statement about the case two days later, after columnist Joseph Kraft, who was better known in Washington than Beech, wrote an article expanding on Beech's story.

The press stories and Fulbright's offensive on behalf of Chau stirred Elliot Richardson to send, on February 7, 1970, what amounted to, in the politely worded context of State Department messages, a tough cable to Bunker. "In your message of December 31 you indicated that you would take personal action with Thieu when and if approaches by Mission officers to lower levels appeared to be unsuccessful," said Richardson. "It seems clear to me that time has come for a direct and forceful approach by you. I leave the timing and manner of your approach to you of course, but it should be soon and Thieu should be left in no doubt of high level concern here that he is unnecessarily harming our mutual objectives."

Bunker was left with no choice. He could disobey a direct order from State, or raise the matter with Thieu face-to-face. He arranged to see the Vietnamese president four days later, on February 11, 1970, and, according to his report of the meeting, laid out the case for not arresting Chau along the lines suggested by Richardson. But Bunker reported that he got nowhere with Thieu, who said he "favored letting justice take its course." "While this is not entirely satisfactory," Bunker ended his cable, "I think we have gone about as far as we can at this juncture."

A wire service report about Fulbright's support of Chau was slightly garbled and misidentified Chau as a CIA agent. Chau responded with a cable thanking Fulbright for his support but pointing out that he had never been a CIA agent. "I strongly ask your consideration for a U.S. Senate investigation on American officials and CIA operations in Vietnam which have been destroying both Vietnamese nationalist ideology and patriots and American image," Chau cabled Fulbright.

That was not a bad idea, Fulbright thought. Maybe it was time to get William Colby before the committee to explain what was going on in an organization that had turned against one of its earliest Vietnamese friends.

AN INVESTIGATION BY A CONGRESSIONAL COMMITTEE thrives or dies on media coverage. It is too much to expect the public to plow through the voluminous transcripts of the hearings to make sense of what has been said. The two-column story in the morning paper and a sound bite on the evening news set the tone of the hearings and create the impression left with the public.

Any good bureaucrat knew that the best way to thwart committee members was to overwhelm them with a mass of boring details, to arrive with a lengthy opening statement that would send journalists into daydreams and leave the investigators with an itch to be elsewhere. Above all, one should not give the legislators a chance to engage in the kind of pithy exchanges with the witness that journalists could lift as crisp quotes to use as zingers in their stories. And as George Jacobson, who was promoted as Colby's deputy at CORDS, said, "Colby was one of the greatest bureaucrats I have known in my lifetime."

After Colby received a cable from the Foreign Relations Committee saying it wanted to look into pacification, he got busy preparing a team to take to Washington that would give Fulbright a comprehensive report on the operations of CORDS.

" 'Let's give them a full picture,' I said," Colby recalled. " 'Here's a chance to tell the story, so let's tell it well.' I'm not sure what Fulbright had on his mind."

Perhaps Colby was not sure what Fulbright, a well-known opponent of the war, had on his mind, but he might have guessed that it had little to do with taking a look at the full picture of pacification. Fulbright was basically interested in two things—first, exploring the

Phoenix program, which had become a focal point for antiwar protest; and second, trying to help Chau by publicizing his case. Fulbright shared the perception in the United States that the Phoenix program was a discreditable operation. Ironically, he had no idea that its roots could be traced back to Chau, the person he was trying to save.

From his opening statement before the committee on February 17, 1970, Colby moved in with a load of stultifying details about the pacification program. After sparring with him inconclusively on the history of the war, Fulbright stopped, inserted into the record a story from the *Washington Post* about the Phoenix program, and turned the questioning over to the other committee members. Senator Stuart Symington of Missouri proved no better at handling Colby, though he managed to introduce Chau's name into the hearings. By the time the committee members maneuvered Colby into a discussion of Phoenix, the eyelids of journalists were beginning to droop.

The next day, when Colby brought John Paul Vann along with him, attendance had fallen off. Colby explained that he wanted to give the committee a look at each level of the pacification program and that Vann represented the top level outside of Saigon. Fulbright wryly thanked Colby and told him he appeared to have a very thorough organization. "You prompt me to comment that I had the idea this was a very primitive country made up of villages and Buddhist monks who went about doing good," said Fulbright. "It seems to have become very complicated. You wouldn't say that we are Americanizing it, would you?"

No, he wouldn't, Colby replied.

John Paul Vann knew the questions about Chau were coming, and he was uncomfortable. The Vann who was appearing before the Fulbright committee was not the same Vann who had served seven years earlier as a major source for the pessimistic reporting of David Halberstam and Neil Sheehan, who had provided the early sparks for the antiwar movement. Some who knew Vann suspected that his change of attitude stemmed at least partly from the fact that Vietnam had become his life's work and his obsession. But there was no question either that Vann believed the United States was finally on the right track to winning, though, in his estimate, the time period involved could run as long as another decade and a half. Once a confirmed anti-bureaucrat, he told the committee that he was pleased to be part of CORDS and that he believed it was working well.

Colby and Vann had developed a good relationship. They shared the same ideas about the political nature of the war (Vann's ideas coming mainly from Chau) and both thought that Westmoreland's meat-grinder strategy had been a mistake, though they realized that the big American military victories of 1967 had probably pushed the Viet Cong into the desperate act of launching the Tet offensive in 1968, which, no matter what the public in the United States thought about Tet, they considered to be a disaster for the communists. Colby was a subtle manager who knew how to guide a maverick like Vann. Besides, he truly admired Vann, not only for his competence and energy, but also for his great physical courage. Colby was brave too, and he enjoyed roving the roads of the delta on motor scooters with Vann. It kept the juices flowing. But Vann had not become a single-minded bureaucrat like Colby, who was able to tell Jean Sauvageot that the Chau case was simply "unfortunate."

What Vann was to tell Fulbright, he realized, could get him fired by Ambassador Bunker in Saigon. Colby had already interceded with the ambassador on Vann's behalf, but Bunker was still angry. Vann had decided to avoid saying anything in an open session where he would be quoted in press reports that Bunker would read. Colby, sitting next to him, tried to deflect Fulbright's questions about Chau as best he could, but Vann finally had to present the senator with the excuse that he didn't want to talk about Chau except in a closed session, "so as not to jeopardize either pro or con the judicial action that is underway in Saigon."

"Mr. Chau seems to be in no way reluctant to talk to the press about this matter," Fulbright told Vann. "Of course, I would gather that he believes he is about to be, in the parlance of the old days, railroaded because his immunity has been lifted, not by a vote in the assembly, but by a petition with 102 names. It is a very odd situation, but if you do not wish to discuss it in open session, I will not pursue the matter."

The next day, after Colby and his team buried the committee under more details of the pacification program, Fulbright changed his mind. Press attention had fallen off; committee members were ducking out. He was losing the attention of everyone. He told Colby that the following day he would get back into the Chau case. Vann was brought back to testify, and he gave a cautious but telling account of his dealings with Chau regarding his brother, which demolished the Saigon embassy's contention that no one had encouraged Chau to talk to

Hien. Fulbright asked if Vann had been told by his superiors not to see Chau after his troubles with Thieu began.

"Ambassador Bunker, sir, and Ambassador Colby have told me since July that it is advisable not to become involved in this matter since it is a matter between the government of Vietnam and one of its officials," Vann said.

Did he believe Chau was a communist?

"Sir, I have to have reservations because Ambassador Bunker has informed me that there are things about the case of which I am not aware. I do not know what these things are," said Vann, adding, "Nothing in my personal relationship with Colonel Chau and my knowledge of him since 1962 would lead me to doubt that he is other than a dedicated nationalist anticommunist person."

"What is Ambassador Bunker's attitude?" Fulbright asked.

"Ambassador Bunker's attitude, and his instructions to me, sir, were that I should tend to pacification in the delta and he would tend to the political situation in Vietnam."

"That is a very clear answer," Fulbright said, after the laughter in the hearing room subsided. "Mr. Colby, since you were so closely identified previously with the CIA, did the CIA chief there know about these meetings of Chau with his brother?"

Colby, who had been on leave from the CIA for two years, said "As I said, Mr. Chairman, my memory frankly is a little dim, and I am not that close to the situation today. I don't have access to the files. I really would have to defer that to the CIA." Colby admitted that Chau had a troubled relationship with the CIA. Fulbright asked which intelligence official was involved. "I don't remember, Mr. Chairman," Colby replied. "I think it was the station as a whole." The thread of questioning about Chau was dropped, then picked up again, and finally lost in the welter of details about the Phoenix program. The hearings finished on a weak note, barely noticed by the press.

"There was good press coverage of the hearings the first day and then it tapered off," Colby said. "I think they were expecting some fireworks and they didn't get them."

"Colby was a very skillful, a very slick guy," Norvill Jones, Fulbright's assistant, said. "And boring as hell. How are you going to keep the committee members' interest when you have a guy like that who's ready with all kinds of facts and figures? It just adds up to a great blob of nothing."

Not exactly nothing. The hearings provided some of the best and most detailed information on the pacification program to come out of the war. Colby did an excellent job in describing the various programs. But, as for bringing the war to a quicker conclusion and helping Chau, which were Fulbright and his staff's original intentions, the hearings were a failure.

AS THE FULBRIGHT HEARINGS FIZZLED, Chau emerged from hiding and entered the National Assembly building, a converted French opera house, where he said he would remain under the protection of parliamentary immunity. The assembly was a half-minute's walk from the Caravelle and the Continental hotels, which served as headquarters for the press corps, and pretty soon a number of journalists had joined Chau to wish him well and to await Thieu's reaction. Chau ordered two cases of beer, a case of orange soda, some French pastries and sandwiches, and the vigil took on the atmosphere of a party.

Two days later, on February 25, 1970, a military field court tried Chau in absentia and sentenced him to twenty years' imprisonment. Chau held a press conference, answering questions in English, French, and Vietnamese, saying he knew he would be arrested but that the government would have to come get him with guns and bayonets. At four-thirty the following afternoon, Thieu's police did just that. Chau heard them arrive and he pinned to his jacket South Vietnam's highest decoration, which had been awarded him for his military service. The police agents first pushed fifty journalists out of the way, then one of them ripped Chau's decoration off his jacket, another knocked him to the floor. He was dragged out of the building, tossed into a jeep, and taken to the Chi Hoa prison.

The manner of Chau's arrest and his imprisonment appalled Elliot Richardson and officials at the State Department. Bunker's embassy, however, took the news calmly. In a cable entitled "Reflections on the Chau Case," the embassy tried to put the affair into perspective for Washington. "At the core of the Chau case probably lies President Thieu's belief that he must gear up his people and army for a long war, and that to do this it is necessary to take a strong and unequivocal anticommunist stance," the embassy wrote. "Thus once it became widely known last year, after the arrest of Tran Ngoc Hien, that Deputy Tran Ngoc Chau had regular contacts with the communists, it would have been difficult for President Thieu not to take action." The embassy conceded that Thieu had made some mistakes, but laid the blame for much of the trouble on the press. "In press handling, the Chau camp was very skillful—from leaking the prosecution's case with annotations by Chau, to cries that he was tried for being an oppositionist, which almost completely detracted from the actual charges, to exaggerated claims of physical mistreatment. The government press handling, on the other hand, was as usual lamentable. The press itself, of course, also did not try to make the government's job any easier. Some of the more outlandish things said by Chau were played down or simply not reported. In the maneuvering preceding and accompanying Chau's final arrest, the press was as much a participant as were Chau's supporters and the government."

The cable reflected the attitude of Ambassador Bunker and CIA station chief Ted Shackley, as well as William Colby, who, suffering a "dim" memory, was trying to stay as far away from the case as possible, since he considered it a political matter unconnected to pacification. The three of them constituted a shrewd combination that understood the limits of the bureaucracy for imposing its will upon anyone. Elliot Richardson, the esteemed under secretary, could send a blizzard of cables on behalf of Chau to Ellsworth Bunker, the esteemed ambassador, and in reply would receive a blizzard of cables assuring him that all was being done that could be done. As usual in cases that found the bureaucracy in strong disagreement, the fight moved to the less civil grounds of press leaks.

"I saw John Vann when he was in Washington to testify at the Fulbright hearings," Dan Ellsberg, who was back working for Rand, said. " 'My ass is on the line,' he told me. 'Bunker has ordered me not to have any dealings with Chau, and told me he'll kick me out of Vietnam.' But at that very moment Vann was talking to newsmen about Chau, trying to help him. About that time I was called over to the State Department by Elliot Richardson's assistant, whom I'd known in Saigon. He brought out the cables Bunker had sent and picked up the phone and started talking to Joe Kraft, telling him stuff right out of the cables. Secret! NoDis! Eyes Only! He hung up and called another reporter. I said, 'Does your boss know you are doing this?' He said, 'Of course. He wants me to do it. Listen, I'll put you in touch with a couple of reporters. Are you willing to talk to them?' "

Ellsberg was. Soon stories were going off in the press like mortar shells. Bunker was outraged, in particular by a story written by the columnist Flora Lewis, who knew John Vann on a personal basis. The *New York Times* turned her column into a news article describing, as the headline said, a "Bunker-State Department Split on Chau." According to the story, the State Department ordered Bunker not to make a public statement about the Chau case because it conflicted with Vann's testimony before the Foreign Relations Committee. "That was a diplomatic way of saying the Department knew Bunker's proposed comment was untrue and was aware that Bunker also knew it was untrue," Lewis wrote. She ended with a snapper: "Bunker, 75, is a traditional type of New England Yankee with a record of high personal integrity. However, it was he who picked Thieu as America's favorite candidate for the presidency and, in effect, created the Thieu government. He is deeply committed to its maintenance in power."

The Lewis story was not correct in all the particulars, but it did point to a curious aspect of the Chau case. Bunker, as Flora Lewis noted, a man of high personal integrity, tried not once but several times to get the State Department to issue a statement that no American official had ever encouraged Chau to talk to his brother. Did he not know the truth? Quite possibly he didn't, Frank Snepp and William Kohlmann believed, because he was drawing from the selective files Ted Shackley had the CIA analysts assemble.

At any rate, it appeared to Bunker, based on the news stories, that he was being set up by someone at State. William Sullivan, the former ambassador to Laos who was now coordinating Vietnam policy for the department, had deflected Bunker's request to make a public statement about Chau. Sullivan's office therefore seemed an obvious place where the leaking might have occurred. Not trusting State's cable traffic, Sullivan sent Bunker a personal letter, headed "Dear Ellsworth," to assure him that he was conducting the investigation himself. It was his conclusion, he said, "That we have here a concerted effort of the most scurrilous type, designed to target you and using the Chau affair as an avenue for that purpose." The evidence he had collected so far suggested "that the effort is well coordinated and that its tracks are probably well covered.

"Nevertheless," Sullivan told Bunker, "we can generally assume that we know the clique who are involved in this business. They are the ones who are greatly enamored of Chau personally, who favor some sort of 'third force solution' to Vietnam, and who regard you and Thieu as major obstacles to their panacea. Most of them are now outside the government but they seem to maintain shadowy influence and connections which give them access to information which makes their continuing operations possible."

Bunker was not mollified. He sat down and, with the help of his chief political officer, drafted a nine-page cable entitled "Press Allegations about the Chau Case." "The most troublesome aspect of the campaign on behalf of Chau," said Bunker, "is the allegation that 'agents of the CIA and members of the U.S. Mission in Saigon knew about Chau's dealings with his brother, and implicitly approved.' It is true that Chau mentioned to U.S. personnel from time to time that he was in contact with a representative or representatives from Hanoi but he never revealed the substance of his discussions with them, merely impressing us with the fact that he had a contact of some importance. We tried to find out through him who the contact was and what the contact had to say. At one point Chau offered to arrange a meeting between his contact and Ambassador Lodge, which was refused by my predecessor, quite properly in my opinion because such a meeting would have gravely compromised our relations with the GVN." Bunker said that John Vann was then authorized to meet with Chau's brother, but the meeting never took place. "In any case," Bunker said, "there could not possibly have been any implication that the U.S. approved of Chau's unauthorized contact, still less that his revelation to us about that contact placed the U.S. under any obligation to protect him from prosecution by his own government when his brother was discovered by the Vietnamese police." Bunker believed he knew what the press was after. "I think it is clear that the press criticism of the GVN and U.S. over the Chau case is motivated in many cases by a belief that we should have explored some kind of deal that the enemy was prepared to offer us when Chau tried to promote a meeting between Hien and Lodge and that we should have supported Chau's later advocacy of a compromise solution to the war."

With Bunker's anger apparent, Sullivan intensified his search for the source of the leaks. The tracks led to Richardson's office.

"I talked to the reporters Richardson's assistant set me up with, and then he called me and said, 'Oh, my God, there's a big flap about this,'" Dan Ellsberg said. "'You told one of the reporters something that came out of a NoDis cable that had very little circulation, and

Sullivan is very excited about it.' I said, 'Look, it's Chau and he's my buddy, and if somebody has to take the rap for this, I'll do it.' He called again and said, 'They've started an investigation and we told them you were the source of the leaks.' I said, 'Jesus Christ, I said I'd be the fall guy if it had to be, but now you're telling me the first minute they arrived you gave them my name.' He said, 'Frankly, I got flustered and didn't know what to say.' I said, 'All the leaks, I did *all* the leaking, old buddy?' He said, 'Well, yes, that's their impression.' "

Within forty-eight hours of being alerted that State Department investigators were on his trail, Ellsberg was told by his former wife that the FBI was also on to him for copying the Pentagon Papers. Ellsberg's former wife had learned Dan was copying the Papers a few months earlier, when he told her his alimony payments would stop if he were arrested and sent to prison. After he involved his two children in helping him copy the Papers, his former wife became angry, and she mentioned to her stepmother, the marine general's wife, what Ellsberg was doing. Unknown to either her or Ellsberg, the stepmother went to the FBI and told them everything.

It was not the first time the government had identified Ellsberg as a leaker. He had begun to leak around the time of the 1968 Tet offensive, when he was called to the Pentagon to work as a consultant on a reexamination of the war led by the new secretary of defense, Clark Clifford. Ellsberg provided secret information to Senator Robert Kennedy, who was on the verge of challenging Lyndon Johnson for the presidency as an opponent of the war. Ellsberg had seen the request from the chairman of the joint chiefs of staff asking Johnson for 206,000 additional troops, some of them to be used in Vietnam, which suggested in the most dramatic manner possible, when soon turned into a *New York Times* headline, that the war was not going as well as General Westmoreland claimed. Ellsberg told Kennedy about the 206,000 request though he was not certain that Kennedy told the *Times*.

"That was my first leak," Ellsberg said. "I gave it to Kennedy, but I didn't think of giving it to the newspapers, and when I saw the impact it had after the press got it, I said, 'How crazy. I've been a fool. I should have been affecting policy this way.' " Ellsberg got in touch with Neil Sheehan, who was now Pentagon correspondent for the *Times*. "I ended up giving Sheehan a leak a day," Ellsberg said. "I gave him a lot of stuff that got Westmoreland fired."

Some reporters at the *Times* disputed the value of Ellsberg's leaks and said that he did not provide the documentation they requested in the form of cables. Whatever his initial impact as a leaker, Ellsberg did not talk about it. "I often said the Pentagon Papers were my first leak, and I was absolutely sincere about that, having repressed this episode. I never told anyone, and I would tend to forget it."

The Pentagon's chief security officer identified Ellsberg as the source of the leaks that were appearing in the *New York Times.* "To my surprise, at the end, it tailed off and they didn't come after me," Ellsberg said. He believed that Defense Secretary Clark Clifford put an end to the investigation, perhaps because Clifford personally sympathized with the thrust of Ellsberg's leaks, perhaps more so because a high official of the Pentagon, Clifford's friend, was also leaking to the press and might have been caught in the investigation.

In any case, the same thing happened two years later, in 1970, when the government, within a forty-eight-hour period, discovered that Ellsberg was not only leaking the secret Bunker cables about Chau but also turning over the Pentagon Papers to Fulbright. Realizing that the FBI would get in touch with the Rand Corporation, from which he had lifted the Pentagon documents, Ellsberg made a hasty trip to see his boss. Ellsberg's position at Rand had become precarious since the previous October when he and several Rand employees drafted an antiwar letter that appeared in the press and was widely discussed. Other Rand employees believed that Ellsberg was out to destroy the think tank, which made its money from government contracts, and that he should be fired. His boss supported him through the furor, but Ellsberg knew it was too much to ask for further understanding when he had the FBI on his tail for stealing documents entrusted to Rand. He decided not to tell his boss about the Pentagon Papers but to use his leaking of the cables about Chau as an excuse to resign.

Ellsberg learned much later that the FBI had appeared at Rand and that his boss had told the agents that the Pentagon documents were not a matter of national security, that Fulbright could get them if he wanted them, and that Ellsberg had resigned from Rand, which meant his security clearance would be canceled. The FBI decided that pursuing the matter with a powerful senator like Fulbright had the potential for embarrassing the bureau, so they dropped the investigation.

The State Department also decided to drop the investigation of the Chau leaks, which, if pursued to its conclusion, would have revealed that Ambassador Bunker was being attacked by the office of the number two official at State, possibly with the tacit approval of the secretary himself. The leaks stopped, and two weeks later the press's attention was shifted to one of the most controversial events of the war—the invasion of Cambodia. Chau's small band of supporters continued to fight on, but they were not joined by others who knew the truth.

Stu Methven, Chau's primary CIA contact, was serving in Indonesia as deputy chief of station when the case broke. Chau revealed his name, and Methven's son, in prep school, sent him the *New York Times* clipping, with a note, "Dad, you never told me you were in the CIA." Methven thought that what had happened to Chau was predictable. "The minute a Vietnamese became a favorite of the Americans he became suspect by the government in power," Methven said. "The best thing was not to build a guy up too far or he was going to get chopped down. Chau became the dandy, and American congressmen who came over on visits were taken out to see him. A guy like Thieu saw that as a threat."

Chau said that he had told Mike Dunn, Lodge's assistant, about his contacts with his brother. Dunn had his own explanation as to why more Americans didn't rush to Chau's defense.

"There were so many Americans interested in Vietnam and so few interesting Vietnamese," Dunn said. "But Chau was an extraordinary fellow. The big problem I had was that I could never set my mind straight as to which Chau was the real Chau. He was at least a triple personality.

"Many people thought Chau was a very dangerous man, as indeed he was. In the first place, anybody with ideas is dangerous. And the connections he had were remarkable. We've been talking all along here in a very frank manner about the bureaucracy, and, I mean, who wants to get caught with—you know, who wants to be the last guy to hold Chau, if this thing blows up. You see what I'm saying?"

18

SAIGON 1973

PRISON LIFE WAS NOT TOO BAD. Chau was given a special room, not a cell, which had a bed and a table. His door was left open when regular inmates were confined and closed when they were allowed out. His wife visited him in the reception area once a week. His food was supplied by his family; he became a vegetarian. He practiced yoga each day, and studied Mandarin Chinese. He received newspapers, books, a radio, eventually a television. Thieu seemed interested in one thing: keeping him quiet and out of circulation. The months turned into years, and Chau followed from his prison room the changes and dispersals of his American friends who had supported him and supported a different strategy for fighting the war.

Two years before the cease-fire was signed in 1973, Chau learned along with everybody else that the *New York Times* had published the Pentagon Papers and that Dan Ellsberg was revealed as their source. Finally realizing that the Fulbright committee wasn't going to release the papers as he had hoped, Ellsberg took the advice of Norvill Jones, Fulbright's assistant, and turned them over to the *Times* via Neil Sheehan, the past receiver of his leaks. Chau understood why Ellsberg had become antiwar; he had contributed to his change of attitude by his own pessimism with the way things were going. Earlier, in his fifteen-year reunion report to his Harvard classmates, Ellsberg had written of how proud he was to have served in Vietnam with Lansdale. "I'm more convinced than I could have been before," he said, "that Lansdale's basic thoughts on political development, on nationalistic and democratic rivalry with communists for leadership of revolutionary forces, and on counter-guerrilla tactics are sound, relevant to Vietnam, and desperately needed here; but *none* of them are being applied, in any degree." As he realized that Chau's and Lansdale's ideas would never be applied, Ellsberg grew first disenchanted and then turned against the war with the kind of zeal that he approached everything he did, from holding a simple conversation to having sex.

For a while, after the *Times* published the Pentagon Papers in June 1971, Ellsberg was treated as something of a hero by the antiwar movement. He was indicted for conspiracy and violations of the Espionage Act, along with Anthony J. Russo, Jr., a former employee of Rand who had helped him photocopy the papers; and he made the rounds of television talk shows and joined the lecture circuit. But then came reports that Ellsberg had gone out on combat operations in Vietnam, and his intense manner, emphasized by the nervous movements and piercing blue eyes, put off many people who had once been ready to consider him an antiwar hero and a champion of First Amendment rights. Moreover, Ellsberg disappointed some of the college students who were in the vanguard of the antiwar movement. When they told him the Viet Cong were the good guys, Ellsberg, being true to what he knew of Vietnam, could only reply "Not necessarily," and that seemed incomprehensible to the students, because they believed that either you were against the war or you weren't, and if you were, then of course the Viet Cong were the good guys. Eventually Ellsberg's reputation was to curve toward that of Lansdale's—smart, maybe, but a little kooky.

Lansdale himself, after bobbing up for so many years to try to influence Vietnam policy, had finally sunk into semi-obscurity. He re-emerged at the time of Chau's troubles with Thieu to call a press conference to drum up congressional support for the Vietnamese politician for whom he had once held such high hopes. But his pleas for Chau were politely received and largely ignored. Then he published his memoirs, which failed to interest the public. Lansdale's attempts to change the thrust of American strategy in Vietnam had really never been understood, and his book appeared at the moment when public debate about the war had solidified into a single question: when and how to get out.

The other prominent supporter of Chau, John Paul Vann, was also out of the picture, killed in a helicopter crash on June 9, 1972. Vann died not while carrying out a pacification project but while fighting a conventional military offensive launched by regular North Vietnamese troops. In May 1971 he was made senior adviser of the military region in the central part of South Vietnam and given extraordinary authority over all U.S. military forces in the area, the only civilian in American history authorized to command troops, making him the equivalent of a major general. Though some of his friends who had once served and supported the war believed that Vann had become totally absorbed by Vietnam and had lost his "compass," Vann thought that they had become fainthearted after all the pressure over the years and had given in to the antiwar movement at precisely the time when progress was finally being made.

In early 1973, Chau heard that a cease-fire had been signed and that prisoners of war would be released. After the peace agreement was announced, the prison director appeared and told Chau that he could no longer live by himself. He was transferred to a larger room, which held four Vietnamese accused of being communists. Only one of them was truly a communist, Chau learned over the next few months—his brother Hien. He tried to understand why the other three hated the Saigon government and preferred the National Liberation Front. One, a lawyer, had many friends on the other side and had purchased medical supplies for them. Another, a student, was antigovernment because his father had been killed by Saigon forces. Chau debated with them each day. Look at Thieu, they said, and consider him alongside Ho Chi Minh or Pham Van Dong. Chau responded that his cause was right, but that unfortunately South Vietnam did not have the right people as leaders. "How can you have a good cause with bad people?" Hien asked. People can be changed, replied Chau, but communism as a cause—never. They argued in a friendly fashion, aware that they had to share the room. Hien did not reveal how he had been captured, nor did he say much about his work as an intelligence officer.

Near the end of 1973 Chau was informed that he and the other four would be transferred to the communist side as prisoners of war. Chau had a choice, he was told. He could write a statement requesting Thieu to release him. The statement would be an apology to the government. Chau refused. If anything, he said, the government should apologize to him. One morning before daybreak the guards opened the door and took one of the prisoners away. The others learned by listening to the BBC that he had been turned over to the communists. For the next three days one person was removed from the cell until only Chau was left. Two officers came to talk to him. The president doesn't want to send you to the communists, they said. But you must write a statement. It will not be released to the press. Chau shouted for them to get out of his room. Do you think I don't want to be released after four and a half years? he yelled. But I won't sign anything.

In August 1974, two emissaries from the president arrived with the news that Thieu had decided to free Chau, on one condition. He could not return home because Thieu feared he would contact the press and resume his campaign against the government. He was taken to a house on Hai Ba Trung Street, where he was guarded by six policemen. When his family wanted to visit, the police provided transportation. This went on for several months, until one morning he was allowed to return to his own home, accompanied by a single guard.

Chau kept quiet. His friends who were able to communicate with him said that Thieu would soon have to step down. The country was coming apart.

19

SAIGON 1975

IN MARCH 1975, GENERAL VAN TIEN DUNG, chief of staff of the North Vietnamese army, was massing his troops outside the central highlands town of Ban Me Thuot. His location was not far from the area where North Vietnamese regulars had met American troops at Ia Drang nearly ten years earlier in the first major battle between conventional forces. The North Vietnamese had been defeated in that battle and had readjusted their tactics, presenting an elusive target to the Americans for the next seven years until they finally considered the time ripe to fight in the open with their tanks and artillery. But they had been beaten by American airpower in their 1972 Easter offensive, when they ventured out, and had once again retreated to the shadows, biding their time until the Americans and their airplanes were gone. Now they were ready to attack.

The guerrilla war, which had been launched by the Viet Cong in the early 1960s, had, for all intents and purposes, ended around 1970. It could be said that the Americans, possessing the balance of terror with their bombs and artillery, and aided by certain pacification projects such as Phoenix, had won that war. The victory had gone unperceived by the American public, which, by that point, simply wanted to be done with Vietnam. But, essentially, the American withdrawal in 1973 left a situation where a conventional South Vietnamese force faced a conventional North Vietnamese force. Despite the optimistic reports emanating from the Pentagon about the success of "Vietnamization"—the emphasis on improving the South Vietnamese army—it was clearly the North Vietnamese who held the upper hand.

Nobody doubted—certainly not Nguyen Van Thieu—that the North Vietnamese would launch another conventional attack in due time after the 1973 peace agreements had brought about the complete withdrawal of American combat troops, and Thieu had developed an emergency plan for dealing with the predicted onslaught of North Vietnamese firepower. He intended to abandon the two military regions closest to North Vietnam and concentrate his forces in a strong defensive perimeter around Saigon, thus protecting the country's economic and administrative center, along with the vital rice bowl of the Mekong Delta.

The emergency plan was promoted by an Australian brigadier general named Ted Sarong, who arrived in Saigon after the American withdrawal, unbidden, as a self-styled military adviser to Thieu, but the idea of partitioning South Vietnam into a more defensible area had been around for years and was not without its logic considering that the North Vietnamese, on attack, could produce more troops at any one point than the South Vietnamese, who were strung out in defensive positions over a wide area and had few reserves.

In March 1975, when the North Vietnamese overran the strategic highland town of Ban Me Thuot, they prompted Thieu, almost by inadvertence, to put his emergency plan into effect. Hanoi had assigned General Van Tien Dung the mission of capturing Ban Me Thuot as part of a long-range campaign that the North Vietnamese hoped would lead to the fall of Saigon—or, more specifically, cause a general uprising—in 1976, when the Americans would be preoccupied with their presidential election and presumably disinclined to respond. In his victory, General Dung captured a high-ranking Saigon officer who didn't know the details of Thieu's emergency plan but who understood the attitudes behind it, and he told Dung under interrogation that Thieu would probably abandon the key highland towns of Pleiku and Kontum if pressed hard enough. Dung cabled his comrades in Hanoi, recommending new and stronger attacks in the upper two military regions. The leadership in Hanoi convened and within two days approved Dung's recommendations, scrapping their old plan and unleashing what would become the final offensive of the war.

One of the many flaws in Thieu's emergency plan was that nothing had changed since Diem's time in the way leadership positions were assigned in the Saigon army. The chief of the general staff had no command authority. The corps commanders reported directly to

Thieu, who made his assignments based on his generals' loyalty to him, in order to prevent a coup, just as Diem had done.

Thieu's loyal commander of the military region he chose to abandon as the first phase of his emergency plan was Major General Pham Van Phu, who, like Thieu, had served with the French. In fact, Phu had been captured with the French garrison at Dien Bien Phu in 1954, had spent several years in a prison camp, and had emerged from the experience shaken and gripped by a phobia that he confided to his friend Lou Conein. "It will finish me," Phu told Conein. "I'm determined never to be captured again." When Thieu told Phu to begin a withdrawal of his troops in Military Region Two, Phu lost his nerve and fled to the safety of a coastal enclave, and the supposed orderly withdrawal from Pleiku and Kontum turned into a chaotic and frenzied retreat, step one in the total collapse of the Saigon army.

The North Vietnamese had always referred to the Saigon army as "the puppet troops," but even they were surprised at how much the collapse resembled the sudden and awkward sprawl of a military marionette whose strings had been snipped. In a manner of speaking, the Saigon army had been cut loose by the U.S. Congress, which had shown a determination after the 1973 cease-fire and the return of American POWs to end the war once and for all, even if it meant a North Vietnamese victory. Instead of giving South Vietnam the $1.45 billion as requested by the Nixon administration for 1975, Congress gave the Thieu regime less than half that amount—$700 million—and was inclined to cut off all aid. After the North Vietnamese overran Ban Me Thuot at the beginning of the final offensive, the Ford administration asked for an emergency $300 million for the South Vietnamese, but that too was turned down.

The atmosphere of Saigon in collapse seemed to have been drawn by some natural atavism to resemble the early days of the war when things were falling apart. Even the cast of characters seemed interchangeable. Instead of Diem there was Thieu, now openly admiring of the murdered former dictator's style of leadership and often withdrawing into his own cocoon. Another controversial American ambassador was running the embassy. Graham Martin had replaced Ellsworth Bunker in 1973 and was admired by some of his subordinates as a hardnosed professional, while others, who grew in number as time passed, saw him as a pigheaded egomaniac who refused to accept the reality of the collapse until it was almost too late to arrange a proper evacuation. Both groups conceded, however, that Martin, who arrived when the American public had turned against the war and Congress was in a mood to cut off aid, was given an assignment that carried high odds for failure.

Also, in the final days, Charles Timmes was to play a role similar to Lou Conein's before the Diem coup. He was the CIA's contact with the Vietnamese generals during the last upheavals. William Colby had personally recruited Timmes for the job over lunch at a Washington restaurant in 1967. The two were old friends, and Timmes was approaching his sixtieth birthday, due to retire soon from the army, where he had attained the rank of major general. Colby and Timmes were so similar as to suggest that Colby was recruiting somebody cast in his own image. Both men were physically unimpressive, softspoken, meticulous, temperate, courteous—and both were deceptively tough and unusually brave. Timmes had wanted to be an opera singer, but he wound up jumping into Normandy as a battalion commander with the 82nd Airborne during the predawn hours of D-Day, where he won the nation's second-highest medal for heroism. In 1962, he was selected to head the military advisory group in Vietnam, and during his tour he made friends with a number of young Vietnamese officers who later became generals. One of them, then a major, was Nguyen Van Thieu. Colby's idea was to make use of Timmes's friendships to keep in close touch with the new Vietnamese leadership, as a replacement for Lou Conein, who had been in close touch with the old. While Conein had spent long hours drinking and gossiping with them, Timmes offered to play tennis and listen to their complaints, which by 1974 he was hearing a lot.

"The Vietnamese officers knew that Congress was cutting back on aid," Timmes said. "The commanders all talked about that. They said, 'Why should we go on and give our blood in vain?' They thought the U.S. was not living up to its obligations."

Politics was back to the same old Saigon standard in the final days, and rumors of coups d'état filled the air. Shortly after the North Vietnamese offensive began, Nguyen Cao Ky started agitating to overthrow Thieu, who had beat him during an earlier power struggle. Ky would meet with a general and try to recruit him for a coup, and the CIA would send Charles Timmes to talk the general out of joining with Ky. Seeking to buy time, Timmes drove Ambassador Graham Martin in his old Volkswagen to meet Ky at his house, and the two men led Ky to believe that they would support him as the future head of state if only he would stay patient and not move against Thieu. But there were other signs that a coup attempt could take place at any time. Tran Van Don had gone through various transformations as a general and a senator and a defense minister, yet remained the same indefatigable schemer until the end, and he was plotting to get rid of Thieu and replace him with his fellow conspirator in the Diem coup, Duong Van Minh, whose decisiveness and intelligence quotient had not improved with the years.

Finally Ambassador Martin realized that Thieu would have to go if there were to be the slightest hope of negotiating a cease-fire with the North Vietnamese, who were racing toward Saigon with their tanks. He arranged to meet with Thieu and began by reviewing the military situation in detail, working his way around to the point.

"The military situation is very bad," Martin concluded. "And the people hold you responsible for it."

Thieu did not agree immediately to resign, but after thinking it over he made a rambling, tearful speech on television, in which he attacked Henry Kissinger and the peace accords that led to the removal of American combat troops in 1973, and then bowed out, leaving Saigon in the hands of Tran Van Huong, the seventy-one-year-old vice president and born-again Frenchman, who began gabbling about destiny picking him to lead the country, as if in his encroaching senility he believed himself to be Charles de Gaulle.

Two days after Thieu resigned, Huong asked Graham Martin to remove Thieu from the country, so that he would not be a factor in Huong's efforts to start negotiations with the communists. Martin assigned Timmes the job of arranging for Thieu's departure. Timmes phoned Thieu and told him he could have a helicopter pick him up at the palace, but Thieu suggested instead that he drive to military head-quarters at the Saigon airport, where they would meet and have drinks before his departure with his entourage of twenty-two mostly generals and colonels. Frank Snepp was assigned to drive the limousine that carried Thieu and Timmes on the ten-minute drive to the airplane, which was headed to Taiwan.

Then Martin and Timmes began working to get Huong to resign in favor of Big Minh. Tran Van Don and the French ambassador, Jean-Marie Mérrillon, had impressed Martin and Tom Polgar, the CIA station chief, with their belief that only Big Minh could negotiate with the communists to bring about a cease-fire that would save Saigon. The French were making a play in the final days to reassert their influence in Indochina, and their instruments were the same old born-again Frenchmen like Tran Van Don, who had learned to speak English but never changed his cultural allegiance. CIA chief Polgar sent Timmes to ask Big Minh if he would be willing to take over and negotiate with the communists if Huong could be pushed aside.

"Big Minh was confident that the communists would deal with him and that he'd be able to bargain with them," Charles Timmes said. "Then the artillery started coming in. I asked Minh to talk to the communists to try to shut it down. They wouldn't listen to him. It looked to me like everything was over. I left that night."

So did as many Vietnamese as could push through the mad scramble to leave Saigon before the first North Vietnamese tanks entered the city on April 30, 1975. Nguyen Cao Ky and a dozen members of his entourage piled into a helicopter and headed toward the sea, where, shortly before running out of fuel, he spotted the USS *Midway* and landed on the carrier. Ky was too choked up to speak when he got out of the helicopter, and he went to a room assigned to him and cried.

CHAU WAS ALSO TRYING to leave Saigon before the city fell to the communists. The only person he could think of who might be able to help him was Keyes Beech, the journalist, who had returned to cover the end of the war for his newspaper and was staying at the Caravelle Hotel. Beech was pleased to see Chau and anxious to help. The press corps had its own evacuation system, and Beech had already gotten a number of Vietnamese employees of American media out of the country that way, and he thought he might be able to do the same for Chau. But after considering the problem, Beech decided that the press system wasn't a good idea after all, since Chau was not employed by an American organization. Beech had good contacts at the CIA station, good enough he thought that they would help him get Chau and his family out of the country with their system. So he telephoned the deputy chief of the station and asked him for help. The CIA officer's reaction was rather strange, Beech thought. He said, "Why not ask us to evacuate Ho Chi Minh?" but then hastily added that he would see what he could do.

"A CIA officer arrived to talk to Chau," said Beech. "What he wanted, I discovered, was to recruit him as a stay-behind agent for the CIA after the communists took over. He concluded that Chau wouldn't make a very good stay-behind, though, and then consented to handle his evacuation."

But Chau heard nothing further from the CIA, and on the morning of April 29, 1975, the day before Saigon fell, he called Beech to ask if he was in touch with the station. Beech was surprised and told Chau, "I'll try to find out how and when you are to be evacuated." Beech dialed the CIA station, embassy extension 615, but nobody could locate the CIA officer who was supposedly handling Chau's evacuation. Beech called Chau's home and spoke to his son, telling him he wasn't able to learn anything but to hold on. In the next few chaotic hours, most of the American journalists left Saigon, and Beech was among them. He heard nothing further about Chau.

"Several years later, when I was living in the Washington suburbs, Frank Snepp told me that Ted Shackley, who was the East Asia division chief in Langley, had in effect vetoed Chau's evacuation from Saigon by the CIA," Keyes Beech said. "Shackley and I were then neighbors, and he dropped by my house from time to time. I asked him about it. 'Was it true you vetoed Tran Ngoc Chau's evacuation from Saigon?' He said, 'I'll have to check the back channel copies on that. But I can assure you he was not one of my priorities.'"

Beech took Shackley's ambiguous reply to mean that Snepp was telling the truth: the CIA had intentionally left Chau behind. "I didn't think anyone would do a thing like that, I really didn't," Beech said. "If someone from the station had said, 'Look, Chau's your responsibility. We don't like the son of a bitch and we're not going to help him,' then I would have known what to do. I was asking them for a favor. The CIA had better facilities than I had, and they were getting a lot of people out who didn't deserve to get out."

When it appeared that Beech's attempt to arrange his evacuation had failed, Chau called the embassy and asked to speak to Charles Timmes. He was surprised by the warmth of Timmes's greeting. Yes, of course, he would help him, Timmes told Chau. To avoid the chaos at the embassy, Chau should meet him the next morning at Timmes's house. But when Chau arrived, Timmes had already left for his meeting with Big Minh. It was impossible to get through the crowds gathered at the embassy, clamoring for evacuation. He rushed to the port, hoping to get his family out on a boat. There, too, the crowds were impossible. One of his children was pregnant, and he didn't want to risk injury to her by joining the desperate shoving to reach the boats. With Buddhist resignation, Chau accepted his fate and returned home.

Three days after the fall of Saigon, his brother Hien came to see him. Chau did not ask for help, and Hien did not offer it. Hien had been appointed the head of the Patriotic Intellectuals Association in the South, an important position with the purpose of guiding educated Vietnamese in the "correct" thinking about the revolution, but not so important a job as Hien might have been expected to merit by his long years of service to the communist cause. One of Chau's relatives on the Central Committee in Hanoi confided that Hien had been demoted because it was thought that he had revealed too much to Thieu's police during his captivity. Nevertheless, Hien showed no signs that he had lessened his devotion to communism, and Chau was careful to keep their conversation on safe family matters. Chau believed that Hien, having devoted his life to the cause, was trapped into supporting uncritically whatever policies were established by Hanoi. After so many sacrifices and years of hardships, to let himself think that the communists were not entirely right would have been self-destructive.

One night at 2:00 A.M., six weeks after Saigon's fall, troops surrounded Chau's house. Why hadn't he turned himself in to the government to prepare for internment in a re-education camp? the leader demanded. Chau replied that he thought it their policy not to incarcerate anyone who had ceased working for the Saigon government by 1972 and by then he was in Thieu's jail. The soldiers knew nothing of his case; it was futile to argue with them. Chau went along quietly.

He was taken to a re-education camp on the road to Vung Tau, where high-ranking civilians and former members of the Saigon government were held. Chau knew most of them. Some he had fought in political battles; others were old friends. All of them had been, like Chau, confident, almost arrogant, when they were riding high, often contemptuous of both the Americans and the Vietnamese communists. Now they walked, eyes averted, heads half-bowed, in the presence of their captors.

Chau's group, which included 303 former officials, spent the first two months clearing and organizing the camp. They were given one bowl of rice daily, and they began to lose the padding that had accumulated during the days of restaurant living. For the next year, their schedule was unchanged. They spent a half-day in the amphitheater listening to political indoctrination and afterward returned to the camp for group discussions, during which everyone was required to stand and give his ideas about the lecture. The prisoners regurgitated whatever line they thought their captors wanted to hear. Were the Americans criminals and rapists, and the Vietnamese who supported them their puppets? Yes was the dutiful reply—heads half-bowed, eyes averted. The thrust of the indoctrination course was concerned less with proving the superiority of Marxism than with emphasizing the superiority of the Vietnamese communists. The winners no longer resembled the thread-bare guerrillas once thought to be determined yet ascetic and self-effacing. In victory they became braggarts, practically strutting before Chau and his group. We are superior to the Americans, the communists repeated. They rolled out their history: thirty years of fighting in triumph over the Japanese, the French, the Americans. Consider the presidents we defeated, they said, starting with Dwight Eisenhower and ending with Gerald Ford. We beat all the American generals (they listed their names). Does this not prove undeniably that we are superior? Yes, yes, came the dutiful reply— heads half-bowed, eyes averted.

Actually the communist propaganda had an impact on Chau and his group. It started them to thinking. Boastful or not, the communists had done exactly as they said—defeated the best of the West. Chau and the other government officials discussed among themselves in private why this had happened. Their answers, then and later, tended to exculpate themselves and lay the blame on the Americans. Chau thought that the majority of the Americans he had met were unable to understand anything that wasn't American. The exceptions such as Lansdale and Vann were in a tiny minority. The cultural conflict, Chau decided, was the reason the war was lost. The Americans couldn't possibly win because they couldn't understand what and whom they were fighting.

Chau underwent frequent interrogation. During his fight with Thieu, many South Vietnamese had come to believe that he was a communist. His communist captors believed he was a CIA agent. He was questioned relentlessly about his contacts with the agency. He was not tortured, but under the poor diet and constant stress he lost forty-four pounds, and when, after fourteen months of "re-education," families were allowed their first visit, his wife did not recognize him.

Chau's wife was pleading his case with the new administration. The communists allowed family members to petition the release of their relatives from the camps, on the condition that they served as guarantors that the relative, once freed, would not oppose the revolution. Chau's wife took the petition to his communist kin from the North who had come to the South after Saigon's fall. They gave their endorsement to free Chau. She asked Hien to sign. He considered for a while, then wrote: "During my discussions with Chau, I became convinced that he is a man who will never change his way of thinking and that he will never accept the revolution. So I sign this petition as a brother. But as a member of the communist party, I cannot guarantee him." Chau's wife was furious. She showed his note to the other family members who had signed. They stuck with their unqualified endorsement. Later, after Chau learned what Hien had done, he tried to be understanding. Hien, after all, knew him better than anyone and was only being honest. But Chau's wife remained unforgiving.

After nearly two years in the camp, Chau's group received word they were to be transferred to the North. They were considered the most criminal of all, and the trip north meant the communists had no intention of releasing them, at least for many years. They realized that some of them would never see their families again. Shortly after they were moved to the transshipment point, Chau was separated from the group. Only he and the former chief justice of South Vietnam's Supreme Court were not sent north. He was taken to the former headquarters of the National Police in Saigon and put in a small cell. He saw no one. His food and water came through a hole cut in the door. He was certain that the communists had decided to execute him for his actions in Kien Hoa in setting up the counterterror teams.

Late one night, after two weeks of solitary confinement, he was marched to an office where two men, one a northerner in his mid-fifties, the other a young southerner, were waiting for him. The northerner told Chau they wanted to work with him but hadn't had the time until now to talk. His first assignment was to write his life's story from elementary school till the day he entered the re-education camp. After that he was to write a second biography, covering the period of the camp until the present. Chau told them he had already written the first story four times; they could get it from the re-education camp. No, they said, this is different. We want you to re-write your whole story. They moved him to a small room, which had a reading light, a table, and a bed. The prison director arrived and said he had been ordered to give Chau whatever food he desired. Just give me whatever you have, Chau said. That afternoon he was brought rice and meat and mango—a feast. He knew the communists wanted something from him, but he was past caring, and he ate it all.

Two weeks later, after examining the material Chau had written, his interrogators called him back to the office and thanked him for his cooperation. They needed more information, however; they asked him to take notes and answer specific questions. The questions were focused on his relationships with Americans. They wanted their names, the kind of work they did together, a description of their personalities. Other questions concerned the Vietnamese leaders of religious organizations such as the Buddhists, the Catholics, Cao Dai, and Hoa Hao. The constant requests for more information went on for four months. It was nerve-racking for Chau, a form of torture. He tried to be careful not to tell them anything he thought they didn't already know, to protect the others, but it was depressing and desperate work. At the end, ordered by his interrogators to engage in self-criticism, he became so critical of himself that he was ready to take responsibility for anything, even for starting the war. He yearned to get it over with, to be executed. He was a broken man.

When Chau was at his lowest point psychologically, an official arrived and said, "The revolution has completed its examination of your case. I have been requested to ask you to sign a promise to cooperate with us after you return to normal life, and also to agree to reveal the names of any people who are acting against the revolution." Chau did not believe they would free him, but he said, okay, fine, just dictate what you want me to say and I'll sign it. "No," said the official, "we want you to write it in your own words." Chau wrote the statement.

The next day he was taken to a room where his family was waiting. They were served tea and cakes. The communist official told Chau's wife that the revolution was still skeptical of her husband but that he wasn't as bad as the others. "We are releasing him," he said, "but we hold the whole family responsible." It was policy to send people released from the camps to a rural New Economic Area, where they were required to clear the land, dispose of mines and unexploded shells left over from the war, and begin farming. Chau hoped to live in his old province of Kien Hoa. One of his interrogators said, however, that Chau would not be assigned to a New Economic Area. The revolution wanted him to remain in Saigon and lead a normal life. After one of his former colleagues in the Saigon government tried to visit him and Chau refused to see him, the interrogator returned and gave him more pointed instructions. "You should see people," the interrogator said. "Do not act like you are under control. The reason the revolution set you free is because we believe you have the potential to help the country. So go back to your friends and lead a normal life. Sometimes we will expect you to give us your impression of these people." They were serious, Chau realized. Informing was the price of his liberty. He began plotting to escape.

While he worked on his escape plans, Chau was assigned to the Social Studies Center, an elite group composed of northerners and southerners who were linked to a similar organization in Moscow. The purpose of the center was to analyze all aspects of the war and to draw lessons that would help communist revolutions succeed in other underdeveloped countries. Chau was assigned to conduct a study on how the Saigon leadership was created and developed. With his study, the Moscow organization would be able to devise more sophisticated means to counter the development of noncommunist leadership in other Asian countries.

CHAU HAD ALWAYS BEEN A SUPPORTER of the Buddhists, and it was to them he turned as a first step to escaping. The Buddhists had accumulated a hidden store of gold during the war, and they were ready to invest in Chau's escape, with the hope that, once outside, he would be able to help them in some undetermined way. They gave him sixty-three thousand dollars worth of gold sheets, and he secretly visited his Chinese contacts in Cholon, the Chinese quarter of Saigon. The Chinese had been the country's main businessmen and entrepreneurs; during the war they were thought by the South Vietnamese to have a stranglehold on the economy. Not long after Chau was released from the re-education camp, the communists decided to expel the Chinese from the country. Hanoi was fighting with Peking, and it was thought the Cholon Chinese might turn out to be a Fifth Column. It was relatively easy for Chau's contacts to bribe minor communist functionaries into providing Chau and his family with Chinese identification cards. This way they might escape with the mass of Chinese refugees who were being forced out.

Chau learned of a woman who owned a boat and paid her a large sum to accept him and his family. The remainder of the gold he invested in Rolex watches and told his children to hide them on their bodies. He intended to use the watches for barter purposes. In February 1979, after a number of delays, Chau and his family joined a group of Chinese refugees who passed through a police checkpoint without problem. They boarded the creaky fishing boat, and shoved off toward Vung Tau and the open sea. As they approached Vung Tau, they were stopped by the local police, who said they wanted to inspect the boat to make sure no Vietnamese were leaving illegally with the Chinese.

Everyone on the boat grew tense. They knew what the police were really after. The woman who owned the boat refused to be shaken down for more. She argued that she had already paid the necessary "dues" to the police in Ho Chi Minh City, as Saigon was now called. The police ordered everybody off the boat. The ninety-seven males were separated from the women and children, who didn't interest the police, and the interrogation began. It was after midnight before Chau and his oldest son reached the table where two Chinese interrogators sat between two Vietnamese communist officials.

Chau's son was questioned in Chinese and, unable to respond, was arrested. Chau sat down at the table. He told them he was of mixed blood, Chinese-Vietnamese, a professor of languages. Perspiring, his heart ripping at his chest, he tried to recall the Mandarin words he had learned while in Thieu's jail. The Chinese questioners, like most of the Chinese in Vietnam, spoke Cantonese but little more Mandarin than Chau. Unable to break his story, they asked him to write something in Mandarin. He took the paper and made a few bold strokes. Perhaps not wanting the Vietnamese communist officials to know they did not speak Mandarin, one of the Chinese examined what Chau had written and nodded his head.

Chau was free to join the Chinese group and reboard the ship. The tension overwhelmed him. He lost control of his muscles and was unable to stand. The interrogators asked him what was the matter. He said he was very tired, stalling for time until he was able to rise. Only twenty-seven of the men were recognized as Chinese; the others had to remain behind. When they reboarded, the men went to their places to lie down. Chau found a place on the deck and knelt in prayer. As he prayed for his family and the freedom of his sons, someone touched his shoulder. He looked around and saw his younger son, who had hidden below decks and had not been discovered by the communists.

A few hours later, the women and children reboarded. Only Chau's oldest son was missing from the family. The police boat taking the captured Vietnamese back to Saigon drew near as the refugee ship headed to the open sea. One of the detained Vietnamese was the brother of the ship's owner, and the police were offering him for sale. When Chau saw that the woman was going to pay, he asked her to buy his oldest son's freedom. He had no money left, he said, but he would repay her after they reached the United States. She said she could not afford it, but she asked the police to include Chau's son as part of the deal for her brother. The police refused and began to haggle. The boat people shouted, "Let him go! Please let him go!" Chau was crying, begging the police for his son's freedom. At the last moment before the police boat turned toward Saigon, Chau's son was allowed to jump to the refugee ship.

They steered a true course for Malaysia. Before the shoreline was spotted, the boat sprang a leak. Everybody began bailing with whatever containers they could find. It was a losing battle. Chau estimated that they had another hour before they went down. Then a murmur swept the boat, turning into a cheer. The coastline was dead ahead.

After they landed the Malaysian police arrived and surrounded the group with barbed wire. The police asked for eight thousand dollars to arrange their freedom. The boat people were convinced they could not be harmed, and they refused to pay, even the ones who still had money. Red Cross workers brought them food. It seemed everything was going to be okay. But the police continued to demand money.

After a month of their refusing to pay the bribe, the Malaysians herded the refugees back to their boat and towed them out to sea. The boat drifted back to the shore that night. The police interned them once more and brought a powerful navy ship to pull them farther out to sea. Many refugee boats, unable to maintain the speed of the navy ships while being towed, capsized and sank, killing all aboard. But Buddha smiled on Chau's group, and after the towline was cut, they drifted to a small, sparsely populated island, one of the many that made up the Indonesian archipelago.

For the next four months the boat people lived a Robinson Crusoe existence. The island was so small, Indonesia so large, that there was no government administration. Fish were plentiful and easy to catch, the weather mellow and warm. Finally, Indonesian police arrived and took control of the refugee camp. Chau saw that the police leader, a sergeant, had a small radio. He proposed a swap. A thousand-dollar

Rolex for a small radio was an offer the sergeant could not turn down, and Chau began listening each night to the BBC and VOA. One evening the announcer read an article by an American journalist who was based in Thailand. Chau sat up when he heard the journalist's name: Keyes Beech of the *Los Angeles Times*.

Chau had one Rolex left. The others had been bartered for food or favors. He decided to take a gamble. He wrote a telegram to Beech, addressed it in care of the United States Embassy in Bangkok, and offered the police sergeant the Rolex if he would send the message when he returned to the mainland. The sergeant accepted, but Chau didn't rate the odds very high that it would ever get sent, and after a few weeks he almost forgot about it.

Keyes Beech had just returned from a reporting trip in the Philippines and was startled to find the message from Chau on his desk. He wondered how Chau knew he was in Bangkok. He turned to a map to try to pinpoint the island where Chau had washed up and then got in touch with American refugee officials and asked them to help. He gave one official two hundred and fifty dollars to pass on to Chau. Later, he and an NBC reporter made it to the island and interviewed Chau, who told them he hoped to get to the States as quickly as possible. Beech advised him to be patient. Back in Bangkok, Beech talked to the American ambassador, who mentioned Chau's case to Richard Holbrooke, an assistant secretary of state who had been one of the bright young men in Vietnam, and soon Chau was notified that he would be transferred. Every refugee needed a sponsor, and since Beech was living in Bangkok, he did not qualify. He talked to George McArthur, a friend who had also worked for the *Los Angeles Times* in Saigon, and McArthur agreed to sponsor Chau.

"Landing in America was a great cultural shock to Chau," said Keyes Beech. "Nobody knew who he was. Nobody cared. He was just another Vietnamese refugee."

20

LOS ANGELES 1980

As Chau was settling his family into a leaky two-room apartment in Van Nuys, California, a suburb of Los Angeles, he received word that Neil Sheehan wanted to interview him about his experiences as a prisoner of the communists for an article that would appear in the *New York Times*. Sheehan's request came at a time when America was entering into a debate with itself, almost subconscious at first, in search of a suitable interpretation of the Vietnam War that the country could agree upon. No one disputed that the war had been a disaster. But why? Had it been fought badly? Or had the Americans lost because they were wrong and the communists right? And how was one to consider the soldiers who had served in the war? Were they murderous psychopaths? Or spit-upon heroes?

The search for an interpretation of the war, a nationally agreed-upon idea of what it all meant, had begun in the early 1960s, slowly and tentatively, limited at first to books and magazine articles. Before the American buildup in 1965, the books on Vietnam were generally educational in nature, with several predicting disaster for the United States. From 1965 until the 1968 Tet offensive, the interpretation of the war became "an agonizing moral dilemma."

In 1968 books, like much of the country, turned antiwar. Many of those published in the first year or so after the Tet offensive reflected a sympathetic interest in North Vietnam or an outrage at the American-caused destruction in the South. This was the beginning of the "bad American/deserving Viet Cong" interpretation of the war. The proponents of this explanation believed that America was wrong in

351

Vietnam, and they admired the tenacity and discipline, if not the ideology, of the Vietnamese opposition and thought the Viet Cong deserved to win, especially considering the corrupt nature of the Saigon government.

The intellectual community was exposed to an impassioned version of this theory, as a result of the ascendance in the late 1960s of the *New York Review of Books* and its chief polemicist Noam Chomsky. Chomsky's Americans, as viewed in his *At War with Asia,* were murderous imperialists and his North Vietnamese were possessed of a thousand virtues. Chomsky was reinforced in 1970 by the publication of Seymour Hersh's *My Lai 4,* which told of a massacre of Vietnamese civilians by American soldiers. His interpretation reached its most influential point in 1971, when Neil Sheehan wrote a lead article for the *New York Times Book Review,* entitled "Should We Have War Crime Trials?" in which he suggested that U.S. military officers and Lyndon Johnson were war criminals.

The following year Frances FitzGerald published *Fire in the Lake,* which took its thesis (the American destruction of the Vietnamese village and hamlet structure) from French scholar Paul Mus, under whom FitzGerald had studied at Princeton after spending some time in Vietnam. FitzGerald was a propagator of the "bad American/deserving Viet Cong" interpretation, but she did not stop there in her book. She also attempted to discredit an earlier interpretation offered by Robert Shaplen of *The New Yorker,* whose influential work on the war, in particular his book *The Lost Revolution,* had acted as a subtle brake on members of the Saigon press corps for years and possibly kept some of them from embracing the "bad American/deserving Viet Cong" theory.

Frances FitzGerald charged that Shaplen had always blamed the failures of the Saigon government on American officials, who, he believed, had not given the Vietnamese good advice at the right time. As Shaplen put it, "The 'lost revolution' in Vietnam represents more than the failure of the United States to capture a revolution from the communists. It demonstrates that we were incapable, over the period of the last twenty years, of encouraging and supporting the cause of a true nationalism against a spurious one." FitzGerald believed, on the other hand, it appeared from her book, that the communists represented the true nationalism and that their ideology melded well with the traditions of Vietnam. "Like Confucianism," she asserted, "Marxism was a social morality."

Shaplen's interpretation was pure Lansdale, of course. Shaplen had been Lansdale's closest journalist friend since the operative's days in the Philippines. A large man who smoked big cigars and looked like a truck driver rather than the intellectual he was, Shaplen was stung by FitzGerald's attack, even more so since excerpts of the book first appeared in his own *New Yorker.* In private, he made unchivalrous remarks that suggested FitzGerald's book grew from Freudian motives directed against her late father, Desmond FitzGerald, the CIA official and Lansdale and Colby friend who shared responsibility for developing many of the programs that FitzGerald attacked.

Whatever the case, it was Frances FitzGerald's interpretation of the war, not Robert Shaplen's, which would gain wide public acceptance. Combined with David Halberstam's *The Best and the Brightest,* which fleshed out and then eviscerated the government officials whose war reports and memos were offered in the Pentagon Papers, her book remained for years the chief influence in forming opinions about the political side of the war, though it suffered curious lapses. Subtitled "The Vietnamese and the Americans in Vietnam," *Fire in the Lake* failed to mention William Colby a single time.

FitzGerald's and Halberstam's influence came partly as a matter of timing. Their books were published only a year or two before the American war ended with the signing of the 1973 cease-fire agreement. Tired of hearing about Vietnam, some critics seemed ready to shut off any further discussion of the war. When James Jones's *Viet Journal* came out in 1974, the *New York Times* began its review like this: "Quick—before your mind fogs up at the prospect of yet another report on Vietnam. . . ." And *Time*'s chief critic called Jones's work "a book about Vietnam for a public that does not want to hear anything more about Vietnam."

The nation was undeniably war weary. Still, such a negative attitude toward the publication of Vietnam books by two of the country's most powerful organs was close to being an act of censorship. The ripple effect was immediately noticeable in the attitude of other reviewers across America. Moreover, their reading of the book public's mind did not hold up in the light of available evidence. Vietnam books had been bestsellers for the previous four years, and there were never more than thirty new titles (out of over thirty-five thousand books published annually) printed on Vietnam in any given year. But for whatever combination of reasons, the publication of Vietnam books dropped after 1974, to about a dozen titles a year.

The most notable works of the post-cease-fire period were by American prisoners of war. Their reports of torture did much to suggest that the North Vietnamese and Viet Cong were not necessarily possessed of the full thousand virtues. The Chomsky interpretation, it became clear during this time, was unsatisfactory—too filled with self-righteousness and finger-pointing, inappropriate now that the war was over and passions had begun to cool. The men who fought in Vietnam posed the first difficulty in the formulation of a suitable new interpretation. Obviously America was to have no Sergeant Yorks or Audie Murphys. But was every soldier to be considered a Private Meadlo of My Lai?

In 1977 came *A Rumor of War* by Philip Caputo, a well-crafted account of his tour as a marine lieutenant, shocking in its revelation near the end that he shared responsibility for the murder of two innocent Vietnamese teenagers. Caputo argued that the insanity of the war had made him do it, and the critics agreed. Theodore Solotaroff said in the *New York Times Book Review,* "The ultimate effect of this book is to make the personal and public responsibility [for the war] merge into a nightmare of horror and waste."

Then a few months later John Leonard announced in the *New York Times:* "If you think you don't want to read any more about Vietnam, you are wrong." Leonard liked to boast that as the *Book Review* editor he had been responsible for publishing Neil Sheehan's war crimes piece, and his enthusiasm for Vietnam writing was revitalized by Michael Herr's *Dispatches,* an ironic celebration of violence and death whose recurring theme was of drugs and madness of the freaky/spooky type. The Sunday *Book Review* critic called *Dispatches* the best book written about the Vietnam War and said, "Herr's literary style derives from the era of acid rock, the Beatles films, of that druggy, Hunter Thompson once-removed-from-reality appreciation of The Great Cosmic Joke."

Herr's once-removed-from-reality interpretation coincided with the direction in which Hollywood was moving and contained elements that the whole country had begun to agree upon: the concept of the veteran as a victim of the war's madness. If America could not give its admiration to veterans as in past wars, it could at least treat them solicitously like outpatients of an insane asylum. In this interpretation, the paraplegic became the heroic victim, the sad equivalent of World War Two's Medal of Honor winner, his paralysis symbolic of both the physical and the psychological maiming of American soldiers.

Born on the Fourth of July by Ron Kovic, an antiwar paraplegic, had been given laudatory treatment by the critics a year or so before *Dispatches* came out, and actress Jane Fonda gave the theme of the paraplegic as victim and hero its widest dissemination with her movie *Coming Home.* President Jimmy Carter did his part to legitimize the interpretation by appointing a paraplegic as head of his administration's veterans affairs.

An indication that the concept of the veteran as a victim of the war's madness was beginning to take hold could be seen by the number of Vietnam vets who were portrayed as psychopaths on television melodramas in the late 1970s. Then Francis Ford Coppola offered up the ultimate psychopath as played by Marlon Brando in *Apocalypse Now,* with a narration written by Mike Herr. Coppola's version of the war quickly clashed, however, with Michael Cimino's version as found in his film *The Deer Hunter,* which, to the dismay of some critics, seemed to suggest with its final scene of Vietnam veterans singing "God Bless America" that the country had not necessarily been wrong in the war and that the men who served had been young innocents doing their duty and confronted by sadistic Viet Cong.

This led to a debate about what was truly authentic. Was the real thing Marlon Brando as a psychopath? Or was the war more accurately represented by the sadistic Viet Cong of *The Deer Hunter?* The search for authenticity was finally ended, according to many critics, by Oliver Stone's *Platoon,* which, with excellent editing and special effects, produced some of the most vivid battle scenes ever filmed. This . . . *was* . . . the real thing, critics said. What *Platoon* said about Vietnam, though, beyond advancing the hardly novel proposition that war is hell, was clear only to those who assumed it said something important.

The Vietnam veterans began to react to their portrayal as psychopaths and baby-killers. Perhaps they were victims of the war, they said, but they were men who should be treated with dignity and respect. The public acceptance of this idea was helped by a number of factors. First, the antiwar movement was silenced by the spectacle of the boat people and the Cambodian holocaust. And the unveiling in 1982 of the Vietnam Veterans Memorial in Washington—the Wall— gave a focus to national sympathy for veterans, as did the attitude of President Ronald Reagan, who was unrepentant in his belief that the war had been an honorable undertaking. Books began to shift their view of the veterans, and even the long-ignored blacks, as portrayed in Wallace Terry's *Bloods,* were given favorable attention for having served on the front lines. Suddenly Vietnam vets depicted in television melodramas became strong and sympathetic figures.

So when Tran Ngoc Chau arrived in Los Angeles, in November 1979, America's search for an interpretation of the war that would later lead to a recasting of the national image of the Vietnam veteran was underway. Proceeding more slowly was the search for a general explanation for the war and its loss.

NEIL SHEEHAN, LIKE PROBABLY EVERY JOURNALIST who had spent any time in Vietnam, had developed an emotional stake in the war, and his was greater than most. While other journalists could and usually did claim—publicly, at least—that they had reported the story dispassionately with "objectivity," it was obvious that Sheehan had crossed a line that was hard to define by those in the business. Sheehan would have been less than human had he not harbored an antipathy for the government bureaucracy that had hounded him and David Halberstam for their reports during the early stages of the war. And no one could doubt that he had been touched in a deeply personal way by the destruction he had witnessed. Yet the editors of journalists serving in the trenches operated from their own ideas of what constituted "objectivity," and though the *New York Times* had turned firmly against the war, it was the impression of some at the paper that Sheehan had gone too far. His war crimes piece in the *Book Review* was particularly looked on with disfavor by some reporters, and it was said that the *Times*'s Washington bureau chief, Max Frankel, was not Sheehan's greatest admirer.

For whatever reasons, Sheehan left the *Times* after John Paul Vann was killed in a helicopter crash in 1972 to write a biography of the man he and Halberstam had considered their hero. It was, some thought, a peculiar matching of subject and author, for Vann, though critical of American actions during the Halberstam-Sheehan era and their best source, had become convinced in the latter stages of the war that America was on the right track and could win, or at least stave off a communist victory. To write a flattering biography of his hero would also, one might assume, lend credibility to the hero's hawkish beliefs about the war. As it turned out, Sheehan discovered with the help of Vann's former wife that his hero had been a womanizer of epic appetites, had even told a lie here and there, and thus had misrepresented himself to the young reporters like Sheehan who had admired him, and was, just as the war itself, Sheehan concluded, *A Bright Shining Lie*—a tarnished hero for a tarnished war.

It was in connection with his research for the Vann biography, already seven years underway, that Sheehan decided to try to interview Chau after he arrived in California. Chau, feeling lost and unsure of himself in his new environment, got in touch with Dan Ellsberg, who had given Neil his number, and asked his advice about whether or not he should cooperate with Sheehan. Ellsberg had reacted like a true friend when Chau landed in the States. He quickly made a visit and, understanding the nature of Chau's pride, gently pressed a thousand dollars on him. He returned again, sleeping in one room of Chau's shabby apartment, and insisted that Chau take more money to buy a second-hand car, so the family would be able to look for jobs.

IT HAD NOT BEEN a very happy period for Ellsberg. Subtly thwarted by Senator Fulbright's assistant Norvill Jones, he had not been able to get Congress to release the Pentagon Papers, which he had once hoped would end the war. Not even George McGovern, the antiwar presidential candidate, would touch them, and a McGovern assistant put out the word that they thought Ellsberg was a kook, or at best a former hawk with a guilty conscience. Norvill Jones suggested that he give the documents to the *New York Times,* and Ellsberg reluctantly agreed. The Papers made a big splash when they were published in June 1971, but in the aftermath Ellsberg's reputation suffered. He was indicted a few weeks later, and Nixon's White House secretly put the "Plumbers" on his trail, in an attempt to destroy him. The Plumbers, headed by former CIA employee Howard Hunt, learned that Ellsberg had engaged in orgies for a brief period during the late 1960s, and they broke into the office of his Los Angeles psychoanalyst, probably looking for information that would link him to homosexual activities. But the orgies had been heterosexual and not a particular concern to the L.A. analyst, such things being relatively common to that period. Ellsberg was seeing the analyst to try to break a writer's block (unsuccessfully) and to try to work out why he had taken so many risks in

Vietnam. The break-in became public at the time of the Watergate investigations, and Ellsberg's trial was cancelled and the indictment dropped. Still, all the gossip about orgies and psychoanalysis did nothing for his reputation. Ellsberg believed he was further damaged by the attitude of the editors of the *New York Times*. After he revealed that he was source for the Papers, "They acted," he said, "like they hated me." He thought it was because he had stolen some of the newspaper's glory.

As a result of the publicity stemming from the release of the Papers, which Ellsberg turned over to the reporter he had leaked to numerous times before, Neil Sheehan, the names of the two men were often linked, and it was assumed they were friends. But this did not exactly describe their relationship. When he gave Sheehan the first batch of documents, three months before the *Times* published them, Ellsberg made it clear that he still hoped to get Congress to release them. Ellsberg later believed that Sheehan, fearing Ellsberg might succeed in getting Congress to put out the Papers before the *Times* was able to publish them, began to mislead him about if and when the newspaper was going to print the material. "He lied," Ellsberg said. "He said the *Times* was not interested when in fact they were going full blast on the thing." Journalism was a thistle of small betrayals, and Sheehan probably did no more than any other reporter would have done under the circumstances, but Ellsberg continued to hold it against him.

Still, Ellsberg thought it might be a good idea for Chau to sit for an interview with Sheehan. Chau, Ellsberg believed, was better qualified to speak about what had happened after the communists took over South Vietnam than any other refugee. He and Chau had stayed up all night talking about his experiences. "I was tremendously impressed at how judicious he was," Ellsberg said. "He was critical of the communists, but in a judicious manner. He was disappointed in the way they had turned out."

Neil Sheehan wrote an article based on his interview with Chau, which appeared in the *New York Times* on Monday, January 14, 1980, captioned "Ex-Saigon Official Tells of 'Re-education' by Hanoi." The first three paragraphs set the tone.

> Van Nuys, Calif.—A former South Vietnamese Army officer and official who spent four years in Vietnam under the Communists, more than half of them in a "re-education camp" and prisons, says the Hanoi leadership

undertook an unprecedented experiment to convert and reconcile its former opponents because it had decided not to liquidate them.

American Presidents had predicted for decades that a Communist military victory in Vietnam would result in a mass liquidation of Hanoi's opponents. The prediction of a blood bath had been one of the abiding justifications for continuing the war.

"There was no blood bath," as many feared would occur after a Communist takeover, said the former official, Tran Ngoc Chau. "There have been some trials and long prison terms have been handed out," he said, but he said he did not know of a single person on the South Vietnamese side who had been executed for acts committed during the war.

Though Sheehan's lengthy article contained nothing that wasn't true, as related to him by Chau, the overall slant of the story suggested to the reader that the communists were rather benign fellows and that Chau's experiences as a prisoner had been hardly more difficult than enduring a tough summer camp. The reaction of the Vietnamese refugee community in America was immediate and violent: Chau and his family began to receive death threats.

"The Sheehan article was a shocker," Dan Ellsberg said. "All he did was tell the nice things Chau said about the communists and not the other things. I called him and said, 'Neil, that's certainly a different impression from what he gave me. Didn't he say *this* and *this?*' Sheehan said, 'Yeah, he said all that. But that wasn't the news. The news was that there was no blood bath.' 'You got him in trouble,' I said."

Chau and his family had no money and were unable to move away from the neighborhood where they were known and being threatened by the other refugees. There was no doubt that their lives were in danger. Chau believed that Sheehan had not told both sides of the story, as he had related it to him. But Chau, as forgiving as ever, did not hold it against Sheehan, and even imagined that the reporter was embarrassed by the effect of his story. In his analysis, Chau believed that the *New York Times* had decided to use him to make a we-told-you-so point about the lack of a bloodbath in order to justify the paper's position against the war. In fact, there was no basis for believing that the story represented anything but Sheehan's personal interpretation of Chau's experiences.

Keyes Beech, the conservative journalist who had vigorously supported the war and who disliked Ellsberg, was also shocked by Sheehan's story. "When I read it," said Beech, "I thought, 'This is not the

Chau that I talked to.' But I don't think Sheehan knew he was hurting Chau. All of us were emotionally involved in Vietnam one way or another. I think Neil had lost whatever objectivity he once may have had. Of course, a lot of people did, and some reporters would suggest that I lost some of my objectivity too—which I did."

Chau's family was shaken and isolated. Though he had accepted money from Ellsberg and Beech when they volunteered it, Chau's pride was too great to ask anybody for help. They would have to make it on their own, he told his family. The point was that they had to pay for their freedom. They would have to take precautions when they left the apartment, but the death threats from the other refugees would have to be endured.

The Chau family set out to study English and to find whatever jobs they could at the minimum wage. His youngest daughter spoke no English when they arrived, but after three and a half years she graduated at the top of her high school class and was admitted to UCLA, on her way to becoming a doctor. His eldest son, who at the last moment had jumped to the boat taking them to freedom, graduated from college as an engineer and was soon making nearly fifty thousand dollars a year, working from seven in the morning till eleven at night. Chau went to computer school and after he finished worked his way up the ladder of a private company to be placed in charge of six programmers.

Five years later they applied for citizenship. Chau cried the day he was sworn in as an American. The family continued to live frugally, paying off debts that had been incurred, even to the Buddhists, who had provided them with escape money. Finally they were able to leave the two-room apartment and buy a six-bedroom house located not far from that endless strip of suburban concrete known as Ventura Boulevard. To some the congested and polluted area might have seemed more a part of the American nightmare, but to Chau and his family it was truly a dream. After having been betrayed by his brother, jailed by his friend Thieu, abandoned by the CIA, shackled by the communists, and used by antiwar journalism, Chau had experienced a rebirth.

Like a phoenix, a true phoenix, Chau had risen from the ashes of the Vietnam War.

EPILOGUE

EDWARD LANSDALE WAS DYING, and we both knew it. I had begun my research for this book a few weeks earlier, in the summer of 1986, and I'd telephoned Lansdale without much hope that he would cooperate with me. He had taken some hard licks from journalists in the years following the war. But after I described my project, he grew enthusiastic and invited me to his home in McLean, Virginia, the next day. I had already scheduled another appointment, but we arranged to meet later in the week, and when I arrived he was anxious to get started. After taking one look at him, I knew that it was only a matter of months, if not weeks; and his wife, Pat, who also knew, was dedicated to making sure that he did not exhaust himself. Thus began several days of difficult and intensive interviews, with Lansdale cheerfully giving it his all, as I tried to reconcile my conflicting desires not to drain too much of his precious energy while taking advantage of his willingness to be extraordinarily candid.

Lansdale had met Pat Kelly (née Yapcinco) during his tour in the Philippines. She was of mixed Chinese and Filipino blood, the widow of an Irish-Filipino who had died during World War Two. She was working as a journalist when Lansdale met her, and she later took a job with the United States Information Service. Lansdale arranged for her temporary transfer to Saigon after he arrived in 1954, and they continued their friendship. After his first wife died nearly twenty years later, they were married. It seemed appropriate that Pat Yapcinco Lansdale, an Asian, was destined to care for, in his final years, the man who so uncompromisingly had loved Asians.

361

Lansdale, I discovered, was enthusiastic about my project because I had mentioned that I intended to portray a Vietnamese side to the story, something rarely found in other books on the war, and would focus on the personal actions of the Americans involved in pacification, not on the kind of bureaucratic details that he detested. A formal biography of him by a military historian was already in the works, but Lansdale believed to the end that the emphasis should be on the Vietnamese, and the day we finished our interviews he inscribed his memoirs, *In the Midst of Wars,* to me this way: "To Zalin Grant, who also has a deep affection for the Vietnamese and is still writing books about their long war." He died eight months later, on February 23, 1987.

Unlike Lansdale, William Colby was in good health, but he seemed to be suffering, in his quiet way, from a case of boredom, as he went through the motions of working as an international lawyer. Colby had returned from Vietnam and had been appointed as director of the Central Intelligence Agency, only to be caught in the congressional tornado that uprooted the CIA in the mid-1970s. Colby was fired by the Ford administration, apparently at the urging of Henry Kissinger, not for practicing the craft of duplicity that had been turned into a low art form during the Nixon-Kissinger years, but for not being duplicitous enough when dealing with the elected representatives of the American people. Opinion at the CIA was split about Colby's tenure as director, with some intelligence officers frankly hating his guts and charging that he had destroyed the agency, and others contending that he had done the right thing as an honorable man.

Whatever Colby's reputation at CIA headquarters, it was hard to find anyone who had known him in Vietnam, journalist or government official, who had very much bad to say about him. In fact, he was considered such a straight arrow by the Vietnam crowd that the gossip about him after the war concerned his divorce and remarriage. Colby the good Catholic—*divorced?* Worse, as Colby obviously and painfully saw it, were the lingering rumors that his daughter Catherine, who died of complications resulting from anorexia in 1973 at age twenty-four, had in effect committed suicide in protest against her father's role in the Phoenix program. Colby was frequently confronted by this charge when he spoke at colleges and universities after his return from Vietnam. His most difficult moment, he told me, came one day at Princeton when a girl stood to accuse him of being an assassin and the reason why Catherine had committed suicide. He was shocked, Colby said, because the student resembled his daughter and even had the same red hair. Colby tried to explain that Catherine had suffered from epilepsy as a child, which led to a troubled adolescence, complicated by poor vision (and an operation for crossed eyes that wasn't entirely successful), and that in reality her happiest moments had been spent in Saigon. His explanation was confirmed by friends of the family, and no one who knew the Colbys gave credence to the rumors, though Colby's sensitivity to the tragedy and his continuing need to set the story straight perhaps suggested, understandably, the remorse of an absentee father.

A number of other former officials I interviewed were, like Colby, fighting their own boredom and letdown from the war and trying to put a brave face on it. George (Jake) Jacobson, who had served as Colby's deputy in the pacification program, asked me to tell everybody that he was thoroughly enjoying retirement and drinking a lot of scotch, though I suspected that only part of his statement was totally true. He died before this book was completed.

Lou Conein, too, claimed that supreme happiness was to be found sitting in his suburban Virginia home doing nothing. Actually Conein told me that he was spending his time reading the Bible from beginning to end. When I relayed this startling bit of news to several of Conein's friends, they laughed and said, "Same ol' Lou—still doing the unexpected." Conein was in and out of the news in the years following his return from Vietnam. He was closely identified with the Diem coup; and then E. Howard Hunt, a former CIA operative whom he'd known in the OSS, called him to the White House at the time Daniel Ellsberg was under investigation for stealing the Pentagon Papers. Hunt was head of the "Plumbers," the group that carried out the Watergate burglary and set in motion the events that brought Richard Nixon down. Hunt's idea was to get Conein drunk, while secretly tape recording the lowdown on Ellsberg. But Conein, as he told me with relish, turned the tables on Hunt—or rather drank him under the table—and the ploy failed. Similarly, Conein proved too slippery for Hunt when Nixon's agents tried to link him to a plan to discredit the Kennedys by forging documents about the Diem coup. Conein served for a time with the drug enforcement agency and then retired completely from government service. His wife, Elyette, became a successful real estate agent.

Conein was in poor health when we talked. He had suffered a minor stroke not long before, and all the years of hard living were etched in

his face. But, although the springy step was gone, the go-to-hell attitude was not. After I turned off the tape recorder, we were speaking
about the publicity he had received, much of it negative, and he said,
"I don't care what the sons of bitches write about me. Nobody can
hurt me now."

Daniel Ellsberg, who lived in California near Berkeley with his
wife, Patricia Marx, and their young son, Michael, had evolved into
the professional man of protest. The very thing that made Ellsberg an
interesting personality—his complex and contradictory intellect—
worked against his ever truly succeeding as a protester who could
inspire others by word or deed, though I had no doubt that given his
energy and dedication he would wind up in some sort of book of
records for the most demonstrations attended, most times arrested.
One might have assumed that Ellsberg's apostasy on the war would
have cost him the friendship of those with whom he had once served
in Vietnam, but I discovered that, to a man, all of them continued to
like him, especially Lansdale, even if they did not necessarily agree
with what he had done.

The one person (besides Colby) in this account who actively disliked Ellsberg and his stand on the war died before his time—at least
according to a book of memoirs published in 1989 by a former Vietnam correspondent, who wrote, "Keyes Beech, who had covered so
many wars, passed away peacefully in his sleep." The journalists who
knew Beech were appalled by the error, but Keyes himself, tough as
ever, just laughed. Beech thought that the reporter, who was against
the war, never got much straight, anyway. The premature obituary
proved not far off the mark, however. Beech died the following year,
in February 1990, at age seventy-six.

Happily, not all the stories about the people who had left the war
concerned death and boredom. Some of them were doing just fine.
Mike Dunn became the head of the Can Manufacturers Institute in
Washington; Barry Zorthian also worked in a plush office, sometimes
giving lectures and attending conferences for the "cottage industry,"
as he called it, that had grown up around the Vietnam War. Rufus
Phillips still had his business, and Stuart Methven was connected to a
defense-related think tank. Vint Lawrence had carved out a reputation
as a Washington-based artist and illustrator.

Even after so many years, Chau was still on the minds of many of
them. During my interviews, when we talked about him, the moment
often turned emotional. Some of the Americans looked away at the

mention of his name; several of them were ready to cry. Chau had become a symbol to them, a symbol of everything that had been lost in Vietnam. I, too, felt tears welling in my eyes as we spoke. But the tears, I knew, were not so much for Chau, as for ourselves.

ACKNOWLEDGMENTS

I WOULD LIKE TO EXPRESS my gratitude to the following persons for making this work unusual, perhaps even unique, in the sense that there are no anonymous sources. Whether one agrees with them or not, I think that their willingness to be open, candid, and responsible for their thoughts and actions is wholly admirable—and a virtue not always to be found nowadays. They include Keyes Beech, Evert Bumgardner, Carol Laise Bunker, Samuel Bunker, Tran Ngoc Chau, William Colby, Elyette Bruchot Conein, Lucien Conein, William Connell, John Michael Dunn, Daniel Ellsberg, J. William Fulbright, Mark Huss, George Jacobson, Norvill Jones, William Kohlmann, Edward Lansdale, Vint Lawrence, Stuart Methven, Rufus Phillips, Joe Redick, Jean-André Sauvageot, Frank Snepp, Charles Timmes, Barry Zorthian; and for interviews given earlier, Robert Komer, Frank McCulloch, Patrick McGarvey, Jason McManus.

The men and women responsible for seeing this book to production have also been straightforward and professional. They include Starling Lawrence, my editor at W. W. Norton, who kept an eye on the compass during the long voyage; Jeannie Luciano; Marian Johnson, a copyeditor with a delicate touch; Andy Marasia and his staff. I would also like to thank Peter Shepherd of Harold Ober Associates.

Friends and relatives, forgiving of inattentions and understanding of excesses, play a supporting role in the writing of a book, and I thank the following: my mother, my sister and her husband, J. David Smith; Barbara Dean and James David; George Sturrock; Sam Abt; William Gibbons; Patricia and John Paton Davies; Annie Miccio;

Deborah Palmer; Sally Ann Palmer, a friend from one continent to another; and Philippe Muller, whose arrival is always heralded by bells and chimes.

I would also like to thank A. M. Secrest, Frank McCulloch, Gilbert A. Harrison, and William Tuohy for help and advice given in past years.

Wallace and Janice Terry are not only our best of friends but also highly valued colleagues who have added their knowledge of the business to this book. A special note of thanks goes to Janice Terry, who shepherded my Freedom of Information request through the State Department; anyone who has gone through that experience will recognize and appreciate the degree of her perseverance.

My thanks, finally, to Claude. I could list a dozen personal reasons, all of them deeply felt, as to why she was indispensable to the writing of this book, but I'll stop at one professional reason: she helped me understand the role of the French in Vietnam—and that was the first step of the journey.

SOURCE NOTES

THIS BOOK IS BASED FOR THE MOST PART on face-to-face interviews. Those interviews are not limited to the tape-recorded principals of this story, but include an accumulation of literally hundreds—I'd not hesitate to say several thousand—of interviews accorded me from 1964, when I first went to Vietnam, until 1973, when I made my last visit after the ceasefire was signed. I'd like to express my gratitude to John Stacks and Jean Bodine of Time, Inc., who made it possible for me to go through the files I wrote as a *Time* reporter; also to Susan Harrigan, later of *Newsday*, whose excellent note-keeping and transcribing of tapes made it easy for me to retrace my interview steps as *The New Republic*'s correspondent in Saigon.

What struck me, as I went through my old files and reread the articles and files of journalists who had reported from Vietnam, was how elusive the story had proved for all of us. It was as though we of the Saigon press corps were standing outside a concert hall peering through a thick glass, able to see and describe the movements of the orchestra but unable to hear the music. It became clear during my research that if the United States is ever to reach an understanding of Vietnam, aside from drawing the obvious conclusion that it was a disaster, more books of a probing historical nature are needed.

The most frequently cited research document for Vietnam is the Pentagon Papers, and I have used all three versions—the *New York Times* edition published by Bantam Books; the fuller version known as the Gravel edition and published by Beacon Press; and the comprehensive study backed by supporting documents, which was released

369

by the Pentagon and can be found in the Library of Congress. None of us should forget, however, that the Pentagon Papers stop at 1968, and the war continued for American troops until 1973 and ultimately until 1975. To use the Pentagon Papers as one's primary research document for Vietnam would be like writing a history of World War Two and ending in 1943; it would not change anything in terms of the eventual outcome of the war, but neither would it give a full picture of what happened.

Fortunately, there are a number of scholars and researchers now embarked on in-depth historical studies of the war. One of them, William Conrad Gibbons, has already published three volumes of his projected multivolume work, *The U.S. Government and the Vietnam War* (Princeton University Press), and it belongs, I believe, in the library of every student of the war. I have drawn from Gibbons's study, with his permission, particularly to illustrate the early history of American involvement in Vietnam.

Another valuable source, though only a brief oral history, is *Many Reasons Why* by Michael Charlton and Anthony Moncrieff (New York: Hill and Wang, 1978), which appeared first as a series of interviews with former Vietnam officials on the BBC. I can remember tuning in to the BBC and hearing by chance the beginning of Charlton's series. Its impact hit me with the same force as when I picked up the *New York Times* and read the first installment of the Pentagon Papers. But Charlton's series needs to be heard, as well as read, because many nuances are unavoidably lost when transferred from audio to print.

Other researchers are taking a more considered look at the war, now that passions have receded, including the veterans themselves. Some of their new analyses can be found in the magazine called *Vietnam,* and the quotation that serves as an epigraph to this book (on p. 9) comes from its editor, Colonel Harry G. Summers, Jr., as recounted in the August 1989 issue, page 62.

CHAPTER 1

The account of Tran Ngoc Chau is based on my conversations with him (interview with Tran Ngoc Chau, December 11, 1986) and the supplementary material he sent me. I have somewhat simplified Chau's ideas to make it easier for the general reader, but anyone who is interested in a more detailed investigation into his strategy for pacification should consult the *Hearings Before the Committee on Foreign Relations, United States Senate, Ninety-First Congress, Second Session, on Civil Operations and Rural Development Support Program,* which were held in February and March 1970.

"That mistake came when the Viet Cong launched a massive attack against the cities" (p. 29). The 1968 Tet offensive was a pivotal point in the war and a source of enduring controversy. For a look at the role the press played during Tet see Peter Braestrup's *Big Story: How the American Press and Television Reported and Interpreted the Crisis of Tet 1968 in Vietnam and Washington* (Boulder, Colorado: Westview Press, 1977). I too was quite skeptical of General Westmoreland's claim, made in 1968, that Tet was a defeat for the Viet Cong. I changed my mind in early 1970, when I went to Vietnam on behalf of CBS and *Time* to investigate the capture of the newsmen who disappeared in Cambodia around the time of the American invasion. At the Tay Ninh amnesty center, near the Cambodian border, I personally interviewed over three hundred Viet Cong who had been more or less forced to surrender because of the invasion, many of them officials of the political/administrative organization. Their candid admissions about their failures convinced me that the Tet offensive had been both a major military defeat and a great psychological victory for them.

"Just how badly they were hurting was apparent to the CIA station in Saigon" (p. 30) Interview with Frank Snepp, December 12, 1986. Snepp later broke with the agency and wrote a book about the American withdrawal from Vietnam, *Decent Interval: An Insider's Account of Saigon's Indecent End* (New York: Random House, 1977), whereupon the CIA garnished his royalties on the ground that he had violated his secrecy agreement. Snepp sued but lost on appeal to the Supreme Court. When I talked to him, he was living in California and working on a screenplay for Marlon Brando, though he didn't seem exceedingly happy with the Hollywood life.

"At the same time, a Vietnamese-speaking official of the pacification program" (p. 30). The official was Jean-André Sauvageot. Interview with Jean-André Sauvageot, November 10, 1986.

"I think Bunker very strongly believed that Thieu was pretty much the only hope" (p. 34). Interview with William Kohlmann, December 12, 1986 (joint interview with Frank Snepp).

CHAPTER 2

"Chau wanted to keep his independence" (p. 35). Interview with Daniel Ellsberg, December 8, 1986.

"We were informed . . . that Chau had received" (p. 40). Department of State Telegram, Saigon 12881, June 26, 1969; declassified under the Freedom of Information Act at my request.

"the tidal wave he was creating by stealing the Pentagon Papers" (p. 40). Frank Snepp wrote in *Decent Interval* that Ellsberg decided to steal the Pentagon Papers because of what was happening to his friend Chau, but Ellsberg told me that the trigger for his action came when the army failed to prosecute the Special Forces men who were involved in the murder of their translator, Thai Khac Chuyen.

CHAPTER 3

"Elyette Bruchot, get away from that window!" (p. 43). Interview with Elyette Bruchot Conein, November 1, 1986.

The account of the Patti mission on August 22, 1945, comes from Elyette Bruchot Conein, who later knew Jean Sainteny and worked in a bank with several of his former assistants. Lou Conein himself was rather elusive about his role in the Patti mission, and I discovered when talking to those who later knew him that he preferred to downplay his actions during that period. It appeared to me that Conein didn't like talking about his participation in a mission that had led to the installation of Ho Chi Minh and his communists in Hanoi possibly because he then turned around and spent the remainder of his career trying to overthrow them. Archimedes Patti is not very helpful in resolving the question in his book *Why Viet Nam? Prelude to America's Albatross* (University of California Press, 1981). Patti makes several cryptic references to Conein, calling him "trustworthy" (p. 113) at one point, "recalcitrant" (p. 199) at another. Conein was equally enigmatic about Patti when I talked to him.

"Personally, Franklin D. Roosevelt never had a doubt" (p. 45). Much of the historical data in this section, though not necessarily its interpretation, is taken from *The U.S. Government and the Vietnam War, Part 1: 1945–1960* by William Conrad Gibbons (Princeton: Princeton University Press, 1986). Henceforth I will refer to the work as "Gibbons" and list the appropriate volume.

"The policy was—and as given to me by General Donovan" (p. 46). From *Many Reasons Why* by Michael Charlton (New York: Hill and Wang, 1978). I found Patti's account of that period, given to Charlton as a spontaneous interview, more persuasive than Patti's own book, which was published three years later with the help of an antiwar activist.

"Lou Conein was preparing to parachute into the South of France" (p. 47). Interview with Lucien Conein, September 16, 1986.

"Really he didn't impress me very much" (p. 50). Archimedes Patti in his interview with Michael Charlton of the BBC.

"Was it obvious to you the Americans were vital" (p. 51). Ibid.
"As Sainteny later admitted" (p. 53). Ibid.

CHAPTER 4

"Ironically, while a handful of reporters were privately criticized" (p. 60). David Halberstam, *Esquire,* Nov. 1964.

"Disgusted and apparently at the end of his possibilities for promotion" (p. 60). See *A Bright Shining Lie* by Neil Sheehan (New York: Random House, 1988).

"John Vann and Ev Bumgardner decided to hide Chau" (p. 61). Interview with Evert Bumgardner, November 21, 1986.

CHAPTER 5

The material in this chapter is largely based on interviews with Elyette Bruchot Conein and Tran Ngoc Chau.

CHAPTER 6

"So when President Truman asked for advisers to be sent" (p. 80). Gibbons, Part 1, contains a revealing discussion about the evolution of the American advisory effort around the world.

CHAPTER 7

"Mindful of the part played by Americans in the recent Greek struggle" (p. 83). *In the Midst of Wars* by Edward Geary Lansdale (New York: Harper & Row, 1972).

"Many years later, when asked what he considered the oddest aspect of Lansdale" (p. 83). Interview with William Colby, June 12, 1986.

"The Office of Policy Coordination eventually merged into the CIA's covert action branch" (p. 87). See *Edward Lansdale: The Unquiet American* by Cecil B. Currey (Boston: Houghton Mifflin, 1988).

CHAPTER 8

"During the year preceding the fall of Dien Bien Phu, Washington had been concerned" (p. 94). For a discussion of this period, see Gibbons, Part 1.

"The first was the Lansdale who was reputed to have a magical touch with foreigners" (p. 98). Interview with Daniel Ellsberg, December 9, 1986.

"Joe Redick, a CIA officer who served with Lansdale" (p. 98). Interview with Joe Redick, September 26, 1986.

"Rufus Phillips, a second lieutenant just turned twenty-five" (p. 105). Interview with Rufus Phillips, October 17, 1986.

"Years later David Halberstam would write in a book" (p. 107). *The Best and the Brightest* by David Halberstam (New York: Random House, 1972), p. 126.

"The journalistic attack was bearable" (p. 125). *In the Midst of Wars* by Edward Geary Lansdale (New York: Harper & Row, 1972).

CHAPTER 9

The material in this chapter largely comes from my interview with Tran Ngoc Chau and our subsequent correspondence.

CHAPTER 10

"It was at the beginning of this sequence of chaotic events, in the summer of 1959" (p. 140). Interview with Stuart Methven, November 9, 1986.

"As Stu Methven was preparing to leave Laos in late 1961, a twenty-two-year-old New Yorker" (p. 145). Interview with Vint Lawrence, November 17, 1986.

CHAPTER 11

"His openness was not a clever device to hide an intractability" (p. 162). Interview with Paul Colby, June 18, 1986.

"I always thought it really doesn't pay for Americans to be telling other people" (p. 163). Interview with William Colby, June 16, 1986.

"I said in my book that there's the traditional gray man" (p. 163). The book is *Honorable Men: My Life in the CIA* by William Colby and Peter Forbath (New York: Simon and Schuster, 1978).

"At 3:30 A.M., November 11, 1960, Colonel Thi began his attack" (p. 176). For a fine account of the events leading to Ngo Dinh Diem's overthrow and murder, see *Kennedy in Vietnam* by William J. Rust and the editors of U.S. News Books (New York: Charles Scribner's Sons, 1985).

"He told me on the phone that I had five minutes to give him a briefing" (p. 180). Gibbons, Part II.

"Lansdale was an idea man, Maxwell Taylor said" (p. 181). *Kennedy in Vietnam* by William J. Rust, page 45.

CHAPTER 12

"just a *pied noir,* a derogatory phrase implying that he was something of a half-breed" (p. 183). David Halberstam tried once more to tackle *pied noir* seven years later in *The Best and the Brightest*—and missed again. On page 252 he writes: "Sully was a *pied-noir* (a term to describe the French lower class in Algeria, like calling an American a redneck.)" Nope. It is applied to a Frenchman of any class born in Algeria when it was considered part of France; or, more loosely, to anyone French who was born or lived for a long time in North Africa during the colonial period.

"We all personalized the struggle" (p. 187). *A Bright Shining Lie* by Neil Sheehan (New York: Random House, 1988).

"The difficulty at Ap Bac" (p. 189). Interview with Charles Timmes, October 27, 1986.

"In a biography of Vann written many years later" (p. 190). *A Bright Shining Lie* by Neil Sheehan.

"They were characters in the story" (p. 190). Interview with Barry Zorthian, November 15, 1986.

"Mike Dunn believed that Henry Cabot Lodge" (p. 191). Interview with John Michael Dunn, November 6, 1986.

"the message turned out to be breathtakingly close to a warrant for a coup d'etat" (p. 194). A facsimile of page 1 of the August 24, 1963, cable to Lodge can be found in *Kennedy in Vietnam* by William J. Rust, p. 113.

"He turned out to be a shrewd, tough operator" (p. 196). *The Making of a Quagmire* by David Halberstam (New York: Random House, 1965).

"Lou Conein got into the coup business" (p. 198). Interview with Lucien Conein, September 24, 1986.

"In my contacts here, Harkins said" (p. 204). *The Pentagon Papers* (New York: Bantam Books, 1971), p. 221.

"Although Conein was a collector of details and a connoisseur of gossip" (p. 212). The author of *Kennedy in Vietnam*, William J. Rust, also found Conein to be less than forthcoming when discussing the assassination of Diem, calling him "Delphic on the subject." On page 174 of his book, Rust writes: "In an interview years after the coup, the usually direct CIA operative ducked the question of responsibility for Diem's murder by cryptically observing, 'My co-conspirators let me down.'"

"He told Khiem his whereabouts at the church in Cholon" (p. 211). *Our Endless War* by Tran Van Don (San Rafael, California: Presidio Press, 1978), p. 108.

"According to Tran Van Don, Conein himself became rather peeved" (p. 213). Ibid., p. 107.

"The hypothesis that Lodge gave Diem up that morning was not inconsistent" (p. 214). William J. Rust writes in *Kennedy in Vietnam* (p. 177) that Diem's brother Can, later executed, was turned over to Lou Conein at the Saigon airport and he then turned Can over to the coup leaders. Rust cites an interview with Conein on August 22, 1983, in which the former CIA operative said, "[Lodge] told me that he was going to make special arrangements for landing this airplane at a certain place at Tan Son Nhut, and that the person on board was to be turned over to the Vietnamese authorities." Rust further asserts that Lodge made his decision to give up Can without consulting Washington.

"The newsmen had prejudices that prevented them from seeing the truth" (p. 215). Interview with Edward Lansdale, June 19, 1986.

CHAPTER 13

"Wonderful, Norvill Jones said" (p. 219). Interview with Norvill Jones, October 21, 1986.

"Fulbright himself grumpily dismissed" (p. 222). Interview with J. William Fulbright, October 20, 1986.

"I knew Dave and Neil in the early days" (p. 228). Interview with Keyes Beech, November 16, 1987.

CHAPTER 14

"But even without the gaffe, it was clear that Lansdale" (p. 238). A number of books have covered Operation Mongoose and the CIA during this period. Two of the most informative are *The Man Who Kept the Secrets* by Thomas Powers (New York: Alfred A. Knopf, 1979) and *The Agency* by John Ranelagh (New York: Simon and Schuster, 1986).

"Connell was impressed by Rufe Phillips and quickly converted" (p. 239). Interview with William J. Connell, November 3, 1986.

"Hubert Humphrey became Lansdale's chief supporter" (p. 239). *The Education of a Public Man* by Hubert H. Humphrey, ed. Norman Sherman (Garden City: Doubleday, 1976).

"Taylor called the generals to the embassy" (p. 242). Saigon Embassy Telegram, December 24, 1964, Pentagon Papers.

"Ambassador Taylor objected to bringing in American ground troops" (p. 244). This and the following quotations attributed to Westmoreland appear in *A Soldier Reports* by General William C. Westmoreland (New York: Doubleday, 1976).

"Taylor had outlived his usefulness" (p. 246). To his obvious surprise, Taylor's biographer—his son John—stumbled upon a memo that McGeorge Bundy had written President Johnson on March 5, 1965, which said in part: "McNamara and I, if the decision were ours to make, would bring Taylor back and put Alex Johnson in charge. . . . Max has been gallant, determined, and honorable to a fault, but he has also been rigid, remote and sometimes abrupt." Bundy recommended that Johnson take up Taylor's original commitment to stay only a year and get him out of Saigon no later than June 1. When Taylor *fils* asked McNamara and Bundy about the memo in 1987, McNamara said he didn't remember and Bundy waffled. See *General Maxwell Taylor: The Sword and the Pen* by John M. Taylor (New York: Doubleday, 1989), pp. 311–12.

"Lodge asked to see me for lunch" (p. 249). Interview with Edward Lansdale, June 21, 1986.

"The first had to do with his belief in the domino theory" (p. 251). *The Vantage Point: Perspectives of the Presidency, 1963–1969* by Lyndon Baines Johnson (New York: Holt, Rinehart and Winston, 1971).

"Not that print journalists didn't get caught" (p. 254). Interview with Jason McManus, June 1, 1971.

"A clique grew up around Zorro" (p. 255). Interview with Frank McCulloch, May 30, 1971.

"The two most influential Vietnamese legmen" (p. 256). H. D. S. (David) Greenway, who had worked as a *Time* correspondent with Pham Xuan An and sought his advice about the political situation many times, tried to establish on his several trips back to Saigon after the war whether his friend really had been a communist spy. Greenway finally made contact in 1989, and he reported that An told him, yes, he had worked for the communists since the French ruled Indochina. An also told Greenway that Saigon's new masters did not really trust him after he had associated with Americans for so many years and that he "had been forced to study the principles of communism. The lesson he had learned, albeit belatedly, he said, was that this was 'really about power' rather than ideals." See article by H. D. S. Greenway, *The Washington Post,* January 21, 1990.

In the March 11, 1990 issue of the *New York Times Magazine,* Morley Safer of CBS wrote about Pham Xuan An: "I do not think of him as a communist, though he is still a loyal party member. I can't even think of him as a nationalist. . . . No, An is a genuine patriot, I decide, one of the few I have known."

I found the retrospective romanticizing of Pham Xuan An, whom I knew for nearly ten years, a bit rich for my stomach, especially considering that An hadn't the foresight, as had his best friend and intellectual superior Nguyen Hung Vuong, who was a patriot too, to see where the communists were leading.

"An, that son of a bitch" (p. 257) Murray Gart to Zalin Grant, November 6, 1986.

"Though he liked Lansdale, Jake Jacobson" (p. 279). Interview with George Jacobson, October 24, 1986.

"Dave and I were both dismayed as we were talked over" (p. 283). *Sub Rosa: The CIA and the Uses of Intelligence* by Peer de Silva (New York: New York Times Books, 1978).

CHAPTER 15

"Most of the critics take off on HES" (p. 292). Interview with Robert Komer, May 25, 1968. The Komer interview provided a little insight into how journalism worked in Vietnam. I was writing an article on pacification for *The New Republic,* a journal that openly flew its colors as being opposed to the war, and Komer at first turned down my request to see him. I asked Barry

Zorthian to intercede, which he did, and Komer then gave me nearly two hours of his time, during which he was pleasant and responsive. He didn't like my article, though, and he wrote a critical note about it to Zorthian, who shrugged and handed it to me without comment. Whatever the problems journalists had in Vietnam, gaining access to American officials was seldom one of them.

"Phoenix wasn't all that effective" (p. 296). Interview with William Colby, June 18, 1986.

"One guy who was a source of information" (p. 297). Interview with Patrick McGarvey, April 17, 1971.

CHAPTER 16

"I told Colby how concerned I was" (p. 302). Interview with Jean-André Sauvagcot, November 10, 1986.

"the only page missing from the files" (p. 304). William Gibbons, who had requested the State Department declassify Bunker's reports for his study, *The U.S. Government and the Vietnam War,* turned them over to me, and I noticed that the page was missing. Gibbons checked with the State Department and found they had no explanation for the missing page, but he, too, was struck by the coincidence.

"His mission was to make it possible" (p. 304). Interview with Carol Laise Bunker, October 5, 1986.

"Bruce Palmer and Bunker served together" (p. 304). *The 25-Year War: America's Military Role in Vietnam* by General Bruce Palmer, Jr. (Lexington: The University Press of Kentucky, 1984), pp. 47–48.

"He became gun-shy of the press" (p. 306). Interview with Samuel Bunker, October 17, 1986.

"Thieu believed that he had made Richard Nixon president" (p. 310). See *The Palace File* by Nguyen Tien Hung and Jerrold L. Schecter (New York: Harper & Row, 1986). Also *Nixon: Volume Two: The Triumph of a Politician, 1962–1972* by Stephen E. Ambrose (New York: Simon & Schuster, 1989).

"Thieu listened, said Humphrey" (p. 311). *The Education of a Public Man* by Hubert H. Humphrey, ed. Norman Sherman (Garden City: Doubleday, 1976).

"Thieu was not nearly as corrupt as others" (p. 315). Interview with Mark Huss, October 16, 1986.

CHAPTER 17

"On December 27, 1969, Elliot Richardson sent Ambassador Bunker a cable" (p. 317). All references to cables in the following pages refer to State Department and Saigon Embassy telegrams that were declassified under the Freedom of Information Act.

"From his opening statement before the committee" (p. 321). See the *Hearings Before the Committee on Foreign Relations, United States Senate, Ninety-First Congress, Second Session, on Civil Operations and Rural Development Support Program.* The following quotations by Fulbright, Colby, and Vann are taken from the transcript of the hearings.

"He brought out the cables Bunker had sent and picked up the phone" (p. 325). In fact, Ellsberg already possessed a number of the documents that were later declassified for me under the long Freedom of Information process.

CHAPTER 18

The material in this chapter comes primarily from my interview with Tran Ngoc Chau and his supplementary material.

SOURCE NOTES

CHAPTER 19

"In March 1975, General Van Tien Dung, chief of staff of the North Vietnamese army" (p. 335). For a detailed account of the fall of Saigon see *Decent Interval* by Frank Snepp and *The Fall of Saigon* by David Butler (New York: Simon and Schuster, 1985).

"The Vietnamese officers knew that Congress was cutting" (p. 338). Interview with Charles Timmes, October 27, 1986.

"A CIA officer arrived to talk to Chau" (p. 341). Interview with Keyes Beech, November 16, 1987.

CHAPTER 20

"As Shaplen put it" (p. 352). *The Lost Revolution: The U.S. in Vietnam, 1946–1966* by Robert Shaplen (New York: Harper & Row, 1966).

"Like Confucianism, she asserted" (p. 352). *Fire in the Lake: The Vietnamese and the Americans in Vietnam* by Frances FitzGerald (Boston: Little, Brown, 1972)

"Theodore Solotaroff said" (p. 354). *The New York Times Book Review,* May 29, 1977.

"The Sunday *Book Review* critic called *Dispatches*" (p. 354). *The New York Times Book Review,* November 20, 1977.

"Born on the Fourth of July by Ron Kovic, an antiwar paraplegic" (p. 355). Based on this analysis, already written at the time, I was able to predict that the film made by Oliver Stone from Kovic's book would not win an Oscar for the best movie in March 1990, even though it was highly touted for the award by the press. My analysis had nothing to do with the film's artistic merit or Kovic's courageous struggle after his return from Vietnam but was based on the fact that the public's interpretation of the role of the Vietnam veteran had changed. Had the movie appeared a decade earlier, there was no question in my mind but that it would have won most of the eight Oscars for which it was nominated, instead of the two it received.

"All of us were emotionally involved in Vietnam one way or another" (p. 360). Interview with Keyes Beech, November 16, 1987.

INDEX

ABOUT THE AUTHOR

ZALIN GRANT spent a total of five years in Vietnam between 1964 and 1973. He worked as a reporter for *Time,* then as a correspondent for *The New Republic,* and was one of only several Americans in the Saigon press corps who spoke Vietnamese. He is the author of *Survivors* and *Over the Beach.*